Readings & Cases in Direct Marketing

Readings & Cases in Direct Marketing

Herbert E. Brown
Bruce Buskirk

NTC Business Books
a division of *NTC Publishing Group* • Lincolnwood, Illinois USA

1992 Printing

 ʾrary of Congress Catalog Number: 88-61140

  6 7 8 9 0 ML 9 8 7 6 5 4 3 2

Contents

Foreword   by Bob Stone   **ix**

SECTION ONE
Direct Marketing Readings

CHAPTER ONE   Where Direct Marketing Is Today   1

Direct Marketing—What Is It?   1
MARTIN BAIER, HENRY R. HOKE, JR., AND BOB STONE

Understanding Direct Marketing Concept Is Vitally Important   3
VIN JENKINS

Don't Cry for Us Madison Avenue   15
RICHARD ARMSTRONG

Two Faces, Two Revolutions, Two Opportunities   17
STAN RAPP

Data-based Targeted Advertising: New Age of
Marketing Relevance   24
LESTER WUNDERMAN

CHAPTER TWO   Strategy in Direct Marketing   31

Marketing Strategies for Maximum Growth   31
JIM KOBS

Integrated Direct Marketing: Maximizing Media Mix   40
ERNAN ROMAN

Make Your Dealer a Direct Marketing Co-Star   44
DIANE LYNN KASTIEL

CHAPTER THREE   Offer and Creative   51

Creativity Retooled to Fit New Concept   51
MARGARET LEROUX

Seven-Step Creative Process Adds "Eureka!" to
Your Vocabulary   53
WILLIAM STEINHARDT

Back to the Basics, or 50 Rules to Live By   57
HERSCHELL GORDON LEWIS

Creating Direct Response Commercials   62
AL EICOFF

CHAPTER FOUR   The Classic Package   67

Designing for Your Market and Budget   67
DAVE WILKISON

The Envelope   70
DAVE WILKISON

The Letter and the Personalized Letter   71
DAVE WILKISON

The Brochure   73
DAVE WILKISON

Pros Tell How to Produce Effective Brochures   75
URI DOWBENKO

Peripherals   77
DAVE WILKISON

CHAPTER FIVE   Media   79

Direct Mail: Advertising's Best-Kept Secret   79
KEN ERDMAN

Tailoring Catalogs to Fit Corporate Personality   84
ANITA M. BUSCH

Seven Myths That Keep You Off TV   87
DONALD D. LEWIS

CHAPTER SIX   Lists and Databases   93

Database Techniques: How to Tap a Key Company Resource   93
RICHARD J. COURTHEOUX

List Segmentation: How to Find Your Best Direct
Marketing Prospects   103
BEHRAM J. HANSOTIA

CHAPTER SEVEN   Lead Generation and
                 Qualification   113

The Application of an Effective Inquiry-Handling System for
Business-to-Business Marketing   113
ROBERT H. HUTCHINGS

Bingo Card Junkies: Why They Could Be Your
Best Prospects   123
ROGER W. BRUCKER

CHAPTER EIGHT   Research and Testing   **129**

Don't Change Your Offer without Testing   129
JOHN KLINGEL

Research Methods   132
JOSEPH CASTELLI

Quantitative Direct Response Market Segmentation   137
RICHARD A. HAMILTON

CHAPTER NINE   Production   **149**

Production: The Last Strategic Frontier   149
MARK GRUEN

CHAPTER TEN   Mail-Order Financial Analysis   **155**

The Dollars and Sense of Direct Mail: Practical Concepts of
Math and Finance   155
PIERRE A. PASSAVANT

CHAPTER ELEVEN   Telemarketing   **165**

When to Use Telemarketing . . . And When Not To!   165
RICHARD L. BENCIN

How to Get More Direct Orders   168
BOB STONE

The Mathematics of Telemarketing   172
BOB STONE AND JOHN WYMAN

Telemarketing SOS   180
RUDY OETTING AND BRAD TURLEY

SECTION TWO
Case Analysis and Presentation

Introduction to Case Analysis and Presentation   185

What's Your Presentation Quotient?   199
  RON HOFF

Direct Response "Rules" Test   209

Warm-Up Exercises   213

SECTION THREE
Direct Marketing Cases

1.	Bull Markets	221
2.	Sealant Marketing	222
3.	Dudes	223
4.	Reliable Bearings	226
5.	Direct Woodworking	227
6.	The Skirting Man Cometh	228
7.	Keowee Grinding	230
8.	Major Computer	232
9.	Letters	235
10.	Total Fitness Machine	239
11.	Magna Deca	242
12.	The Royer Corporation	243
13.	WENCO, INC.	255
14.	Allwood Chef, Inc.	260
15.	Workmate Pricing Problem	265
16.	Shopsmith, Inc.	266
17.	Blue Chip Grinding	273
18.	Kestnbaum & Company	281
19.	Western Wear Inc.	286
20.	PQ Systems	294
21.	Wall Drug Store	315
22.	Fairfax Cab Company	331

Foreword

This is a unique book. Its publication is a classic case of serendipity.

Meeting quite by accident, two prominent marketing professors learned that they were of the same mind about a void in direct marketing literature. Both had a vision of a book that would take direct marketing practitioners into the upper strata of achievement.

What Herbert E. Brown, Ph.D. at Wright State University and Bruce D. Buskirk, Ph.D. at Northwestern University saw was a need for a book that would take practitioners beyond the basic "how-tos," a book that would provide easy access to state-of-the-art applications, a book that would show the way to professional problem solving. *Readings and Cases in Direct Marketing* fills the need.

Herb Brown and Bruce Buskirk know direct marketing as few marketing professors do. Their credentials are outstanding. Each is completely comfortable in the "real world" business environment; each teaches direct marketing at his respective university.

Brown and Buskirk have divided *Readings and Cases in Direct Marketing* into three parts. For Section One—"Direct Marketing Readings"—they reviewed thousands of articles, selecting only those which qualified as "state of the art." Then they organized these articles under eleven direct marketing classifications, everything from strategic planning to direct marketing success requirements. The result is that the reader has a treasure house of knowledge and experience to draw from.

Section Two, "Case Analysis and Presentation," and Section Three, "Direct Marketing Cases," are reminiscent of the famous Harvard Business School approach. The reader is shown, step-by-step, how top-echelon marketers solve marketing problems.

With twenty-two cases to choose from, you learn how to apply the five main elements in a well-developed case analysis, how to write cases, how to make case evaluations, how to give oral and group presentations. The bottom line is that the reader, with this new-found knowledge, will now be able to solve direct marketing problems previously considered "unsolvable."

It is time for direct marketing practitioners to move beyond the basics. *Readings and Cases in Direct Marketing* shows the way.

Bob Stone, Chairman Emeritus
Stone & Adler, Inc.

Preface

Readings and Cases in Direct Marketing was conceived as a book for use in both the college and professional direct marketing fields.

As this is being written, bachelor's and master's degrees in direct marketing are offered at several universities. One or more direct marketing courses are offered at hundreds more. Theoretical perspectives are now being advanced and researched by scholars. Journals have been established as outlets for scholarly research. Trade journals have become numerous. Basic and specialized trade books are increasingly in evidence. Foundation books for use in collegiate settings have appeared.

However, there is still a void. Much of the burgeoning direct marketing literature emphasizes principles, concepts, definitions, and "what works" material, as it must. This information is of immense utility to the aspiring professional. At some point, however, a practice context should be provided for direct marketing study. One of the best ways to provide this is a representative set of direct marketing problems. This is the void and the role this book seeks to fill.

In direct marketing, a good rule of thumb is to discover the rules before implementing a program, rather than after a program has failed. Effective direct marketing practice requires a knowledge of the rules in such major areas as lists or media, offers, creative, direct marketing math/numbers, and databases. To this end, the selection of readings included in this book is designed to focus the reader's attention on, and challenge his or her understanding of, the really critical success factors in direct marketing—as a prelude to, or at least simultaneously with, problem solving.

A second direct marketing rule of thumb is that once the rules are known, major breakthroughs often come from applying the rules in creative ways, or from breaking them in equally creative ways. Thus, the problems and cases included in this book were selected or designed to challenge the user's ability to understand the *rules* of direct marketing; to apply them in the basic, conventional ways; and even to break them in creative, and possibly unconventional, ways, should this be suggested by the problem at hand.

To this end, this book challenges the reader with a variety of cases and problems—some large and some small, some rich in data and some data poor—but all reflecting the reality of the direct marketing channel and industry.

Database marketing increasingly reflects the direction in which the field is evolving. In the process, the field is not breaking away from its mail-order origins, nor should it, for mail-order principles represent the strength of the emerging new order in marketing—whatever it is called. Direct marketing does not conflict with other forms of marketing. Instead, it overlays, melds with, and enriches traditional concepts, techniques, and approaches.

Accordingly, though this book focuses on those marketing perspectives and technologies that are distinctly direct marketing, it does not overlook the interrelationships of direct marketing with the general marketing field. In view of this, the articles and cases selected for inclusion in this book challenge the reader to reflect on the blending and melding of direct and general marketing, and in the process discover that this blending is, in fact, the reality of both direct and general marketing.

Both the authors and publisher wish to thank the people who so graciously granted us permission to reprint the following readings and case histories.

Herbert E. Brown
Bruce D. Buskirk

Direct Marketing Readings

Where Direct Marketing Is Today

Direct Marketing— What Is It?

Martin Baier, Henry R. Hoke, Jr., and Bob Stone

Written by three leaders in the direct marketing field, this is a definitional piece that appears regularly in *Direct Marketing*. In it, direct marketing is described as having the same broad function as marketing in general. *General* and *direct marketing* are distinguished in a primary sense by the fact that the latter requires a database. Other major characteristics of direct marketing include buyer–seller interaction, system, measurable response, and media variety. Telemarketing is the number one direct response medium, followed by broadcast, newspapers, miscellaneous media, direct mail, magazines, and interactive TV.

An Aspect of Total Marketing— Not a Fancy Term for Mail Order

MARKETING IS THE TOTAL OF ACTIVITIES OF moving goods and services from seller to buyer. (See chart.) Direct Marketing has the same broad function except that Direct Marketing requires the existence and maintenance of database:

a. To record names of customers, expires, and prospects
b. To provide a vehicle for storing, then measuring, results of advertising, usually direct response advertising
c. To provide a vehicle for storing, then measuring, purchasing performance
d. To provide a vehicle for continuing direct communication by mail and/or phone

Direct Marketing Flow Chart

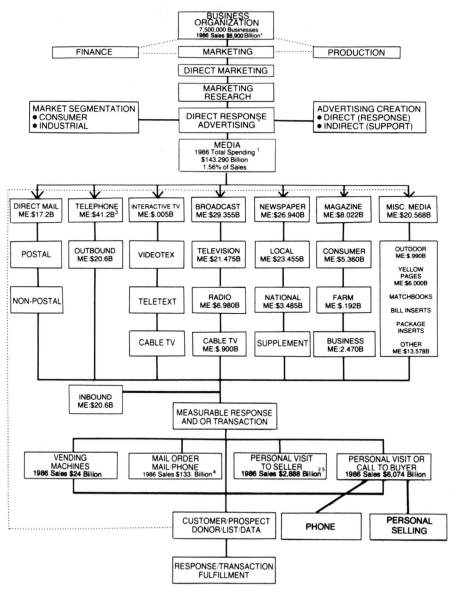

¹Source: Arnold Fishman, U.S. Census, Robert Coen, McCann Erickson (Media Figures).

²Personal visit to seller includes $1.204 billion of Consumer Product Sales at retail plus 90% of Consumer Services Sales. 10% of Consumer Services Sales are conducted by salespeople visiting the buyer.

³Rudy Oetting, Telephone Marketing Resources, New York City, working with AT&T figures, says that roughly half of Telemarketing Expenditures are for Outbound Calls; 50% for inbound.

⁴The Mail Order Sales Figure includes roughly $33 billion of charitable contributions which are not included in the $9,300 billion of U.S. Aggregate Sales.

⁵This total does not include $870 billion in investment spending minus $75 billion in Net Exports.

*Dollars in Billions

ME: Media Expenditures

Thus, *Direct Marketing* is interactive, requiring database for controlled activity: by mail, by phone, through other media selected on the basis of previous results.

Direct Marketing makes direct response advertising generally desirable since response (inquiries or purchasing transactions) can be recorded on database for building the list, providing marketing information.

Direct Marketing plays no favorites in terms of Methods of Selling . . . and there are only three:

a. Where buyer seeks out seller—retailing, exhibits
b. Where seller seeks out buyer—personal selling
c. Where buyer seeks seller by mail or phone—mail order

Direct Marketing requires that a response or transaction at any location be recorded on cards, mechanical equipment or, preferably, on computer.

Direct Marketing can be embraced by any kind of business as defined by the U.S. Census Standard Industrial Classification system:

Agriculture	0100-0999
Mining/Construction	1000-1799
Manufacturing	2000-4999
Wholesale	5010-5199
Retail	5210-5999
Department Stores (5311)	
Financial Services	6010-6799
Services	7010-7999
Advertising Agencies (7311)	
Computer Houses (7372)	
List Brokers (7388)	
Non-Profit	8010-8999
Public Administration	9100-9999

Direct Marketing is an interactive system of marketing which uses one or more advertising media to effect a measurable response and/or transaction at any location.

Martin Baier, Henry R. Hoke, Jr., and Bob Stone, "Direct Marketing—What Is It?" *Direct Marketing*, January 1988. Reprinted by permission of *Direct Marketing* magazine.

Understanding Direct Marketing Concept Is Vitally Important
VIN JENKINS

Direct marketing is the system that best suits the needs of target marketers, but it is much, much more than that. Two factors clearly distinguish direct marketing from general marketing: direct one-to-one relationships and interactive two-way communications. Basic to direct marketing is the concept that each and every direct response campaign should be carried on with as much concern for long-term image building as with the short-term cost per reply. Not only are direct and general marketing harmonious, but the two systems should be embraced in a total marketing plan which creates a synergistic effect. The use of databases of customer records is what makes possible overpowering service, especially after-sale service. Any business activity that encourages better relations between marketers and customers and a communication dialogue is a positive step forward. In this sense, direct marketing may prove to be the ultimate marketing concept to better satisfy consumer wants and needs.

Probably the most important management fundamental that is being ignored today is staying close to the consumer to satisfy his needs and anticipate his wants. In too many companies, the customer has become a bloody nuisance whose unpredictable behavior damages carefully made strategic plans, whose activities mess up computer operations, and who stubbornly insists that purchased products should work.

THE ABOVE STATEMENT WAS ATTRIBUTED TO Lew Young, the editor in chief of *Business Week*. It appeared in the book entitled *In Search of Excellence*. We are now living in an age where people, and the businesses they represent, can really only succeed if they genuinely embrace the concept of marketing.

It has become exceedingly difficult, if not impossible, to derive satisfaction, a sense of achievement, and the profit necessary to sustain business livelihood, unless one satisfies the needs and wants of today's consumers. Those who truly embrace the marketing concept try to find out what consumers really want. They pull out all stops to fulfill identified needs and wants. They compete fiercely.

Successful marketing people have a genuine interest in mankind, in people from all walks of life. They are motivated by the satisfaction that comes from being successful. Through success which is measured in terms of fulfilling consumer needs and not just by the generation of a profit. They realize that profit is, in fact, simply a consequence of successful marketing and not an end in itself.

And yet, for all of this, for all of the lessons of recent decades, there still remains a large section of the business community who pay lip service to marketing. Whose only concern is self-expression through the creation of products or services which are of interest to them, and not necessarily of interest to the consumer.

Let us now consider direct marketing within the context of the marketing concept. The system of direct marketing has certain inherent features which can make it easier to achieve marketing success. In fact, direct marketing is a concept whose time has come.

In our efforts as marketers to fulfill consumer wants we have an unprecedented volume of products, and variations of products, to meet the consumer's every whim. Some mass marketed products are customized to the point where only a small proportion of total production output is exactly alike.

This has resulted in the need for "targeted marketing." And direct marketing is the system which best suits the needs of target marketers.

But, direct marketing is much, much more than that. It fully embraces the communication process creating a dynamic and ongoing dialogue with the consumer. This application opens the door to direct marketing for all marketers including those who approach audiences of mass proportions.

However, while direct marketing is rapidly proliferating, its potential is far from being fulfilled. Direct marketing is still underdeveloped in Australia. Before direct marketing can achieve the level of acceptance it deserves, it is essential that all people responsible for the marketing function attempt to fully understand the concept of direct marketing.

So, what is direct marketing?

A number of definitions have been created over the years. But, the following one really embodies the heart of the concept of direct marketing.

> Direct marketing is a marketing system in which the marketer establishes direct relations with the consumer via interactive communication.

Therefore, the two most important elements of direct marketing are firstly, the fact that a *direct one-to-one relationship* is established with the consumer, and secondly, that this relationship is created through *interactive (two-way) communication*. These two factors clearly distinguish direct marketing from general marketing.

Once the product has been created or the service is in place, marketers do embrace both general marketing and direct marketing. When you look at these two systems, you'll realize that all marketers embrace direct marketing, even if in some cases it is confined to personal selling to an audience such as the retail trade.

In a nutshell, in the general marketing communications mix, we have publicity, general advertising, and the form of sales promotion which does not seek a direct response. Direct marketing embraces personal selling, general advertising by direct mail, direct response advertising, direct support advertising, and sales promotion which does call for a direct response.

General marketing embraces the retail and vending distribution channels. Direct marketing, on the other hand, embraces direct selling, and mail order, and the retail distribution channel as well.

The subject of mental and emotional response raises the very important topic of the awareness creation and image-building by-products of direct response advertising. The trap with direct response is that it is all too easy to concern ourselves with the volume of today's response, to measure our results by cost-per-reply alone. This is very short-term thinking.

Each and every direct response campaign should be created with as much concern for the long-term image building aspect of the communication as with the short-term cost-per-reply. After all, the cost of tomorrow's response will be greatly influenced by whether or not you have built a favorable image of your company.

Applications of Direct Marketing

Most people believe that the potential of direct marketing is confined to particular needs of businesses or special marketing circumstances. Let's explode those myths!

To simplify the issue let's divide all businesses into two basic groups. Firstly, there are companies that market their products or services to the masses. Secondly, there are companies that market to specific target audiences. Any organization that needs to reach and influence a select target group should attempt to capture the names of current and prospective customers.

Direct communication mainly by direct mail is likely to be far more cost-effective than use of the mass media in circumstances such as these. In fact, the narrower the audience profile, the more likely that the creation of a direct marketing database will improve marketing performance. Database marketing is the most overt form of direct marketing.

This brings me to the least understood form of direct marketing. And that is the creation of a dialogue with the consumer through the mass media. Any mass media communication which seeks a direct response is direct marketing.

More importantly, if the advertising seeks genuine feedback of consumer understanding or interpretation of the advertising message, or consumer opinions about the product or service, then this is interactive communication at work. And this interactive communication is the cornerstone of the direct marketing concept.

This brings us to the communication process itself. Of all the elements which affect marketing, the process of communication is not very well-understood. Apart from the physical exchange process, communication is the only link between the marketer and the consumer. It is the vital link because, without it, physical exchange is most unlikely to take place.

Let's look at the process of communication itself. Take a look at the chart, The Communication Model, which is featured in the classic marketing textbook by Kotler. Note that the process of communication is complete only when there is feedback from the receiver to the sender.

The Communication Model

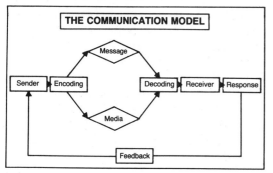

It is our task as marketers, therefore, to ensure that we encourage as much consumer feedback as possible. Through split-run testing of our direct response advertising, we can generate genuinely meaningful feedback about how the consumer has interpreted our message or our offer.

What this model suggests is that communication is an interactive two-way exchange process. It is not simply transmitting messages. It is not simply a process of injecting our thoughts into the minds of consumers.

With general marketing, the communication is, in effect, a monologue. It is a one-way process. Messages are transmitted and received. But, consumers are not asked or expected to engage in the communication process. There is no feedback, other than that stimulated by market research—which, of course, must be conducted on a limited scale.

With direct marketing, however, we do ask the consumer to respond. To engage in the communication process. To take part in interactive communication. This two-way communication, to be sure, is basically at a minimum. When we ask consumers to complete an order form or to simply "accept an offer," the feedback is minimal.

At the other end of the spectrum, though, two-way communication is at its best when we encourage and allow the consumer to feedback answers or opinions in response to our communications. With general marketing, the limitations of the research feedback process may not

be detected until things go awfully wrong in the marketplace.

With direct marketing, there is a much greater opportunity through the direct measurement of actual consumer behavior to adjust our communications to suit the needs, the wants, the values and the aspirations of the consumer.

Programmed Learning

People approach a communication differently if it is obvious that the marketer is asking for a reply, an answer, or any kind of physical response. Programmed learning motivates consumers to take a more active and meaningful role in the communication process. Essentially, programmed learning is an education technique which has a valid application in marketing communications.

In marketing situations, we take the advertising message and break it down into its component parts. The consumer is then asked to answer questions relating to each part and feed back his or her understanding of the message. This leads consumers to better comprehension of detailed complex advertising messages.

For example, Sperry New Holland released 11 new items of equipment to the rural market this year. A 12-page buyer's guide was produced which was inserted into three major farming journals. Sperry New Holland generated a 14 percent response from the total circulation. This is a fantastic result when you consider the detailed readership of the buyer's guide that was required to correctly answer the eight programmed learning questions.

Incidentally, over 50 percent of the respondents requested one or more of the product brochures on offer. This goes to prove that many consumers or users are anxious to learn more about their purchasing options. Just imagine also the huge benefit that Sperry New Holland gained through adding the names of qualified prospects to their database and through feeding leads to their dealer network.

Let's now turn our attention to the task of understanding the relationship between direct marketing and general marketing. It may appear that when it comes to strategic planning we have this choice: embrace either general marketing or direct marketing. In fact, the marketing model we examined earlier may have created the impression that the two systems are mutually exclusive. But, of course, they're not.

Not only are general marketing and direct marketing harmonious, the two systems should be embraced in a total marketing plan which creates a synergistic effect. Ed Nash, of BBDO Direct in the United States, called this synergy "interdynamic marketing."

Let's see how this concept works. (See charts Interdynamic Marketing.) First of all, let's examine the model of interrelated marketing which is on the left-hand side of the chart.

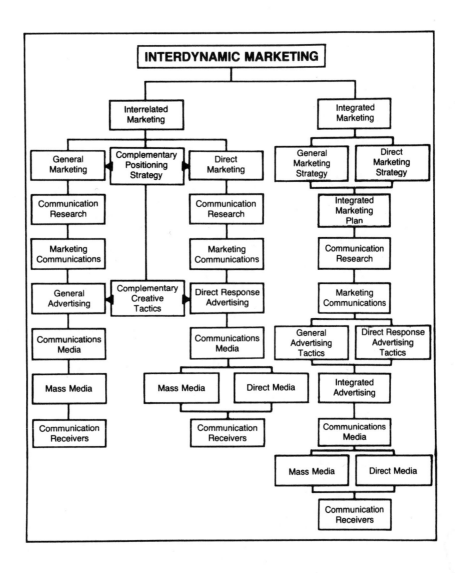

We won't go into all the details of this model. But, let's concentrate on the fact that in this strategy plan, the general advertising and the direct response advertising will be executed in totally separate campaigns.

Our task then is one of making certain that the positioning strategy and the creative tactics are entirely complementary. In a plan of this kind, a decision is taken to prepare and execute general advertising for the purpose of creating awareness and building an image.

As part of the overall plan, it is decided to run a direct response advertising campaign which makes a specific offer—one which is relevant in the environment created by the general advertising. This may not appear to be an unusual approach, and it isn't. It is perfectly valid under numerous marketing circumstances.

The other major strategic option is to execute general marketing and direct marketing programs through a totally integrated communications campaign. I refer now to the right-hand side of the chart. Where the addition of a direct response solicitation does *not* interfere with or compromise the important general advertising message, there may be no reason to keep the two elements apart.

On the contrary, greater effectiveness may be achieved through integrated marketing which is executed through an integrated advertising campaign. This area of strategic planning can be approached in a number of ways. For instance, the major purpose of the advertising may be to create awareness and, at the same time, skim off the available response from the core prospect market through a modest motivation to respond.

On the other hand, integrated advertising may be created to present a special offer in a very powerful fashion which principally aims to generate a high volume of response but, at the same time, create positive awareness as a by-product of the campaign.

This is strategy planning at its best—looking at all the options, being aware of all the opportunities, and making conscious decisions to take a very deliberate tack with either inter-related marketing or integrated marketing.

When one is invited to conduct a marketing audit, it's amazing but all too often true that the most fundamental elements are not planned and are, therefore, not actioned. Each and every direct marketing plan should cover these five key components:

1. Current customer retention and activation
2. Current customer upgrading
3. Cross selling to current customers
4. Past customer reactivation
5. New customer acquisition strategies

One of the fabulous benefits of the direct marketing system is that it is possible to create and maintain a database of customer records. What is the value of a customer to a business? Obviously the value varies significantly according to the particular product or service.

But, in any business where there is a repeat sale or an ongoing sales potential, a current customer will be worth much more to the business than most people realize. Customer goodwill is probably the most undervalued of all business assets.

Let me quote once again from *In Search of Excellence:*

> In observing the excellent companies, and specifically the way they interact with customers, what we found most striking was the consistent presence of obsession.

> Service, quality, reliability are strategies aimed at loyalty and long-term revenue stream growth (and maintenance).

So, the first priority in a direct marketing plan should be to maximize current customer performance. Let's look at each of these five key elements in turn.

Current customer retention and activation. If you're involved in a marketing situation where the product or service is of considerable value and/or is purchased infrequently, then a "customer retention" program should be seriously considered. A typical example of this activity is the "owner retention" campaigns that some of the luxury car makers engage in.

Just to support this theory here's another quote from *In Search of Excellence:*

> Although he's not a company, our favorite illustration of closeness to the customer is car salesman Joe Girard. He sold more new cars and trucks, each year, for 11 years running, than any other human being. In fact, in a typical year, Joe sold more than twice as many units as whoever was in second place. In explaining his secret success, Joe said: "I send out over 13,000 cards every month."

> Why start with Joe? Because his magic is the magic of IBM and many of the rest of the excellent companies. It is simply service, overpowering service, especially after-sales service. Out of context, Joe's 13,000 cards sounds like just another sales gimmick. But, like the top companies, Joe seems genuinely to care.

Where goods may be purchased on a reasonably frequent basis, promotions must be mounted to stimulate customer activity. For instance, many of the specialty retailers should have a program of regular contact with their captive customers to maximize sales turnover. Obviously, where products or services are sold on a subscription or membership basis, a multiwave renewal program is essential to minimize the attrition rate.

Current customer upgrading. One of the most productive ways to increase sales is to upgrade the value of business with current customers. Incentives can easily be structured to motivate your customers to buy more of the same or upgrade to a purchase of better quality.

Cross selling to current customers. Any organization that markets a *range* of products or services should offer current customers *other* products or services from the range. Cross selling is a highly productive direct marketing ac-

tivity. Even if your customer base is of huge proportions, a profiling exercise will soon sort out which segments of the file that are suited to cross selling solicitation.

Now we move on to the business of winning new customers.

Past customer reactivation. In many industries people who were customers of the business in the past can be won back to the fold cost-effectively. Often, the only activity that needs to take place is that promotion to current customers be extended to the lapsed customers.

Proper database management is the key to effective past customer reactivation. Careful analysis and evaluation of results according to recency and frequency criteria soon establishes the potential of winning back old customers.

New customer acquisition strategies. Most businesspeople place great emphasis on acquiring new customers. My view is that providing you have done all that you can do to retain, upgrade and cross sell to our existing customers, then by all means start concentrating on the job of conquesting.

With direct marketing, there are four basic strategies to win new business, and these are:

1. One-step acquisition campaigns.
2. Referral programs.
3. Two-step acquisition campaigns.
4. Two-step personal selling programs.

Let's examine each of these briefly. When salespeople engage in cold prospecting, this is one-step direct marketing. In other words, apart from general advertising, there is no lead generation support activity.

When retailers attempt to generate a purchase at the point-of-sale, or when mail-order traders directly solicit an order through direct response advertising, then this is a one-step approach. There is no intermediate step of calling for enquiries.

Alternatively, the direct marketer may decide to use the two-step method to acquire new customers. Essentially, the first step is a process of creating a list of "hot prospects." The principal purpose of the first-step communication is to create consumer enquiries or to generate leads for the salesforce.

First, referral programs. Given the right incentives, current customers of a business are often happy to refer their friends and acquaintances to the marketer. These *referral* programs are called "Member Get a Member" or "Introduce a Friend" or, in the Australian idiom, "Dob in a Cobber."

Step one is simply that—a name solicitation exercise. The second step can be executed through personal selling, telephone selling or by direct mail. No new customer acquisition plan would be complete without at least a test of the referral concept.

Next, we have two-step acquisition campaigns in which we ask the prospect to enquire about the product or service. Therefore, step one is an enquiry generation program. And step two is almost always executed through direct mail. Any product or service which is of a complex nature may benefit considerably from the dissemination of detailed information to interested consumers.

In such circumstances, direct response advertising campaigns which offer more information about the product or service can bridge the buyer-readiness gap between mild interest and desire to purchase. In mail-order programs, a list of enquirers can be used for an extensive step-two follow-up exercise. Direct mail or telephone selling, or a combination of both, can convert a high proportion of those enquirers into customers.

When retail is the distribution channel, again, a follow-up by direct mail can lead people to a purchase through retail stores. And, providing that the right kind of inducements are made, the effectiveness of this two-step approach to retail marketing can be directly measured.

Another major two-step activity is, of course, lead generation. In many industries,

A.I.D.A.—Awareness/Interest/Desire/Action

AWARENESS	INTEREST	DESIRE	ACTION
Presence/Image	Positioning: Product/Audience	Information Dissemination	Commitment Solicitation
GENERAL MARKETING		**DIRECT MARKETING**	
GENERAL ADVERTISING IN THE MASS MEDIA		TWO-STEP PLAN: • Step One: Enquiry Generation or Lead Generation (through Direct Response Advertising) • Step Two: Direct Mail Follow-up or Personal Selling Presentation	

two-step personal selling is now a permanent feature of the direct marketing plan. So, rather than have sales personnel waste valuable selling time "knocking on doors," they are now encouraged to concentrate on making professional presentations to people who have asked for a representative to call.

In many marketing situations and in particular the marketing of consumer services or business-to-business marketing, we may see a plan of the kind summarized in the chart AIDA. Most people are familiar with the AIDA formula to win new business. Here's how it can be executed in an interdynamic marketing plan.

The awareness or attention, resulting in corporate or brand presence and image, can be created through general advertising. Similarly, interest can be heightened through a positive strategy to position the product vis-à-vis its competition and to the appropriate audience, again through general advertising.

In such an environment, direct marketing can play a positive role in creating desire and generating action. Both the information dissemination and commitment solicitation activities can be executed through the two-step customer acquisition programs we've just discussed.

Personally, I am utterly convinced that the concept of direct marketing can be of great benefit to *all businesses*. I believe that direct marketing should not only be part of the total mix, it should be adopted as part of every organization's marketing philosophy.

Let's see how direct marketing works in a practical sense for the great variety of business activities in today's marketplace. There are, of course, so many different kinds of businesses, to simplify the discussion they have been grouped as shown.

1. Companies that market directly to consumers.
2. Companies that sell through intermediaries.
3. Business-to-business marketers.

However, as we confine our examination to these representative groups, stretch your imagination to draw similarities with the type of business activity in which you are engaged.

First, let's consider the companies that market directly to consumers. We'll start with the vast number of *consumer service* marketing organizations: All the financial service companies—from banks to building societies, insurance companies to credit unions, stockbrokers to cash management trusts, and so on.

Add in the travel, accommodation and entertainment industries. The car rental companies, the airlines, the hotel groups, the travel agents, and restaurants. These, and many others, have huge opportunities if they embrace direct marketing. All of these businesses, in effect, retail their services directly to the public. If not, they use the personal selling aspect of direct marketing to reach the consumer.

So, all of the consumer service organizations already have an existing relationship with their customers. And most of them capture their names and addresses. Some of them, in particular financial and insurance companies, capture and store vast amounts of data about each of their clients.

So, where is the interactive communication? Is there an attitude that the individual is important? Why do many of the service organizations advertise only to the masses when they could very effectively also be creating a productive dialogue with the most important people in the world—their current customers?

Only in recent years have we begun to see signs that consumer service organizations are realizing the potential of direct marketing. In this category, of course, we must look at retailers, the service organizations that, on behalf of manufacturers and importers, deal one-to-one with the consumer.

Most retailers can benefit from direct marketing. In particular, those retailers that place more emphasis on personal service—the department stores, the boutiques, and the specialty stores, have huge opportunities to communicate directly with their customers. They also have opportunities to promote store traffic with new customers.

Obviously in this category we have also the mail-order traders—the likes of Reader's Digest, Time Life, Franklin Mint, etc. These organizations fully embrace the direct marketing concept at the distribution end. Mail-order traders embrace direct response advertising but, generally do not seize on their opportunities to engage in a more meaningful interactive dialogue with their customers.

Direct selling organizations are also in this marketing category. Companies like Tupperware and Avon also fully embrace direct marketing at the distribution end.

The second group is companies that sell through intermediaries. Those businesses, which sell through such intermediaries as distributors, wholesalers and particularly through retailers, also have outstanding opportunities to embrace direct marketing in their own right. And by suggesting this, let me make it categorically clear that I'm not suggesting that these marketers abandon retail distribution in favor of mail order. Far from it.

On the contrary, the direct marketing concept should be embraced in order that performance through the retail channel can be optimized. The key is that mass communications through general advertising campaigns should be extended to include two-way communication through direct response advertising.

Let me quote just two examples, one of an opportunity for marketers of consumer durables and one for marketers of packaged goods. First, the consumer durables: Let's say you market a product which has, as most goods of a durable nature do, a lengthy list of features and benefits. What can you do? Do you try to communicate all these worthwhile copy points in your general advertising?

Do you try to be all things to all people? Do you try to appeal to a wide audience purely on the image aspect of the brand? Obviously, general advertising in the mass media is not the way to communicate all that could be said about your product. Nor is this approach good enough to satisfy the consumer's need for detailed information prior to a purchase.

This communication gap can be filled by direct marketing. Information of a detailed nature can be offered through direct response advertising in the mass media. People who have their interest aroused can respond seeking the information they need. You can communicate all the features and benefits to qualified prospects in a follow-up program.

The packaged goods marketers essentially embrace direct marketing through sales promotion programs, such as sweepstakes, competitions, cash-back offers, and so on. But, in my view, they should go beyond this and attempt to create a dialogue with the consumer through interactive communication. These concepts do, of course, support the existing retail distribution system.

The third category is the business-to-business marketers. Any business which markets its products or services to other businesses generally embraces direct marketing as *the major system* in the mix.

Quite frankly, the important issue here is that these organizations should perceive themselves as direct marketers. With the concept in mind, the right balance with general advertis-

ing is more likely to occur. And in this frame of mind the company is much more likely to take a flexible approach to the communications mix and the distribution mix.

There is no doubt, for instance, that the order-taker style of salesperson has largely been replaced by two-step personal selling and by mail-order systems. With products or services that are complex, professional personal selling is usually essential.

On the other hand, replenishment of accessories to current customers, for example, can be more cost-effectively stimulated through business-to-business mail-order marketing. The IBM mail-order catalog is a fine example of this approach. All in all, there are marvelous opportunities for all kinds of businesses and organizations to embrace direct marketing.

Initially, all it takes is a better understanding of the concept we've discussed today and a willingness to appraise the existing marketing plan and to look for ways to better balance the general marketing and direct marketing mix.

Having outlined the concept of direct marketing, I think it's only fair that I try to put the direct marketing system into proper perspective for you. We hear so much these days about the explosive growth of direct marketing activity that it makes one really wonder about the facts. (See Direct Response Advertising— Estimate A.)

Let's examine direct response advertising. According to the Australian Direct Marketing Association research, the expenditure on direct response for the generation of mail-order sales, subscriptions, and donations was $253.1 million in 1982-1983. To that, we must add the expenditure on direct response advertising for sales leads generation, enquiry generation, and sales promotion.

There is no research to show the value of expenditure in any of these categories, but at Clemenger Direct Response, our desk research indicates that it would add at least $250 million

Direct Response Advertising Expenditure—1982-83 (Estimate A)

1. Generation of mail-order sales, subscriptions, donations. (Source: ADMA)	$253,100,000
2. Sales leads generation 3. Enquiry generation (for brochures, samples, etc.) 4. Sales promotion programs	$250,000,000
Total (approximate)	$500,000,000

Direct Response Advertising Expenditure—1982-83 (Estimate B)

1. Generation of mail-order sales, subscriptions, donations. (Source: ADMA)	$253,100,000
2. Sales leads generation 3. Enquiry generation (for brochures, samples, etc.) 4. Sales promotion programs	$500,000,000
Total (approximate)	$750,000,000

Direct Mail Advertising Expenditure—1982-83 (Estimate A)

1. Generation of mail-order sales, subscriptions, donations. (Source: ADMA)	$ 97,100,000
2. Sales leads generation 3. Enquiry generation and fulfillment 4. Sales promotion programs 5. General advertising (business-to-business)	$ 50,000,000
Total (approximate)	$150,000,000

Direct Mail Advertising Expenditure—1982-83 (Estimate B)

1. Generation of mail-order sales, subscriptions, donations. (Source: ADMA)	$ 97,100,000
2. Sales leads generation 3. Enquiry generation and fulfillment 4. Sales promotion programs 5. General advertising (business-to-business	$100,000,000
Total (approximate)	$200,000,000

Direct Response Advertising Expenditure—1982-83

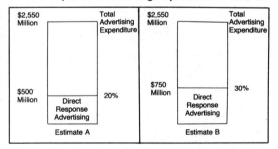

to the ADMA figure for a total of $500 million. (See Direct Response Advertising—Estimate B.)

However, the expenditure in the areas not measured could be as high as $500 million and this would yield a total of $750 million. (See Bar Chart: Direct Response Advertising.)

Comparing these estimates with total advertising expenditure in Australia, direct response may represent around 20 percent to 30 percent of all advertising expenditure. Over the last two decades, there certainly have been significant changes in the way media have been used.

Let's consider direct mail. (See Direct Mail Advertising: Estimate A.) This has always been the main advertising medium for direct marketing. Direct mail is the medium for communication with customers and captive prospects. It is, and will remain, a major medium for business-to-business advertising campaigns.

ADMA research indicates that the value of direct mail advertising expenditure for the generation of mail-order sales, subscriptions and donations was $97.1 million for 1982-1983. If you add to that the anticipated expenditure of $50 million on direct mail for lead generation promotions, enquiry generation campaigns, consumer sales promotion campaigns and business-to-business general advertising, then the annual value of direct mail advertising is more likely to be at least $150 million.

It is possible that the value of direct mail in categories two to five could be as high as $100 million. This would suggest that expenditure on direct mail could be as high as $200 million. (See Direct Mail Advertising: Estimate B.) Therefore, our estimates indicate that direct mail represents around 6 percent to 8 percent of all advertising expenditure in Australia.

Telephone Selling Expenditure—1982-83 (Estimate A)

1. Generation of mail-order sales, subscriptions, donations. (Source: ADMA)	$16,700,000
2. Sales leads generation	$33,000,000
Total (approximate)	$50,000,000

Telephone Selling Expenditure—1982-84 (Estimate B)

1. Generation of mail-order sales, subscriptions, donations. (Source: ADMA)	$ 16,700,000
2. Sales leads generation	$ 83,000,000
Total (approximate)	$100,000,000

Mail-Order Sales 1982-83—Consumer Market

In recent years, we have seen the emergence of telephone marketing and, in particular, the outbound telephone selling aspect. (See Telephone Selling: Estimate A.) If we add a low $33 million for lead generation to the ADMA figure of $16.7 million for mail-order sales, then the telephone selling investment would be around $50 million.

Alternatively, if we optimistically value lead generation at $83 million, then telephone selling may be worth around $100 million in Australia. (See Telephone Selling: Estimate B.) These rough estimates suggest that the telephone is an important communications medium, particularly for business-to-business marketing.

How big is the mail-order industry? And is it growing in Australia? Let's try to answer these often-asked questions. First, the ADMA research indicates that the value of consumer mail-order sales (that is, excluding business-to-business mail-order sales and fund raising income) was $953 million in 1982-1983. According to the Australian Bureau of Statistics, the value of retail sales of all goods for 1982-1983 was $40,539 million. On this basis, *mail order represents only 2.35 percent of all retail sales.*

However, if one excludes groceries and food from overall retail sales—that is, products that are generally not suited to mail-order marketing—then mail order represents 3.77 percent of general merchandise sales (goods that are typically sold through department stores, specialty stores, and boutiques).

By any measure, mail order is only a relatively small part of the total retail scene. However, changing socioeconomic patterns, new technology, and changing lifestyles will see greater use of the mail-order system in the future.

In a complex world, it would be imprudent to dogmatically state the reasons why direct marketing is gaining greater acceptance. The reasons really do not matter greatly, but the fact that direct marketing is proliferating is an important business trend.

Philosophically, any business activity which encourages better relations between marketers and consumers and which encourages a communication dialogue is a positive step forward. In this sense, direct marketing may prove to be the ultimate marketing concept to better satisfy consumer needs and wants.

To conclude, I want to relate yet another quote from *In Search of Excellence:*

> The excellent companies really are close to their customers. Other companies talk about it. The excellent companies do it.

Vin Jenkins, "Understanding Direct Marketing Concept Is Vitally Important," *Direct Marketing,* October 1984. Reprinted by permission of *Direct Marketing* magazine.

Don't Cry for Us Madison Avenue

RICHARD ARMSTRONG

In recent years, general advertising agencies have proceeded to buy out or otherwise obtain direct marketing advertising agencies. These general agency personnel have the notion that direct marketing seeks to generate responses, while ignoring image. In reality, however, image building has been and continues to be an important part of the direct marketers concept. General agency personnel can profit a great deal by learning how direct marketers deal with the image issue.

EVER SINCE MADISON AVENUE FINISHED ITS feeding frenzy on the direct-marketing industry, there's been a lot of talk in the trade press about "a new era of creativity in direct response." With an influx of creative talent from Madison Avenue, so the argument goes, direct marketers at last will learn something about building an image for their clients.

It has been suggested that old-fashioned direct marketers like myself are the advertising industry's equivalent of hit-and-run drivers. In our reckless pursuit of profits, we neglect the long-term consequences of our actions. We would, for example, gladly print our direct mail on toilet paper if we thought it would cut the cost-per-thousand.

All this is about to change, however, now that Madison Avenue has taken over the direct-marketing agencies. At last, we junk mailers are going to discover the secrets of Madison Avenue creativity. Specifically, we're going to learn—fanfare and timpani roll—how to create an image.

Well, speaking on behalf of my fellow direct marketers:

Thanks, but no thanks. Or, to put it more bluntly, if the people responsible for Mr. Whipple have something to say about "image" to the people responsible for L.L. Bean ... well, we're listening. Meanwhile, maybe there's a thing or two you can learn from *us*. In fact, there are five ways direct marketers build an image that general advertisers would be wise to remember.

1. Direct marketers offer ironclad guarantees.

Nothing builds a company's image in the customer's mind better than a good guarantee and a commitment to honor it, yet general advertisers rarely use this age-old technique. The value of a guarantee was forcefully brought home to me on a recent trip to Maine. Nearly every native I met had a story to tell me about L.L. Bean, and most of these tales revolved around Bean's legendary guarantee. I heard about kayaks returned after 10 years and cheerfully replaced, refunds made for scuffed hiking boots and moth-eaten sweaters, all after years of use. Surely some of these accounts were exaggerated, but does it matter? A company whose customers are willing to stretch the truth to convince others certainly doesn't have an image problem.

2. Direct marketers go beyond building an "image" toward building a "relationship."

Does your grandmother have an "image"? Does your wife, or husband? I guess they do. But you actually have more than just an *image* of these people; you have a *relationship* with them. Thanks to general advertising, I have an image of IBM. But thanks to direct marketing, I have a relationship with Lillian Vernon. Nothing carnal, mind you, but my relationship with Lillian is based on intimate transactions which have been maintained over a period of years. I've received letters from her, I've spoken with her assistants on the phone, I've had my problems resolved, my questions answered and—in return for being such a good friend—I've received gifts and discounts. As far as I'm concerned, Lillian Vernon's image couldn't be better.

3. Direct marketers seldom change their image; they merely add to it.

Pepsi-Cola has had about five images in my lifetime. Coca-Cola has had three images in the last month. The "Kiplinger Letter," however—a financial newsletter sold primarily by direct mail—has not only kept the same image for the past 35 years; they've literally been mailing the same letter. Madison Avenue's first instinct is to change a product and tell their customers it's "new and improved." The direct marketer's first instinct is to tell his customers that his company has been in business since the turn of the century, that the product has never changed, that millions have used it in the past with great results. Direct marketers take an additive approach to their image to let it grow and sink deep roots in the consumer's mind. General advertisers, on the other hand, take an *overhaul* approach: When the product's image shows signs of fading, wipe it out and create a new one. Thus the $25 million that a client spends on one campaign will be rendered worthless by the $30 million he spends on the next. In the long run, which approach works best?

4. Direct marketers personalize their companies.

To their credit, general advertisers have caught on to this technique in recent years, but as thrilled as Madison Avenue was with the success of Frank Perdue and Lee Iacocca as spokesmen for their own companies, we direct marketers reacted with a huge yawn. We've been doing this for years! What better way to create an image for your company than to incarnate it in the form of a real human being? From the homegrown peaches of Harry & Da-

vid to the electronic gadgetry of Richard Thalheimer, customers trust the product because they trust the man behind it.

5. Direct marketers create a good image for themselves by maintaining a good image of their customers.

When a company has a good image of me, I have a good image of it. When a company treats me like a fool, my image of it goes down. It's as simple as that.

Direct mail has had a bad rap recently and, unfortunately, much of the criticism has come from the hybrid agencies that were spawned by Madison Avenue's seduction of direct-marketing companies. I'm thinking especially of a recent advertisement by Scali, McCabe, Sloves Direct that attacked "junk mail" for being ugly, insulting and demeaning to its readers.

I don't agree. I do confess that much of the direct mail I receive contains gimmicky involvement devices—"Yes/No" stickers and so on—but I don't find these particularly insulting ... nowhere near as insulting as "Ring around the collar," for example.

If anything, I find my direct mail treats me as much more of an intellectual than I really am. In recent weeks, I've received mail from the *Nation,* the *New Republic* and the *National Review* which sought to engage my mind on a variety of political, social and economic issues to which I previously had given scarcely a moment's thought. This is heady stuff for a guy who gets a kick out of "The Love Boat."

Granted, these are upscale products, but even my most downscale direct mail makes certain flattering assumptions about me which Madison Avenue TV commercials rarely do: (1) That I can read, (2) that I can think, (3) that I am capable of making a decision, and (4) that I'm an individual who acts on free will.

So, like most Americans, I read or skim almost all of my direct mail. And, like most Americans, I consider Madison Avenue's "creative" TV commercials to be excellent opportunities for going to the bathroom.

Richard Armstrong, "Don't Cry for Us Madison Ave.," *Advertising Age*, Vol. 56, August 26, 1985. Reprinted by permission of Crain News Service.

Two Faces, Two Revolutions, Two Opportunities

STAN RAPP

The wall between direct and general marketers is breaking down. The mass advertising of the past is slowly being enriched by direct-response advertising. Confusion occurs when no distinction is made between direct marketing's mail-order past and its database-driven future. Using the computer, the mass markets of the past have been "demassified." This permits the search for that special person, or firm, who is just right for your special product or service. Then, having made a sale, the database-driven direct marketing approach permits the maximization of follow-on sales and buyer–seller linkage, and leads to stronger buyer–seller relationships.

WHEN THE FIRST SPUTNIK ORBITED THE EARTH in 1957, the idea that it would be possible to photograph an object the size of a human being from a satellite a hundred miles up seemed inconceivable. Yet our ability as marketing people to target individual consumers has advanced no less rapidly. This newfound ability is fueling the growth of the phenomenon we call direct marketing.

During the past year, Tom Collins and I have been writing a book about the new direction in which we see marketing going. We have taken a few steps back from our everyday involvement to look at the impact the computer and other technological changes are having on past assumptions about advertising and promotion.

What we saw was the wall between mass marketers and direct marketers breaking down. The word we heard spoken increasingly in the halls of Colgate and Bristol-Myers, at GTE and IBM, at Phillip Morris, R. J. Reynolds/Nabisco and Kimberly-Clark is direct marketing.

But, it is not *only* direct mail order selling, which eliminates the middleman, that fascinates them. It's something quite different: It's a new direction in marketing strategy, a new way of advertising, selling, thinking, which is affecting and will increasingly affect almost *all* providers of advertised goods and services.

Slowly but steadily, the mass advertising of the past is being enriched by direct response advertising that locates and communicates directly with a company's best prospects and customers. This newfound ability can be equally rewarding—whether selling a product or a service, whether selling by mail or by phone or at a retail location.

Some of the confusion about direct marketing comes from the fact that it has two faces: One looks to direct marketing's mail-order past and the other to its database-driven future.

Let's turn the clock back a hundred years or so to 1878 when *Gody's* fashion magazine offered what they described as an unparalleled premium—one never offered by any magazine either in this country or in Europe. Subscribers were to receive a free Chromo print. The copy frankly states that the purpose of the offer is "to make it difficult for other magazines to compete."

The early years of mail order were the golden years of telling it like it is in advertising copy. Sears, Roebuck customers of 1966 received the Big Book featuring Cheryl Tiegs as a teenager on the cover, and inside were "the headless wonders of yesteryear" and their nononsense sales message.

Then came the revolution—a revolution spawned by the computer, the credit card, free phone calls and demassified markets.

It didn't happen overnight. It required two decades to totally transform what we once called mail order and now call direct marketing. Mail order was a way of selling directly to the public. Direct marketing is a concept many different kinds of advertisers are employing to form relationships with individual consumers.

Norman Rockwell's typical American family consisting of husband, wife and 2.7 children has just about disappeared. Mom's not home watching TV. She's out working, while her VCR records the programs for her; and she zaps the commercials when she plays it back.

No single factor in the revolutionary changes we have seen can rival the computer chip—a quarter-inch square of silicon capable of storing 1 million bits of random access memory. As the cost of computing comes down, down, down, the pace of change goes up, up, up.

Women in Labor Force with Children under 18

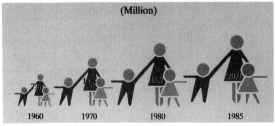

A growing number of working mothers in the labor force continues to increase the demand for more and better products—and the convenience of shopping at home.

In 1973, it cost $7.14 to access 1,000 bits of information. That's about 20 words—enough to recall the name and address of a customer, when a purchase was made and what was purchased. By 1988, that cost will be reduced to about one penny.

The power of the modern computer to economically sort, arrange and analyze vast amounts of data heralds the dawn of a new day for each and every marketer. It provides the power to remember each customer's specific needs, wants and history, and to clone the best customers with computer programs that find people just like them.

The computer supplies the power to motivate an individual purchase based on relevant data. It can target those consumers worth promoting and suggest how much to spend to get them.

800 Numbers and Credit Cards

VISA and MasterCard were introduced in the late 1960s. It is estimated that there were more than 600 million credit cards—possibly as many as 800 million—in use last year. That's better than six or seven cards per household. They are used in 29 million transactions daily.

As staggering as these totals may seem, the number is increasing monthly as Citicorp, BankAmerica, Chase Manhattan and Sears put out tens of millions of pieces of mail offering still more instant credit.

Anyone who is *anyone* can shop by card from home—day or night—by picking up the phone, and they don't even have to pay for the call. Toll-free 800 numbers became a viable service in 1967, but advertisers were slow to realize their enormous potential for many years.

Business-to-business marketers were the first to use the 800 service. Now, more than half the advertisers in *Business Week* and other business publications invite immediate response by phone. By the early 1980s, advertisers reaching the consumer jumped on the bandwagon.

Cap'n Crunch set a world's record for stimulating telephone calls to an 800 number. On a treasure map inside Cap'n Crunch boxes, Quaker Oats printed a free telephone number to call for instructions on finding the villain La Foote. More than *24 million phone calls* were received, and Cap'n Crunch increased its market share by 33 percent with a residual increase of 15 percent.

While Cap'n Crunch was going all out in pursuit of La Foote, the liquor industry was timidly tiptoeing into the free-phone era. Liquor advertising has always been a creative affair, but now something else is creeping into its advertising. Chivas Regal, the most spectacular creative success ever seen in the liquor category, invites prospects to call and send a gift of Chivas. Hennessy added a reminder card bearing their 800 number for the prospect to carry in his pocket for the day he needs to send a gift or respond to a sudden thirst.

The coupling of the free phone call with the credit card established the home as a shopping center in its own right. Once the public accepted 800 numbers, it became easy and relatively economical for advertisers to strike up relationships with prospects, while creating one-to-one dialogue with their prime target audience.

Demass Market

The mass market has splintered into the demassified market. In 1966, a Coke was it. Today, depending on taste and lifestyle, cola drinkers have at least seven varieties to choose from. Revlon makes 157 shades of lipstick; 41 of them are pink. Hair coloring once meant Miss Clairol and little else. Today, Clairol offers *nine* different hair color brands, and right alongside are eight more brands from L'Oréal.

These days, a purchaser needs a consultant to make a buying decision, and the manufacturer needs nine different ad campaigns where there was one mass advertising strategy before.

Splintered markets mean splintered budgets. As the addressed market becomes more segmented, it becomes increasingly uneconomical to advertise to *everybody* just to reach *somebody*. It suddenly makes much more sense to find those special somebodies and talk directly to them. *That's* where direct marketing comes in.

As if there weren't enough to deal with already, there is the changing society. The number of working women with children younger than 18 keeps rising. There are more than 20 million of them. Women who work outside the home have less time to shop in stores. They spend many evenings with their favorite catalogs—choosing the latest gourmet cookware or bath accessories or exquisite chocolates.

Yes, it's a different world and a different marketplace. A data glut. A cashless society. A shattered mass market. A rapidly aging population. A growth of single-person households.

All this and deregulation too.

Godzilla

Do you remember the 1966 Sears catalog with Cheryl Tiegs on the cover? Cheryl is back 20 years later. It's a new Cheryl, and it's a new Sears, aimed at a new generation of upwardly mobile catalog shoppers.

Sears has become the ultimate database marketer. It can identify and satisfy almost every need of each individual customer. Sears offers Allstate insurance, Coldwell Banker real estate, Dean Witter investments and the Sears Savings Bank. An interrelated databank provides each Sears business unit access to a vast customer file. So, if you buy a home through Coldwell Banker, you can expect to receive the Sears Home Furnishings catalog and a home insurance offer from Allstate. And if you have any money left over, you'll hear from Dean Witter. *Now, that's direct database marketing.*

Now comes Sears' Discover credit card—the icing on their marketing cake. The holder can take up to 1 percent as an annual dividend from Discover and use it to reduce his or her current balance, or choose a Sears gift certificate or open a savings account and Sears will double the value.

Sears is today's Godzilla of marketing, doing battle not only with retail and catalog competitors, but with insurers, bankers, real estate brokers and investment houses. Sears is building the ultimate consumer database that knows just about everything about the buying behavior of 40 million customers.

The transformation of Sears is just one reflection of how yesterday's mail order world has changed into a new breed of direct marketers who use computers to enhance and manipulate customer files to locate new marketing opportunities.

Remember the Montgomery Ward catalog from the 1920s? Today we have Victoria's Secret. If there's any doubt about just how upscale and different today's catalogs have become, just try shopping by mail from Tiffany's, or dip into a lush dream book from Gucci, or take a fling with Cartier and order a cushion-cut sapphire ring for $4,250 or a yellow sapphire drop necklace for $22,500.

It all adds up to 8.5 billion catalogs a year targeted to the individual needs of various market segments.

Everybody's Doing It

The biggest single change brought about by the past two revolutionary decades is that suddenly everybody is doing it. Everybody is getting into direct marketing: the airlines, the phone companies, business-to-business marketers, retailers, automobile manufacturers, package goods companies, oil companies, overnight delivery services, insurance companies and banks.

The Second Revolution

The 1960s were the heyday of mass marketing. The 1970s decade of segmentation and

line extension were followed by the intensified niche marketing of the early 1980s. By 1990, the revolution will be complete.

The future does not necessarily belong to direct marketers or to mass marketers. It belongs to companies that understand the new marketplace, the new media and the new technologies.

Tom Collins and I constructed a universal model for maximizing sales—a guide to be used in selling in stores, by mail, by phone, by electronic terminal or with personal salespeople.

MaxiMarketing does not mean a company should give up what it is already doing. It means examining every step of the selling process in light of the new realities.

The first step in the process is *maximized targeting*: finding and focusing on that *special* person who is just right for your *special* product or service.

A public database is one that has already done most of the hard work. It has identified, by name and address, almost every household that uses a given product type but not your brand. Or, every household that has exactly the hobbies or equipment or lifestyle your product or service calls for.

The most ambitious and useful undertaking in profiling households by name, address and brand purchase began with a JFY Audit America questionnaire, mailed to 70 million households last year. JFY now has current data on 21 million households. Big guns like RJR/ Nabisco, Procter & Gamble and General Foods are aiming their sights at competitive brands by mailing to JFY names. Reportedly, they are spending millions of dollars for these golden prospects. Usage in the past eight months has spread to pharmaceuticals, household products, distilled spirits and soft drinks.

Here is how Searle used database prospecting for Metamucil. Searle had already repositioned Metamucil (its laxative product) as a fiber supplement. It targeted three groups for database marketing: dieters, laxative users selected from the JFY database and young urban professionals.

It mailed an unusual calendar of coupons developed to encourage repeat usage. It paid off with an overall response of 15 percent. The coded cents-off coupons were used to track response over a year's time to determine who was or wasn't a trier, and who became a one-, two- or three-time user. Searle then went back into the mail with targeted offers to turn non-triers into triers and triers into regular users.

Ford recently went about building a prospect database by using print media to survey consumers about what they like and don't like about their cars, when they expect to be in the market for a new model, and what type of transportation best fits their family's needs. Ford could then mail the right offer to the right family for the right Ford car.

Spelunking

Spelunking is the exploration of caves. A cave is a deep niche, so spelunking for prospects is another name for niche marketing.

A fascinating example of spelunking is an ingenious promotion from a veteran direct marketer who found an interesting way to sell tours of Ireland. He fills up four busloads a week, at a charge of around $2,000 per tour member, by sending personalized messages to a number of people who have the same Irish surname.

The letter says: "On behalf of the Ancient and Royal Clan McClure and the men, women and children of Ireland, it gives me great pleasure to invite you and your family to attend the historic Grand Reunion of the McClures in Ireland. . . ."

He has found his niche, and it is paying off handsomely. Using *Maximized Synergy,* he is making his advertising do two or three jobs at the same time.

In the era of one-to-one marketing, nobody who is anybody will ever run an ad in a magazine or a newspaper without a sales promotion offer or an 800 number or a direct response coupon.

Double-duty advertising has already changed the face of advertising in the fragrance category. Giorgio of Beverly Hills was the first to combine making an image with making a sale right off the page. Giorgio's perfume became a leading national brand by using double-duty advertising that opened up 250 top retail outlets while taking charge card orders by mail and phone.

Giorgio went from $1.2 million in sales of its own exclusive fragrance in 1982 to total annual sales last year of more than $100 million. Then, the company used scent strips again to introduce a Giorgio fragrance for men. More double-duty advertising—selling by mail and in stores.

Calvin Klein followed Giorgio's example when it launched Obsession. A trail-blazing $17 million campaign took mail and phone orders while pushing image to establish the retail brand.

If Calvin Klein could establish a brand— and get its $17 million back in direct mail-order sales—how much more would the company be able to budget while planning the next launch? The answer came with a smashing introduction of Obsession for men and another blockbuster for their line of lotions and potions for the body. Obsession's advertising has shown that in an era when just about everyone has credit cards and a phone at hand, a manufacturer can sell direct, get reach and frequency, and keep his retailers happy all at the same time.

Maximized Linkage

How often have you sent away for more information for a product or service in answer to a compelling piece of copy and received a reply in a plain brown wrapper. And—horror of horrors—no personal letter. No re-sell. No offer for acting now. And no reflection of the creative strategy used in the ad campaign that got you to ask for the information in the first place. It's as though the people who create the ads never talk to the people who send out the literature.

Most advertisers seem oblivious to the chance to address their best prospects and to send them a series of meaningful follow-ups that will lead to the sale—wherever it is made.

Not so, Cuisinarts. It is creating phenomenal sales success by building in linkage between the advertising and the sale. Cuisinarts starts with whole-brain advertising that appeals to the rational and emotional sides of its target audience. The recipes for the dishes shown are always offered in ads with a toll-free number for the nearest dealer.

But the company doesn't stop there. It offers subscriptions to the Cuisinarts magazine and a Cuisinart Cooking Club with a membership fee of $18. Purchasers of a Cuisinarts appliance can get a three-month membership free. Since it has the names of many Cuisinarts owners and is sending the bulletins as a club member, it takes advantage of the opportunity to offer lots of attachments too. Cuisinarts is an example of getting close to the customers and *staying* close to be sure he or she gets addicted to using the product or service.

We are at a crossroads in advertising comparable to the explosion of creativity that followed the emergence of television as the dominant medium in the 1950s. A few pioneering advertisers, such as Cuisinarts, Air France and

Nikon, are starting to focus creative attention on what to do *after* the advertising runs. The results can be as electrifying as the birth of the 30-second commercial.

The link provided in Air France advertising is the offer of a videocassette, replacing the usual travel brochure sent in the past. When a respondent phones for a tape, the telemarketing representative asks for his credit card number. If the tape isn't returned within 10 days, the respondent's account is charged $29.95. Prospective travelers have a chance to see the very hotels offered in package tours as well as highlights of the cities to be visited. It's a moving demonstration of the fantasy of being in France. At last word, Air France was mailing out 2,500 tapes a week, and the videocassette had become an effective link between the advertising and the sale.

Maximized Sales

The 1980s has seen one group of advertisers after another joining the rush to develop a direct relationship with their best prospects and customers. The innovator in the diaper category was Huggies with a $10 million customer relationship program aimed at new mothers. The point of all the relating—a prenatal-to-toddler booklet series describing stages of development—is these cents-off coupons included with the helpful baby care and guidance materials.

Before deregulation, AT&T advertising was all about reaching out and touching someone. After deregulation, AT&T realized that it had better do something more for a customer than just sending a bill. So, Opportunity Calling was born. AT&T later announced a $100 million budget to sell the idea.

The airlines found that frequent traveler programs could keep them in touch with the 20 percent of the market that provides 80 percent of the profits. Johnson & Johnson discovered it could use the share of mind it gained selling baby care products to become the number-two seller of toys—both direct and in stores—to those very same families who buy the company's baby powder.

The 1980s will be remembered in marketing history as the decade of transition. We are living through a shift from "get a sale *now* at any cost," to the building and management of customer databases that track the lifetime value of the relationship with each customer.

As the cost of accumulating and accessing data drops, the ability to talk directly to prospects and customers—and build one-to-one relationships with them—will continue to grow.

In this new era, there are two major opportunities for those marketers who are ready, willing and able to break out of the box of past assumptions: 1) Add to what is already working well; 2) Expand into new territory.

MaxiMarketing is a continuum that turns likely prospects into lifetime customers. It facilitates targeting prospects who are clones of the best customer in a database. They can be found and communicated with in the most likely media.

The advertiser can appeal to them with whole-brain advertising that invites a response. Sales promotion can be designed to deepen the relationship with prospects, not just make the sale. Prospects' names and addresses can be obtained by building linkage into advertising.

Double-duty advertising can reap a twofold reward. The marketer can build a relationship with the customer database, his company's private advertising medium. And through the database he can begin to develop additional sales of various kinds, with perhaps even different channels of distribution.

This continuum adds up to much more than the sum of its parts, because it makes possible a single unifying marketing strategy. The good will that has been established in a company's brand name over the years can be turned into new products sold directly to the customer database. The company can sell direct while supporting a basic channel of distribution.

When the light of a new day dawns on January 1, 1990, I believe that all service companies and many product manufacturers will be spending as much time and money maximizing their relationships with known customers as they now do on their brand-image advertising to the world at large.

Taken individually, any of the changes discussed here can have a profound effect on the success or failure of a business in reaching its marketing objectives. Taken together, they add up to no less than a new playing field with a new set of ground rules for business decision makers. This unfamiliar terrain requires looking with new eyes at every step in the marketing process: From preliminary research to product development and pricing, all the way through to deciding on advertising and promotion strategies.

It is vital for marketers to re-examine the advertising and promotion assumptions that seemed to work so well just a decade ago and to test them against the new realities.

To fail to do so is to risk falling behind competitors who are already exploring the explosive opportunities of fresh new ideas. These new directions use media technologies to target the most likely prospects, insist on accountability in measuring the effectiveness of each advertising expenditure, and link the advertising to assembling a private database that can be used to convert prospects into triers and transform triers into heavy users.

Tom Collins and I chose a quotation from Bill Bernbach as the frontpiece for our book on *MaxiMarketing:* "Those who are going to be in business tomorrow are those who understand that the future, as always, belongs to the brave."

It also belongs to the quick. Again and again—couponing is just one example—we have seen that when everybody jumps into a good thing, the law of diminishing returns gradually sets in.

But we have also seen—with advertisers as diverse as Coca-Cola and American Airlines—that when a company establishes a strong early lead with a new concept and works at maintaining it, it is very hard to overtake it.

Stan Rapp, "Two Faces, Two Revolutions, Two Opportunities," *Direct Marketing,* September 1986. Reprinted by permission of *Direct Marketing* magazine.

Data-based Targeted Advertising
New Age of Marketing Relevance
LESTER WUNDERMAN

Before the Industrial Revolution, all marketing was direct and all communications relevant to the sale. But the industrial revolution separated buyers and sellers, enhanced the role of intermediaries, and led to loss of producer control of contact quality. To regain some control, the manufacturers began to go out in front of the intermediaries and build awareness, images, and franchises with the customer—to the benefit of the intermediary. This system worked very well, but the overall result was that the two parties who had the most interest in the product, the party that made it and the party that would use it, were not in contact with each other. Furthermore, not being a prime party to the transaction, resellers large-

ly abdicated their role as service intermediaries. In addition, the system required the manufacturer to make contacts with the whole market, not just the relevant part, or parts, of it, leading to waste promotion. The direct marketing approach brings the two primary parties back together and eliminates much of the waste. General advertising modifies attitudes and direct marketing modifies behavior. Modern marketers who look for ways to put direct and general marketing together properly can hope for sales explosions greater than any yet achieved.

MARKETING TODAY IS IN A CRISIS AT A CROSS-road. Two separate paths have come to the same place at a difficult and confusing moment in our economic history.

Let me for the moment label one road as indirect marketing supported by general advertising. And let me label the other as direct marketing supported by transactional targeted data-based advertising.

Discouraging economic results have raised some questions about whether indirect marketing and general advertising are sufficiently accountable in today's difficult business climate. Is the best answer to depressed sales to do more of what we have already been doing?

Or is there finally a real choice? New targeted communications technologies and techniques are about to threaten some of our conventional communications assumptions. Will they grow fast enough, or ever become widespread enough to become the main media method? And even if they do, can we make them effective enough to assume the major task of helping to build businesses.

Do these two roads represent separate directions, each leading to a different marketing objective? Or are both feeder roads, coming from different places but leading to yet another new marketing superhighway where sales speeds will far exceed our current rules of the road?

Let's back up a bit and trace each to their earlier source and see if we can determine where they and we are heading.

There was a time in America, as everywhere, when all marketing was direct and all communication relevant. Before the Industrial Revolution almost everything sold was custom made. Buyer and seller were in direct contact with each other, and they could exchange information as needed. A man who wanted a suit brought his needs to a tailor, and the suit was made for him—and him alone.

Each community had its craftsmen, and each craftsman knew his community and the needs of his individual customers. The buggy maker, for example, knew who needed a buggy and when the family had become affluent enough to afford a better one or a second one.

While the manufacturing process was slow, laborious and inefficient, the marketing process was totally effective. Little, if anything, was made for inventory, and the needs of the consumer were known to, and provided for, by the producer. Advertising, if any, served to encourage such personal connections in areas where competition existed, or to announce the location of a craftsman.

Then came the Industrial Revolution, and suddenly everything changed. Machines made standardized products in volume and at low cost for buyers unknown. Marketing and advertising became necessary and integral parts of the mass production process.

The new system developed quite naturally and with fundamental logic. Machines produced standardized products, at low cost, and in great volume without orders from specific consumers. To distribute the flood of manufactured goods required that they be sold and shipped to resellers, who were wholesalers or retailers. Low prices made it possible for the average consumer to own categories of products heretofore only available to the wealthy.

So began the indirect marketing and distribution system with which we are familiar. When the manufacturer sold his products to a wholesaler or retailer, he lost track of, and control of, his product. It would be sold to the ultimate consumer by a reseller for his own profit, at his own price, and in his own way.

In order to regain some control of the demand for his product, and to remain identified with it, the manufacturer gave the product a brand name or his own name and began to advertise it to the ultimate consumer with whom he would never have any direct contact. The advertising was in the interest of the reseller, helping to create a demand for the products so that reorders would continue for the particular brand offered. The manufacturer could not depend on the loyalty of the reseller to his product or his factory, so the advertising spoke for the manufacturer to the end consumer.

As we know, the system was and is amazingly effective. The consumer welcomed the wide variety of goods made available at low prices, and the distribution system made goods available almost everywhere. A wide variety of new and better products was introduced as the inventive genius of the country was married to the techniques of machine production. Great consumer franchises were created.

New production techniques led to new distribution methods, which led to more advertising, which in turn supported more media. The system was a giant circle which created wealth and work for a growing, expanding and prosperous society.

So what went wrong? Not much. But what happened may have been more significant than we thought. The resellers, who substituted for the manufacturer as the human connection to the consumer, increasingly gave up their service role. Their main interest was in their own efficiency and their own profit. To this end they became more like warehouse depots for the merchandise and increasingly depended on the manufacturers' advertising to create demand for the products.

More and more the competition between manufacturers was expressed in media through advertising rather than between products at the point of sale. The war for the consumer's favor became a media war, because the only access to national media belonged to the manufacturer. The sales transaction belonged to the retailer. The two fundamental partners—the consumer, whose need was to be served, and the manufacturer, whose product satisfied it—remained unknown to each other. This separation of the manufacturer from his ultimate consumer gave rise to general advertising. That is, advertising which created awareness of the product and favorably conditioned the consumer's attitude toward it.

But that advertising had to stop short of trying to complete the sales transaction, because at that point in the marketing process the goods belonged to somebody else. It was advertising done here and now for sales to be made then and there. Manufacturers tried to motivate retailers to act aggressively on their behalf, but were frequently frustrated by the unwillingness or the inability of the resellers to act effectively.

Two Tiers of Advertising

So two tiers of advertising developed: national advertising, which made the product known and attractive; and retail advertising, which attempted to motivate a sales transaction. Because the manufacturer didn't and couldn't know who his specific customers and prospects were, he had to condition the entire marketplace with his message. He couldn't know who would buy his product or when.

The retailer, having largely given up his personal role, frequently didn't know much more. Therefore, both tiers suffered from an underlying structural irrelevance. They could not attain the kind of efficiency which would bring the right product to the attention of the right prospect at the right time. I say this not as criticism. Enormous progress has been made in media efficiency and persuasion technique, but general advertising has not yet developed a communications weapon as precise and as accurate as a rifle. Advertising is still in the shotgun stage.

However, while all the foregoing has been taking place, an alternative system has been improving and sharpening precisely those skills which indirect marketers had given up. The second system is called direct marketing, and it and direct response advertising are the fastest growing advertising and marketing discipline in the world today.

Just as mass production, mass distribution, mass marketing and mass advertising were the logical expressions of the Industrial Revolution, direct, accountable, databased, precision transactional advertising is the perfect expression of the Post Industrial Revolution. If the Industrial Revolution substituted the power and speed of the machine for the endurance and muscle power of man, the Post Industrial Revolution has extended all of his other faculties. Microprocessors, lasers, computers, satellites, robots, speed up and expand the range of: memory, information, computation, precision, communication, and even thinking and reasoning itself.

These extensions of the capability of man begin to make it possible to replicate on a national basis the original person-to-person transactional mode of the preindustrial marketplace. Suddenly men can communicate and deal with each other over great distances. They can match their needs with products that satisfy them, and they can select each other out of the crowd any time they need to. Even products themselves can be custom made on the production line by computer controlled robots.

The computer helps us to find and store information about tens of millions of customers and prospects so that we can find them one at a time. Computerized printing, interactive cable, addressable cable TV, videotex, QUBE, home computers already permit us to initiate and maintain a sales dialogue nationwide, and this ability can only improve. The use of the computer and data-driven communications as a marketing tool is as fundamental a change as the Industrial Revolution itself.

The two prime parties to the great transactional exchange of needs and products are once again in contact with each other. Now we have the same situation nationwide that applied to the buggy maker and his customer locally. The reseller, who has abdicated his role as the service intermediary, will have a radically altered place in this new Post Industrial society. He may cease to be the sole transactor of sales and become the deliverer of service in the interest of buyer and seller. If he does not perform increased and different essential services to both prime parties, he may eventually become redundant.

Now let me try to tell you a bit more about direct marketing and show you how it is used:

• Direct marketing is getting your message direct to the consumer to produce a desired action.

• Direct marketing is a *marketing process* which uses advertising to originate an ongoing dialogue between a prime supplier of goods or services and the ultimate consumer.

• Direct marketing creates a database which is constantly refined as it is used to define, locate and communicate with and sell to prime prospects and customers.

• This database makes possible a unique and totally relevant ongoing dialogue between producer and consumer.

• Direct marketing *creates customers* as well as sales.

• Direct response is a form of advertising which selects and locates targeted prospects in all media, causes them to respond, provides ongoing information, directs purchases through any distribution channel. It results in accountable advertising which creates measurable transactions. Direct marketing uses all media. Let's look at some typical uses of a few of them.

Direct mail. Mail helped in the launching of a major new company—the Advanced Information Systems Division of American Bell. A mailing was sent to 500,000 business prospects of American Bell. It told them what American Bell is and how it can serve them. It asked for a phone inquiry, or if the prospect is not ready to buy, a questionnaire was provided giving information which would update their database for the future.

This database includes customers, prospects, responders, and non-responders. It updates everything known about each prospect or customer company. Each succeeding mailing to each company is computer-printed to guarantee the relevance of each message.

Catalogs. A catalog created for the Consumers Products Division of American Bell acts as a demographic store.

Magazines. A Book-of-the-Month Club ad in *Time* magazine sought to get respondents to subscribe to an ongoing, book-buying service which would offer books each month to customers.

Newspapers. An insert for the Advanced Information Services division of American Bell, which ran in 23 major cities on Sunday was a preprinted insert which in effect carried all of the same information as was contained in the direct mail.

Television. A television commercial for *Time* magazine invited buyers to place an order for a subscription and tells why.

These examples provided just a cursory look at how direct marketing uses a variety of media. Mainly I want you to understand that direct marketing is not just direct mail—it's every medium you can use to create a transaction. Even direct mail is no longer the direct mail you may have experienced. It's not an advertisement in an envelope, but an engineered, scientific, data-driven communication or series of communications which deal individually with a customer or prospect by name and by problem.

Such advertising has no reason to exist if it is not relevant, if it is not accountable, and if it is not used as a way to begin or continue a dialogue between a prime producer and an ultimate consumer.

So there you have the two separate roads that have led us to where we stand today. As I said when I began, we are in a crisis and at a crossroad. So where do we go from here?

I believe the answer is self-evident if we reduce this discussion to two simple definitions:

- General advertising modifies awareness and attitudes.
- Direct response advertising modifies behavior.

Now, if we can put both of these forces together properly, we might create sales explosions greater than any we have yet achieved.

This is already being done, and let me show you how.

The CIT division of RCA is in the business of making loans. Our research in 1981 indicated that inflation had substantially increased the value of individual homes. CIT could lend money on this increased value to help consumers pay for things they needed. There were, however, several problems. CIT was unknown. The company never advertised to the public. They had no loan offices. Inflation had increased the value of homes to a different extent in each major community in the country.

Newspapers as Retail Centers

The solution we chose was a simple one. We would use newspapers to act as a retail center. We created a preprint, which was individualized to each community in which it appeared. The actual inflation rate in that city was shown so that the consumer could calculate the increase in value of his home. The eight-page newspaper insert told all about CIT and how to call or write to borrow money and what it would cost. After preparing this newspaper ad, we held it.

First we ran a television commercial for four weeks to create awareness of CIT and the opportunity. Four weeks later we placed the booklet in the local newspaper.

Starting on the Thursday evening before the Sunday on which the ad was to appear, we began to run commercials which called attention to our newspaper-like store. We also put direct mail into the market at the same time. The campaign was successful and launched a new business for CIT.

Now, I would like to consider how this combination works for a traditional direct marketer such as L.L. Bean. You all recognize the L.L. Bean catalog. It is really a national lifestyle store.

You probably also recognize the characteristic small space ads seeking sales and catalog inquiries. We place some 1,500 of these in about 200 publications each year.

What you may not recognize is the fact that TV commercials serve to support other L.L. Bean efforts. They are helping enormously to accelerate the growth of one of America's fastest growing companies.

TV commercials for Merrill Lynch certainly help to make the public aware of Merrill Lynch and to feel positively about their services.

The commercials make the 2,000 ads we place each year for Merrill Lynch local offices more effective. They also help direct mail work better. And they set the stage for a commercial which sold more government bonds in one week than Merrill Lynch brokers had sold in the previous six months.

If time permitted, I could tell you more about the new ways by which General Foods is selling coffee, Procter & Gamble is selling diapers, Johnson & Johnson is selling toys, CBS is selling records and electronic games and Pan American is marketing air travel.

The combination of general advertising and databased, targeted direct marketing may be a new and better answer to many of our current marketing problems. It has power, precision, efficiency and accountability beyond that of any other marketing/advertising system in history.

It may in fact be the new marketing weapon that America's largest companies need to win their war against economic adversity and foreign competition.

Lester Wunderman, "Data-based Targeted Advertising: New Age of Marketing Relevance," *Direct Marketing*, July 1983. Reprinted by permission of *Direct Marketing* magazine.

Strategy in Direct Marketing

Marketing Strategies for Maximum Growth

Jim Kobs

Historically, direct marketers have tended to emphasize the tactics of creative execution that are readily testable in the marketplace, for example, is a one- or two-page letter better? But brilliant tactical execution can't save a program that is strategically weak. More attention to strategy is needed. The first step in strategy development is a situation analysis to learn about the marketplace, competitors, and the like. Once objectives are set, strategies can be developed, and tactics, or the details of how strategies will be executed, can be pulled together. Different strategies can be used to reach the same objective, and different tactics can be used to implement the same strategy. Acquiring new customers and then maximizing their value are the two broad, basic marketing objectives that should be considered. When deciding on strategy and objectives, several key questions that might usefully be asked are: Is it more important to build sales or profits?; How heavily should a company invest in new customer acquisition?; Can present customers be profitably contacted more often with existing products or services?; Should a company try to grow the product category or penetrate it?; What is the best price position for a product or service?; Can the media or distribution channels being used be explained?; and, Should a company try to add new products, launch new businesses, or develop new markets?

THERE'S LITTLE DOUBT THAT STRATEGIC PLANning is becoming more and more important throughout the business world, regardless of the type or size of the company involved. And strategic planning has special significance for those of us in direct marketing.

There are two main reasons for this. First, direct response marketers have historically always tended to emphasize the tactics of creative execution—tactics that are readily testable in the marketplace. Tactics like, which premium offer will pull the greatest number of orders? Or which of two different headlines in an ad or letter produces the greater response? Or is it better to use a two-page letter or a four-pager? But in emphasizing tactics like these, direct response marketers have often neglected strategy!

Second, even brilliant tactical execution—using the greatest copy and the most attractive graphics—can never save a program that is strategically weak.

Numerous examples of this over the years come to mind. One is a customer club started by a large manufacturer. On the surface, it seemed like a logical idea. It was promoted heavily with elaborate mailing packages. But it failed because people realized that the so-called club really didn't offer them any significant, meaningful benefits. So while the creative execution of the club's promotional materials was very good, the project ultimately failed because it was strategically weak.

Maybe that's why I've always liked what Michael Porter of the Harvard Business School said about the importance of strategic planning:

It is the unity, coherence and internal consistency of a company's strategic decisions that position the company in its environment, and give the firm its identity, its power to mobilize its strengths, and its likelihood of success in the marketplace.

Let's examine the subject of strategic planning for direct response marketing more closely. Despite its importance to direct response marketers, if one goes through all the direct marketing books ever written, my own book included, there is very little good material written about strategic planning.

The first step toward a sound program of strategic planning is to do something most companies have already had the foresight to do. Namely, develop a detailed situation analysis, which is merely a fancy way of saying, in writing, "where are we now?"

If the job was done correctly, the company already knows certain things, such as:

- What are current sales trends, and what do they suggest?
- What are the present strengths and weaknesses?
- What are the key S.T.E.E.P. (social, technological, economic, environmental, political) factors in the current marketing environment?
- What results are expected from the present way of doing things?
- What is the competition doing?

And so on. With that as background, let's quickly review the meaning of marketing objectives or goals, strategies, and tactics:

Objectives are specific, measurable goals for a period of time.

Strategies are the planned actions designed to reach those objectives.

Tactics are the details of how we will execute the strategies.

Note that more than one strategy can be used to reach a certain objective, and more than one tactic can be used to execute a certain strategy.

These definitions are best understood when discussed in relation to an example in order to see how they work. We'll use a gift catalog business for this purpose.

The objective is to boost sales from the house list by 25 percent. Is that a sound objective by the above definition? No, because no time period was specified for reaching that objective.

So, the objective should be amended to say that it could be reached *during 1987*.

Now, one *strategy* that could be used to reach this objective might be to mail the house list more frequently. A second strategy might be to increase the size of the average order from the house list.

The tactics for implementing the first strategy might include doing three mailings during the Christmas season instead of the usual two; also adding a re-mail catalog to the best names, following each regular catalog during the year.

The tactics for the second strategy of increasing the average order might include adding higher-priced merchandise to the catalog, offering more accessories to complement basic items, establishing a higher minimum order, and pushing credit purchases (which usually are larger than cash purchases).

Direct response marketing objectives fall into two broad categories—acquiring new customers or prospects at the lowest possible cost, and maximizing customer value through conversion, retention and repeat sales.

Acquiring new customers at low cost is a mission that is critically important. New customers or prospects are the lifeblood of any business, not the least reason being that many present customers will inevitably leave for one reason or another—age, dissatisfaction, change in lifestyle, etc.

Acquiring new customers or prospects is often called front-end marketing, and it's where most firms spend a big part of their time and budget. A mail order company might spend 25 percent or 30 percent of its sales on acquiring new customers, compared to only 3 percent to 4 percent of sales spent on advertising by many general advertisers.

Maximizing the value of customers is equally important. It is usually not enough to simply make a one-time sale, or generate a new inquiry on a cost-effective basis. Usually, it costs money to make that sale or get that inquiry, and it is then necessary to make sure, through what is called back-end marketing, that what results is a profitable return on investment.

To put it another way: Spend money on the front-end to make money on the back-end.

Most firms do not spend enough time, attention or money in the back-end area, even though it offers great leverage. For example, just a small boost in the inquiry conversion percentage can make a big difference in sales and profits.

Acquiring new customers and then maximizing their value are the two broad, basic direct marketing objectives that should always be considered.

Naturally, the objectives developed in the marketing plan should be more specific. One might have two, three, four or more objectives for the front-end marketing and likewise two or more objectives for the back-end.

But how does one decide what objectives to include in the marketing plan? What are the key strategic issues to address?

Again, it's hard to find any good books or articles that deal with the subject from a direct marketing perspective. But from my own experience, and the many clients I've dealt with in different types of businesses, there are seven key strategic planning questions that come up over and over again.

At this point, the word "strategic" is being used in the broader sense, as it relates to strategic planning, not just as a strategy to reach an objective.

These are the kind of questions one should be asking to develop objectives. To illustrate each of them, I asked a few senior marketing people at Kobs & Brady to suggest some examples, which I'll cite as we discuss each strategy.

Question 1: *Is it more important to build sales or profits?*

In general, in a lean year, most businesses try to maintain as much *profit* as possible. They tend to cut expenses, including marginal advertising. But in a booming year, their concern is usually to make more sales, to maximize the number of dollars they put on the books.

So to some extent, the right answer to Question 1 is a function of the economy, and what results are expected. But it also depends on things like a company's position in the marketplace, and the resources and facilities available, including how many dollars are in the advertising budget.

How the first question is answered has a lot to do with the plans already put in place. If the goal is to build sales, it is necessary to: promote heavily, use marginal lists or media, spend a larger share of the advertising or direct marketing budget on new prospects, and perhaps launch new products.

If the goal is to *build profits,* it is necessary to: spend less on advertising and promotion, concentrate on using proven lists and media, spend a larger share of the advertising on direct marketing budget promoting to present customers and avoid risky expenditures, like new products.

Note that it's relatively easy to "milk" a mail order business and maximize short-term profits; but this can hurt in the long-term, because there won't be as many customers to go back to next year, and in the years ahead.

An example of whether to emphasize sales or profits is Western Publishing Company. A few years ago, when it was still owned by Mattel, which was going through a lean period, Western Publishing was told to maximize its profit. It concentrated on promoting proven, successful products like its Sesame Street Book Club for the juvenile market, and the Knitting Collection for the adult market. Since both were proven and established products, these promotions produced solid and predictable results.

More recently, under a new owner, Western Publishing's mission shifted to building sales. While the company continued to promote old standbys, it shifted its major efforts and dollars to establishing new products like the Scribbler Activity Program for children, a Crocheting continuity program for adult females, plus a number of similar new programs which followed.

So, either building sales or building profits can be a valid goal, but the strategy that's right for one will probably be dead wrong for the other.

Question 2: *How heavily should a company invest in new customer acquisition?*

That seems like a simple question to answer, but I'm repeatedly surprised at how many supposedly sophisticated marketers don't know what it's worth to get a new customer.

Yet, if a company does not know what a new customer is worth, it can't know how much can be profitably invested in order to get the new customer on the books. Thus, two possibilities exist. Either too much is being spent, which is bad, or too little is being spent, and the result is the loss of sales to more aggressive competitors.

Still, this is the most common strategy for building direct marketing sales. It is necessary, then, to know what the repeat business potential is, and what *payback period* is needed from new customers.

For example, if Xerox is selling a $1,500 copier by mail, the odds are it will be a number of years before the small- and medium-sized firms targeted will be ready to buy another one.

Other than some "small change" potential on copier supplies, it is costly to invest in new customers—it is necessary to acquire them on a break-even basis or better.

Maybe a publisher—for example, Encyclopaedia Britannica or World Book—is promoting an annual yearbook. The yearbook business is like a moneymaking machine, because the repeat order rate is excellent. Most customers, once they sign up, will keep buying each new edition year after year. Therefore, one can really afford to invest in new yearbook customers, because that investment will be made back on future sales.

Finally, how about the mail order photofinishing business? Is the repeat business potential good or bad? Despite what one might think, the fact is, it's bad—because it's a deal-oriented business with very little customer loyalty. Whoever is offering the best price on processing is likely to get the customer's next roll of film. So, like Xerox, the photofinisher can't afford to invest too heavily in new customers.

But overall, this is an area where many firms shortchange themselves. They often limit new customer acquisition to the lists or media that they can use on a break-even or better basis. And at the same time, they thereby limit their growth.

If they knew (and understood) the concept of the lifetime value of a customer, they would realize one simple but all-important truth: The *higher* the lifetime value of a customer, the *more* a company can afford to spend to acquire one!

Question 3: *Can present customers be profitably contacted more often with existing products or services?*

Chances are, yes! For example, in a conversion or renewal letter series, a company might make six or eight mailings, because the last one in the series is still paying out. It brings back more sales or revenue than it costs to get and fulfill the order.

Can existing customers be sold more of the same product? Or related products? Are the products consumable, like paper products

or supplies? What really is needed to maximize profits in this area is a contact strategy. It's a concept that I think is best explained by Bob Kestnbaum of R. Kestnbaum & Co., a leading consulting firm:

> Contact strategy refers to the specific decision of how many times each customer segment will be contacted each year. It is not the same issue as list segmentation or development of promotional media. Segmentation specifies who will be reached. Media selection specifies how offers will be delivered. But contact strategy refers to a positive commitment to reach designated buyers and/or inquirers a specified number of times each year.

I share Bob Kestnbaum's opinion that direct marketers often neglect to establish a contact strategy. But there are some sophisticated direct marketers—like Fingerhut—who mails its best house list segments more than 30 times a year. That's 2½ times per month!

The last time I decoyed Franklin Mint, I got almost 50 mailings over the next 12 months—roughly one a week. Even in the catalog business, when one buys something from most catalogs, they get eight to 20 or more catalogs next year. Or place an order with Haband, which sells men's clothes, as I did a year or so ago. I got six mailings from them in January, and that was on top of three in October and four in November.

Developing this strategy usually involves employing some type of *RFM formula* (recency, frequency, monetary) to identify the best customers.

One small catalog firm used to mail all 100,000 of its customers eight times a year—for a total of 800,000 pieces. By developing an RFM formula and assigning point values, the customer list was broken into four segments.

The best segment got 12 catalogs. The other segments got eight, six or three books. This strategy not only boosted sales, but reduced the mailing quantity from 800,000 to 650,000 with corresponding cost savings.

To be able to mail the customer list heavily, a variety of different products or services is needed.

Starcrest goes even further by offering three different product lines under different names. Starcrest is the name the company uses to promote low-cost merchandise for women. Signature offers more upscale merchandise for females, and Handsome Rewards is the name used to offer merchandise to a male audience.

Question 4: *Should a company try to grow the product category or penetrate it?*

This question relates to both the life cycle of the product or service category, as well as the age or life cycle of the firm's product. The typical product life cycle consists of five stages: 1) relatively low sales during the *testing intro* stage; 2) good sales during the *growth* stage; 3) strongest sales during the *maturity* stage; 4) sales start dropping during the *saturation* stage and; 5) sales drop sharply during the *declining* stage.

It's the direct marketer's job, of course, to try to hold off the decline in sales for as long as possible. Some products and services—like electronic products—have shorter life cycles.

But in many cases, the life cycle of the category is more important than the life cycle of the product. Bankers Life and Casualty sells hospital life insurance—a product in an established category. The company does not have to sell someone on the need for insurance, as much as it has to sell a particular policy.

On the other hand, an HMO (health maintenance organization), needs to help educate people on what HMOs are and help grow the category.

We're really talking here about a concept that is more familiar to general advertisers and package goods firms than to direct response marketers—the concept of market share. If the category is expanding—and a company just maintains its share—sales should increase. But

if the category is a *mature* one, with only nominal growth, a company needs to get a bigger share of sales (or steal someone else's share) to see significant growth.

Let's take the air express business as an example. The U.S. market for overnight delivery is about $4 billion a year. And it's a category that's still growing rapidly—roughly 20 percent a year. Federal Express dominates the market in the U.S., with more than 90 million shipments a year, and a 45 percent market share.

Smaller competitors—Emery or DHL—should let Federal grow the category, and then fight for a larger share of it.

Federal, on the other hand, would try to grow the market, partly with new products and services like Saturday delivery, and if it can't increase its share, at least it can be preserved or maintained.

The marketing share concept will become more common to direct response marketers in the next few years, as we get more statistics and competitive data to help us see where we rank vs. the competition. And sometimes, we have to be prepared to shift strategies, like Home Box Office.

When the cable business was booming, HBO maintained a growth strategy and became the leading premium channel. HBO put the emphasis on selling cable—knowing that, as the category leader, it would get its share of the added business.

But now that the cable market has tightened, HBO has had to shift to a penetration strategy. It's the only way it had a chance to maintain a good growth rate. Some people in the cable business are doing poorly, but HBO's strategy shift has paid off in 400,000 new subscribers in 1986 (according to *TV Guide*), while its main pay-cable competitors are losing viewers or just staying even.

Question 5: *How to position and price a product or service?*

There have been books written on the concept of positioning. Some people think of it more as a creative strategy. It's really a marketing-oriented strategy, and it goes hand-in-hand with pricing.

Positioning helps to segment the market. Segments may be identified that can be better served with a flanker product or line extension. Once again, I'm talking about a concept that is more familiar to general advertisers than to direct response marketers. The packaged goods firms that sell everything from cereal to toothpaste are the real masters of positioning.

But positioning doesn't apply just to products. Look at the service category. Years ago, when people wanted to buy or sell stocks, they went to a stockbroker. And the brokers all charged almost the same thing. Then Charles Schwab came along and changed the rules. And now over 4 million people have decided that a discount broker makes sense.

But guess what! The firm that started it all is no longer the cheapest. Today, there are regular brokers, discount brokers like Schwab, and deep discount brokers like Olde. And this same segmentation is going on in many other categories.

It is necessary to have a clear idea of how a product or service is being positioned and priced. Quill is an example of a company that does. It has become the leader in mail order sales of office supplies and products by promising low prices and big savings. And it is smart enough to stick with that positioning year in and year out.

This strategy can apply to a whole company, or to one product line, or to a single product. Take Bally's Lifecycle, for example. Its commercial model, which is sold to health clubs and fitness centers, is priced at $1,998. But to crack the consumer market, the company had to come out with a different model. It's lighter weight and less expensive. In fact, it's priced at $1,438 with monthly payments—or $560 less than the commercial model.

Question 6: *Can the media or distribution channels being used be expanded?*

For a mail order firm, the media used plays the same role that distribution channels play for other advertisers. Maximum sales cannot be expected if the product is only in one or two types of retail outlets. Yet many direct response marketers arbitrarily limit the media options they use. A classic example is Cincinnati Microwave, a leader in radar detectors.

In 1981, its product was sold exclusively by mail order advertising. In 1984, it was still using only space advertisements, in every logical publication, and in many cases, in every issue. Even when Cincinnati Microwave introduced its first new product since the original one, the Passport model, it still relied solely on space ads to promote it.

Yet, what's happened to many other direct response marketers in the last few years? Haband used to rely only on mailings for its prospecting. But in recent years, a major portion of its prospecting budget was shifted to space ads. In fact, Haband's space ad budget *increased* over 200 percent in a recent four-year period. A multimedia approach is becoming increasingly important to the direct response marketer.

To help visualize both the media and distribution channels available, I developed the accompanying flow chart for the course I teach at Northwestern University.

The top half represents the media alternatives. The bottom half shows the distribution alternatives. The database at the very bottom is obviously a key element in direct marketing. The results we get flow back to the top and influence future advertising. The media alternatives can be used either for prospecting or, in the case of direct mail and telephone, can also be used as database media to target customers and inquiries, with virtually no waste circulation.

The bottom half of the chart shows the three main actions the customer or prospect can take, and how those flow into the three distribution channels. And, other than vending

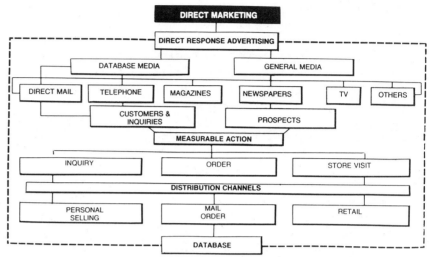

Kobs' flow chart highlights the role that Direct Mail and Telephone play as Database Media. It's adapted from the "Direct Marketing Model" by Vin Jenkins and the "Direct Marketing Flow Chart" by Martin Baier, Pete Hoke, and Bob Stone.

machines, there are only three of them—personal selling, mail order and retail. Over the years, direct marketers have tended to neglect the retail distribution channel. But it's currently getting a lot of attention from catalog firms, ranging from Eddie Bauer to Talbots. Sharper Image has opened 14 new stores in the past year, for a total of 27. These now account for half of Sharper Image's total sales and a typical store carries about 450 items, or almost three times the 160 products carried in the catalog.

On the other side of the spectrum, some traditional retailers are adding direct marketing methods to better serve their customers. Take Florsheim's new Express Service as an example. By adding a video terminal to their stores, customers are offered over 14,000 shoe styles, sizes, and colors, shipped from a central distribution center.

Question 7: *Should a company try to add new products, launch new business, or develop new markets?*

All are somewhat risky. But the alternative to the risk of new ventures and new markets is the certainty of slow stagnation, so it's largely a question of which makes the most sense.

Of course, adding new products is usually more difficult for a manufacturing concern than one that acts as a distributor or retailer. New product start-up for a manufacturer involves considerably more expense—capital, machinery, space, etc.—and necessitates more sales and income potential than does adding a new item or line to a catalog.

But adding new products (even for a manufacturer) is usually less risky, less time-consuming and requires less investment than launching a new business. Take Ace Pecan as an example.

Ace Pecan is a medium-sized firm in the nut business. At retail, it competes with companies like Planters and Fisher Nuts. Ace built its mail order business by selling gourmet nuts with four-color direct mailings to individuals and to companies.

When Ace Pecan expanded from solo mailings to a catalog, it was able to successfully add a number of new products, including Italian sausages. Nuts and sausage might seem like a strange combo, but it's a lot easier to get a few catalog pages to pay out, than launching a separate sausage-by-mail business.

Whether adding new products or new businesses, a key consideration is whether or not they work off the existing database. When Mayo Clinic approached Kobs & Brady a couple of years ago about launching a health newsletter, one of our first questions was, "How many former patients did they have?" The answer was about 5 million (with most of them still alive).

We felt a newsletter would be a low-risk venture, sure to succeed if the editorial product was good. We were right: One year after the launch, the Mayo Clinic newsletter had over 100,000 paid consumer subscriptions.

What about new markets? Normally, opening new markets is less risky and less costly than starting new products or new businesses. Sometimes, a new market can be tested with an existing control mailing. But often it requires a new mailing package, like the one Mayo Clinic used to go after group subscriptions from the business market.

A more elaborate package was called for, and Mayo would have been shortchanging itself not to give this large market segment its best shot. And sometimes, as we saw with Bally's Lifecycle, a different model is needed to really tap the potential of a different market segment.

My final point is not really a strategic planning question but a "checkpoint" question:

Is the advertising execution consistent *with the marketing strategy?*

That includes everything from offers to creative execution. Virtually every direct marketer will immediately answer: "Yes, of course." But that's not always an honest answer because

it's dangerously easy to let these strategies stray in different and wasteful directions.

A photofinisher, for example, may want to promote a quality image, but that would be inconsistent with a deal-oriented business. It could send confusing signals to the consumer.

Let's take a closer look at the creative area, using Ameritech Mobile Communications as an example. Cellular phone technology is new and very few people have car phones. The last figures show there were about 500,000 in the U.S. and 25,000 in the Chicago area.

If a company is trying to grow the category, it does things like concept selling, because it wants to convert non-users into users. But when competition came along and started running very competitive ads, Ameritech shifted its short-term strategy to building and maintaining market share.

So Ameritech's advertising became more benefit and value-oriented. It actually reduced prices, as well as added some new benefits. And, some of its ads included a comparison chart, a common element when fighting for market share. Thus, it is important to always be prepared to shift strategy in order to react to competitive changes in the marketplace.

Hopefully, the marketing strategies discussed will provide something to think about when doing a marketing plan, or developing the next direct marketing program.

Ideally, one should do more than just think about these strategies. Because if direct response marketers really want to *maximize their growth* they can no longer afford to neglect marketing strategy!

Jim Kobs, "Marketing Strategies for Maximum Growth," *Direct Marketing*, May 1987. Reprinted by permission of *Direct Marketing* magazine.

Integrated Direct Marketing
Maximizing Media Mix
Ernan Roman

The key to direct marketing success is not in finding some new medium for reaching prospects. It's in learning to use marketing media together in sophisticated ways to maximize the profitability of every marketing dollar spent. The art and science of achieving synergy in a direct marketing environment can be called Integrated Direct Marketing (IDM). IDM zeros in on a more highly select target market than ever before. It also addresses the prospect's psychographics. Conceptually, IDM is similar to the way the multicomponent direct mail package is designed. Some people read the letter, some the brochure, some the order form, some the lift note. IDM does the same thing by offering different people the opportunity to respond to the medium that suits their individual preferences. When using IDM the issue is not, for example, which medium produced the best results. Instead, it's the relationship between media, for example, a mailing draws minimal response but paves the way for a telephone call.

In the early days of direct marketing, single-shot efforts that were less than perfectly executed often made money, thanks to the raw power of the direct marketing concept. The novelty has worn off. Prospective customers are no longer surprised when they see their name emblazoned on a mailing or receive a phone call soliciting their business.

To succeed today, each piece of marketing communication has to be more convincing than ever before because the media is now familiar and more easily ignored.

Along with the popularity of direct marketing has come clutter. Making an impression on a prospect who is bombarded with multiple messages in the current marketplace is a staggering challenge.

Production costs, increasing at a rate of 10 percent a year, are another problem. It takes more success to make a profit under these demanding economic conditions.

At the same time that direct marketers find budgets tighter, they face higher expectations from top management based on past successes. The demands for performance and bottom-line accountability have never been greater.

There is good news too, of course. As a result of computer technology, the use of demographics and psychographics to pinpoint target markets has advanced light-years beyond the capabilities of even a few years ago. Technology has added to the battery of marketing techniques through laser printing, sophisticated outbound call routing and so on.

In this scenario, the challenge is clear: to develop new, powerful and efficient direct response techniques.

The key is not in finding some new medium for reaching prospects. The media already exists. The key to success is in learning to use these media *together* in sophisticated ways—to maximize the profitability of every marketing dollar spent by using each marketing impression to reinforce and enhance every other marketing impression created.

The art and science of achieving synergy

in a direct marketing environment can be called *Integrated Direct Marketing* or IDM.

Innovative Implementation for Familiar Tools

Integrated Direct Marketing employs broadcast and space advertising, direct mail, telemarketing, point-of-sale and so on, in a new and revolutionary framework. Instead of using clashing and conflicting efforts, IDM creates seamlessly integrated campaigns that produce maximum impact and profitability.

This coordinated combination of media cuts through clutter with its unified, self-reinforcing message.

IDM zeros in on a more highly select target market than ever before, making the most of advanced demographic and psychographic list selection techniques to pinpoint promising market segments, then delivering a persuasive streamlined message to this audience across a variety of media.

IDM addresses the prospect's psychographics. The unique psyche of each individual makes them responsive to a particular marketing stimulus. Conceptually, it is similar to the way multicomponent direct mail packages are designed. Some people read the letter, some the brochure, some the order form, some the lift note. Practitioners of IDM bring the same lessons to bear on designing the media mix for the overall campaign, offering different people the opportunity to respond to the medium that suits their individual preferences, within the context of a unified synergistic effort.

Distinctive Facets

Small-scale applications of media integration are common: Using an 800 number to boost response to a mail solicitation or using a media campaign to generate inquiries that are then followed up with direct mail. There are several significant points that make IDM a breakthrough concept:

● *Integration of marketing efforts across all media.* Instead of occasionally linking two media or halfheartedly picking up a creative concept and echoing it in related campaigns, IDM calls for unified planning up front. To maximize return on a marketing investment, all aspects of the multimedia campaign must be linked across the board—concept, timing, support services and management evaluation procedures.

● *Holistic analysis of results.* Testing has always been a hallmark of successful direct marketers. In an IDM effort, the cross-related testing parameters add new complexity to the task. Not only are segmentation and number gathering more demanding when tracking as many as six integrated marketing media, but analysis of these figures must be undertaken from a new perspective.

Instead of looking at the results and deciding to concentrate budget and effort on the one or two areas which have tested most successfully, we must look for the supportive interrelationships between media demonstrated by the numbers and make decisions accordingly.

For example, if a mailing draws minimal response, but paves the way for a successful outbound telemarketing call, the IDM-aware manager will recognize this relationship and realize that cutting off the seemingly unprofitable mailing would be a false economy.

● *An intensified management role.* When interested in a single marketing medium, the businessperson hires the most talented agency they can afford within that medium and asks them to exert their efforts to achieve maximum response. But what happens if the executive wants to take advantage of IDM synergy?

Most direct marketing agencies specialize in a single medium, seeing any other media employed in a campaign as add-ons to increase response to their core medium. When creating a truly integrated direct response campaign, the media must be balanced to achieve the greatest *overall* profit. The only source for this kind of control is marketing management within the company.

The Integrated Direct Marketer does not have to master all the intricacies of all the available media. However, he or she must have the knowledge and insight to control and coordinate the efforts of the experts, subordinating their individual enthusiasms to the common goal.

So far, I've outlined three different ways IDM differs from traditional marketing. Here's a case study of a campaign by one of our clients that dramatically demonstrates that the integrated combination works better than stand-alone media.

All the Way to the Bank

Citicorp, a leader in breaking down the traditional geographical restrictions on financial institutions, is expanding its business and consumer customer bases across the country.

Regulations still prohibit building bank branches outside the state that grants a bank its charter. To do business with customers who live far from the nearest bricks-and-mortar bank branch, Citicorp relies on direct marketing. They have used each of the familiar direct marketing media for years, individually and in combination. Not long ago, they constructed a program to offer in-depth head-to-head comparisons for four different media combinations.

Citicorp had multiple goals in this marketing effort. The keystone product was a fixed-rate home equity loan. Bank research indicated that the same target market segment would also be interested in a flexible revolving credit line vehicle, so it was desirable to integrate offers of both products.

Citicorp's ultimate goals were geographical expansion and the development of proven

strategies for continued growth in the future. More than the immediate sale of a financial instrument is at stake because each completed transaction produces a new, geographically remote customer for continued solicitation in an on-going banking relationship.

To accurately quantify the impact produced by media integration, four separate test packages were executed, each carefully tracked to allow accurate testing and analysis.

1. The basic control package was a direct mail piece with a lengthy application to be filled in and mailed to the bank. This application requested over 70 pieces of personal and financial information.

2. The same mail package with the addition of an 800 number inviting the customer to call, ask questions and have the application completed by phone.

3. The same mail package complete with 800 service, with the addition of a BRC for requesting more information. People who sent in the coupon received an outbound telephone follow-up call.

4. Finally, timed to coincide with a separate mail drop, newspaper ads featuring an 800 number were run in the target market. The mail package was the same as for test three.

All the mail packages offered only the home equity loan product and not the revolving line of credit account. John Hunter, vice president, Citicorp Telemarketing Services, their in-house state-of-the-art center located in Baltimore, explains, "Due to the complexity of these products, it was impractical to offer both in the same direct mail package. However, once telephone contact had been established, a more flexible offering was possible. If prospects were hesitant about the fixed-rate home equity loan or wanted a product with a lower interest rate, the telephone communicator could shift gears and introduce the revolving credit line option. Of course, this degree of flexibility required an intensive training program along with a de-

TABLE 1.

Test	Accounts Opened	Revenue Per Account	Cost Decrease Per $1,000 Loaned
Mail + 800# vs. Mail Alone	+ 7%	+ 30%	-63%
Mail + Coupon + 800# + Outbound Telemarketing vs. Mail Alone	+ 13%	+ 19%	-72%
Mail + Coupon + 800# + Outbound Telemarketing + Print Advertising vs. Mail Alone	+ 15%	+ 23%	-71%

tailed and lengthy script for telephone communicators."

Evaluating the Response

"An important aspect of the testing process in any direct response program is deciding the proper criteria by which to judge the response," says Mr. Hunter. "For Citicorp, this involved three factors: the number of accounts generated, the revenue per account and the cost per $1,000 loaned."

Based on the presented results in Table 1, Citicorp went with the third choice—the combination of all the media tested. At a 1 percent higher cost than the second test, the third test produced a 15 percent better market share.

Lessons to Be Learned

The Citicorp program illustrates several key considerations in the IDM process. It dramatically illustrates that the IDM strategy works. Were it not for this process, we could not have designed a program that, by adding components to the media mix, ultimately increased the *number* of accounts opened by 15 while driving down the acquisition costs by 71 percent compared to mail alone.

We can clearly see the increased complexity of testing and tracking required by the IDM approach. Of course, the knowledge gained through this testing procedure applies to more than the single program at hand—investment of time, energy and capital in IDM-style testing procedures pays dividends across product lines and marketing campaigns by developing strategies that can be implemented in future efforts and establishing ongoing relationships with customers and potential customers.

Finally, the Citicorp case history provides a fine example of the unique power of an integrated media approach. A completed transaction in this program entailed thousands of dollars and an intense level of trust in a remote financial institution. By carefully combining the impact of media advertising, the persuasive prose of direct mail and the interactive personalization of telemarketing, Citicorp became a presence in people's lives, gaining their trust and their business. As Mr. Hunter explains, "Citicorp is well-known in its home territory of New York, but it is far less familiar in Maryland. However, the results of the marketing efforts for Home Equity were so successful that they helped establish Citicorp as one of the leaders in the mortgage business in the mid-Atlantic region."

Ernan Roman, "Integrated Direct Marketing: Maximizing Media Mix," *Direct Marketing,* September 1986. Reprinted by permission of *Direct Marketing* magazine.

Make Your Dealer a Direct Marketing Co-Star

DIANE LYNN KASTIEL

More and more, business-to-business marketers are finding that "dealer-directed" campaigns—which involve dealers financially and strategically—can fortify their direct marketing efforts while keeping their costs down. Programs in which dealers split half the cost of each mailing are fairly typical, but in some cases the dealers foot the whole bill. Control of the program is an issue, with manufacturers or vendors retaining control in most programs. Some programs, however, are very successful when almost total control is in the hands of dealers. Some straddle the fence, letting each dealer choose how much control and participation they want to have. Most experts agree that acceptance and growth of dealer-directed programs will increase as more people use them and spread the word of their potential.

TWICE A YEAR, GELCO CORP. EMBARKS ON A lead-generating direct mail campaign. Nothing unusual about that.

However, unlike traditional direct marketing programs, where dealers receive their leads passively, the Minneapolis-based leasing firm lets its dealers choose the mailings' target areas. They also place their own names on the material. In return, dealers pay 100% of each mailing's cost—typically about 43 cents apiece.

"We wanted to say, 'Look, we are this huge leasing company, but we also have an office right around the corner from you,'" says Burton Grossman, Gelco's director of marketing and sales development. The program "helps combine that local feeling with a national image. It's sent out under a local name, not by some big organization.

"And people want that—they want to deal with a substantial firm that can meet their needs, but they also want to call their local dealer and say, 'Hey Fred, where's my car?'"

More and more, business-to-business marketers are finding that such "dealer-directed" campaigns—which involve dealers financially and strategically—can fortify their direct marketing efforts while keeping costs down.

They also build goodwill among vendors and their dealers—strengthening their relationships—and increase the saliency of products in the minds of distributors. That's especially important, of course, when vendors are competing for distributors' attention.

"Even if the dealer or distributor you're dealing with doesn't sell products that directly compete with yours, they sell other products, so you're still competing with other manufacturers for the dealer's time and attention," says Mark Morris, president of More Direct Inc., a Minneapolis-based agency.

Further, dealer-directed direct marketing

campaigns often draw more potent leads than traditional programs. That's because members of the distribution channel are usually more familiar with end-users than are the companies they represent, experts say.

Yet before starting dealer-directed campaigns, companies must consider a number of factors. Among them: Who should pay for the program, and how much should they pay?; how much control should dealers have over the campaign?; who's responsible for tracking the leads?; and how much does it cost to get the program off the ground—and keep it strong?

Who Foots the Bill?

Often, getting dealers to participate in a direct marketing program isn't easy, and large financial outlays can discourage them. In fact, some experts contend that the more dealers have to pay, the less likely they are to join in.

On the other hand, some financial investment may make the program more important to them. "They're more committed to making it work if you get the dealer to put their own money in it," says Michael Wikman, president of MW&A, a Minneapolis agency that specializes in direct marketing.

Programs in which dealers split half the cost of each mailing are fairly typical. Yet there are exceptions, such as Gelco, where dealers foot the whole bill.

And Gelco's program seems to be successful. A test program drew a 2% response—double the target rate—last year and Mr. Grossman says all 50 of his dealers now participate.

Likewise, Hayward, Calif.-based ComputerLand Corp. makes its dealers pay for most of each campaign.

While that may seem prohibitive to dealers, they usually realize significant savings—compared with the cost of running a program themselves.

ComputerLand's program "is still much cheaper than we would ever be able to do on our own," says Denny Davies, VP-sales for Weldon Electronics Inc., which owns and operates five ComputerLand stores in Minnesota.

ComputerLand, the country's largest computer retailer, absorbs "a big financial burden in terms of the set-up and implementation of the program; we only pay for what we use," he adds.

MW&A's Mr. Wikman estimates that such "self-liquidating" programs still only cost a dealer one-fourth to one-third of what it would take to run a program on its own.

Who's in Control?

Another important factor: How much control should dealers have over the campaign?

In some programs, dealers and distributors choose not only which geographical areas will be covered but what types of prospects in a given area will receive mailings and how often mailings will be sent.

"There's so many different variables you can throw into the program," says Mike Harris, president of Aldata List Co., Minneapolis. "It can be either very rigid or very flexible, depending on the degree of control you want to give to the dealer organization.

"But the more flexibility you throw into the program, the more expensive and time-consuming it becomes to implement and maintain," he cautions. "If you have rigid controls on the program, it's easier to get it rolling and keep it rolling."

Generally, although there are exceptions, the manufacturer or vendor retains the most control in a dealer-directed program. Experts say that's the best way to ensure success because it centralizes and coordinates the activity, resulting in expeditious mailings and easier measurement and analysis of results.

Fawn Vendors Inc., Des Moines, Iowa, found that out the hard way. It recently switched to a centralized program, controlled by the company with the help of its agency, after previous programs that relied too much on dealers failed.

"If you let the dealer organization do it themselves, they don't get it done," says Phil Masters, dealer development manager of the vending machine company. He adds that "very few" dealers sent out the mailers that Fawn used to provide.

"Company sponsorship is very important," he says. "It's a lot more profitable, a lot more complete, and it's projected out over a year, instead of being done in short spurts."

Fawn's 26 nationwide dealers will continue to pay 100% of the direct mail program's cost—from 40 cents to 45 cents apiece. They will be able to dictate which geographical areas they want mailings sent to, as long as they send out a minimum of 1,000 pieces each mailing, but they must participate in all three annual mailings.

Fawn also developed three different mailing pieces, aimed at different segments: the industrial market, such as factories; the "refreshment service" market, more luxurious office settings that buy fancy, modular-design vending machines; and the "street" market, which includes gasoline stations and rest areas.

Almost Total Control

The Office Systems Division of 3M Co., St. Paul, Minn., is one of the rare companies that put almost total control in the hands of their dealers. Under its long-running dealer-directed program, the division sends direct mail material to dealers and they do the rest, including developing their own mailing lists.

However, 3M charges dealers 100% of the mailings' costs, from 75 cents to as much as $4, says Lovell Baker, national sales manager for file management products, the division's main business. This ensures that the direct mail pieces, which 3M develops from the material used to support its direct sales force, won't go to waste.

"When they put their own money out, you know darn well they're going to use them," Mr. Baker says. 3M also leaves it up to dealers to track results and doesn't keep close records on dealer participation in the program. However, most dealers participate to some extent, Mr. Baker says.

3M is also one of the few companies that provide telemarketing training to dealers. Dealers can either use a free training kit 3M developed for the telemarketing personnel who support its direct sales force, or they can "hire" one of the company's telemarketing sales representatives to provide personal training. Mr. Baker would not disclose the cost of the latter option, however.

Peter Calihan, president of Hughes Calihan Inc., Phoenix, one of 3M's dealers, says "there's pros and cons" to 3M's approach.

"Salespeople like to get a lead that they didn't do anything for," Mr. Calihan says. But 3M's program "allows the salesperson to get more control over what goes out to his territory. It's also easier for us to measure the results for ourselves," rather than relying on the manufacturer's word.

Hughes Calihan regularly buys direct mail from 3M, which it gives to its sales managers and sales representatives to use at their discretion. The dealership also has hired a 3M telemarketing representative to train its personnel. However, Mr. Calihan could not estimate what his company spends on 3M's dealer-directed program each year or provide any response or conversion figures. The reason: So much of that work is left up to the individual salesperson, he says.

Creative Input

Like 3M, ComputerLand gives dealers an unusual amount of say in its direct marketing program. Besides selecting geographical areas for the computer retailer's triannual mailings, dealers have input into the program's creative design.

Namely, the campaign is subject to preview and suggestions by ComputerLand's "marketing council" of elected dealer representatives, which provides input into ComputerLand's marketing in general. Even dealers that are not council members are encouraged to offer their thoughts.

"Oftentimes, we'll call them and say, 'How's it going?' and ask for their input," says Ruth Ann Barrett, direct marketing manager.

But ComputerLand dealers pay a price for their power. The company requires participating dealers to pay the full cost—50 cents—of each mailer they send out. In addition, they pay 100% of the fulfillment costs associated with any necessary follow-up to the initial mailing, such as requests for more information. They also pay for sales leads furnished by ComputerLand.

The company doesn't give dealers a choice in the number of mailings they send out, either; dealers must participate in all three.

"We have a long buying cycle," Ms. Barrett explains. "All our research shows that persistency is important. And, since we only mail three times a year, it's important that dealers participate in all the mailings."

Mr. Davies of Weldon Electronics joined the company's direct marketing program for the second time this year.

"We definitely got a lot more leads than we anticipated initially," Mr. Davies says. Under last year's program, the five Weldon stores mailed out nearly 26,000 direct mail pieces to about 15 counties and got a 2% response.

Straddling the Fence

E. F. Johnson Co., Waseca, Minn., straddles the fence by letting each dealer choose the amount of control and participation it wants.

The mobile communications systems manufacturer, which charges its dealers 50% of the mailing costs, allows them three options: They can request that the company do virtually all the work, including formulating mailing lists and sending out direct mail material; they can supply their own mailing lists, and have the company send out the material to prospects on that list alone, or to that list and the company-generated list; or they can request that the company send them the direct mail material so they can mail to whomever they want.

MW&A, Johnson's agency on the program, offers that option to all its clients.

"In almost every program we've ever done, we've had a minimum of dealers (that want material sent to people on their own mailing lists) and a minimum of dealers that say, 'I want to do my own thing in my own way.'" MW&A's Mr. Wikman says, "So we try to offer a system that can meet everybody's needs."

However, it's "typically a minority" that chooses one of the two options that involve more work on the dealers' part. Generally, fewer than 10% of a company's dealers supply their own mailing lists and fewer than 5% want to do the mailing themselves, Mr. Wikman says.

At Johnson, only 5% of participating dealers offered mailing lists of their own and about 2% mailed out their own material.

24 Mailing Dates

Dealers in the Johnson program have other options besides deciding how much they want to participate in the mailings. They can choose from 24 annual mailing dates, although they send out material at least three times a year and are discouraged from mailing more than once a month.

Dealers also choose the geographic area they want mailings to go to and the types of businesses they want to reach within each area. And like Fawn, Johnson offers three different versions of the direct mail packages, aimed at three different types of businesses.

Although the direct mail program was under way at press time, preliminary results showed "at least a third" of the respondents were requesting demonstrations, Mr. Wikman says.

Star Manufacturing Co., an Oklahoma City, Okla.-based construction products manufacturer, has a similar program. But it requires participating dealers to pay 100% of the cost, up front. Then, at the end of the year, they're eligible for up to 50% reimbursement under the company's cooperative advertising program.

After Star identifies appropriate prospects in a dealer's target market, each dealer chooses the types of end-users it wants to reach: manufacturers, retail stores, or miscellaneous groups such as churches and local governments. The dealer also dictates how many of four annual mailings prospects will receive.

The mailings include letters to presidents of prospect companies, four-color brochures and a small promotional gift. Star sends out all the mailings and furnishes the gifts.

Although Star's program, which is more than 10 years old, has consistently garnered the participation of only 25% of its 520 dealers, they have been the largest and most successful, says Thomas Morris, manager of marketing services.

The response is usually 1.5%, compared with an industry norm of 1%, Mr. Morris says, adding that the response rate has been as high as 1.8% on some mailings.

Lately, Star has been emphasizing its program more, in an effort to increase dealer participation. "We're really promoting direct marketing harder this year than we did last year," Mr. Morris says. "It's the most cost-effective way to reach potential customers."

Who Gets the Leads?

In most dealer-directed programs, dealers want new leads to go directly to them instead of going to the manufacturer first. That's the way 3M does it.

"There is always a strong desire on the

part of the dealers to have the leads come back to them," Aldata's Mr. Harris says. "However, it is preferable to have the leads come back to a central location, whether it's the home office or the agency who puts the program together."

Manufacturers that have done it both ways agree that central control works best. "To see the follow-through, it's so important to have that control," says Fawn's Mr. Masters. "You don't want leads to sit on the shelf and collect dust."

In Star Manufacturing's case, the company gathers leads and sends a list of prospects to the appropriate dealers. If the prospect indicates that he or she plans construction within three months, Star notifies the dealer immediately by telephone.

Gelco handles its leads in a slightly different way. It lets its agency, MW&A, collect them. The agency then generates lead reports for dealers and within 36 hours sends prospects the information they request.

"That way, we make it easier for the dealer to follow up on the leads because we've already done a lot of the work for them and we've done it in a timely fashion," says Mr. Wikman.

Up-Front Costs

Manufacturers should keep in mind that even when dealers pay 100% of mailing costs on a dealer-directed program, there are other, vitally important expenditures that must be made. In addition to the ongoing "maintenance" costs of administering such programs, manufacturers typically invest up to $10,000 to develop a "sell package"—aimed at enlisting dealer participation.

These sell packages include promotional information on the direct mail program, samples of actual mailings and prospects availability reports, which give the dealer an idea of how many prospects the program may reach.

Although sell packages can cost as little as $2,000, they are extremely important in rousing dealer participation, experts say. In fact, ComputerLand says dealer participation in its campaign dropped considerably when its sell package lost its luster.

In 1985, the program's first year, 200 of its 600 dealers participated. But this year, only 115 dealers joined in.

The difference was a decline in the company's "merchandising efforts" to its dealers, says Ms. Barrett, the direct marketing manager. A training tape, used to introduce and explain the program the first year, was omitted this time. And the company didn't announce the program at its annual conference, as it did last year.

"I think the word just didn't get out as well as it did last year," Ms. Barrett says. "Next year, we'll be putting more effort into merchandising, like we did last year."

Fawn, meanwhile, spent about $2,000 developing its sell package, which was scheduled to be mailed to dealers in mid-July. And it hopes the new, centralized approach will encourage crucial dealer participation.

"If you can get the dealer involved and get him to participate, he'll come back because it's very effective," Mr. Masters says. "But the hardest part is getting him to see the results—the net effect in terms of his investment return, dollar for dollar."

While not entirely unheard of, dealer-directed direct marketing programs are still fairly new to most business-to-business marketers.

"The concept has been around for many years, but we've found that easily less than 50% (of companies that could benefit from such programs) do it," Mr. Wikman says.

Most agree, however, that acceptance and growth of dealer-directed programs will grow as more people use them and spread the word of their potential.

"We have, as marketers, been extremely slow to adopt new methods," says More Direct's Mr. Morris. "There's still a great need for sophistication in the marketplace. It's a matter of an evolutionary process."

Diane Lynn Kastiel, "Make Your Dealer a Direct Marketing Co-Star," *Business Marketing,* August 1986. Reprinted by permission of *Business Marketing.* Copyright Crain Communications, Inc.

CHAPTER THREE

Offer and Creative

Creativity Retooled to Fit New Concept

MARGARET LeROUX

Mailboxes and TV will not suddenly be devoid of Publisher's Clearinghouse sweepstakes and Ginsu knife commercials, but direct marketing creativity is changing. This change reflects entrance of the increasingly upscale marketer into the direct response field. The new generation of TV commercials are sophisticated instead of silly, assertive rather than aggressive, as clients apply the same aesthetics to direct marketing that they do to package goods advertising. Direct response creativity differs from general advertising, that is, rhymes don't work, humor is chancy, the best place for some of the cleverest lines is in the wastebasket. Direct response creativity involves one person tapping another on the shoulder in the supermarket checkout line, saying, "You really ought to try this product." Direct marketing's mission is to make a sale, not to make a product more recognizable.

IT'S NOT NECESSARY TO LOOK FAR TO TRACK THE latest influences on direct marketing creativity. They're as close as the nearest magazine or tv set.

Glossy, full-page automotive ads and snappy, 30-second spots for toothpaste represent the new standards against which direct marketing creativity is being measured.

This doesn't mean mailboxes and tv suddenly will be devoid of Publishers' Clearinghouse sweepstakes and Ginsu knife-like commercials. These direct marketing standbys will be joined, not supplanted, by toney appeals from companies like AT&T Communications, Bank of Boston and Citicorp Diners Club.

Instead of blaring "YOU may have WON," however, more direct mail pieces reflect the image of the increasingly upscale advertisers entering the medium.

For example, Boston-based The DR Group created a piece for Bank of Boston that had a primary goal of boosting the bank's upscale image among consumers, as well as generating sales leads.

The mailing, which received a Good Echo Award yesterday at the Direct Marketing Assn. convention bears no resemblance to stereotypical junk mail. The campaign's reproductions of Renoir paintings, its heavy stock portfolio, glossy catalog and invitations to polo matches and museum exhibits are a far cry from the creative executions consumers would have expected to pop through their mail boxes just a few years ago.

Also, the new generation of direct response tv commercials is sophisticated instead of silly, assertive rather than aggressive.

A prime example is a 30-second spot showing a father and daughter discussing how they use their credit cards. Instead of being an image spot for Visa or MasterCard, the commercial is a direct response spot for a Manufacturers Hanover Trust Co. retail banking service.

An 800 number for credit card applications tagged onto the end of the spot has drawn "a phenomenal number of responses," says Bill Butler, exec vp, creative director for Wunderman, Ricotta & Klein, New York, which produced the commercial. "To look at the commercial, you wouldn't say, 'That's a good direct response commercial.' You'd say, 'That's a good tv commercial,'" he says.

Direct response advertising can be judged by the same criteria as general advertising, Mr. Butler says. "Clients are applying the same aesthetics to direct marketing as they are to package goods advertising," he says.

Direct marketers no longer sound much like carnival barkers, says Emily Soell, president, exec creative director, Rapp & Collins, New York. Marketers with larger ad budgets

than the old-line direct marketing companies spend more to present their products to prospects. And more of these companies are now using direct selling methods to move their products and services.

"New non-traditional users of direct marketing such as Bristol-Myers and other package goods advertisers are moving direct marketing closer to the elegance of general advertising," says Ms. Soell.

Companies new to direct marketing are taking advantage of computer technology that allows them to hone in on specific customers. Porsche Cars North America, for example, is making an appeal to a selective audience—owners of 5-year-old Porsches—to test drive a new model. A slick, upscale direct mail piece created by Direct Marketing Agency, Stamford, Conn., directs them to a local dealer, the result of computerized address matching.

AT&T is using direct mail to target specific groups such as frequent users of overseas long-distance lines. "They're able to talk to customers about specific needs and give them information based on their calling patterns," says Ray Dempsey, co-founder of Ad-Direct, a Westport, Conn.-based division of Marketing Corp. of America.

"There's a profound difference between direct marketing today, which emphasizes information dissemination, and the traditional goal of product distribution," he says.

Yet, "there will always be a difference between the objective of direct marketing—to elicit a response—and advertising's goal of creating awareness," says Hank Stromberg, senior vp, creative director at Ogilvy & Mather Direct, New York.

While few refute that assertive general market advertisers have too much vested in their products' images to sacrifice them to sacrilegious direct response campaigns. "When they use direct marketing, they want something that's compatible with that image," says Mr. Dempsey.

As more big-time, general market advertisers are finding a use for direct marketing, the agencies specializing in it are retooling standard creative approaches to the discipline. "Copy today isn't a matter of following a formula," Mr. Stromberg says.

"I think the blurring of the lines between advertising and direct marketing is great," says Jim Punkre, president of Brainstorms, a direct marketing agency in Emmaus, Pa., and winner of the first Caples Award for direct marketing creativity. "I want to know who drew the lines and what's the benefit of drawing them?"

Good direct marketing, he says, is the result of "knowing what audience you're talking to and understanding how their minds work." It's not a matter of using the techniques of one marketing specialty over those of another.

General advertising has a lot to gain by paying attention to some of the basic tenets of direct marketing, Mr. Punkre says. "Advertising should always have been more integrative," he says, adopting direct marketing's efficiencies.

"When you get those response cards and phone calls, you get the bottom line."

Direct marketing is the product and the salesman, says Rapp & Collins' Ms. Soell. "It's the only way the consumer is going to find out about the product. Direct marketing can't have the trendy, staccato tone of general advertising; it's got to be more complete.

"We're creative in different ways from general advertising," she says. "Rhymes don't work, humor is chancy and clowning isn't always apt. The best place for some of our cleverest lines is in the wastebasket.

"We're the person tapping another on the shoulder at the supermarket checkout line saying, 'You really ought to try this product.'"

Direct marketers cannot afford to play the ad game, says William Gregory, exec vp, director-creative services at Kobs & Brady Advertising, Chicago. "Your mission is to make a sale, not to make a product more recognizable." Exciting and memorable general advertising creative executions actually might be counter-productive to achieving established direct marketing goals, he says.

Mr. Gregory envisions a day when a direct response tv commercial will win a Clio award. "It will be the flashiest, glitziest, most contemporary direct response spot ever put in the can," he says.

"But," he says, "we're going to be slightly embarrassed when the word begins to filter out that this award-winning commercial cost $250,000 to produce and pulled 25 orders at a cost of $10,000 each."

Wunderman's Mr. Butler urges marketers to maintain their perspective. The disciplines should be considered as elements that possibly balance and enhance each other, he says, and direct marketers and their clients should take only those elements from general advertising that fit naturally and discard the rest.

"If we keep trying new things in controlled test situations," Mr. Butler says, "we may discover some of the things toothpaste salesmen do work for us."

Margaret LeRoux, "Creativity Retooled to Fit New Concept," *Advertising Age,* October 27, 1986. Reprinted by permission of Crain News Service.

Seven-Step Creative Process Adds "Eureka!" to Your Vocabulary

WILLIAM STEINHARDT

Creative pacesetters of the past appeared to know that the left brain was able to compartmentalize, organize, and match present experiences to past experiences. They also sensed that the right brain was able to respond to both the novel and the unknown, to think in images, to see wholes, and to detect patterns. From recent studies and observations of how the left and right brain interact come a pattern for creating ideas that can help immediately. The pattern is a seven step outline:

1. Aim at your target.
2. Bring in all the facts.
3. Crystalize, chew, and classify your material.
4. If fatigue or frustration set in, defer your thinking temporarily in order to invite help from the subconscious mind.
5. Expect the unexpected entrance of the idea. It will pop into the head out of nowhere.
6. Fine tune your idea.
7. Test your idea out in real life to assess its value and practicality.

THE SCENE IS FAMILIAR TO YOU IF YOU'RE A CREative person who has to produce an idea: you sit and stare at a blank sheet of paper in the typewriter or at an empty sketch pad.

You may have experienced that feeling more than once in your career. You are not alone. Through the ages, men and women have constantly struggled to solve the mystery of the ways ideas are born. Especially the "big idea"—which in a brief phrase or artful stroke capsulizes the essence of a thought and moves masses of people to action.

Thanks to the findings of studies on creativity during the past half century, and particularly since the 1960s, you yourself have the potential to create more ideas than you ever thought possible.

Research on how the brain's right and left hemispheres interact with each other and how each functions by itself has confirmed the observations by a few earlier creative leaders—such as advertising giant James Webb Young in the 1940s—on how to generate ideas.

What we now know of the "verbal" left brain and the "visual" right brain explain the steps these pioneers already seemed to be taking in outlining the creative process.

Without the benefit of the scientific experiments, equipment and vocabulary of today, this older generation of creative pacesetters appeared to know that on the one hand the left brain was able to compartmentalize, organize and match present experiences to past experiences.

These leaders also sensed that on the other hand the right brain was able to respond to both the novel and the unknown, to think in images, to see in wholes and to detect patterns.

These recently diagnosed characteristics of the brain make the early 20th century observations of Italian economist and sociologist Vilfredo Pareto even more remarkable. Pareto then noted that an idea is a new combination of old elements—representing the ability of the creative person to see relationships, with each fact a link in the chain of knowledge. What Pareto saw illustrates the left brain interacting with the right.

A contemporary example of an idea being a new combination of old elements is the nationwide air express delivery service. Combining air transportation at night with surface transportation during the day, both of which existed for decades, has given rise to a new guaranteed next-day long-distance delivery service.

From the influences of brain studies by present-day researchers and from observations of earlier creative guides come a pattern for creative ideas that can help you immediately.

The pattern, a seven-step outline, is simple.

Carrying out all the steps, one at a time and one after the other in strict sequence, will take work. But it will give you results. Best of all, the procedure works not only for writers and artists. It also works for leaders, planners, organizers and anyone else in the company structure.

Follow this outline faithfully, and you'll increase your creative productivity:

1. Aim at your target. Define your goal and state when you want to reach it.

Establishing clear, specific responses to these points will, first, prevent wandering and, second, will give you the self-discipline to guard against the human weakness of inertia.

2. The next step is to bring in all the facts. The fact-gathering will center not only on all the available material for the current project you're working on, but also on general knowledge gained over a period of time from a variety of non-related reading background and living experiences. This combination forms the basis of establishing relationships so necessary to the art of producing ideas.

For this preparation phase the use of index cards will be helpful. By placing one item on a card, you'll have a way of classifying the information when you reach the next step in the pattern.

The gathering of facts will be one of your toughest steps. You must be willing to pay the price of plunging into a wide range of source material. But if done conscientiously, with all the vigor and vitality needed, it will pay dividends later in the results you'll achieve.

One of the important ways of bringing together material is to keep abreast of recent developments in your field. Try to stay on top of new tests, techniques and literature that are pouring out continually.

Have discussions with friends, individually or in groups. Attend conferences. Associate with creative people (you'll also learn how they create!). All of these activities will keep you mentally stimulated, a valuable attribute in the process of helping you produce ideas.

A powerful force to aid you in getting facts and answers is to adapt a questioning attitude. Even be naive so that you take nothing for granted.

A good starting question is "Why?" Why is this product made as it is made? Why is this product sold as it is sold? Why has this product not been made larger or smaller, taller or shorter, heavier or lighter? This list of "Whys" goes on.

"What?" is a good question, too. What other use can be found for this product? What are its present uses? What makes the consumer want the product? The list is just as endless as the list of "Whys."

"How" can we make this product more attractive? How can we make it more durable? How can it be adapted to other uses?

"When?" and "Where?" and "Who?" also will serve you well.

Cultivate and develop a heavy respect for the question-asking ability.

But just as essential to obtaining idea-creating thoughts is the ability to listen. Analyze what the person is saying rather than allowing your mind to wander or letting yourself prepare a response.

3. Now that you've brought in all your facts, you're ready for step three: Crystallize, chew and classify your material. Here is where you put thoughts into combinations as possible ideas. Try for 10 or 20 or 30 such combinations. In a kaleidoscopic fashion, these combinations will shift into new relationships. They'll reveal new patterns.

Swing from the obvious to the ridiculous. Don't let rational, judicial thinking step in the way. Don't let criticism enter the picture. Don't question the quality of thoughts being developed.

All of these simply will stop the flow of additional thoughts. As a result, many possible ideas will be overlooked. At this point, go all out to seek quantity.

This mental digestive process will help you look at facts in different ways.

See what can be modified: color, shape, sound, odor, motion, meaning. Try to rearrange: the sequence, the speed, the pace, the components, the schedule, the pattern. Go for a reversal: put the end at the beginning, put the top at the bottom. Magnify something: units, action, price, anything made higher, longer, thicker, stronger. Reduce something: shorten, condense, even omit. Have a substitute or alternative: ingredients, power, process, approach.

Although this third step may make you tired, don't give up at this point. The mind has a second wind and will carry you a longer distance than you'd expect. Eventually, of course, you'll reach that hopeless stage where you can't go any further.

4. When exhaustion, fatigue and frustration set in, move on to the fourth step: Defer your thinking—temporarily cease your efforts in order to invite help from the subconscious mind.

The step is important because your conscious mind retains less than a third of all your experiences and knowledge. But your subconscious mind—the second section of your mental storehouse—retains all your knowledge and experience.

As you drop the project and let the incubation process synthesize all the material for you, ideas will begin to jell by themselves. Be patient. Don't try to force an idea. You'll only block its conclusion. The non-conscious part of your life continues to work in your behalf and will assist you in reaching a solution.

One of the most effective ways to defer your thinking is to do things like go to a concert, the theater, movies, or poetry reading. Or read a detective story.

5. Now comes exhilarating step number five: Expect the unexpected entrance of the idea. Out of nowhere the idea will pop into your head. But it will happen only when the previous four steps will have been taken. It's a feeling of "Eureka! I have it!"

And you'll suddenly "have it" when you're shaving, with foam all over your face. It will suddenly happen when you're showering, with soap lather all over your body. It will occur when you're half awake in the early morning or suddenly awakened in the middle of the night. It will flash across your mind when you're driving alone on the highway at 2 A.M., halfway between two major cities.

When the illumination—characterized by a sudden insight or combining of parts into a coherent pattern—comes after the rest period, your immediate attention or action is vital. Otherwise the idea may be lost.

That's why you always should carry a notebook with you to jot down the ideas the instant they appear. Many famous inventors, writers and advertising people do this. If you're shaving, keep the notebook by the sink. If you're showering, keep the book by the tub. If you're sleeping, keep the notebook on the night table. And if you're driving, keep the pad on the passenger seat next to you. Pull over to the side of the road immediately after the idea arrives and start jotting.

6. Fine tune your idea. The initial presence of the idea will not be quite perfect. There will be rough edges. Look for loopholes. Search for doubts to be removed. It will be necessary to refine the idea to have it fit exactly.

When you've done this, it would be well to show the idea to others for judicious, constructive criticism. Still further refining may result. A good idea has self-expanding qualities. It stimulates those who see it to add to it. New possibilities you overlooked may come to light.

7. The last step is to gear the idea to action. Now you test out the idea in real life to

assess its value or practicality. Unless the idea is put to use, it benefits no one.

When your next assignment comes to produce ideas, you'll be better prepared for the fact that ideas generally spring from well-filled and well-disciplined minds. The seven steps described above will help you gain the necessary discipline.

Remember, it will be essential to acquire as much background material as is feasible and to learn to think clearly. There will be hard work in applying yourself in a conscientious way both to the assimilation of the facts and to the arrangement and rearrangement of the various patterns possible.

The current studies on the way the brain functions and the observations of earlier creative thinkers are strong assurances that if you follow the above described steps in sequence, you, too, one day out of the blue will suddenly yell, "Eureka!"

William Steinhardt, "Seven-Step Creative Process Adds 'Eureka!' to Your Vocabulary," *Business Journal Magazine,* August 13, 1984. This article originally appeared in the San Jose *Business Journal.* Permission to reprint is granted by the publisher, which retains all domestic and foreign rights.

Back to the Basics, or 50 Rules to Live By
HERSCHELL GORDON LEWIS

This article presents the first ten of fifty reasonably well-tested rules for writing direct response letter copy that sells. These are:

1. Keep your first sentence short.

2. No paragraphs longer than seven lines.

3. Single space the direct response letter; double space between paragraphs.

4. In a multipage letter, don't end a paragraph at the bottom of any page except the last; break in the middle of a sentence.

5. Don't sneak up on the reader— fire your biggest gun first.

6. Don't open up with "Dear Sir" or "Gentlemen"; use "Dear Friend," "Dear Fellow Executive," and so forth.

7. Don't close with "Yours Truly"; use "Sincerely" or "Cordially," and so forth.

8. Use an overline and a P.S., if they aren't stupid.

9. Experiment with marginal notes.

10. Use letters to test appeals such as fear, exclusivity, greed, and guilt.

DURING A CONVERSATION WITH ABOUT A DOZEN people, all of whom earn their livings either as practitioners of some facet of direct response or as paid advisors, I came to an ultimately startling conclusion:

Some of the most basic, primitive information—mechanical as well as creative— hasn't filtered down to everyone in our business.

"Taking nothing for granted!" may be the direct marketing rallying cry to replace, "Take no prisoners!" or "Don't fire until you see the reds of their eyes!" With that assumption, I offer 50 (in mail-order hype words, a full half-hundred) basic rules—all of which are instantly useable, all of which are reasonably well-tested, and none of which requires, as the ads say, "three to five years' experience."

To avoid sensory overload, and accusations of glibness, we'll spread the 50 rules over the next five issues.

Let's start with . . .

Tip No. 1: Keep your first sentence short.

I offer this suggestion because the first sentence is your indicator to the reader. From this early warning your target will form a quick impression: The letter is going to be easy to read, or the letter is going to be hard slogging.

The notion of a short first sentence isn't an absolute, invariable law. It's just a good idea most of the time; and because it's a good idea most of the time as well as an easy idea to implement, it's on this list.

Tip No. 2: No paragraphs longer than seven lines.

When I suggested this very tip to the assemblage of direct response people, I guess I shouldn't have been surprised to get the question, "But, what if a paragraph has to be longer than seven lines," and the question brought several assenting nods.

My answer: No paragraph has to be longer than seven lines. Here's an example, from my own mailbox:

Dear Friend:

It may surprise you, as it surprised me, to learn that even though we have high-powered, knowledgeable accountants, we still wind up paying too much income tax . . . although we don't know it at the time. We pay too much tax because our accountants can only work with the figures we give them; they can't "invent" deductions for us, they can't create unassailable tax shelters out of thin air, and they can't find productive uses for money that just isn't there to start with.

But, what if you could . . .

That's a double whammy, because this is the first paragraph. The writing isn't bad, but the impression is deadly.

I won't rewrite as radically as I would for pay, but here's how I'd have started this letter with the same ammunition:

Does this surprise you? It surprised me.

Like you, I have a high-powered accountant. My surprise came when I found out that even with his hand joining mine on the tiller, I was paying too much income tax.

I was paying too much tax, and you may be paying too much tax, because . . .

One paragraph becomes three, or four, and reader fatigue vanishes.

Tip No. 3: Single space the letter; double space between paragraphs.

This tip is even easier to implement than the first two. It's founded on ease of readership. Manuscript and news releases traditionally are double-spaced, but that's because an editor needs the space between the lines to write in his blue-pencil chicken-scratch.

A letter should set up for easy reading; a double-spaced letter not only is harder to read, but every aspect balloons fatly outward. A two-page letter becomes four pages, and a four-page letter—well, don't even think of it. Worse, the page has an overall gray look because the space between paragraphs is identical to the space within paragraphs. Emphasis is far harder to achieve.

A suggestion, if you disagree on grounds of tradition rather than reader attention: Set your next letter both ways. Ask 50 people which one is easier to read. If you're really scientific, ask questions based on reader comprehension.

Tip No. 4: In a multipage letter, don't end a paragraph at the bottom of any page except the last; break in the middle of a sentence.

Newspapers have known this for decades. Readers demand completeness. If you've ended a paragraph at the bottom of the page, the reader has a reason to read on only if he or she has developed a firm interest in what you're selling. But, if you leave the reader in midsentence, you're in command. That person is your captive until the end of the sentence—which is on the next page.

This is the direct marketing parallel to the movie on the Late Show. The show doesn't open with credits and titles; it opens with action. Once you've seen the first five minutes, it's too late to switch channels, because you'll have missed the opening of the film on the competing channel; it started with action too.

Tip No. 5: Don't sneak up on the reader.

An inverse wording of this tip might be, "Fire a big gun to start the battle." We're in the Age of Skepticism, and letter-openings such as this one betray a 1930's selling attitude:

This story begins around the turn of the century, when times were peaceful and big fortunes could be made.

Way back then, someone took a look at a contraption some people still called a horseless carriage, and they said, "Gee, wouldn't it be great if we could start these vehicles without cranking them by hand? Old Silas broke his arm cranking his machine, and the danged thing never would go."

OK, it isn't dull. As this type of opening goes, it's more intriguing than most. I agree. Now read the next paragraph.

Half a century later, a guy named Al Shepard climbed into a different contraption, and a lot of smoke came out of the bottom end. Wham! Within a couple of minutes our first astronaut was not only out of sight, he'd made history.

Now I'm not so pleased. It's obvious at last—we aren't talking about starters or storage batteries, and we aren't talking about outer space. We still don't know what we are supposed to be talking about, and we're deep into the letter.

Just for the sake of history, I'll tell you. This writer is selling acreage (land). It could have been any of 10,000 other possibilities, including aardvarks and Zoroastrian texts.

Firing your biggest gun first is a good idea, because it can't miss. As the letter opens, you're at point-blank range, and you may never have this advantage over your target-prospect again. Why sneak around, unless you don't think you have the rhetorical power to blast him out of the water?

Tip No. 6: Don't open with "Dear Sir" or "Gentlemen."

Why not? Because they suggest stiff-necked, old-fashioned pomposity. The job of warming up the reader, establishing rapport with him, is one of the great hurdles we face. A greeting such as "Dear Sir" or "Gentlemen" adds sandbags to the obstacle when we should be shoveling it away.

In a unisex age, I occasionally see "Dear Sir or Madame." This is real barf-bait, the kind of opening we might expect from a bill collector but not from our friendly mail-order vendor.

The mail-order industry has pretty much settled on "Dear Friend" as a neutral substitute when we can't personalize the opening. Depending on the list, you can thrust your rhetorical blade closer to the heart:

"Dear Fellow Member"

"Dear Executive"

"Dear World Traveler"

"Dear Collector"

"Dear Tennis Nut" (you can see the benefit of *equivalence* in greetings when you add a word— "Dear Fellow Tennis Nut")

Do we need the "Dear" at all?

I used to attack it on the grounds it's a cliché, worn out, and the reader isn't really dear to us at all, which makes it hypocritical. I don't point a bony finger any longer, because some of the substitutes I've seen are so contrived they make me long for good old Dear.

Some strong useable substitutes for the old-fashioned opening gain their strength from suggesting the communication is limited to a special-interest in-group.

"To the Relative Handful of Homeowners Who Demand Pure Water:"

"This Private Notification Is Limited to Executives Earning More Than $50,000 a Year."

"Information for Experienced Collectors Only."

A nit-picking question: Should we put a comma or a colon after the greeting?

Business letter writing classes teach colon, not comma, and I agree, conditionally. The colon suggests a respect for the reader. It's a subtle point, and it isn't absolute—especially since it's hard to stroke the reader at arm's length. But, mastery of letter writing comes from exalting the reader, *then* sliding in next to him when defenses are down.

I often make the comma/colon decision based on whether or not I'll indent each paragraph. Indenting is less formal, ergo more logical use of a comma.

If you worry about this kind of thing, you're too ulcer-prone to be a direct response writer anyway.

Tip No. 7: Don't close with "Yours truly."

"Yours truly" isn't as stiffly formal as the "Dear Sir" or "Gentlemen" that often begins a letter in which we see it. But, it reeks of antiquity without polish.

Antiquity *with* polish is a standard and often elegant selling technique. "Your servant, sir" is an example of this writing style—which had better match in *all* components or you look foolish.

You'll find "Sincerely," (*not* "Sincerely yours") as the close on most letters; business-to-business often uses "Cordially," on the theory that "Sincerely" is more emotional a close than the text justifies.

Attacking "Sincerely" is like breaking a butterfly on the rack: Why do it? If, though, you're doggedly determined to improve the close of your letters, try adding another pinch of salesmanship:

"Yours for more vigorous health"

"For the Board of Directors"

"Bless you, my dear friend " (fund raising only, please)

Tip No. 8: Use an overline and a p.s., if they aren't stupid.

An overline is a preletter message at the top of the page. You can type it or handwrite it. You can position it toward the right edge, or if you have a neatness complex you can center it.

What you shouldn't do is give away your message in the overline. I read this overline on the letter in a fat, heavily-produced mailing:

If you've driven accident-free for the past three years, you can save 10 percent to 20 percent on your automobile insurance.

I'd have said, ". . . let me show you how to save . . ." rather than ". . . you can save. . . ." My objection to this overline isn't based on this one small refinement but on the notion that instead of accelerating reading, comprehension, and preacceptance, this one blunted my interest and lost me as a reader. Too much too soon.

The purpose of the overline parallels the purpose of envelope copy. Envelope copy is like a kamikaze dive, with one purpose only: to excite someone enough to get him or her to open that envelope. An overline, too, has one purpose only: to get the reader into the letter, with more enthusiasm or anticipation than one could generate without the overline.

In my opinion, "This is a private offer" or "Do you qualify?" are stronger overlines than the "accident-free" wording. Years ago, college courses in advertising passed over outdoor advertising with a single direction: "No message longer than 11 words." We might resuscitate this suggestion today, for overlines.

A p.s. has easier rules. It should reinforce one of the key selling motivators or mention an extra benefit which doesn't require explanation.

Those who study such arcane matters tell us the overline is the most read part of a letter, and the p.s. is next. Automatically the format itself gives us thunderbolts to hurl. Let's not take the electricity out of them.

Tip No. 9: Experiment with marginal notes.

Marginal notes are a specialty. Not every letter benefits from them, which suggests determining from the tone of the letter whether or not they'll be beneficial.

When you do use them . . .

The rules for marginal notes are even more stringent than they are for overlines.

Two of them, in my opinion, are inviolable.

1. Handwrite everything.
2. Never use more than four words.

I'll explain: Marginal notes draw their power from the appearance of a spontaneous outburst of enthusiasm. The writer is so excited, so enthusiastic, that he bubbles over.

Handwritten bubbling over has verisimilitude. Typed bubbling over looks contrived. We fight like tigers to avoid a contrived look, so why take the risk? If the man in charge looks at it and says, "It looks schlocky," you can fight or abandon the idea; don't switch to typing in the margins.

The four word maximum is a good idea mechanically as well as creatively. Imposing this limit means you can write big enough to grab the reader's eye the way you should. There's no handwritten marginal message that can't be transmitted in four words, *maximum*. Some examples of marginal notes:

"Here's your FREE bonus!"

"Read this *extra*-carefully"

"Save 50 percent"

Don't be afraid to use hand-drawn arrows, lines, brackets, or even stars for emphasis. You're creating the impression of spontaneous enthusiasm.

Marginal notes, along with handwritten overlines, should be in a second color. What color? Don't consider any color other than the color in which you print the signature, usually process blue.

For heaven's sake don't have an overline and marginal comments in beautiful writing, a showcase of fine feminine calligraphy, and then have an illegible scrawl for a signature at the end of the letter. The writing should match. (Incidentally, there *never* is an excuse for an illegible signature on a direct mail letter. It may give ego-satisfaction to an executive, but it drains intimacy out of the communication.)

Tip No. 10: Use letters to test.

The letter is the most logical testing instrument in a direct mail package.

Testing one brochure against another is expensive, even if all the changes are in the black plate. Testing response devices such as order forms often gives muddy results, because such tests aren't always logical; a writer, testing response device formats, often throws one to the wolves because the offer doesn't suggest a second approach.

But letters! We can find the Kingdom of Heaven there. The writer becomes a hero because his four-page letter outpulled the one-page letter—or vice versa. The letter can test the four great motivators of the mid-1980s (*Fear, Exclusivity, Greed,* and *Guilt*) against one another.

The letter can test masculine wording against feminine. It can test a harrumphing executive against a hay-chawin' good ol' boy. It can test the validity of some of the tips in this article.

Best of all, letter tests are cheap. It costs next to nothing to print copies of two letters instead of one.

(While you're at it, consider testing a tinted paper stock against white. The text has to be identical, or you destroy the purity of results. This isn't a copy test, I know, but color psychology is itself one of the creative aspects of direct marketing.)

Herschell Gordon Lewis, "Back to the Basics, or 50 Rules to Live By," *Direct Marketing,* June 1984. Reprinted by permission of *Direct Marketing* magazine.

Creating Direct Response Commercials

AL EICOFF

As with all direct marketing, television advertising must motivate immediate actions. Direct marketers get their ratings from NCR (National Cash Register). TV ads need not be dull, drab, and unimaginative. Direct-response TV must simply present the benefits of products and services in the most informative and interesting (though not necessarily the most entertaining) way. And like the old time pitchman, the immediate sale is necessary because tomorrow neither the "pitchman" nor the buyer will likely be there. The essential formula for constructing direct response TV ads is:

1. Describe a "holder." This is usually the promise of free gifts, an amazing offer, and so forth.

2. Present/establish the problem.

3. Demonstrate how your product can solve the problem simply and effectively.

4. Make a "turn." The seller gives the price and tells how the buyer can obtain the product. This often includes extra incentives for immediate action.

5. Make a guarantee. Often part of the "turn," the offer is made with an "unconditional guarantee," the strongest sales closer ever developed.

IN HIS ADDRESS AT THE NATIONAL DIRECT MARketing Convention in 1982 and in both of his books, *Confessions of an Advertising Man* and *Ogilvy on Advertising,* David Ogilvy suggested that no one should be in advertising who had not spent at least his first two years in direct marketing. That's because direct response advertising professionals have to be the best in the advertising industry. As indicated in chapter 2 and restated in chapter 3, people in direct marketing must continually produce immediate, profitable results. There is *no* margin of error for either direct-marketing creative or media people. The direct marketer does not have the luxury of an extended wait-and-see period. Direct marketing truly disregards past performances, yesterday's successes, and fellow direct marketer's opinions. Direct marketing asks, "What did you do for me today?" If that question cannot be answered positively, the direct marketer will have few chances to redeem himself for that specific offer. Continual failure will quickly slam the doors.

The accepted method of evaluating a direct marketer's creative and media personnel is based on today's results. No other branch of marketing—or, more specifically, advertising—is more critical of its participants.

Because an immediate, profitable return is the only way direct marketers keep score, that score must be evaluated daily. The creative objective of all direct marketing exposures must be to motivate immediate actions, that is, profitable leads or sales. Regular advertisers rely on Nielsen or Arbitron, while direct marketers rely only on NCR (National Cash Register).

TV Advertising

The most effective selling method is person to person. If every company could sell its product by having a well-trained salesperson call on the potential customer, there would be no need for any other advertising medium. This, of course, would be not only costly, but impossible. Thus, the next best means of reaching a potential customer on a personal level is through television.

When an advertiser uses television, he is knocking on the door of the potential buyer, who, in effect, invites him into his home. The visit usually is limited to no more than 120 seconds, which is not much time to motivate a potential customer to take postive action.

Think about it.

If you were invited into a customer's inner sanctum for the purpose of motivating a buying action, would you use those precious seconds to tell a joke, mime, sing a song, or entertain with a brass band? Or would you get right down to the business of selling? Isn't it logical that you would take the allotted time to set forth the problems the customer may have relative to the service the product performs and then explain how your product solves those problems?

In the vernacular of the old, experienced direct-marketing creative writer, the secret of direct marketing success lies in *telling the potential customer why he should buy your product. Tell him again. And then tell him what you told him!*

It is important that you make the sales presentation both interesting and effective. The entertainment aspect of advertising did not become part of the creative aspect until the advent of broadcast. By the time broadcast became a reality, the creative personnel were so far removed from most clients' overall marketing program and sales thrusts that they lost the ability to evaluate their efforts. In effect, they lost the scorekeeping mechanism. As pointed out in *The One Minute Manager* by Kenneth Blanchard and Spencer Johnson, "No one wants to play a game in which there is no way to keep score."

Therefore, advertising's creative community made up its own way to keep score: awards!

To score, you must win an award! And so the hot-dog creative was born. Being a hot-dog creative means being unique and entertaining, and that's what the CLIO judges (advertising's answer to the Oscar) looked for in the selection of winners. Many of the advertising community's agencies zeroed in on the hot-dog creative of Stan Freeberg, Jerry Della Femina, Doyle Dane Bernbach, Mary Wells, etc. The mainstream agencies, such as J. Walter Thompson, Ogilvy & Mather, Leo Burnett, and McCann-Erickson, stayed with a more conservative approach, though they paid homage to the entertainment trend by adding celebrities, music, and sometimes a little light-hearted humor to their advertising efforts.

So that you get a better understanding of the 1960s and the history of the hot-dog CLIO winners, let's look at the record. Here is what *Advertising Age* had to say about CLIO awards in an article that appeared July 10, 1967:

> Without a doubt this is the funniest reel of winners in all of television's history . . . but the laughter has begun to die away, less than two months later, as the agencies that won four of the CLIOs have lost the accounts. Another CLIO winner is out of business. Another CLIO winner has taken $5 million out of television. Another has taken one half of its brand business to another shop. Another CLIO winner refused to put its entry on the air. Two others are in serious jeopardy at this time.

This situation was not unusual. Out of 81 CLIO winners from years gone by, 36 of the represented agencies either lost the account or had gone out of business.

The two creative sensations of 1983-84 were the "Where's the Beef" campaign for Wendy's and the Michael Jackson "Thriller" commercial for Pepsi-Cola, neither of which were on the air three months after their initial exposure.

Does this mean that direct-marketing commercials are dull, drab, unimaginative? No, it means just the opposite. A direct-marketing commercial must simply present the benefits of its products or services in the most informative and interesting way. Notice that I use the word "interesting," as opposed to "entertaining." Effective television advertising often is interesting rather than entertaining. In the early days of television, "interesting" 30-minute sales pitches were the norm. Though they aired constantly, viewers responded positively to them. In fact, they created as much discussion as the "hot dog" commercials did.

The boardwalk pitchman and the traveling medicine man always presented their wares in an interesting way in order to attract crowds and hold their attention long enough to make a sale. Their approach, with the rough edges smoothed and the pitch condensed, is relevant to broadcast direct marketing today.

Whether pitchmen's presentations were five minutes or two hours, they all used the same format. The presentation included a holder, that is, a promise of something sensational to come, ranging from free prizes to a never-before-seen miracle. The presentation of the problem involved an ailment, a difficult chore, or a substandard product performance. Then came a solution with a visual demonstration or verbal description of how the seller's product would solve the problem. The pitchman used the "tell 'em, tell 'em again, and tell 'em what you told 'em" technique. Then came the *turn,* that part of the presentation that asked the potential customer to reach in his pocket for the money. The turn was always reinforced by a guarantee of satisfaction that ended with "or your money will be cheerfully refunded." No other phrase was so powerful in

bridging the credibility gap as a money-back guarantee. The pitchman had to make an immediate sale because neither the buyer nor the seller would probably be there tomorrow.

The Anatomy of a Sales Presentation

No creative writer has ever been able to approach the effectiveness of the boardwalk huckster, who often sold 50 percent to 75 percent of his entire audience. His sales presentation was born of evolution. He watched and listened to the responses of his audience and was able to counter their negative reactions. He saw what made them pull out their wallets and what made them walk away. He accentuated the positive, eliminated the negative, and sired the perfect sales presentation.

In the early days of television, a pitchman was often used as the presenter. First he would work before a live audience on the boardwalk, in a department store, or on a street corner. We took him to the TV station only after we were satisfied that we had the most effective presentation. Although this technique has not been used in many years, there is no reason why it should not be reinstated today. One can learn much from in-store demonstrations, and a perceptive direct marketer can often learn more from a person-to-person technique than from all the research that money can buy.

Let's look more closely at the basic elements of the pitchman's presentation. Many pitchmen held their audience with stinging verbal warnings. They called attention to an imaginary pickpocket in the audience whom they gave "just five minutes to leave"; they insulted the audience by shouting, "anyone who thinks he's so smart that he has nothing more to learn should leave now." With either of these two holders, anyone who starts to leave is branded a pickpocket or a wise guy.

In television commercials, a holder is a promise of free gifts, a product's "miraculous" performance, an "amzing offer," a "sensational price," or a "revolutionary new concept." The commercials use a series of buzzwords that keep the audience's attention.

In the presentation of a "problem," the seller of a coleslaw maker demonstrated the old-fashioned "knuckle-bustin'" utensils mom used to make coldslaw with: clumsy hand graters and dangerous kitchen knives. The problems presented by sellers of health tonics ranged from sexual impotence, bad eyesight, and bad teeth to the problem of having a husband "that never won a blue ribbon at a fair." The household always provided a full gamut of problems ranging from the "stooping and wringing" that is necessary with an old-fashioned wringer-type mop to the "rubbing and scrubbing" that characterizes cleaning your silver, polishing your car, and removing stains from pots and pans. The more common and catastrophic the malady or problem, the greater chance one has in selling the cure or solution. Ultimately, you create a universal problem and solve it by providing a universal cure.

Once you've established the problem or need, you are ready to discuss its solution; you must demonstrate how your product can solve the problem simply and effectively. You mop the floor without stooping, bending, or scrubbing. You touch the silver and it instantly shines. You turn a handle and you have a mountain of coleslaw or a pan full of perfectly textured potato pancake batter. On television, the magic is performed before your very eyes. On radio, the miracle occurs through words that conjure up images.

The buyer is now ready for the turn. The seller gives the price and tells how the buyer can obtain the product. The turn often includes extra incentives for an immediate reaction: a free attachment, an added product, or a reduction in price. It is this segment of a commercial that demands an immediate action. As part of the turn—and in order to bridge the credibility gap that may exist between the con-

sumer and an unknown manufacturer—the offer is made with an unconditional money-back guarantee. The money-back guarantee is the strongest sales closer ever developed.

The Anatomy of a Sales Presentation

holder→problem→product presentation→ solution→turn→guarantee

In the construction of a commercial, it is not always necessary to have a "problem" and a "holder." For example, in selling magazine subscriptions or music tapes, no problem exists. Today, few commercials are constructed with a "holder," although it is a powerful aspect of selling. Certain elements, however, must be present in an effective direct-marketing commercial.

I have said that the description or demonstration of benefits is an essential aspect of good commercials. The word "benefit" in effect, replaces the word "sizzle" in the old selling adage "sell the sizzle, not the steak." It is imperative, therefore, to know the difference between a "feature" and a "benefit." The difference may seem obvious. However, on numerous tests given to professional direct-marketing copywriters, as well as to university advertising students and professors, an amazing number were unable to differentiate between a benefit and a feature. So that you can better understand the difference, here is a list of features and benefits:

Feature	Benefit
Remote-control television	You don't have to get up to change channels
Programmable thermostat	Greater comfort and higher economy
Rack-and-pinion steering	Easier handling, quicker turns
One calorie per can	Helps you watch your weight
Automatic focusing	Never pay for developing an out-of-focus picture

(continued)

Feature	Benefit	Feature	Benefit
24-hour automatic teller	Get money when you need it, even in the middle of the night	Long-lasting scent	Smell good all day; use less product, so you can save money
Push-button dialing	Saves time in dialing, prevents broken nails	Computer fuel injection	Faster starts, smoother ignition, greater mileage, so you save money
Golf club with solid metal head	Gives greater distance and accuracy		
Ceramic tile roofing	Lowers heating and cooling costs, saves on reroofing expenses		
Money-back guarantee	Assurance of satisfaction, purchase without risk		

Al Eicoff, "Creating Direct Response Commercials," from *Al Eicoff On Broadcast Direct Marketing,* Chapter V, NTC Business Books, 1987. Excerpted, with permission, from *Eicoff On Broadcast Direct Marketing,* by Al Eicoff (NTC Business Books, Lincolnwood, Illinois, 1987).

The Classic Package

Designing for Your Market and Budget

Dave Wilkison

Your mailing format and materials should reflect who you're mailing it to, and what you're selling. Customers and prospects need different materials. For instance, upscale markets deserve different treatment than downscale. Ideally, the copywriter and graphics designer should work together. The roll-out cost of design options must be examined before testing. The order form is the most important part of the mailing. Order forms can be improved with "action devices" that make it easy for the prospect to accept the offer. The order form should contain a summary of the offer blocked in easy-to-read sections. Instructions on how to fill out the order form should be highlighted. Using the back of the order form can often enhance the effectiveness of this part of the package.

How your mailing should look depends on who you're sending it to and what you're selling. The key factor is the prospect. You should design (and of course, write) differently to the person who is your customer rather than a cold prospect.

Your envelope should tell former customers that it's "you" again, but be different and intriguing enough to alert them that there's something important for them inside.

If your product is upscale, the look, texture of stock, and production quality of your components should reflect it. The prospect should feel, on seeing your package, that this is indeed a message of value and importance worthy of his or her attention.

By the same token, if you're promoting sales or low-ticket items, you should telegraph this message by your look and appearance.

If your product is upscale, the look, texture of stock and production quality of your components should reflect it.

"Thank you for being there and for being what you are: an unabashed, informative, and glitz-free celebration of good wooden boats."

Charles W. Smith   Durham, N.H.

Do you have a reputation? If your firm is well-known, by all means use your reputation as a door-opener. Your logo and design should be used to "brand" your package to take advantage of your reputation. Blank envelopes using just a well-known logo are an example of this reputation advantage.

Designing for your market requires designing around the offer.

Ideally, writer and designer should write and work out the package problem together. When that is not possible, the designer should examine the copy he or she is presented with and *really* read it. Understand what the copy is saying. Even ask the writer questions about it. Ask the writer what he sees as the most important parts of the package.

The designer should emphasize elements about the offer, copy and the benefits of the product or service that are *positive*. If it's a trial offer, for example, this should be emphasized by the type treatment wherever it appears.

If it's a firm "cash-up" offer with a guarantee, on the other hand, the designer should make the guarantee stand out, while highlight-

ing the offer copy. Negatives should not stand out, while positives and instructions should be laid out prominently.

Every organization cannot afford its own direct mail production expert. But, you should be given an idea of a basic direct mail budget. This way you can figure approximately how much more (or *less*) you might be able to invest in a package to bring you a winner, not only on pull but on costs, too.

Start the Creative

Armed with an overall budget figure, designer and writer can work together to come up with a package. And I hope you will be given time to do an adequate job. (Though from experience, creative design is usually done under intense time pressure.)

Once you have the idea, cost it out. Check out with your lettershop whether the package can be inserted with their equipment. Ask the printers and direct mail production houses for alternatives on stocks and printing processes.

Don't automatically go for the low bid, or the low-cost stock.

Consider the Feasibility

Included in any judgment of package cost is the ability to produce the package in quantities. There is a fine-tuning adjustment any designer has to make. It is possible to test a package that's elaborately beautiful, beat the control, but lose on roll-out costs or production incompatibility.

What happens next? Then you have to retest it in a less expensive version and see if it still works—or you may have to adjust it so it can be inserted in bulk quantities without hurting response. This not only costs time, it costs profits. Get it right the first time out.

The order form is the most important part of your mailing. Yet, it is often the dullest and most uninspiring piece in the mail package. Order forms should look like order forms, of course. That does not mean they have to look dull.

In designing an order form, designer and writer should contemplate the use of "action devices" the prospect uses to accept the offer. A typical action device is a punch-out token placed in a slot on the form. The action device could also be a plastic card, a real coin, a tear-off strip, rub-off strip, even a stamp taken from somewhere else in the package.

Of course they cost more. Dynamically designed action devices can make your offer more acceptable because they *involve* the prospect. They invite the prospect to use them and they give your package more impact. They cry out to be used and that is why action devices help your order form.

Design of Order Form Elements

With the exception of sweepstakes mailings, most order forms should contain a summary of the offer blocked out in easy-to-read sections. Positive aspects of the offer should be driven home in easy-to-grasp boxes.

If there is a guarantee it should be enhanced with ornate borders and set in aggressive yet "trustworthy" typography. Examples of good guarantee typefaces are from the serifed fonts such as Times Roman, Palatino or Garamond.

Positives about the offer deserve strong headline treatment.

If there is a deadline—box it—put it in color. Make it one of the first things the reader notices.

Actual contract copy mentioning prices should be set low key and writers should be advised to make the order copy as short as possible. The longer the contract copy, the more intimidating the feeling of commitment.

Don't be afraid to demonstrate on the order form. Instructions as to what to do should be highlighted. If there is filling out to do, point to it. If there is tearing out to do, tell them and have tiny arrows pointing to printed dotted lines over your perforations. If there is an action to be taken, illustrate it in a miniature box.

I believe in receipts and "keepers." Set aside a portion of the order form as a receipt, often with the guarantee included on it that the customer can keep as a record of his transaction. It is one more action feature to an order form that solidifies the commitment and secures the trust of the customer.

If the order form is your address vehicle, provide a place for the label. It looks neater and more businesslike.

Also, talk your writers into writing copy for the back of your order forms, too. Use the space for an enhancement of the guarantee, description of bonuses, if any, or advantages of the offer.

Backgrounds

Design should include consideration of screens and backgrounds for portions of the order form to make it look valuable. Order forms may take the look of financial documents, credit card sales slips, shipping labels, and more. Using check-like backgrounds adds to the customer's perceived value of your offer, while drawing his close inspection of your order form.

Dave Wilkison, "Designing for Your Market and Budget," *Direct Marketing,* February 1987. Reprinted by permission of *Direct Marketing* magazine.

The Envelope
DAVE WILKISON

The envelope and order form can work together to create a visual effect that intrigues the reader. Blank envelopes almost always get opened, but a good envelope with good teaser copy should pull more qualified buyers. Selection of paper stock depends on the idea concept behind the mailing. Look for stock that says what you are. Windows should be used to isolate important things about the mailing, but should not reveal the whole story. Action tabs (pull-back tabs and die-cuts, etc.) beg, like a zipper, to be opened. Envelope teasers should set the tone for the mailing and deliver the character of the mailing.

I HAVE DISCUSSED THE ENVELOPE SECOND BE-cause often the envelope and the order form can work together to create a visual effect that intrigues the reader.

But, before we get started, I'd like to say a word about blank (logo and address only) envelopes. They are good. They almost always get opened. And you should test them from time to time.

However, a good envelope with good teaser copy and solid design should pull more qualified buyers in most cases, because it sets your inside message up. With no promise or benefit on the envelope, the first enclosure your prospect sees has to have a great impact to grab his/her attention. The concept envelope whets your prospect's appetite and gets him to read more of your inside message. Blank envelopes should be considered when going to your present customers, or if your firm has a national reputation.

Stocks

The heavier the stock you choose, the more important and valuable looking your envelope. However, light stocks with an interesting feel to them can add a fiduciary look to your envelope while adding to its perceived value. Selection of stock depends on the idea concept behind your mailing. Look for a stock that says what you are.

If selling financial services, sift through valuable looking stocks to keep that fiduciary feel. If selling a classy book or gourmet food, lean to glossy stocks. There is no rule of thumb except that the envelope should have a look and a feel to it that match the product or service. Beware of heavy stocks in multimillion quantities. They are hard to manufacture in quantity when you are on a tight time schedule.

Windows

Windows should be used to isolate important things about the mailing. If a free bonus is offered, you might show it through one window. If there's a deadline date, you might show it through another window. Windows should not reveal the whole story, though. Use them as teasers, showing part of a dollar amount, or showing a "pay to the order of" line. Think about pistol-shaped windows to add differences to your envelopes.

Tabs and Openers

Just as action devices invite ordering, pull-back tabs and die-cuts invite opening. They beg, like a zipper, to be opened. People like to fiddle with them. If looking for a twist to your envelope, put in a pull-back tab device But it should work with the copy on the envelope, perhaps to reveal a message underneath, or a special bonus. Remember, always make a device be part of an ongoing building process that leads the prospect to the order action.

Teasers

Type for a teaser should deliver the character of the message. The look has to grab the prospect and force him/her to read it. Small teasers won't be read as quickly as large ones. Boxing your copy helps. "Urgent" stamps often increase pull 10 percent to 15 percent. Be careful with the word "Urgent"—the message really should be urgent, as in the case of a final billing notice.

Dave Wilkison, "The Envelope," *Direct Marketing*, March 1987. Reprinted by permission of *Direct Marketing* magazine.

The Letter and the Personalized Letter

DAVE WILKISON

Lots of different letter "looks" work in direct mail. Looks won't matter if strong sell copy is not there. Headline elements should let the reader know immediately

what the best things you're offering him/her are. Letters should be typed, or look typewritten. Plenty of short paragraphs and indented sections help the reader "stockpile" benefits in his mind. Short two-to-three word bursts in the margins often help. A P.S. is normally effective also. Multiple page letters on single sheets, mailed unfolded, are recommended. The three forms of personalization (impact, laser, and inkjet) offer different advantages. Use windows on your envelope to reveal personalized portions of your order form or personalized documents inside.

THERE ARE A LOT OF LETTER LOOKS OUT THERE in direct mail. You have to find out through testing what look works best for you. If the strong sell copy isn't there, the response won't be there either, and what it looks like doesn't matter. The following are strictly Direct Marketing Graphics' ideas on what makes a letter more readable and compelling.

Headline Elements

A letter should start with a strong benefit headline, crystalizing the benefits of the offer in a nutshell. You can get the reader to focus on the offer by placing this copy in a box of stars (called a Johnson Box, named after Frank Johnson who created the device) or use bold dramatic headlines. This way the prospect immediately knows the best things you're offering him.

Copy Flow

In my opinion, letters should be *typed* in typefaces like Courier and Prestige elite. Typesetting a letter does not make it look like a letter. Ideally, a typewritten look with plenty of short paragraphs and indented sections draws the reader again and again to different sections of a letter, so the benefits of what you're selling "stockpile" in his mind.

The first page of the letter, after the headline, should have several short sentences as openers. The offer copy should be stated near the bottom of the first page, or if it's not, the action to be taken to say "yes" should be highlighted.

Reading Aids

The letter can be enhanced by *handwriting* in the margin in short two- to three-word bursts to draw the eye in. This is particularly helpful in longer letters of six pages or more. Don't be afraid to put other action words, such as "urgent" or "reply now" in strategic spots. Ask the writer to write you a few. Ask the writer for a P.S. message, if he or she doesn't supply one. It's the most read part of the letter. Also think about isolating any guarantees or special bonuses in boxes at the end of the letter, in the middle, or on the first page.

Folds and Stocks

The more a letter can look like a letter, the better. Multiple page letters on single loose sheets give the reader the feeling the letter is more important. Mail it unfolded if possible. Select stocks that make the letter look special. Experiment with outsized letters, like 8½-by-14 inches, for different looks. But, any design of a letter should enhance its readability and attract attention to the offer.

The Personalized Letter

There are three types of personalization technology being used today. They are *impact* (done by a computer printer where keys actually strike in the personalization), *laser* (where all copy is fixed on a computer form via a heat or cold process), and *inkjet* (where copy is sprayed on). This is a simple description of each process.

Each technique requires a special continuous computer form to be created and designed to the personalization house specifications. In creating this form you have to be aware of the length of your longest possible fill-ins (such as how many characters in your longest name), and the maximum print area available to you. Generally, your order form is also part of your computer form and can be slit off during the insertion process and made a separate piece in the mailing.

Laser and inkjet have the ability to print in different directions, and both offer you a variety of typefaces to choose from.

Impact delivers more of a personal typed look. Most of the time this is done with a match-fill process where portions of the letter are pre-printed. You have to be careful to have your personalization fill-in come at the end of lines, because the impact continuous form always allows a maximum number of characters (usually 132 characters on a two-up form) for the fill-in. Laser and inkjet can "close the gaps" because the entire letter is printed out and the computer controls the personalization positioning.

The Best Looks for Different Personalized Effects

Impact personalization does not give as good a look as laser for straight letter copy. I do like it, though, for telegrams and sweepstakes mailings because of its feeling of immediacy.

Laster gives you the cleanest, sharpest image, making it a natural choice for business and financial mailings, and a good all-around choice for any market.

Laying Out a Personalized Letter

Read the above section on "The Letter" again. The same rules apply. Talk the writer into short personalized paragraphs. Discuss the possibilities, when using laser, of putting personalized messages by the side of the copy to draw the eye to it.

On most personalized letter forms you have about four pages to work with, only two of which can be personalized. But, with some technologies you can personalize on both sides of the form. Consider that possibility when choosing printers.

Prepare a personalization grid or "schematic" to show your forms house how the piece personalizes before you set type. Work closely with the programmer.

Working Personalization with Your Envelope

Remember what I said about windows? Use windows on your envelope to reveal personalized portions of your order form or personalized documents inside. It helps get the prospect's interest.

Time

Allow at least 10 weeks to develop a personalized package, including writing, programming and production.

Dave Wilkison, "The Letter & the Personalized Letter," *Direct Marketing*, April 1987. Reprinted by permission of *Direct Marketing* magazine.

The Brochure

Dave Wilkison

A brochure can take many forms. Type selection is very important when products don't lend themselves to demonstration. Information presentation has to be tight and airy all at once. Graphic elements increase in significance when promoting a luxury book or a deluxe product. Graphics have the burden of delivering the flavor and feeling of the product. Call-outs and blocks, and arrows leading to copy blocks, and the like, are recommended. Headlines should be weighted and emphasized in relation to their importance. Never emphasize the price. Models, if used, should emphasize the product in use. Showing real people is more effective than illustrations or line drawings. The fold of the brochure should be "bedsheet," with each logically proceeding panel building excitement. An overall signature typeface should be used to tie the entire brochure together.

There are a number of pieces that qualify as brochures in our business. Demands on the designer vary according to the product or service.

For example, if you're promoting a meeting or conference, or a product not lending itself to demonstration, type selection is very important, and design of your listings and explanations has to be readable, but deliver the information with impact. It has to be both "tight" and "airy" all at once.

If you're promoting a luxury book or a deluxe product, your graphic elements have to deliver the "flavor" and "feeling" of what you're selling, yet have to "coordinate" with the headlines and body copy.

The design can "compartmentalize" the elements, lending a formality to the piece. This is useful when designing for financial groups or products requiring a formal image. But, if the brochure needs to create an excitement about the product, then an effective way to do this is to have graphic elements overlapping.

Call Outs and Boxes

Copy blocks should be no more than four or five lines long and should be broken up by subheads to draw the eye.

Boxes are good devices to use, but they should be placed so they stand out, yet blend with the overall design. Use call-outs to make pictures come alive, instead of just lie there. Call-outs with arrows leading to copy blocks make prospects read the copy squibs that may get overlooked if not pointed out. Ask your writers what elements in the copy they feel are important and figure how you can tie them to an illustration.

Elements to Emphasize

Headlines should be weighted in relation to their importance. Major promises deserve major typeface treatment. *Offer headlines* should stand out strongly, especially when offering items on trial or money back. *Guarantees* should be granted a special graphics treatment, using signatures and tints behind the copy to deliver a trustworthy, honest tone.

Listings of importance to the product, like features, endorsements, clients, etc., should be isolated in boxes. *Order form areas* should be separated out by dotted lines. Think about captions for every illustration, because they are noticed. Think about placing "emphasis boxes" in or near pictures.

NEVER EMPHASIZE THE PRICE, EMPHASIZE THE ADVANTAGE OF THE PRICE (like amount of saving) AND THE NATURE OF THE OFFER (like "No-Risk Free Trial").

Photographs

Photographs using models involved with a product should emphasize the product in use, so persons can put themselves in the picture. Models are very expensive to use, so you should have them demonstrate the product in a way that a standard shot of the product won't.

Illustrations

Illustration with line drawings, diagrams or original painting is not as effective as showing real people using your product. It doesn't allow that human impact or mysterious process of "transference" (where a person looking at your brochure mentally exchanges places with the persons in your picture) to take place.

In shots of the product, create a mood for the product by photographing it with objects connected with its use. (An expensive luxury, but it creates an aura that is part of what the prospect is buying.) Show features of the product close up, but be sure to explain each feature with copy. Can you develop a good sequence photo-shot demonstrating the product? They are always worth a thousand words.

Folds

Bedsheet brochures, like 24-by-38-inch sheets, should fold logically, with each panel building excitement for the product, because that is the way a writer usually writes the copy. Back panels are usually reserved for a restatement of the offer.

Folds should proceed logically, with some sections of other fold panels showing, if possible. Think about overflaps for long listings of features.

The inside spread should show the product in full glory in a manner in which there are lots of little sections that the prospect can pore over or skim quickly to get the salient features.

By breaking up the copy in boxes rather than placing it all in one block, more of it will get read.

Small brochures, such as 5½-by-8½-inches or billing stuffer foldouts, require organization along the same principles as outlined above, only with closer attention to the type size. Eight point is the minimum you should go for optimum readability. Order forms should be highlighted with dotted lines and instructions supplemented with arrows.

All-Type Brochure with Limited Illustration

Here's the test of a great designer. Here selection of type is paramount, and breakout and organization of the copy depend on close coordination of writer and artist.

An overall signature typeface should be used to tie together each panel of the brochure. . . . Liberal use of that signature typeface should introduce different sections. Build in air. It allows the copy to invite readership. Consider non-coated, heavyweight stocks to give the all-type brochure more presence and impact.

Dave Wilkison, "The Brochure," *Direct Marketing*, May 1987. Reprinted by permission of *Direct Marketing* magazine.

Pros Tell How to Produce Effective Brochures

Uri Dowbenko

The brochure is the television of the direct mail package. Like television, it offers immense credibility. It offers the prospect an opportunity to see for themselves. It offers the seller the space to diagram the most complex of working parts or the most elaborate of details. Some guidelines for producing more effective direct mail brochures include:

1. Define your offer and its major benefits in the headline.
2. Use the front page of the brochure to attract attention with a dramatic photograph.
3. Use editorial-style layouts and simple graphic design for credibility.
4. Use photographs to show the prospect how the product is used.
5. Use photo captions to emphasize key benefits.
6. Use typography that helps people read your messages.
7. Prove your story with case histories and testimonials.
8. Emphasize the guarantee.
9. Use coupons to make it easy for your prospect to respond.
10. Use full-color printing and quality paper to convey a first-class image.

"A BROCHURE IS THE TELEVISION OF DIRECT mail," says Ed Nash, known as "the master strategist of direct marketing." "Like television, it offers immense credibility because words can lie, but the eye cannot be fooled. It offers the prospect a chance to 'see for yourself' the beauty of the product offered and how it will look at home, garden, or office. It provides space to diagram the most complex of working parts or the most elaborate of details."

It also makes a very important first impression to your prospect.

Here are some guidelines for producing a more effective brochure in your direct mail, mail order, and sales lead generation:

Define your offer and its major benefits in the headline. "The headlines which work best," says David Ogilvy, founder of Ogilvy and Mather, "are those which promise the reader a benefit." Make a list of every selling point and be sure to include it in your brochure—either as a headline, a subhead, or as a part of your copy. For example: "The Hired Hand will feed your horses automatically even when you're not there"—a headline for an automatic horse feeder brochure; "How chiropractic can help improve your health naturally"—a headline for a patient education doctor's brochure; "Sunrooms, Smartest Home Improvement of the 80's"—headline for a sales lead generation brochure, and "Freedom fighters of the world unite"—a headline for a fund-raising brochure.

Use the front page of the brochure to attract attention with a dramatic photograph. For example, a striking photo of a horse, nose to the dirt, arouses the reader's curiosity with the headline "Don't leave your horse without it."

A photo of a girl, arms in a V-for-victory formation, jumping out of the water, emphasizes the impact of the headline "Relief of pain."

Use editorial-style layouts and simple graphic design for credibility. "If you make them (ads) look like editorial pages, you will attract more readers," says ad magnate David Ogilvy. "Roughly six times as many people read the average article as the average advertisement."

Take a hint from magazine editors who set shorter articles (called sidebars) next to the main piece. Other information about your offer—how to use your product or a step-by-step demonstration, or a short history of the product can be included in your brochure set aside from the main sales copy by a tinted color box or another device.

Use photographs to show the prospect how the product is used. Never assume that your prospect will instantly understand how your product or service will make life easier—unless you explicitly show it.

For a brochure to sell an English-as-a-second-language audiocassette course, photos showing people listening to cassettes while doing housework, driving in a car, eating, and so on are crucial in communicating the ways the product can be used when the target audience is not fluent in English. For a new product, an automatic horse feeder, for example, a visual demonstration of the step-by-step process of how to use it is also vital in showing the bene-

fits. For a physician capabilities brochure, photos emphasize how chiropractic can be used— "These problems can be relieved: whiplash, on-the-job injuries, sports injuries."

Use photo-captions to emphasize key benefits. Your beautiful photographs essentially buy readership for the photo-captions, so highlight key benefits in your captions. Don't waste caption space by describing what's in the picture. Use it to promote the offer.

Use typography that helps people read your message. "All our reading is done in upper and lower case type," writes Claude Hopkins. "We are accustomed to that. When we meet lines set in capitals, we have to study them out. This may not be a severe handicap, but it is always a detriment."

Prove your story with case histories and testimonials. Customer testimonials, a celebrity endorsement, a report of a testing laboratory or other proof that your offer is worthwhile should always be included because people are always interested in what a third party has to say about your products, services or your firm.

However, be careful. It was only several decades ago that the tobacco companies were buying endorsements from doctors and opera singers who endorsed cigarettes as a healthy way to relax and improve the voice.

Emphasize the guarantee. If one guarantee works well, then two guarantees should work better, contends direct marketer Rene Gnam. Give your prospect as many reasons as you can to trust you. After all, you are asking a customer to trust you by placing an order and sometimes sending payment for items they have never seen before or handled.

"I believe that it is not at all coincidental that the companies with the most generous policies seem to be consistently among the most successful," says Ed Nash.

Use coupons to make it easy for your prospect to respond. "Countless tests have proven that coupons multiply returns. I have seen many tests made by mail-order houses offering catalogs.

Some ads had coupons; some did not. The difference in returns was enormous," says John Caples, author of *How to Make Your Advertising Make Money.*

Use full-color printing and quality paper to convey a first-class image. Today people are used to seeing everything in color because of color TV, and because of their God-given eyesight. It's natural and obviously life-like. Likewise your brochure should be in color—to reflect the quality of your company and products— and to be as memorable and convincing as possible. Color brochures are cost-effective because color sells better.

Uri Dowbenko, "Pros Tell How to Produce Effective Brochures," *Target Marketing,* October 1986. Reprinted from *Target Marketing* magazine, published by North American Publishing Company.

Peripherals
DAVE WILKISON

Direct mail peripherals include postcards, bonus inserts, and lift letters. The postcard headline should immediately telegraph what the purpose of the postcard is. A bonus insert should really stand out, though it need not be based on a "big idea." A "free" something or other can often suffice. Don't typeset lift letters. Make them look like actual typewritten letters. Use a different stock for the lift letter and seal it with a gluespot or seal. Break lift letters up into paragraphs of just a couple of sentences each. Use a typewriter style like Prestige or Elite, preferably a serifed typeface.

POST CARDS, BONUS INSERTS AND LIFT LETTERS are three types of peripherals that can be used in a direct mail package. Decide which will best suit your needs.

Postcards

Design should revolve around the typeface and purpose of the post card. Headlines should immediately telegraph what the purpose of the post card is. Use different stocks to invite interest. Use arrows to point to what is important.

Bonus Inserts

A bonus insert should really stand out. There does not necessarily have to be a big idea behind it. It should be screamingly functional. If it's a FREE bonus, make the word "FREE" big. Also emphasize the headline *how you get the bonus,* referring back to the main order form.

Is there a special action they have to do involving another form? *Illustrate it in a small diagram on your bonus insert.* It is involving and makes maximum use of your order form. In fact, it's a good idea to have your bonus insert refer back to the order form by telling again how to order.

Is there a deadline? Make the deadline prominent on your bonus insert. Make the insert jumpy in look so it attracts attention to the three points:

1. What the bonus is.
2. How you get it.
3. If there's a time limit.

Make the bonus insert of an unusual size, fold, or different stock. It must stand out!

Lift Letters

Don't use typesetting, make them look like actual typewritten letters. Handwritten teasers should be readable! Use arrows to point the way inside. Select a stock different from your four-page letter to enhance the illusion of the "extra letter" concept. Seal it closed with a gluespot or sticker seal, if you can afford it.

Insist that the writer break up his or her paragraphs into just a couple of sentences each. Keep them readable and don't arbitrarily tell the writer to cut the copy. On the other hand, don't let the writer talk you into setting it in 6 point just to squeeze all the copy in.

Use a typewriter style like Prestige Elite or Courier, preferably a serifed style. The sans-serif styles are more difficult to read.

Dave Wilkison, "Peripherals," *Direct Marketing,* June 1987. Reprinted by permission of *Direct Marketing* magazine.

Media

Direct Mail
Advertising's Best-Kept Secret

Ken Erdman

Direct mail is essentially sales messages by mail. Direct mail can be used to sell products for later delivery. It can also be used to bring customers and prospects to your place of business. It can pave the way and introduce sales people before personal calls. It is the most personal of all media. It can be directed to those likely to be especially interested in your offer. Surprisingly, most people, particularly business people, not only read direct advertising mail but like it and act on it. Cost per mailing depends on the number of pieces, but can usually be done for less than $1.00 per mailing piece. Professionals who prepare direct mail pieces abound, but direct mail can be a do-it-yourself medium. It's an ideal medium for the business or professional person. Its measurability lets you determine quickly whether it is or isn't cost effective. Some experts believe that dollar for dollar, nothing will return as much to your business as direct mail. It should be a part of every manufacturer's marketing plan, regardless of the size of the company. Continued success is based on creativity and keeping your mailing list up to date.

EXCITEMENT WAS ELECTRIC—IN THE INDUS VALley between India and Pakistan—when the citizens first heard that an organized message-delivery system was starting in business. No, it was not United Parcel Service or even the

India/Pakistan mail system. It was a private business concern that thought it would be profitable and informative to send messages from one remote group to another. It didn't make the papers, and you never saw it on television because it happened about 4000 B.C.

"The roots of direct mail go back thousands of years and include messages written in hieroglyphics on papyrus and fabric sent throughout the Egyptian kingdom about 3000 B.C.," says Nat Ross, of the New York University Center for Direct Marketing.

The Assyrians, Babylonians, and Persians used clay tablets and cuneiform inscriptions in the year 2000 B.C. A Babylonian clay wrapper, perhaps the very first envelope, dates back to that year.

Ever since, in evermore sophisticated forms, people have been sending selling messages by mail. And that's basically what *direct* mail is: *sales messages* by mail.

Here's how direct mail works for a typical small businessman:

In the early spring the proprietor of the camera store on Main Street orders 1,000 instant camera brochures from a supplier (probably free). He orders envelopes, a printed letter, and a simple business reply card from the local print shop. The copy on one envelope says: "Now you can have a picture-perfect graduation instantly." These will be sent to the parents of graduates of the local high school. The other envelope is printed: "Now you can have a picture-perfect vacation instantly." It is sent to existing customers. The letters are written with an attention-getting first paragraph, followed by several paragraphs of short words and sentences outlining the benefits of a camera that can give you a good-quality picture without waiting. They also include a short paragraph with pricing information, an offer to ship and bill the camera to charge customers, and an invitation to open a charge account. The body of the letter concludes with an invitation to come to the store for a special graduation/vacation offer. Then a postscript (the sec-

ond most important part of the letter) offers a free package of film, if the customer orders by mail or visits the store by a certain date. The package might also include a free imprinted guide to better photography, purchased by the owner of the camera store from an advertising specialty distributor.

At U.S. $150 each, the sale of only a few cameras, along with the resulting film sales, will pay for the mailing. Other benefits: a chance to reinforce the store's image, prospective new film customers for each camera sold, and a reminder for any camera user, instant or otherwise, to buy film. This basic technique can be modified to fit almost any business with equally successful results.

Note that direct mail is a *sales* message delivered by *mail*. It is not to be confused with mail-order or catalog selling, where the sales message might appear in a variety of media such as newspapers, magazines, radio, or television, and is intended strictly for the ordering of merchandise to be deliverd to the consumer.

Though direct mail can be used to sell products that will subsequently be shipped to consumers, it can also bring customers and prospects to your place of business or to trade shows or seminars. It can pave the way and introduce salespeople before personal calls. It can help establish your business, organization, or professional image. It can be used for market research, fund-raising, public relations, announcements, greetings, and distribution of news and educational and social information.

Direct mail is the most personal of all media. Your sales messages are usually enclosed in an envelope and directed to some specific person. Through careful mailing-list selection, the person receiving your letter should be especially interested in your offer. You can tailor your message to your audience, and waste less effort and money.

Contrary to a long-popular image of direct mail as unwanted mail, most people—and particularly business people—not only read advertising mail but like it and act on it. Scientific opinion research supports these facts, and more importantly, the sales and service dollar figures generated by direct mail attest to its effectiveness. Nobody likes an empty mailbox.

Direct mail offers many advantages not found in most other media. Creative options include a wide variety of envelope sizes, shapes, and colors; different grades and colors of paper to suit particular situations; a selection of typefaces to complement almost any message. Your package can carry product samples, catalogs, recordings on tape or on paper-thin records. You can include imprinted gifts to attract attention or say "thank you." Your mailing can even take advantage of the sense of smell, with scented paper and attachments ranging from roses to root beer. For the element of surprise and fun, direct-mail pieces can be designed as pop-ups, literally jumping out at you as the envelope is opened.

How much does all this cost? Surprisingly little—in contrast, it's been estimated that the cost of an industrial sales call averages over U.S. $200. Other media base costs on the number of readers, listeners, or viewers. But there is often tremendous waste.

Direct mail, targeted to specific prospects, can be produced and mailed, depending on numbers of pieces, for well under $1.00 per mailer.

Best of all, direct mail can be a do-it-yourself medium. Think about it. Someone comes to sell you newspaper or radio space or time. Specialty salespeople stop in to sell you imprinted items. A volunteer solicits an ad for an organization's program booklet. But who comes to sell you direct mail? Most people, with the help of readily available books, magazines, cassettes, and seminars, can produce results with direct mail on their own. For those who can afford it, advertising agencies specializing in direct mail and direct marketing can offer professional help.

One of the least recognized but most important advantages of direct mail is its measurability. You send out a certain number of pieces

and receive a certain number of replies. If your response justifies the cost, you're successful. If not, you can test a new approach.

Direct mail is an ideal medium for the business or professional person, the fund-raiser, or the organizer of a committee or event. Consultant Murray Raphel, of Atlantic City, New Jersey, U.S.A., one of direct mail's leading authorities, proclaims in all of his writings and speeches: "Dollar for dollar, nothing will return as much to your business as direct mail."

Practitioners generally agree that the most effective direct-mail package consists of an envelope with teaser copy on the outside, a personal letter, a brochure or descriptive piece to reinforce the letter, and a business reply card or order form and envelope. If cost-effective, an imprinted specialty or other attention-getting device may be included.

But the traditional package is not the only way to go. An even less expensive approach is the self-mailer. Here you save the cost of the envelope and the labor to stuff it. A great advantage of the self-mailer is its *lack* of privacy. The offer can be on the front or back, right out there for everyone to read and make a quick decision about whether or not to read further. Self-mailers work especially well when you're sure that your audience has some interest in the product or service you're promoting.

Let's go back to the Main Street camera shop. If it sponsors a photography clinic in cooperation with its suppliers, and a mailing regarding the clinic is sent out to the shop's customers, it's a sure bet there will be a higher-than-usual interest level. Therefore, copy on the outside of the self-mailer will get most interested people inside. In lieu of the factory-supplied brochure, you can print a picture and description of the camera with free factory-supplied art. The business reply card, perforated for easy detachment, is an integral part of the mailer.

There's an even less expensive way to go. The camera-shop proprietor can buy full-color postcards showing the camera on one side along with the addressing space, the ad copy on the inside of that panel, and the order form on the other panel with the camera shop's return address on the inside. Again, the color photo for the outside comes from the manufacturer and the postcards can be printed by specialists listed in the classified telephone directory. (Since postcards are "gang-printed" with other jobs, they are probably the least expensive full-color printed pieces available.)

Yet, there's something even less expensive than postcards—in fact, virtually free. If you use a computer for billing, you can add a sales message to your bill or statement.

Other forms of direct mail include sales letters, invitations, and greeting cards. Our camera-shop proprietor can send a personal letter in a plain envelope to customers who have purchased cameras, offering a free camera-cleaning service. It will bring the customers back to the shop and you can be sure they will buy something while there. Or an invitation might be sent to come and see a new line of merchandise or a new model of camera, and offering free refreshments.

When the proprietor travels, a letter can be printed in advance for mailing to good customers, including photos from the vacation trip. The best part about these mailing styles is that they are highly personal and the customer gets a feeling of importance from being among the select few recognized.

If you are a manufacturer, your direct-mail efforts can be as simple as mailing catalogs and technical literature. But even here, they should be accompanied by a letter and a reply form requesting further information, a quotation, or perhaps just a request to stay on the mailing list. Now you can measure the effectiveness of your efforts. Or you can use mailings to build traffic at your trade show, introduce new products, gain sales appointments, or make seasonal mailings for seasonal products. Direct mail should be an integral part of every manufacturer's marketing plan, regardless of the size of the company.

Doctors, lawyers, dentists, and other professionals who are advertising more frequently are turning to direct mail, because its personal nature befits their conservative, low-key approach. Here again, direct mail can be simple, inexpensive, and effective. Typically, the doctor and dentist can send reminders for checkups—often producing a substantial increase in appointments and the added benefit of better dental or health care for the patient.

• A group of five California, U.S.A., periodontists joined in a mailing to 10,000 college-educated, married prospects with a median age of 47, minimum incomes of $35,000, and three family members living under the same roof. The mailing contained a letter, a color brochure that enables the reader to do a periodontal self-examination, and an American Dental Association photo brochure on dental flossing. The novel part of the mailing was the actual piece of waxed dental floss included in a protective container. The five dentists report little time for golf these days.

• A plastic surgeon seeking opportunities to testify as an expert witness directed a mailing to trial lawyers and included a business card punched to fit a rotary telephone file.

• An accountant in Hawaii, U.S.A., routinely sends out postcard income-tax reminders in January. The response to the less than 25-cent-per-piece mailing is spectacular.

Fund-raising is a natural for direct mail. The audience can be carefully preselected, the message personal and private, and an envelope included to make contributing easy.

• A Gettysburg, Pennsylvania, U.S.A., college parents-support group used creative direct mail to substantially increase both the number and size of contributions. First they moved the mailing date from early December, when people were busy with holiday planning, to Valentine's Day, when recipients were more relaxed but still had love and charity in their hearts. The heart became the trademark of each year's mailing. The copy followed a valentine theme and was printed in red on pink stationery. As an added inducement, inexpensive imprinted advertising specialties were included, accentuating each message. One year a heart-shaped magnet was held to the letter by a small metal strip. The message: "Open your heart for Gettysburg." Another year a compressed sponge which expanded when dipped into water carried the theme, "Help Gettysburg Expand." Mailings also included heart-shaped paper clips and heart-shaped cloth appliqués to be worn on Valentine's Day. Since most of the work was done by volunteers, costs were minimal.

If you're running for political office, direct mail is almost indispensable. It's the extension of the handshake—the most personal appeal to the voter. This me-to-thee communication receives attention not always afforded handouts and other promotions. Direct mail is inexpensive and has a well-defined and easy-to-obtain mailing list—registered voters.

But how often have you wished you had more information about customers, prospects, donors, and members of a group? Direct mail is an ideal way to gather market information. A carefully designed survey with an incentive for its completion, even if small, will usually bring good results. Alert hotel managers can send selected guests critique forms with a personalized letter following their stays. The same plan works for restaurants and other service businesses.

In producing mailings, the do-it-yourself approach encompasses anything from design and copywriting to actual production through computer-generated, desktop typesetting and illustration.

Success is based on creativity. Much successful direct mail is do-it-yourself or in-house. Advertising agencies can handle your direct mail, but their interest in your account and their fees will be reflected in the amount you

do. For larger users, direct-response agencies in major cities have particular expertise in direct mail as well as in mail order and telemarketing. Here again, the cost factor is predicated on your mailing budget. If you produce your own direct mail you'll probably need the help of a free-lance artist, typesetter, and printer. Consult each before you complete your package. They can offer money-saving tips. Plan your mailing well in advance to accommodate delays (remember Murphy's Law). Be sure to get cost estimates and establish a budget. Many mailings fail because a cost was left out of the proposed budget.

Now that you have produced your mailing, what next? Many authorities believe your mailing list is the critical element in the direct mail process. Your best list is probably your customer list. You usually get more business from current or past customers than from any other source. The three basic ways to increase your business are: getting new customers, getting established customers to buy more often, and getting them to spend more money each time they buy. Two of three involve existing customers.

If you ask most small-business people whether or not they have a mailing list, they will probably say "No." If you ask *any* business or professional person if he has a customer database, the "No" will be emphatic. Yet a database is just a list of customer names and addresses with some additional information— how often they buy, what they buy, and how much they spend. Where is this information? If yours is a charge-account business, it is in the accounting records. With a computer, it is easily retrievable. You can also gather information from cash slips or keep a mailing-list card form next to the cash register. The more you get into direct mail, the more easily your list will develop.

The next step is keep the list up to date. The average family moves every five years. The average employee also changes jobs once every five years. Thus one fifth of your mailing list is outdated every year.

In addition to your own mailing list, you

can rent lists of prospects, selecting your own demographics and psychographics. Remember the periodontists and their selection of prospects by age, income, housing, and geography? Check your classified directory for mailing-list brokers. Another alternative is to swap lists with a friendly but noncompetitive business. In some communities, retailers and professionals combine names into one list, eliminating duplications.

And now let's think about postage. First-class mail is the most expensive, but it has the advantage of speed and gives access to forwarding and address corrections. Bulk-mail rates are cheaper, since the mailer does part of the work—sorting by zip code, bagging and labeling, and delivering to the post office. It's also slower and not nearly as predictable as first-class mail. Many invitations mailed bulk are received after the function. But both classes of mail fit particular needs. For most direct mail, the method of affixing postage makes little difference. Consumers and business people alike are used to metered mail and preprinted postage.

The last stop in the direct-mail process is assumed to be the post office. Actually a visit to the post office should come before your mail is printed, to make sure that the design, size, and weight meet the applicable standards for the postage rate in your budget. At one time a trip to the U.S. post office was an awesome experience. You entered a stone-cold building, spoke in hushed tones, and were surrounded by pictures of the FBI's most-wanted criminals. An infraction or mistake on your part could be a serious government offense, punishable by fine or jail sentence—or both. Times have changed. In most post offices, direct mailers can expect prompt, courteous service. The postal service needs your business.

Speaking of the postal service, former postmaster general of the United States William F. Bolger had this to say about direct mail: "Direct mail is an appreciated, effective, re-

sults-oriented medium. It's a medium many people utilize without the aid of outside help. It's a medium that can produce significant results even on a do-it-yourself basis. Direct mail really is advertising's best-kept secret!"

Ken Erdman, "Direct Mail: Advertising's Best-Kept Secret," *The Rotarian*, January 1987. Reprinted by permission of *The Rotarian*.

Tailoring Catalogs to Fit Corporate Personality
ANITA M. BUSCH

Both specialty and mass market retailers have become increasingly aware of the catalog's role in reaching their customers. Some ad agencies believe the most important thing when creating a catalog is selling the image of the client. Today's consumer is better educated and desires a more modern, sophisticated approach, they claim. "You have to sell glamour." These spokesmen are speaking for the retailing industry. Those who speak for the direct response industry still feel the best catalogs are not of the type just described. Retailers are actually leaving mail order and concentrating on traffic generation with the glamour catalogs that are often produced. As they move away from direct response and toward traffic generation, not all are experiencing a jump in costs, due in large part to fulfillment cost savings.

LOOKS AREN'T EVERYTHING ... UNLESS, OF course, the subject happens to be catalog design.

Some direct marketers and retailers are so concerned with their image they are changing the look and the style of one of their main marketing tools. Both specialty and mass market retailers have become increasingly aware of the catalog's role in reaching consumers, creating an image for their stores and moving merchandise. As a result, some catalogs have become soft-sell appeals that play on consumer's buying motivations rather than those based on price.

When creating a catalog, "the most important thing is selling the image of the client," says Stan Freeman, vp-creative director of New York-based Allied Graphic Arts, the nation's largest producer and designer of retail and direct mail catalogs.

Anita Treasch, San Francisco-based Esprit De Corp.'s advertising director, agrees. "Image advertising vs. product advertising ... that's been [Espirit's] philosophy all along."

The rhetoric used to describe the look of the '80s is varied, but the underlying message is clear: Customers do not want the hard-sell approach any longer.

"There's a natural evolution [under way] in advertising and marketing. Consumers are tired of hard sell because they've heard it so much, they don't know what to believe anymore," says Robert Petrick, creator of Chicago-based CITY catalog, which displays an eclectic mix of designer furniture and accessories. Mr. Petrick, a former vp-creative director at Burson-Marsteller, Chicago, describes CITY's catalog as an "image piece, a very soft-sell, sophisticated presentation. It's a reflection of the owners."

In addition to giving the catalogs more personality, an editorial approach fits better with the buying audience's demographics. Today's consumer is better educated, says Robert Wyker, president-ceo of AGA, and desires a more modern, more sophisticated approach.

"You have to sell appeal and glamor," he says. "Pretty much everybody is going in the editorial direction, and I mean editorial in all facets of the catalog—photography and production."

Some catalog business observers disagree. Joan Throckmorton, president of the New York-based catalog consultancy that bears her name, says mail order catalog style still is best characterized by those produced by Horchow, Land's End and Lillian Vernon. "Esprit and The Gap are not representative of the mail order industry."

A shift to the editorial approach is quite evident in catalogs for San Bruno, Cal.-based The Gap, Esprit, CITY and Bigsby & Kruthers, a men's specialty clothing store based in Chicago, whose catalog is very heavy on images and light on copy. Those that are written, like Esprit's catalog, often follow a stream-of-consciousness style that provides little direct product information, focusing more on the models and providing a strictly defined image of the store.

Esprit's current "Real People" campaign, conceived by owners Susie and Doug Tompkins, began in 1984. Delrae Roth, graphic designer and assistant art director, says the company chose to use customers instead of models for their catalogs because it "wanted to show consumers that the clothes and image are made for real people, not just for models."

The copy in Esprit's catalog reads like a short, personal profile of its "real people" models. For example, 33-year-old Rebecca Street, who Esprit describes as "Esprit customer and actress," poses with her 8-year-old daughter and 11-year-old son, all wearing Esprit clothes. The copy on the page profiles all three individually.

Ms. Street, her hair wrapped in a black scarf and a shock of blond hair tousled on her forehead, says in the customer profile: "Esprit lets people know that life should be easy and fun and that people shouldn't take everything so seriously. I love my work because I get to be in a new reality in the whole world of make-believe. When I was little, I liked St. Theresa, but that was before I discovered Greta Garbo and Marilyn Monroe."

Specialty stores such as CITY and Bigsby & Kruthers have the chore of calling attention to themselves in the face of the mass retailers' mammoth ad budgets and high profiles. They rely heavily on unique advertising to create and define their niche.

Mr. Petrick places only one item per page in CITY's catalog and uses a unique, synthetic paper, creating a visual effect that superimposes one product over the next.

For design purposes, product descriptions and costs and the mail order form were reserved for the final page of the catalog, says Mr. Petrick.

H. Gene Silverberg, president and co-founder of Bigsby & Kruthers and the producer of its catalog, says specialty stores have to do something special in advertising to set themselves apart from their main competitors, the mass retailers. He uses third-party endorsements, selecting well-known local heroes like Chicago Bears defensive back Gary Fencik, U.S. Rep. Dan Rostenkowski, Illinois Gov. James Thompson and Bob Bell, formerly Bozo the Clown.

All the featured models were photographed by portraitist Jean Moss. The intention of the catalog, which looks more like a photographer's portfolio, is to illustrate that "the men make the clothes," not vice versa, says Mr. Silverberg. The copy in the company's catalog, "The Suit Book," only identifies the model and concentrates on his accomplishments in one or two short sentences. Downplayed is the brand name of the suit, which does not appear until the catalog's last page.

Specialty stores aren't the only retailers worrying about competition. Those designing catalogs for larger chains are feeling more pressure to produce something that rises out of the crowd.

"There's a lot of catalogs competing for attention," says AGA's Mr. Wyker. "Any well-produced catalog will reach the consumer. The [catalogs] that reach the wastebasket are the ones that aren't well-produced."

The catalog cover is the most important tool in catching the consumer's eye, says Mr. Freeman. "It is the first impression the consumer gets of the company." In light of the new editorial style, the talent of the writer and art director have become even more important in determining a catalog's success, he says.

Mr. Wyker says AGA's biggest competitors are catalogs that are produced in-house. Money often is the determining factor in whether a company chooses a catalog service or decides to do the work internally. Some retailers select a service like AGA to see the catalog through from inception to distribution, he says.

Others, like The Talbots, The Gap, Esprit and Bigsby & Kruthers, are produced in-house. The Talbots moved in-house last year after a four-year stint with AGA.

In 1984 Maggie Gross, senior vp-advertising, fell into The Gap from Ann Taylor where she was marketing director, and the company brought its advertising in-house from its agency Wells, Rich, Greene, New York, "because no one can take care of yourself as well as you can," says Ms. Gross. Also, the agency fees the company saved have been converted into a new print campaign, she says.

Both Bigsby & Kruthers and The Gap used their catalogs to reposition themselves as more upscale, sophisticated companies, and more importantly, to expand their consumer base.

Bigsby & Kruthers, which opened as a jeans store in 1971, has evolved into a suitery serving corporate executives. "The customer base grew to include a different income bracket and different professions," says Mr. Silverberg. As the store evolved, "the company had to keep or create a pace that the consumer wanted," he says, and therefore the advertising mirrored its customer and changed to a more creative, up-scale approach.

The Gap made the decision to redirect its advertising because "the company wanted to expand the consumer base, which had been defined as teen agers looking for inexpensive clothing," says Ms. Gross. "We began focusing on more tasteful and classier styling, yet still be very, very affordable."

To get the news out concerning The Gap's transformation, a million catalogs were mailed to customers. "The catalogs were designed to lure the consumers into the store and to make the shopper aware of The Gap's change in image," she says.

This was done by downplaying the price, which in earlier advertising had been presented in large, boldface type. Now, shot in a country setting, the soft, earth-tone colors of The Gap's catalogs presents a classier, less price-oriented image.

Although the company will not release sales figures, Ms. Gross attributes "phenomenal growth" to "the combination of merchandising, advertising and the way the stores are looking."

Interestingly, as sales have reportedly increased, some catalogs no longer are direct sales tools. In 1985, Esprit discontinued mail order because that segment of its business had served its purpose in increasing consumer awareness, and its sales were shifting from mail order to retail, says Laurie Davison, Esprit's print production coordinator.

By leaving mail order and concentrating more on retail, the company had better control of the presentation of the product, says a company spokeswoman. Now the catalogs are designed mainly to increase customer traffic, says Ms. Treash.

"The catalog now is a preview of the sea-son and focuses on where to buy," she says. "Through the catalogs, we are essentially telling the consumer, 'Don't wait for the mail, come into the store.'"

As more catalogs change from hard-sell mail order books to glossier, soft-sell, long-form ads, catalog producers are either not experiencing a jump in expenses or are finding ways to compensate for the higher costs. "We have definitely saved on fulfillment costs" because of the discontinuation of mail order, so printing catalogs on a higher grade of paper stock has not altered costs much, says Ms. Davison.

The company spends "as much or maybe more" on the catalogs, she says.

"Production costs haven't increased, strangely enough . . . well, at least not significantly," says AGA's Mr. Freeman, who oversees Bloomingdale's, Samuel Roberts, Chadwicks of Boston, Raleigh's and Appleseed's catalogs.

Still, marketers realize the power of the catalog. AGA's Mr. Wyker says, "An outstanding catalog could add another 2% to 3% in sales for the retailer." Looks aren't everything . . . or are they?

Anita M. Busch, "Tailoring Catalogs to Fit Corporate Personality," *Advertising Age*, October 27, 1986. Reprinted by permission of Crain News Service.

Seven Myths That Keep You Off TV

Donald D. Lewis

Behind each of the myths that keep direct marketers off television is a truth that can work in their favor. These myths and truths are:

1. Making TV commercials is too expensive. In truth, a solid direct response commercial can be very affordable. As little as $10,000 is not unusual.

2. TV time is too expensive. In truth, effective direct response TV time can often be had for as little as $50 for two minutes. In any event, cost is relative, and TV often offers the lowest cost per order and highest return on investment.

3. TV only works for low-priced products. In truth successful programs exist for products at all price levels.

4. A TV special offer is too hard to change. In truth, video technology and the nature of most direct response commercials can permit a 24-hour turn around.

5. TV results are too hard to track and control. In truth, when the telephone response option is used, results are almost instantaneously known, and are usually known with surgical precision within 24 hours.

6. A TV commercial is too short to sell my product. In truth, if it is, TV can be used to sell the most exciting part of the story and get a lead, leaving the rest for later, in the mail or over the phone.

7. TV is too difficult to precisely target. It is more difficult than direct mail, but time slotting and selective program buying can be amazingly effective in reaching job seekers, gardeners, people interested in home improvements, and so forth. Like all media, TV is a choice that can work for the marketer who knows how to use it.

IF YOU'RE LIKE MANY DIRECT RESPONSE MARKETERS, you know a lot about newspaper, magazine and direct mail advertising. Everyday, you deal with layouts, lists, printing deadlines, column inches and other print facts of life.

But when it comes to television, you're not quite so knowledgeable. In fact, you might even be rejecting TV as a possible medium because you've fallen for one of the seven widely believed myths about response TV.

But don't despair. Behind each of these myths is a truth that may be better news for you than you think.

Myth 1: TV commercials are too expensive to make.

Myth 1 is the most common and probably the hardest to shake, especially when you hear the horror stories about commercials like Apple's "1984" supposedly costing $400,000 to produce. It's true, making a top-notch spot can certainly be expensive.

But other TV commercials, if they're done right, can also be very inexpensive—sometimes as little as a few hundred dollars.

When you see that Coke or McDonald's commercial that simply blows your mind, it was probably done on a budget of $200,000 or more, using the best creative talent and technology that money can buy. Many of these commercials involve a shooting crew of 40 or more people. From concept to completion, they might take six months or more to make.

But what is right for McDonald's isn't necessarily right for the direct response marketer.

In fact, typical, hard-hitting direct response commercials these days can easily be made for around $10,000.

How is that possible when the national advertisers spend an average of $125,000 per spot?

> ### How to make a $10,000 commercial:
>
> Every commercial is different, but here is a typical budget breakdown of a $10,000 TV commercial done on a non-union basis, with the ad agency supplying the copywriting and producing services.
>
> | | |
> |---|---:|
> | *Director* | $ 500 |
> | *1 day Video Shoot:* | |
> | 5 man crew | 1,200 |
> | Camera and tape machines | 1,000 |
> | Tape | 300 |
> | Actors (extras) | 500 |
> | Location or studio rental | 250 |
> | Props | 500 |
> | *Post Production* | |
> | Voice-over talent | 250 |
> | Recording voice and music | 300 |
> | 1½ days rough editing | 1,000 |
> | 1 day final editing | 2,500 |
> | *Miscellaneous* | 200 |
> | *Subtotal* | 8,500 |
> | *Ad agency's 15% commission* | 1,500 |
> | *Total* | $10,000 |

First off, direct response commercials are simpler and cheaper to make. Instead of using celebrity spokespeople (who can demand fees of up to $100,000 or more), many direct response commercials use a simple "voice-over" in which the presenter is never seen, only heard. Voice-overs cost far less than actors on camera.

Another reason is production costs. While the big boys use their dozens of singers and dancers and spectacular helicopter shots, the typical direct response spot relies on a simple product demonstration. The simpler the demonstration, the less costly it is to shoot.

Other factors contribute to the cost savings. Many response spots are shot on videotape instead of the more expensive film. Sometimes they're done with non-union crews and talent. Some ad agencies even have in-house produc-

tion departments that can save their clients even more money.

When all is said and done, a good, solid direct response commercial can be very affordable. My recommendation is that it should never cost any more than 10 percent of your ad budget.

Myth 2: TV time is too expensive to buy.

Do you know what they wanted for a 30-second spot in this year's Super Bowl? $450,000. It's no wonder that a lot of potential advertisers consider TV too expensive!

But in the world of direct response, Super Bowl spot prices mean nothing—because the response marketer never buys them!

Instead, he spends his money where the values are. It might be cable. Smaller markets. Local independent stations. Late night and

What a 2-minute costs to air:

The cost of airing a TV spot can vary dramatically. Below is a selection of markets with rates and households reached by an independent station in daytime.

	Cost	Households Reached
NBC network	$60,000	4,630,000
New York	750	170,000
Los Angeles	800	98,000
Boise	25	3,000
Fresno	100	21,000
Orlando	140	16,000

daytime. The direct marketer knows that media cost is relative and goes for the media offering lowest cost per order and the highest return on investment.

In these areas, it's not uncommon to find yourself paying as little as $50 for a two minute commercial. Or even less, because TV time is the ultimate negotiable commodity, subject to the ups and downs of supply and demand.

Although newspaper and magazine rates are only now becoming subject to negotiation, TV is the ultimate supply and demand marketplace. If you are good, you can be paying as little as half the going or published rate—particularly in today's times, when stations and networks are scrambling for business.

Myth 3: TV only works for low-priced products.

Another myth about TV is that it is only effective for inexpensive offers of $9.99, $29.99 or the like. People who believe this miss the point, because it's not the price, it's the value that people are looking for.

Successful television offers have included weight loss programs that retail for $500, doll collections that cost $30 a month, real estate home study courses that sell for $400, even precious gems for $200 and more. These offers were successful because the viewer perceived value.

Want even more evidence that you can sell expensive products on TV? Look at the sofa and electronics retailers who continually use TV to sell high ticket goods. Or watch one of the new TV auction programs. They sell product after product of every possible description in almost every price category.

Myth 4: A TV special offer is too hard to change.

Some advertisers shy away from TV because they don't think it offers merchandising flexibility. They are concerned that TV won't allow them to test special offers or react to changing competitive conditions in their market.

Actually, nothing could be farther from the truth. Because, unlike a direct mail campaign which can require a lead time of weeks or even months, today's videotape technology allows a television commercial to be changed almost overnight. And if the commercial is planned properly, it can be done very inexpensively.

For example, one of our clients discovered that his sales increased dramatically if he offered overnight delivery of the product. So we went into the studio at 9 a.m. the next morning and recorded a new voice-over tag onto his commercial. By noon, we were adding a new graphic to it; by 3 p.m. the commercial was being duplicated, and by 5 p.m. it was in the mail. The commercial was broadcast the very next day!

Speaking of lead times, TV can be even better than direct mail for many test situations. TV orders generally come in within hours of the commercial airing. Instead of waiting weeks for direct mail responses to trickle in, the TV advertiser can know his results in days.

Myth 5: TV results are too hard to track and control.

Again, this is nothing more than a myth. A direct response commercial demands action. In most cases, it asks you to call an 800 phone number. And responses come in fast—usually 80 percent of all responses are made within 24 hours of a commercial's airing.

By carefully tallying the number of phone calls a particular commercial generates in a particular time slot, the marketer can let his computers track leads and cost per order with almost surgical precision.

These results can be used to test the impact of different commercials, different stations or different time slots. They can be used to test action offers, copy points and product names. They can even be used to develop a formula for media buy that ties a stations cost per thousand to your cost per order and rate of return targets.

Myth 6: A TV commercial is too short to sell my product.

Many direct marketers are used to relying on lots of copy. They use direct mail pieces that may have thousands, even tens of thousands of words. The idea is to involve the prospect in a deluge of information, telling as complete a sales story as possible.

Obviously, you can't do that in a 60-second or 120-second commercial. You only have

time to sell the most exciting benefits and differences, leaving the rest of the sales story to be told later.

While that approach is far different from the traditional long copy used in direct mail, it is an approach that is working. Virtually every product you see in direct mail is now being successfully marketed on TV by somebody . . . and I mean everything—from books, to record collections, to toys, foods and clothing.

But what if you really can't sell the product in a minute or two?

You have several choices. The first is the two-stage sale. Say that your product is a vacation time sharing property. In the commercial, you might ask the viewer to call a special telephone number simply for a brochure. Stage one is when the viewer calls to give you his name, address and phone number where the information is to be sent.

After you send the brochure, you follow up with stage two, an outbound telemarketing call. Your salespeople now have the chance to give more information than ever and hopefully close the sale.

But there is also a second alternative, and it is a new and exciting one. Sometimes called the "infomercial" concept, it is the idea of placing a commercial inside a TV program that has been specially created with entertainment and information that augments the commercial.

You may have seen some of these programs on the air already, talking about weight loss or self-improvement courses. In today's highly competitive and deregulated television industry, more and more stations and networks are now running them. These program lengths can run to 30 minutes, one hour, even two or more hours. But while these vehicles may look like programs, their content is very supportive of the commercial.

Imagine being able to take a full hour to tell a prospect about your product, complete with demonstrations and testimonials from actual users. It's being done now on cable, independent and even network stations across the country.

Myth 7: TV is too difficult to precisely target.

OK, it's not as easy to hit a target audience with TV as it is with direct mail. TV viewers don't fill out questionnaires or reader surveys. But you would be amazed how well a TV audience can be reached and identified.

Want to reach overweight people? Job seekers? Gardeners? People interested in home improvement? You can do it on TV with the kinds of programming and cable that are available.

The key to targeting lies in the time slots and programming you buy, because that is what the viewer is watching. And, with today's proliferation of cable services, the trend is toward more and more segmentation of the viewing audience, making it easier than ever to reach a specific target.

Keep these myths and realities in mind when you map out your next media campaign because television, like all media, is a choice that can work for the marketer who knows how to use it.

Donald D. Lewis, "Seven Myths That Keep You Off TV," *Direct Marketing*, January 1987. Reprinted by permission of *Direct Marketing* magazine.

Lists and Databases

Database Techniques
How to Tap a Key Company Resource
RICHARD J. COURTHEOUX

New technological and economic developments permit the direct marketer to focus on the customer as never before. Computer capability is up. Computer costs are down. Software friendliness has increased. Printing technologies have advanced. Database management has emerged. A database permits more sophisticated and flexible manipulation of information than in the past. The difference between a file and a database must be understood. Database components include customer infor-mation, transaction information, product information, media information, promotion information, and geodemo-graphic information. To function properly, all components of a database must be linked and become part of an integrated entity. Database manage-ment should include accuracy checks, audit trails, and security systems.

WE ALL KNOW THAT FOR THE PAST SEVERAL decades computer technology has been an engine driving enormous economic and social changes. Its first applications have been in highly structured areas where the impact has been immediate, quantifiable and dramatic. In contrast, the current era is characterized by the application of computer technology to more unstructured areas, including marketing. In this article our focus will be on database technology and its use in direct marketing.

This article will explore:

● The basic terminology and concepts of data-bases and database marketing.

Table 1. Classical and Modern Direct Marketing

Classical	*Modern*
• Analyze profit and loss per offer.	• Analyze profit and loss plus business development per offer.
• Merchandise or media driven.	• Customer or market driven.
• Rudimentary customer record.	• Substantial customer information stored in database.
• Simple, cell-based segmentations (usually recency/frequency/monetary).	• Advanced multivariate statistical models optimized for long-term results.

- The necessary steps in database marketing.
- The components of direct marketing databases.

A second article will examine some general database marketing applications.

The dramatic improvements in direct marketing will come from those who understand database marketing, internalize it and become comfortable enough with it so that they can generate creative new modes of direct marketing.

Throughout the world, direct marketing practice is in transition from a "classical" pattern to a "modern" one. The difference between the classical and modern approaches can be summarized by Table 1.

The modern direct marketer focuses on the customer. Offers are designed and merchandise is chosen so as to develop an ongoing relationship with the customer.

These developments have occurred because there are new opportunities presented by economic and technological change. These changes can be grouped as follows:

a) Computer hardware capabilities have increased dramatically.

b) Computer costs have declined drastically.

c) State-of-the-art software is both more powerful and more user-friendly.

d) Many direct marketing-related technologies have advanced.

A quick review of major trends in computer capability advances shows that there is much faster instruction execution giving greater throughput and faster access times. This is combined with vastly increased on-line storage which makes more data immediately accessible. Decreased data communication costs have made remote site computers (and databases) easily accessible and networks of computers feasible. At the same time, microcomputers have put cheap computing power in the hands of end users.

While technology has advanced, the machine-related computing costs have been falling dramatically. Computer hardware costs have declined 20 percent to 25 percent per year for about a generation, a trend which is projected to continue indefinitely into the future. Such declines result in a doubling of the performance per dollar every three years. Thus, at current prices, $1 buys (approximately) execution of 100 million computer machine instructions or on-line storage of 50,000 characters for one year. Overall, computer hardware costs typically average about 30 percent of all data processing costs. This percentage has been consistently declining.

The revolution in hardware technology and costs has brought about a revolution in software. Systems are designed to be on-line and interactive, rather than tape-oriented batch processing. The software is written in increasingly higher level languages to enhance programmer productivity and give non-programmer users the ability to access and manipulate data. These capabilities are often obtained by use of Database Management Systems (DBMS).

Technology has been moving forward in other areas of significance for direct marketing. Printing technology has improved to include personalization of messages on mailing pieces and customized catalog composition. Telephone communications are cheaper and more efficient, supporting operation of both inbound and outbound telephones. New electronic media such as cable television and videotex are emerging. Computer databases can be enormously useful in combination with each of these technologies.

These technological developments come at a time when several sociological trends which support direct marketing are also at work. There are an increased number of households with all adults employed. Time is at a premium so shopping must be satisfying and gratifying. Moreover, the populations of developed countries are becoming increasingly diverse in terms of tastes and interests, household composition and ethnicity.

Not surprisingly, then, two of the most common reasons for mail-order purchases are convenience and selection. A database of information allows the direct marketer to exploit these strengths by targeting the right type of offer to each consumer.

What Is Database Marketing?

What is database marketing and what is a database? First, let us define the term "database." A database is:

—*A comprehensive collection of interrelated data.*

—*Serving multiple applications.*

—*Allowing timely and accurate retrieval or manipulation of data.*

The term "database" is not a synonym for the term "file." A real database will typically consist of many files which can be linked together relatively easily and cheaply as needed. A file is typically a single collection of records of the same type. These differences are illustrated in Figures 1 and 2. Table 2 gives a point by point comparison of database and file characteristics.

Similarly, the term "database" is not a synonym for the term "list." A list is usually a collection of names and addresses from a single source. The list is usually used to support one principal application and is often difficult to access. Many companies are developing customer databases. A key element of most databases will be one or more lists.

What is new in the database concept? The database is regarded as a major resource of the direct marketing company. Like other major resources it needs careful management and at-

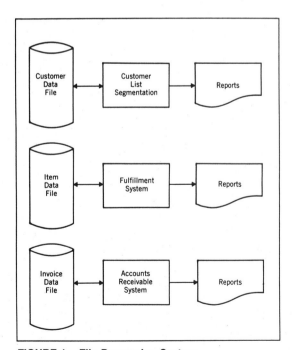

FIGURE 1. File Processing System

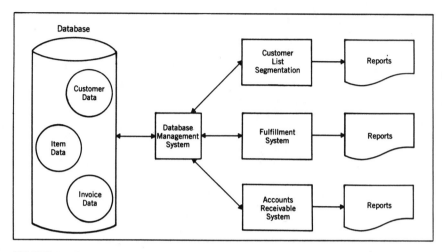

FIGURE 2. Database Processing System

Table 2.   Databases and Files

Database	*File*
• Contains many types of data which can be linked together.	• Usually contains only a single type of information (or record type).
• Derives information from multiple sources and supports multiple applications.	• Usually derives information from a single source and supports a very limited number of applications.
• Can be accessed easily and in multiple ways, especially for ad-hoc queries.	• Often allows only a single method of access, making ad-hoc queries difficult.
• Is viewed as a major corporate resource (or asset).	• Is designed to support a narrow range of applications.

tention. The capabilities exist to manipulate information more extensively and more flexibly than in the past. Much more sophisticated analyses can be performed which explore relationships among different types of data. Unanticipated needs for information can be serviced at reasonable cost and in an acceptable time frame. On some systems users who are not programmers can access the data directly.

Database marketing uses the database to support all phases of the direct marketing process. Each direct marketing effort has two effects:

• *It produces sales, inquiries, leads or some other measurable response.*

• *It enhances the information in the database. This information has real, quantifiable value.*

The database is the foundation for planning, execution and measurement of direct marketing efforts. All marketing efforts are linked together by the database. Current efforts make use of information accumulated from the past, and they contribute to the body of information which will be available in the future. The fundamental principle of database marketing can be stated as follows: *Marketing efforts are designed, executed and measured on the basis of the long-term impact.*

The process of database marketing can be broken into the following steps:

1. Specify data to be retained.
2. Specify outputs, reports and methods for accessing data.
3. Collect, insert and update database information.
4. Analyze and plan.
5. Execute and measure.

Specifying the data to retain requires brainstorming to identify all potentially useful information from all sources. It is important to be future-oriented by considering what a business will be like in three to five years. One should use expected future costs, rather than current costs, in many situations.

The database will have to supply a number of outputs. These typically include: selection of customer names for mailings or other marketing efforts; extracts of the customer database for analytical work; fulfillment of list rental orders; and personal computer interfaces to allow for manipulation of data on small systems.

Many times the database will be used to support managerial decisions. The effectiveness of decision making will depend on the ease of access to the data. Most desirable is ad-hoc access directly by end-users via a user-friendly query language. This eliminates extra communication steps, avoids DP personnel availability problems, but may be computationally expensive or interfere with production processing.

Another alternative is to develop parameter driven programs to generate reports on demand. Here, end-users specify among choices via "menus." Old-fashioned access procedures require requesting services from the data processing department. This is a machine-oriented approach which gives data processing

maximal control over access to the database. In many instances, marketing needs may not receive quick service.

Database information will come from many sources. We know that information is only useful if it is correct. To maintain correctness make all sources of data check data accuracy, apply reasonability checks, keep audit trails and generate subtotals that can be cross-checked.

Initial loading of information into a database can be especially problematic. All the information to be used should be checked for errors and undocumented codes. Conversion rules will need to be developed.

Ongoing databases require updating. This updating may be:
Batch (all at once) mode.
Transaction (on-line) mode.

For security, database information should be backed up on computer readable tape periodically.

Analysis and Planning

Of course, database development is not the objective. The database information supports descriptive and predictive analysis. This, in turn, supports business synthesis of information for decision making.

Analysis attempts to break down the business functioning into component parts. The database is used to get quantitative descriptions of various components. Whenever appropriate, statistical techniques are used to describe component characteristics.

Synthesis attempts to integrate the individual components into a comprehensive description of the business. Quantitative descriptions of individual parts are linked together. Financial modeling software is used to express relationships and generate reports. Financial models can be used in "business-as-usual" planning of future requirements and alternative ("what-if") scenarios. They can also be used for evaluating totally new business ideas.

The database will support execution of direct marketing efforts, including segmentation of customers, counting necessary for mail planning, order entry, fulfillment and handling of telephone interactions. Problems may be spotted early enough to correct them or minimize their effect (for example, mail may not have been delivered in a particular area). In many cases the database will be used to improve inventory control.

Database Components

In direct marketing, it is often useful to construct the database from the following components:

Customer information.
Transaction information (i.e., orders, returns).
Product information.
Media information.
Promotion information.
Geodemographic information.

For the components to function together as a true database, there must be linkages among them as illustrated in Figure 3. All information should be part of an integrated entity (the database), rather than separate pieces.

Direct marketing databases are a key resource for marketing purposes. Marketers should be involved in database specification to guarantee that all marketing needs are satisfied. Marketers should focus on the information needed to support current and planned activities, provide a base for new business development, and gain a competitive edge (or avoid a competitive disadvantage).

Marketers need to focus on and quantify benefits derived from information. Good database design requires attention to a number of points. Data of various types and from different sources should be stored so it can be easily linked together. Part of database development is the specification of how data can be accessed.

Data being entered into the database should be checked for accuracy. There should be audit trails which can detect corruption of data accuracy. Data security mechanisms should be built into the system. Often, information should be collected and retained on tape even before the database is specified. It is difficult, costly and sometimes impossible to reconstruct data which were not retained at the time they became available.

The major data elements of direct marketing databases are shown in Tables 3 through 9.

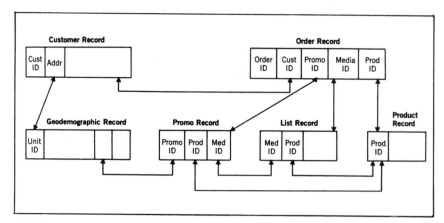

FIGURE 3.   Linkages among Database Components

In the tables the justification for each element is given. Any direct marketer establishing a database will want to expand upon and customize the elements listed in these tables.

Table 3. Consumer Elements

Element	Use
● ID number	Unique identification; linkage to other data.
● First name	Sex coding; identify multiple buyers in a household.
● Last name	Ethnic coding.
● Title	Sex coding; professional classification.
● Address	Necessary for mailing; links to geodemographic information.
● Sex	Men and women have different propensities to respond to various offers.
● Age	Often an important factor in products purchased.
● Acquisition source	Evaluation of customer sources.
● Acquisition date	Allows tracking of cohort groups; used for normalizing purchase rates.
● Offer exposure	Necessary for response analysis; necessary for evaluating interactions among offers.
● Offer response	Necessary for response analysis; necessary for evaluating interactions among offers.
● Purchase history summary information —Orders —Items —Sales —Returns —Service	Useful for crude segmentations; may be used for customer service.
● Lifestyle information	Segmentation for targeted offerings.
● Predictive scores	Segmentation for circulation; measurements of offer success.

Table 4. Business-to-Business Elements

Element	Use
● ID number	Unique identification; linkage to other data.
● Company name	Identification.
● Buyer's name	Important for getting mail to the decision maker.
● Buyer's title	Important if buying person changes.
● Address	Necessary for mailing; often identifies multiple names in a company.

(continued)

Table 4.   Business-to-Business Elements (continued)

Element	Use
● Industry classification (SIC code)	Important for segmentation.
● Business size —Revenue —Number of employees	Important for assignment to proper distribution channel; may determine frequency of contacts.
● Estimated demand for relevant products	Important for assignment to proper distribution channel; may determine frequency of contacts.
● Telephone number	Telemarketing; customer service.
● Channels used for ordering	Understand customer channel preference.
● Offer exposure ● Offer response ● Purchase history ● Predictive scores	Same as for consumer elements.

Table 5.   Order Elements

Element	Use
● Buyer ID for linkage	Link transaction to buyer information.
● Date	Analyze frequency of orders; analyze timing between marketing actions and transactions.
● Medium (source) ordered from	Analyze source effectiveness.
● Amount of transaction	Important measure of activity.
● Placement method	Track mail, phone or other placement methods.
● Payment method	Track use of credit cards, checks, house credit, etc.
● For each item —Item ID —Quantity —Returns —Out-of-stock —Dollar sales	Detailed information on product purchases may reveal lifestyle information; returns and out-of-stocks may affect customer loyalty.

Table 6.   Product Elements

Element	*Use*
• Item ID	Unique identification; linkage to other parts of the database.
• Price	Important product characteristic; may contribute to customer segmentation.
• Product category	Important for segmentation; may be useful for developing new, specialized offers.
• Style, taste or other classifications	Important for segmentation; may be useful for developing new, specialized offers.
• Sales	Evaluate item success.
• Returns	Identify poor merchandise.
• Service problems	Identify problematic merchandise.
• Inventory control data —On hand/on order —Order lead time —Warehouse location	Aid customer service; control inventory costs.
• Media used for selling —ID for linkage —Cost allocated to item —Response	Evaluate marketing efforts for an item.

Table 7.   Promotion Elements

Element	*Use*
• ID for linkage	Unique identification; linkage.
• Cost	Evaluate profitability.
• Format or offer code	Generalize about success of formats or offers.
• Media used —Lists —Space	Locate optimal combinations.
• Results —Orders —Sales —Returns —Bad debt	Evaluate performance.

Table 8. List Elements

Element	Use
● List ID	Unique identification; linkage.
● Selection codes —Recency —Frequency —Monetary —Category	Describe selections used; analyze importance of various factors.
● Mailing code	Identify piece mailed; necessary for evaluating list performance.
● Mailing date	Track recency and frequency of list use.
● List classifications	Generalize about types of lists which work well.
● Percent postal qualified —ZIP code —Carrier route	Estimate postage costs; often an indication of list maintenance quality.
● Performance —Quantity mailed —Orders —Sales —Returns —Bad debt	Evaluate list profitability.
● Cost to rent	Evaluate list profitability.

Table 9. Geodemographic Elements

Element	Use
● Geographic unit ID (for example, ZIP code)	Unique identification; linkage.
● More general unit ID (for example, state)	Aggregation to larger geographic units.
● Demographic information (usually purchased from a demographic service)	Allows for generalizations about types of areas which are successful.
● House list information —Penetration —Response	Used to understand house list characteristics; may correlate with outside media success.
● Performance by mailing —Quantity —Orders —Sales —Returns —Bad debt	Evaluate best areas for marketing.

Richard J. Courtheoux, "Database Techniques: How to Tap a Key Company Resource," *Direct Marketing*, August 1984. Reprinted by permission of *Direct Marketing* magazine.

List Segmentation
How to Find Your Best Direct Marketing Prospects
Behram J. Hansotia

Direct marketers need to make sure their best prospects are at the top of their file. Some number crunching sophistication is required to accomplish this, and computerized database management is virtually mandatory. Good prospect data is essential. Effective segmentation involves scoring each record on a database or purchased list for purchase probability. This usually requires robust statistical techniques such as discriminant analysis, cluster analysis, and automatic interaction detection (A.I.D.). Once records are scored, the next step is to segment the database or list and calculate cumulative response rates and internal rates of return (IRR). The mailer then mails until the incremental cost of mailing equals the incremental return from the mailings.

THE KEY TO YOUR SUCCESS IN DIRECT RESPONSE marketing, be it consumer- or business-oriented, by mail or by telephone, is to organize your prospect data base to ensure that the best prospects are found at the top of the file where they'll be used first.

In other words, direct marketing lists should be segmented into productive and non-productive names. Whether you qualify prospects according to their likelihood of response, likely order size or expected long-term profitability, you want to concentrate effort on the most productive portions of your list. And you want to avoid those market segments to which you cannot sell profitably.

But identifying the best prospects can be difficult, particularly when lists are complex and you suspect that a variety of prospect characteristics could affect response rates and order sizes. Fortunately, statistical analysis offers a number of modeling approaches to cut through that complexity and improve your ability to spot the best names on your lists.

As a marketer who manages, among other things, a direct response program, you need to understand how segmentation maximizes the profitability of your mail and phone campaigns. Of course, you won't be doing the actual statistical number crunching yourself; you have staff people or you hire outside experts to do that for you. But you need to know the principles underlying segmentation modeling in order to manage the process properly.

With that objective in mind, we'll examine three fundamental modeling approaches in this article. We'll see how to segment any direct marketing list, particularly large ones, so that your mail and phone programs concentrate on hot names and avoid the duds.

Data Base Management

For today's sophisticated marketers, direct response marketing is synonymous with "data base marketing," the logical manipulation of customer and prospect lists in order to maximize the return on the direct marketing investment. Needless to say, list—that is, data base—decisions are driven by the information the marketer has collected, or has available, on each of his prospects. Information typically contained in business-to-business marketer house files includes prospect company demographics (industrial classification, number of employees, sales, products/services, management names and titles, processes used, markets served, etc.), previous purchase behavior (type of purchase, recency, frequency, volume) of the company's own products, purchasing behavior with respect to competitive or complementary goods, etc., and credit behavior.

The more the per-record (per-name) information, the more a list can be segmented. For example, adding plant square-footage information to an in-house file can make a big difference in picking likely prospects for an industrial maintenance and repair product manufacturer. Additionally, information about previous purchase behavior and credit history can be very valuable in identifying the most desirable prospects.

So far, we've been using the term "data base" loosely, as if it were synonymous with "lists." But the modern direct response data base is, at the minimum, a computer-readable file. And it is extremely valuable for segmentation purposes if it is a relational data base, or one that is fully networked. Those allow users to sort and select records in a variety of ways simultaneously and interactively.

Computerization is essential for the three well-known segmentation modeling techniques examined here:

- scoring the value of each record via multiple regression analysis and related statistical methods;
- cluster analysis using a variety of techniques to classify records in homogeneous categories; and
- "tree analysis," formally known as automatic interaction detection (AID).

Scoring the Data Base

Scoring is a robust analytical technique which assigns a score to each individual name in a file, depending on the profile of the person or company. Scores can be determined for the prospect's likelihood of response, expected long-term profitability as a customer, the pros-

pect's likely purchase volume, or other marketing performance criteria. The higher the score the more desirable the prospect. The method is based on multiple linear regression analysis or some variation thereof.

Although the method is extremely powerful and the end result easy to use, building scoring models does require some expertise in statistical modeling. Nonetheless, it's important for a marketer who wants to manage the overall direct response program to know what scoring models can accomplish.

Scores are based on statistical analysis of mail or telephone list test results. The tests indicate which individuals or companies respond to an offer. The model examines the characteristics of the responders (their demographics, etc.) and creates a mathematical formula that indicates which characteristics are coincident with response or some other marketing performance measure.

Rather than rely on simple cross-tabulations, statisticians use multivariate techniques such as regression because they examine all variables simultaneously. Because a dozen or more variables likely have impact in direct marketing models, simpler methods like cross-tabulation are too unwieldy for segmentation analysis, nor can they measure how all those variables interact with each other.

By plugging the characteristics of a new, untested name into the formula, the model will assign a score to that name. For example, a common variant of multiple regression modeling, two-group discriminant analysis, uses formulas which assign a binomial score: "1" if a name is likely to be a responder, or "0" if it's not likely. Those kinds of scores are known as "categorical" or "discrete," rather than "continuous." In other words, the score is either black or white, not indicating shades of gray.

Figure 1 illustrates a discrete variable with five levels. Rather than treat variable X as continuous, with values lying along either the straight solid line or the curved dotted line, the

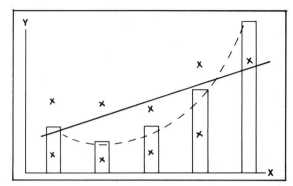

Figure 1. Discrete and Continuous Variables

model treats X as discrete steps as shown by the vertical bars. An actual direct marketing model might have a dozen or more different variables, each with five or six discrete steps.

The continuous versus discrete distinction is important because, in practice, most scoring models also use categorical variables for independent variables—the types of prospect characteristics plugged into the formulas. Statisticians do that because a number of useful variables are categorical by nature—profession or SIC code, for example.

Also, even if an independent variable is continuous (such as age, income, sales or number of employees), its relationship to the dependent variable (the score) may not be linear and may defy attempts to model it in a nonlinear fashion.

Finally, using categorical rather than continuous variables allows a regression model to handle variables with missing values. Missing data are common in marketing analysis. Seldom will you find data bases where every piece of information is known for every individual or business.

One other point about scoring models; they need to be tested. Typically the analyst will apply the model to names with known response rates, for instance—names different from those used to build the model—and see if the model correctly estimated those response rates.

Using the "Scorecard"

The end product of the model is a scorecard assigning points to company or individual names in the data base. It indicates how many points are associated with each level of each prospect profile characteristic (the independent variables). The sum of points assigned to a company or individual name, or to a segment of the list, is the total score.

Table 1 shows a simplified version of a scorecard derived from a model used by a hypothetical insurance company selling casualty auto insurance to commercial fleet owners. The table shows point values associated with each of four levels of the number of employees characteristic, and three levels of company type. (Company type is an example of a categorical variable that cannot be quantified directly.) Those point values are determined by the mathematics of the regression analysis.

Table 1. Two Insurance Market Variables

No. Employees	Points	Company Type	Points
<100	100	Service	50
100-1,000	60	Light Mfg	80
1,000-10,000	30	Heavy Mfg	20
>10,000	10		

The company has a typical direct marketing program. It encloses lead cards in its mailings to corporations. An insurance agent contacts those prospects who return the card seeking more information. The agent collects more information about the prospect, then mails a proposal.

The insurance company cannot afford to mail lead-generating letters to all companies in the nation. It needs to identify those most likely to want fleet coverage. It needs list segmentation.

The company's prior experience indicates that, typically, it can generate four lead cards for every 1,000 letters mailed. A statistician recommends that building a scoring system requires a test producing at least 400 to 500 responses. The company needs, therefore, a random test sample of 125,000.

The company decides to pick 130,000 companies on an n-th name basis from the Dun & Bradstreet Inc. data base. Analysts code response cards to help identify respondents. Returns number 494, for an overall response rate of 0.0038.

The company's statistician considers these independent variables for his regression model: company type, number of employees, company sales and capital assets. He constructs the company type variable using standard industrial classification (sic) codes to designate prospects as service organizations, light manufacturing or heavy manufacturing. He codes his dependent (response) variable as either a "1" or a "0."

Once calculated, the regression formula shows, for purposes of our simplified example here, that company type and number of employees are the two most important characteristics discriminating between responders and non-responders. Table 1 shows the scores at each level of those variables.

Ranking Segments

Note that four levels of number of employees and three company types create 12 combinations, each a market segment, as shown in Table 2. Not all segments actually have to exist in reality; some are just theoretical. (In actual practice, where, say, eight variables could each have five levels, the analyst will want to ignore most of the 390,625 theoretical market segments!)

Each name in the data base receives the score of the segment to which it belongs. As Table 2 shows, the segment score is the sum of the points attributed to the relevant level of each variable. The last two columns of Table 2 show the incremental response rates (irr: the average response rate, as determined by regression mathematics, expected from each name in a segment) and the percentage of file represented by the segment.

Note that two segments have a total score of 110: service companies with 100 to 1,000 employees; and light manufacturing companies with 1,000 to 10,000 employees. Both have the same response rate of 0.0029. A similar situation exists for a score of 80 points.

Table 2. Twelve-Segment Scorecard

No. of Employees		Company Type		Score	Incremental	Percent of
Category	Points	Category	Points	Ttl. Pts.	RR (IRR)	File (POF)
<100	100	Svc.	50	150	0.0040	17
100-1,000	60	Svc.	50	110	0.0029	15
1,000-10,000	30	Svc.	50	80	0.0024	8
>10,000	10	Svc.	50	60	0.0022	7
<100	100	Lt. Mfg.	80	180	0.0050	10
100-1,000	60	Lt. Mfg.	80	140	0.0035	12
1,000-10,000	30	Lt. Mfg.	80	110	0.0029	6
>10,000	10	Lt. Mfg.	80	90	0.0025	1
<100	100	Hvy. Mfg.	20	120	0.0031	5
100-1,000	60	Hvy. Mfg.	20	80	0.0024	4
1,000-10,000	30	Hvy. Mfg.	20	50	0.0021	9
>10,000	10	Hvy. Mfg.	20	30	0.0020	6
						100%

That's an important observation. A score is not necessarily exclusive to one segment. The two segments with scores of 150 are quite dissimilar, as are the two with scores of 80. For purposes of response-oriented segmentation, we consider segments with the same score to be homogenous regardless of their demographic differences. For that reason, although scoring is very powerful as a segmentation technique, its results are somewhat more difficult to interpret than models clustering prospects by similar demographics (but quite possibly dissimilar response rates!).

Table 3 ranks the 10 response-oriented segments in Table 2 by score. The last two columns display the cumulative percentage of file and the cumulative response rate (CRR: the overall average rate expected by mailing to the segment and all the segments preceding it).

Figure 2 graphs the relationship between the IRR and the CRR. Once the curves are developed they can be used for some time to forecast response rates, if the marketing climate is fairly stable. Generally, the shape of the curves remains stable; however, their amplitude often needs to be adjusted with changes in factors such as seasonality, file recovery and marketing conditions.

Note too how the IRR decreases faster than the CRR. The distinction is important because, as we'll see later in this article, a mailer wants to use a file only down to a target IRR level, *not* to a target CRR level. As illustrated in Figure 2, because of the economics of his direct marketing offer, the marketer wants to use only the top 70% of the file—the point associated with the break-even response rate on the incremental response rate curve.

So far we've concentrated the discussion on response scores, assuming the values of all responses are the same. Yet a similar approach can be used when the potential value of each customer is different. In such a case it makes eminent sense not to use values of "1" or "0" as the only dependent variable scores; the analyst might use the discounted net-present value of a customer over his forecasted life cycle, for example. The non-responder of course still receives a zero score.

The regression model then searches for factors which try and identify not only responders, but the most profitable responders. At the end of the model development phase, instead of obtaining a table which relates score to incremental response rates only, we would have a table which would show the relationship

Table 3. Ranking Ten Response Segments

No.	Score	Segment	IRR	POF	Cumulative POF	Cumulative RR (CRR)
1	180	(<100, Lt. Mfg.)	0.0050	10	10	0.0050
2	150	(<100, Svc.)	0.0040	17	27	0.0044
3	140	(100-1000, Lt. Mfg.)	0.0035	12	39	0.0041
4	120	(<100, Hvy. Mfg.)	0.0031	5	44	0.0040
5	110	(100-1,000, Svc.) & (1,000-10,000, Lt. Mfg.)	0.0029	21	65	0.0036
6	90	(>10,000, Lt. Mfg.)	0.0025	1	66	0.0036
7	80	(1,000-10,000, Svc.) & (100-1,000 Hvy. Mfg.)	0.0024	12	78	0.0034
8	60	(>10,000, Svc.)	0.0022	7	85	0.0031
9	50	(1,000-10,000, Hvy. Mfg.)	0.0021	9	94	0.0030
10	30	(>10,0000, Hvy. Mfg.)	0.0020	6	100	0.0029

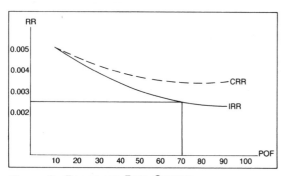

Figure 2. Response Rate Curves

between score and incremental and average expected profits.

For example, suppose a prospect company has a probability of responding (IRR) of 1%. Because of the information we have on it (past purchase behavior, number of employees, etc.), we forecast that if the prospect company buys, it will become a $100,000 account. Then that prospect's expected value is 1% of $100,000, or $1,000.

Another prospect, with a 1.1% response probability, is expected to buy only $90,000, if it buys. Its expected value is just 1.1% of $99,000, or $990. Of the two companies, the one with the smaller expected response rate nonetheless seems to be the more valuable prospect.

Cluster Analysis

Regression-based scoring identifies segments that may appear to be dissimilar at first glance, although they are homogeneous in terms of marketing performance (response rate, expected profits, etc.).

On the other hand, cluster analysis, another multivariate segmentation technique, groups prospects into clusters or segments that are homogeneous in terms of demographics. The segments aren't necessarily homogeneous in terms of performance. Specifically, the analyst strives to achieve performance homo-

geneity within each cluster even though he's defining clusters indirectly, according to demographics and other prospect characteristics.

The weaknesses of the method for direct response segmentation purposes, is that it makes no explicit effort to identify variables which help explain variations in performance. We are forced to use all the variables that seem to be right for the names in our data bases. Some variables may be important in explaining response behavior; others may be just excess baggage. So unlike regression analysis which identifies the key factors which help explain response behavior, we do not have that feature in cluster analysis.

Returning to the insurance company example, the statistician wants to classify the companies in his random sample to see if he can segment on the basis of company profile. Cluster analysis is a natural analytical technique which comes to his mind, but it's a technique used only on continuous variables.

The method works by measuring each segment's degree of differentiation, or "distance," from an overall average for a group. But company type, one of the key variables in the regression analysis, is a categorical variable. It definitely is not continuous because there's no measurable distance between, say, a service firm and a light manufacturing organization.

The statistician therefore employs a new variable, capital assets-to-sales, as a stand-in for type of firm. He reasons that service organizations generally have low capital assets-to-sales ratios. Heavy manufacturing, however, has high ratios.

His cluster analysis then uses two variables: number of employees and capital assets-to-sales. After examining groupings from six to twelve clusters he finally settles on a group of nine clusters. His computer output includes the percentage of the file included in each cluster, the average values of the two variables and the response rate for each of the nine clusters. Table 4 shows the data.

Table 4. Segmentation by Cluster Analysis Mean

Cluster	Percent of File	No. Employees	Capital Assets to Sales	Response Rate
1	22	191	0.01	0.0037
2	17	585	0.05	0.0029
3	10	9,100	0.03	0.0023
4	12	165	0.30	0.0046
5	8	856	0.35	0.0038
6	3	11,200	0.28	0.0027
7	6	211	0.75	0.0028
8	7	810	0.95	0.0024
9	15	10,300	0.88	0.0021

Table 5. Ranked Clusters

Cluster	POF	Response Rate	Company Size	Utilization of Capital Assets
4	12	0.0046	Small	Medium
5	8	0.0038	Medium	Medium
1	22	0.0037	Small	Low
2	17	0.0029	Medium	Low
7	6	0.0028	Small	High
6	3	0.0027	Large	Medium
8	7	0.0024	Medium	High
3	10	0.0023	Large	Low
9	15	0.0021	Large	High

The cluster sizes are somewhat different from the segments developed with the regression approach. Discrimination among the clusters is also somewhat less than what we saw earlier. The best cluster here, cluster four, has a response rate of 0.46% compared with the 0.50% rate of the best segment identified by regression. The two worst clusters in Table 4, numbers nine and three, have a slightly higher response rate than the two worst segments on Table 3, however.

The approach in this example is simplified, of course. It's only two-dimensional, basically with small, medium and large companies and companies with low, medium and high us-age of capital assets, as shown in Table 5. If a cluster analysis had been carried out using, say, 40 additional variables, almost certainly there would be very little discrimination among the clusters' response rates.

Scoring Beats Clustering

In practice, cluster analysis has not been used to a great extent when marketers have had their own data. As we saw above, although cluster analysis allows us to group customers who have similar profiles, there is no guarantee that the individuals in a given cluster have the same response probabilities. Also, while we can develop response rate curves with clustering, in this author's experience one can develop steeper and hence more discriminating curves with regression analysis.

In addition to those two major reasons for not employing cluster analysis, there are other technical considerations, such as a lack of well-known statistical rules for identifying the optimal grouping of clusters. And clusters generally have mediocre to poor stability when marketers try to validate them in subsequent list tests. That is, when cluster analysis is carried out on two randomly drawn samples, often the resulting clusters can be substantially different, particularly when large samples have several variables. In such instances the calculations of cluster analysis depend more on judgment than mathematical rules.

All of that implies some serious shortcomings in cluster analysis. Yet the method has earned a significant following in marketing where researchers frequently have little or no profile information about a data base. After a random sample has been tested, the analyst computes response rates for easily identified clusters of demographic similarity.

The widely-used zip code segmentation models used in consumer marketing, for example, are such cases. Working from the assumption that "birds of a feather flock together,"

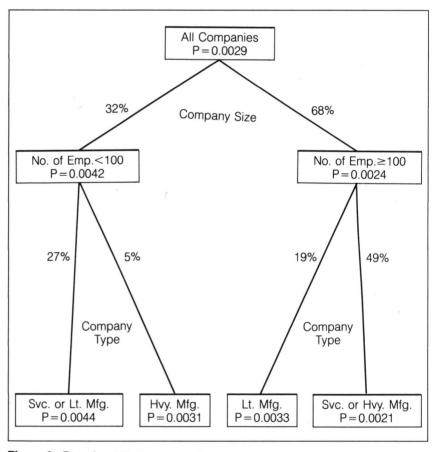

Figure 3. Data for AID Tree

analysts apply test response data to each zip-defined segment, often without regard to how much people in the same zip codes really are similar in terms of their consumption of the product or service being offered.

Automatic interaction detection (AID) is a statistical technique that identifies segments within a market, particularly segments which might not be obvious to casual observation.

The AID Tree

The tree-like diagrams produced by an AID study, as shown in Figure 3, help to illustrate the process. The AID technique sequentially splits a sample into two parts according to a dichotomy in the independent variable. The analyst, or rather the computer program which automatically tests the data, makes the splits so that the subgroups produced by each split are as widely separated as possible in terms of their scores on the dependent variable.

In other words, and in terms of the list segmentation task, AID will split a sample into two groups, say large and small companies (two levels of an independent variable), according to the response rate (dependent variable) of each. The computer program looks first for those splits that produce subgroups with the largest differences in response rate.

An AID for our insurance company example might produce the tree in Figure 3. The full sample is split into two subgroups, small companies on one hand, and medium and large companies on the other. There's a wide difference in each subgroup's response rate. But each subgroup can be split further according to the company type variable, as shown.

As a result, we get segmentation that's similar to the patterns produced by the scoring and cluster analysis methods. But with AID, we find fewer segments, just three, because two of the four segments shown at the bottom of Figure 3 have nearly identical response rates.

Although AID is a very useful tool in creating well-defined, easy to understand segments, the method is quite sample-sensitive. As a result, attempts to validate an AID-determined segmentation plan by resampling a list often result in entirely different segments. Again, regression-based scoring seems to be a superior approach for creating accurate segmentation plans.

However, AID can be a useful first step in an analysis. Because it does show the interaction among variables, AID can suggest which variables should be included in developing a regression model, for example. If any interaction term turns out to be statistically insignificant, it can be dropped from the regression model.

How Much to Mail

Again, the important thing is that the marketer, who isn't actually running the statistical tests himself, understand the principles of list and data base segmentation in order to manage the process properly. The marketer's main interest, of course, is what to do with the modeling output.

We've seen how segmentation patterns allow us to calculate the incremental and cumulative response rates, IRR and CRR respectively. And we noted in Figure 2 that a mailer, or telemarketer, wants to promote only to a certain portion of his list—to names with an expected response rate greater than the break-even point required for his direct marketing program.

In other words, he mails or phones the most productive names first, moving down the list until the incremental response rate is equal to the break-even response rate. The break-even response rate is calculated by dividing the in-mail cost per piece (the marginal cost of mailing that single, additional piece) by the gross profit of a direct sale. (Short-term deci-

sions such as mailing depth don't have to account for long-term fixed manufacturing or
service costs.)

For example, if a package costs $0.90 to
produce and mail and it's designed to make a
$100 sale, the break-even IRR is $0.9/$100 0.9%.
That is the depth where the incremental expected profit is equal to the mailing cost. The
incremental expected profit of all names and
segments below that point will be less than the
in-mail cost of the offering and should be ignored.

In situations such as our insurance example, where the mailing is designed to further
the selling process but not necessarily close a
sale, the marketer must estimate how much a
response is worth. In other words, what's the
value of the insurance company of finding a
corporate fleet manager who wants to know
more about insurance and may be ready to buy
a new policy?

Response rates are not the only way to
calculate mailing or telemarketing depth. In
continuity programs or in markets with long-
term customer loyalty, the net present value of
a newly acquired customer may be a more
meaningful performance criterion. As mentioned earlier, you can calculate an incremental
expected net present value for each name or
each segment in the file. The break-even point
required for the program is the rate of return
on investment you require from a program.
And your break-even mailing point becomes
the in-mail cost of the package divided by the
net present value of the new customer. Of
course, it is crucial that you keep excellent records and calculate the order rates, cancel rates,
depletion rates, etc. of your customer base, so
your planning is accurate.

It is very important to note that all deci-

sions should be made not on an average basis,
but on an incremental basis. That is, with segmentation we have the unique ability of priori-
tizing our prospects according to their profitability. One way of looking at segmentation is
that it splits the file into several smaller homogeneous files and we mail to only those individual smaller files which are profitable. If we
made our decision on a cumulative or average
basis, as shown by the CRR curve, we would end
up mailing to some of the non-profitable
names or segments as well.

Direct response segmentation modeling
has made significant strides in consumer marketing, and the same class of models can be
developed for business-to-business marketing.
The most important requirement is the availability of good prospect data. Once you develop
the discipline of recording every customer contact and the different transactions associated
with each customer, you are well on the way to
successful, profitable data base segmentation.

Then you'll be ready for the state-of-the-
art approaches discussed in this article: scoring
models based on regression analysis; cluster
analysis models and the tree models of the
automatic interaction detector. Building them
requires substantial knowledge of statistical
mathematics. But you should understand what
the models produce, and what your suppliers
and in-house experts should provide to you in
order to successfully manage your direct marketing program and selectively go after your
best prospects first.

Behram J. Hansotia, "List Segmentation: How to Find
Your Best Direct Marketing Prospects," *Business Marketing*,
August 1986. Reprinted by permission of *Business Market-
ing*. Copyright Crain Communications, Inc.

Lead Generation and Qualification

The Application of an Effective Inquiry-Handling System for Business-to-Business Marketing

Robert H. Hutchings

The problem many companies have is not so much how to generate inquiries, but rather how to separate suspects from prospects. A computer-based inquiry handling system is required for this. The computer system should be located in the advertising department. The system starts with inquiry-oriented advertising and alternative choice offers—offers which include hard offers for example, send a salesman, and soft offers, such as, send information. "Send a salesman" choices are classified as "A" inquiries, and followed up immediately. The soft-offer responses are fulfilled with a package that includes a bounce back card. Bounce back card choices that indicate continuing interest represent "B" inquiries and are sent to salespeople for development through personal contact. All other inquiries are labeled "D" for database and direct advertising. The entire advertising and sales effort should be summarized in report form. Some especially helpful reports include (a) the Company Profile Report, (b) the Trip Planning Guide, (c) the Quarterly Inquiry Listing, (d) the Purchase Potential Report, (e) the Product Inquiry Report, (f) the Regional Report, (g) the Daily Flash Report, (h) the Publication Effectiveness Report, and (i) the Cost To Potential Effectiveness Report.

Introduction

A SALES FORCE IS ONE OF THE BEST ASSETS A company has, but at today's cost of closing an order, it has become one of the most expensive assets in marketing.

With the rapidly increasing cost of a personal sales call—McGraw-Hill Research estimates $229.70 in 1985 (4)—many companies now give advertising more prominence in the selling process by using it to secure inquiries.

The common approach is to use various advertising media to generate response. The inquiries may take the form of business reply cards, coupons, publication bingo cards, phone calls or letters. Volume can vary based on the perceived value of the offer made in the advertising.

The problem many companies face today is not how to generate enough inquiries, but how to separate suspects from prospects. Identifying prospects and managing inquiries is a problem of substantial proportions.

The majority of today's business-to-business companies fail to make the most of inquiry potential. Most spend hundreds of thousands of dollars on supporting a sales organization, yet they treat inquiries as intrusions, and lack a system to manage them. A study by The Center For Marketing Communications (1) determined that 18 percent of customers requesting information did not receive it, and that 43 percent of those who inquired received their material too late to consider it in the purchasing decision. This unresponsive pattern has widespread consequences in terms of wasted advertising dollars and disenchanted customers.

Inquiries are handled inadequately because many business-to-business companies do not have systematic, managerially responsive systems for fulfilling requests and capturing data

that will qualify an inquiry for a follow-up sales call. Establishing an inquiry system to address these problems requires a careful look at the selling process itself.

Business-to-business buying in general is an evolutionary decision-making process, rather than the impulse response characterized by consumer marketing. Many salespeople use the traditional AIDA formula in the persuasion process: they (1) create *attention,* (2) generate *interest,* (3) develop *desire,* and (4) initiate *action.*

Advertising has accepted a similar model developed by Lavidge and Steiner (3) to explain how advertising works. Their model, like the AIDA formula, is based on a hierarchy of effects in the communication process. It is possible to borrow from this model in order to establish a hierarchy of effects for the selling process (Exhibit 1). The model assumes that before purchasing action occurs, an evolution takes place during which the prospect moves mentally through a series of steps, starting with awareness and ending in the purchase action.

There are a number of discrete steps between awareness and purchase. Along the way there are also maximal opportunities to increase the efficiency of personal selling. It is here that advertising assumes increased importance in the selling process.

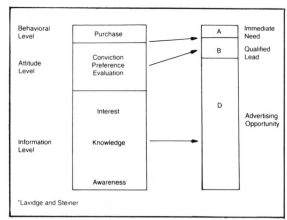

EXHIBIT 1. Hierarchy of Effects*

Salespeople and advertising specialists both start at the same place, at the information level. However, advertising can do a more cost-efficient job of creating awareness, developing knowledge and generating interest. This level of the hierarchy can be described as the area of opportunity for advertising.

However, the attitude and behavioral levels of evaluation, conviction, and purchase are more appropriate for salespeople than advertising. These steps often require a face-to-face dialogue or a product demonstration to progress through the hierarchy. The greatest efficiency and lowest costs result when sales and advertising people do respectively what they do best. An effective inquiry system assigns specific roles to each.

The Ingredients in an Inquiry-Handling System

A good inquiry follow-up system should address the interaction problems often associated with the activities of the salespeople, the marketing manager, and the advertising manager.

Insofar as generalities can be made, sales representatives dislike and avoid paperwork. They often resent any perceived intrusions into their territories and resist measurement and control. A good inquiry-handling system minimizes these objections. It also must be simple to use, easy to work with, and seen by salespeople as a help rather than a burden.

Marketing and sales managers are bottom-line oriented; they are charged with developing company revenue. Their success is related to identifying sources of business and securing that business. Most have limited marketing budgets with which to achieve quota goals. They are sometimes suspicious of the advertising component because it is difficult to measure. A good inquiry-handling system must have the ability to extract information from a database that is pertinent to these managers,

and to present it in clear and understandable form.

Advertising managers are charged with generating response from the advertising programs, forwarding the sales leads to the sales representatives, and then reporting the result of the advertising investment. This is difficult to assess with precision. Many times, sales representatives do not supply all the information necessary for proper evaluation.

A good inquiry system must be able to supply the necessary analysis without total reliance on the sales representative. This system should identify the effectiveness of advertising expenditures as related to inquiries, and should be designed to offer direct benefits to everyone involved in the process.

Many good inquiry systems have been disbanded because of failure to get the support of salespeople and marketing management. There is a shade of irony in the need to "sell" sales specialists on procedures that benefit them significantly.

Requirements for Success

1. It is advisable to locate the computer for the inquiry system in the advertising department.

Advertising people are good landlords for the system because they have a natural interest in justifying advertising programs. The personal computer with its easy-to-use inquiry handling software makes the advertising department installation relatively easy.

When the system resides in the advertising department, controls can be structured to eliminate delays in responding to inquiries. When inquiries are handled by other departments, delays often intrude because of other priorities. Other departments often do not associate sales value with the inquiry handling, not understanding that time cools the inquiries. The sales opportunities are then lost.

Sales representatives frequently believe that leads generated by headquarters are questionable. Cold inquiries sent for follow-up contribute to that belief. An unfortunate reality is that salespeople often discard an entire bundle of sales leads when the first few are unproductive.

The inquiry system will survive if emphasis is placed on its ability to measure the promotion and identify its contribution to completed sales.

2. Advertising objectives should be inquiry-oriented.

There is a difference between direct response and general advertising. General advertising is used to create awareness or images and shape attitudes. When inquiries are required, the creative techniques associated with general advertising often do not produce efficient response. Forcing a coupon into an ad or simply adding a phone number does not adequately address the response needed.

Advertising objectives must be clearly defined as inquiry-driven advertising. The creation of advertising that employs known response techniques should be the mission of agency or staff copywriters and art directors. Their advertising should be measured against response-oriented goals.

The Inquiry System Starts with the Offer

A response-oriented advertisement should employ alternative offers.

Hard offers such as "Send a Salesperson," and *soft* offers (e.g., "Send information"), position the inquirer's interest in the obvious way. A request to send a salesperson indicates an immediate need. A response asking for information indicates a lower interest level. Still other types of offers can position the inquirer along intermediate steps of the buying decision hierarchy. One such example is "Put me on your mailing list." This type of offer identifies continuing interest in the product or subject presented in the advertising.

Hard offers are associated with an immediate need, and require no further qualification before they are implemented as sales leads. Most inquiries, however, are responses to soft offers. Unfortunately, 77 percent of them are not yet qualified for a personal follow-up (2). Soft offers must be investigated and qualified before release to salespeople. It is at this point where many inquiry systems fail. Too often, unqualified inquiries are sent to the sales representative in bulk and turn out to be unproductive, wasting time and effort.

Qualifying Soft Offers

The package that is used to fulfill the inquiry obviously has purposes that go beyond supplying product information. When used effectively, it is a vehicle that can gather information about the inquirer's level of interest in buying. But the fulfillment package is often misused; it is frequently a haphazard collection of material assembled as an afterthought. Too often, for example, the response card is similar to the original offer: it is unlikely that the same person will respond to the same offer twice. The successful fulfillment package must be an integral part of the initial creative planning process for the direct response advertising program.

A bounce back card should be inserted with the fulfillment package. This card is the key to qualifying inquiries (Exhibit 2). This reply card differs from an inquiry business reply card. Its purpose is to get information about the inquirer, his ability to buy, and his potential as a prospect. The bounce back card is not offer-oriented and therefore a reason must be given as to why the prospect should return it. Here is one way to position it:

We hope your inquiry has been answered to your complete satisfaction. If it hasn't we'd like to know about it. We would appreciate your taking a minute to respond

We hope your inquiry has been answered to your complete satisfaction. If it hasn't, we'd like to know about it and would appreciate your taking a minute to respond to these few questions. This will help us to provide you with the thorough service we want you to have.

1. Was the information you received adequate?
   ☐ Yes ☐ No

2. If you need additional information, please specify.
   _____

3. Are you contemplating purchasing analytical instruments? ☐ Yes ☐ No If yes, are your requirements ☐ immediate ☐ 3-6 months ☐ 6-12 months ☐ over 12 months

4. What is your application? _____

5. Would you like an IBM Technical Marketing Representative to call? ☐ Yes

   Phone No. _____

6. Do you wish to remain on our mailing list?
   ☐ Yes ☐ No

7. Comments _____
   _____

If your address is incorrect,
please make corrections.

```
Baker80208B NMR2
B Baker
Sr Research Physicist
Denver University
University Park
Denver CO 80208
```

Please help us by completing this postage free card and returning it to us.

EXHIBIT 2. Bounce Back BRC

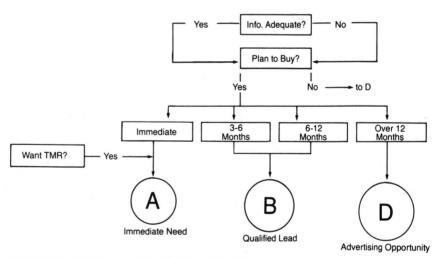

EXHIBIT 3. Follow-up Inquiry Classification

to these few questions. This will help us to provide you with the thorough service we want you to have.

The bounce back card questions are easy to answer. A simple check-mark supplies most of the information, with space for brief additional comments.

From these questions and answers a profile can be drawn which places the respondent in one of a series of follow-up categories (Exhibit 3).

Monitoring the Fulfillment Follow-up

The computer monitors the time from the shipment date of the fulfillment package. If the bounce back card is not returned within thirty days, a follow-up letter and another bounce back card are sent. The letter appeals for response by asking, "Has your recent inquiry been answered properly?" A second follow-up message is sent fifteen to thirty days later if there is still no response. This letter is more direct: "We're back again because we haven't heard from you." The envelope includes another bounce back card, the third and usually last. After two follow-up letters and three bounce backs, the requests usually stop. Additional follow-up has generally been found unproductive.

It is information drawn from both the original inquiry card and the bounce back card, compiled and analyzed, that identifies an inquirer as a qualified sales lead.

Some inquiry management systems use the telephone to qualify inquiries, but this is a costly approach when the volume of inquiries is high. A preferable method is to use the telephone for upgrading promising bounce back respondents. The calls are fewer and the success rate is higher.

Classifying Responses: A, B, and D

When a request for a sales representative to call is marked on either the inquiry card or the bounce back card, it is classified as "A" in the computer and sent for follow-up as "immediate need." The "A" classification will be used for forecasting sales potential and generating management reports.

Bounce back cards that are analyzed as being of "continuing interest" are classified as "B." They are sent to the sales representative as qualified leads that need development through personal contact.

All other inquiries reside in the computer and are classified as "D," for database and direct advertising. They are the emerging mar-

ket, and constitute a very responsive mailing list.

It is the "D" group that represents the advertising opportunity. Advertising follow-up with direct mail programs drives the group up the purchasing decision hierarchy at less cost than that of personal selling. When "D" respondents arrive at the qualification level, the sales representative takes over.

Too often companies discard inquiry names if they are not immediately productive. This is a major error and a waste of excellent business potential.

Sales Representative Follow-up

Unqualified inquiries sent to salespeople are mostly unproductive and consequently tend to lower sales morale. A qualification system that supplies productive sales leads can change morale for the better. Criticism about bad leads gives way to requests for more leads. Better sales leads stimulate a cooperative spirit and make the follow-up reports easier to obtain.

Advertising management and marketing management need to know the potential of sales leads for future business. In most companies, it is unlikely that an order is closed on the first call. The follow-up report is critical in the evaluation of the various advertising programs: many inquiry systems have failed because accurate information was not supplied about the follow-up process.

Getting salespeople to report on the follow-up call is a problem. One way to overcome it is to design a simple, easy-to-use report form. The "Follow-up Report" illustrated in Exhibit 4 is a self-mailer that requires only a check-mark in the "Excellent" or "Good" columns within the four categories shown. These categories represent the segments for forecasting the closing of the order.

Sales Inquiry Information Record

Today's
Date: 04/6/84   Product Interest: CS
Territory   DANIEL SPARKS   Fulfillment Sent: 03/15/84

INQUIRY
FROM: H. BARGER
                                                        Inquiry Classification: B
          GENERAL ELECTRIC COMPANY
          175 Curtner Ave.
          San Jose, CA 95125
                                                        Special Requests:

SOURCE: CHEM & ENG NEWS

Follow Up Report: BARGER95125H   Product Interest: CS

Contact Date: **Closing Potential**
                                                       (check one box)
Responded By: ☐ Phone   ☐ On Site   ☐ Other   1-3 Months*   ☐1 Excellent   ☐2 Good
Next Step Planned: 3-6 Months   ☐3 Excellent   ☐4 Good
  ☐ Demonstration   6-12 Months   ☐5 Excellent   ☐6 Good
  ☐ CSC Visit   Over 12 Months   ☐7 Excellent   ☐8 Good
  ☐ Sample Evaluation   No Potential   ☐ Excellent
  ☐ Price Quote   *Forecast? ☐ Yes ☐ No If Yes, $ _____ Revenue
  ☐ Proposal

COMMENTS: _____   Type of Funding
_____   ☐ Internal   ☐ Grant   Seeking funds
                                                       ☐ No Funding   ☐ Don't Know
_____
_____   What competition if any? _____
                                                       _____

Return Follow Up Report   Marketing Rep. Sig. _____

EXHIBIT 4. Follow-up Report

Each box on the form is assigned a number. These numbers become the basis for advertising evaluations and other management reports.

Inquiry systems seldom have all follow-up reports returned for evaluation. Most companies are content if they achieve 50 percent to 75 percent of the follow-up reports. The best solution is to make the reporting task easier, rather than to pressure the sales force. If their support for the inquiry system is undermined, the loss is greater than the value of the missing data.

Inquiry System Reports

The information collected forms a database which represents a wealth of useful information. The computer summarizes the results of the advertising and sales efforts. It can sort in countless ways and will produce printed reports or graphs.

The resulting information can be put to work in many ways and can help provide advertising accountability. Such reports prove useful in researching and evaluating new markets. They can evaluate publication effectiveness and provide insight into the value of various creative appeals. Some reports can be used to evaluate the effectiveness of sales follow-up activity and equilibrate sales territory assignments. Reports can be generated as needed, but they should be prepared and circulated monthly. Certain types of reports have particular value for the different categories of participants in the system, as in the following examples.

```
REPORT UXM010                        ***COMPANY PROFILE***                        PAGE: 1
SPEC ID: 1047                                                                      DATE:
------------------------------------------------------------------------------------------
WILLIAM H RORER INC                                                       SIC: 283-DRUGS
500 VIRGINIA DRIVE                                                      REGION: NORTHEAST
PORT WASHINGTON PA 19034                                           TERRITORY JIM CIOBAN


-----------------------------------INQUIRIES RECEIVED FROM:--------------------------------
                                                        PROD     PROM/     DATE/      INQRY
NAME              PHONE              TITLE               INT      MEDIA     SOURCE*    CLASS
L M SATTLER       215/628-6388                           LO      12 PF     03/11/82 TS   B
E KELLY           215/628-6621                           LO      12 PF     03/15/82 TS   B
L M SATTLER       215/628-6388      CHEMIST              LO      17 VG     09/22/82 S    A


---------------------------------- LAST INQUIRY FOLLOW UP RECORD --------------------------
              NAME:   L M SATTLER
      CONTACT DATE:   9/28/82
  PRODUCT INTEREST:   LO
            ACTION:   PROP PLANNED
       COMPETITION:
         POTENTIAL:   1
   TYPE OF FUNDING:   INTERNAL
      RESPONDED BY:   ON SITE

          COMMENTS:

*CODES:
(TS) TRADE SHOW — (S) SPACE — (L) LIT — (DM) DIR MAIL — (BB) BOUNCE BACK
```

EXHIBIT 5. Company Profile Report

Here are some reports that are especially helpful to *sales representatives:*

1. The Company Profile Report (Exhibit 5). This report documents an historical record of inquiries received from a single company. People who responded to the advertising are listed along with their qualification rating, date of inquiry, and product interest. This report also has value in maintaining sales territory coverage when representatives change.

2. The Trip Planning Guide (not shown). The inquiry data can be sorted in zip code sequence to supply a reference to the sales representative for planning a more orderly coverage of territory. When appointments are scheduled in one zip code location, another nearby company can be called upon.

3. Quarterly Inquiry Listing (not shown). An inquiry report can be prepared which lists the total respondents by territory. Labels can be made and used for local mailing programs.

These following reports are useful to *sales management:*

1. The Purchase Potential Report (Exhibit 6). The source of information for the purchase potential report is the sales lead follow-up card. The closing potential numbers assigned by the salespeople establish a ratio norm against which other programs are evaluated. This norm becomes a stronger management tool as the inquiry system database grows.

Norms are useful in comparing current-month activity against previous-month activity and in comparing achievements against year-to-date objectives. They are also useful in comparing sales region and sales representative effectiveness.

The "Purchase Potential" identifies the volume of potential sales. This report is useful for manufacturing planning. The same report also helps sales managers plan for appropriate sales closing action. For instance, a potential rating of "1" may require only a special incen-

```
┌─────────────────────────────────────────────────────────────────────────────────────┐
│                        NATIONAL POTENTIAL FOR LEAD CLOSING              DATE: JUNE     │
│                                                                        PAGE: 1        │
│                                                                                       │
│  NAME            COMPANY                    CITY            ST   POT   PROD  TER   REG  │
│                                                                                       │
│  R P SLOANE      HONEYWELL                  PHOENIX         AZ    1    E2    RK    DW   │
│  A P MASINO      HANSENS LAB INC.           ROCHESTER       NY    1    VO    CD    PC   │
│  D HALPERN       EATON CORP                 MURRAY HILL     NJ    1    U1    JK    PC   │
│  C A CHANG       WYETH LABS                 TOLEDO          OH    1    I3    LL    HD   │
│  G LARSON        A W LYONS                  RARITAN         NJ    1    LO    LC    PC   │
│  C K KIM         ORTHO PHARM CORP           SPRING HOUSE    PA    1    I9    JC    TM   │
│                                                                                       │
│  J R BRECO       SHERWIN WILLIAMS           PHILADELPHIA    PA    2    NB    JC    TM   │
│  C T KITCHEN     KITCHEN MICROTECH          MORGAN TOWN     WV    2    L9    GC    HD   │
│  F RANDA         PARKER CORP                DES PLAINES     IL    2    G1    GO    HD   │
│  S G WEBER       PENNWALT CORP              AURORA          IL    2    VO    DC    TM   │
│  D JUNG          GENERAL GRAIN              CRANBURY        NJ    2    VO    JK    PC   │
│  R LA CORTE      SMITH KLINE & FRENCH       PITTSBURGH      PA    2    VO    DC    TM   │
│  B PEPPE         UNIV. PITTSBURG            PITTSBURGH      PA    2    VO    DC    TM   │
│  E N PLOSED      S C JOHNSON CO             RACINE          WI    2    I3    GO    HD   │
│                                                                                       │
│  B SWARIN        CITY OF BARTLESVILLE       BARTLESVILLE    OK    3    E2    JB    JM   │
│  K P KOSITIO     GLYCO CHEMICALS            PASADENA        CA    3    I3    SB    DW   │
│  P LENAHAN       ELECTRONIC PROP. CO        ALBUQUERQUE     NM    3    RO    FH    JM   │
│  A C SHAIKI      AVACARE                    PLANO           TX    3    VO    JB    JM   │
│  K NOMURA        UNIV. CALIFORNIA           PACIFIC PAL     CA    3    I3    JB    JM   │
│  H L WALDRAM     PROPELLANT LAB             WARREN          PA    3    N8    MF    HD   │
│  R E LIVINGS     GENERAL MOTORS             WILLIAMSPORT    PA    3    U9    DC    JM   │
│  M T LITTLE      NORTHROP CORP              IRVINE          CA    3    E2    FS    DW   │
│  C M OAKLEY      PARKER CHEMICAL CORP       LANCASTER       PA    3    VO    DC    TM   │
│  J F SHALLA      CARTER WALLACE CORP        GLENVILLE       IL    3    VO    DC    HD   │
│                                                                                       │
│  R W CASE        RIVERFRONT MERTS           COVINGTON       KY    4    P2    GC    HD   │
│  M W KIRBY       FOOD MATERIALS             HAWTHORNE       CA    4    I3    FS    DW   │
│  F N FRY         ALLIED CHEMICAL            MIDLAND         MI    4    U9    LL    HD   │
│  G J BEYER       UPJOHN COMPANY             CRANBURY        NJ    4    VO    JK    PC   │
│  T C ALLEN       SQUARE DEAL CO             NEWARK          DE    4    U9    JC    TM   │
│  W E BRAKES      COOK COUNTY HOSPITAL       CHICAGO         IL    4    I3    GO    HD   │
│  R C BUTTERHOP   DUPONG CORP                NEWARK          NJ    4    VO    JK    PC   │
│  J R BOLANDS     ECHO SOUND CORP            CHICAGO         IL    4    VO    GO    HD   │
│  B N AMAND       US FDA                     WASHINGTON      DC    4    U1    BG    TM   │
│  I SIEGE         ARMSTRONG WORK CORP        LEWISTOWN       PA    4    VO    DC    TM   │
│  J ROP           CARTER WALLACE             SANTA CLARA     CA    4    VO    DD    DW   │
│  T W ALLEN       DRAFT INC                  NORWOOD         PA    4    I3    DC    TM   │
│  L GOLHY         ALLERGAN PHARM             INDIANAPOLIS    IN    4    VO    JV    HD   │
│  M JUHA          BTI CORPORATION            DUARTE          CA    4    VO    FS    DW   │
│  F LIPARI        GENERAL STORE COMPANY      PEORIA          IL    4    VO    GO    HD   │
│  W E BAKER       UNIV. CINCINNATI           CINCINNATI      OH    4    VO    GC    HD   │
│  J PARHUA        KEYSTONE CARBON CO         READING         PA    4    VI    DC    TM   │
└─────────────────────────────────────────────────────────────────────────────────────┘
```

EXHIBIT 6. Purchase Potential Report

tive to get the order, while a "3" may need more sales contact, including a product demonstration.

2. The Product Inquiry Report (Exhibit 7). The product inquiry report maintains a running record of the numbers of inquiries received for each product in the line. Quite often, there is a correlation between product inquiries and product sales volume. This report can highlight those areas in which more advertising is needed to inrease the number of inquiries.

3. The Regional Inquiry Report (Exhibit 8). This report compares the effectiveness of one region with another in scoring inquiry potentials. Another similar report compares the records of sales representatives within a single region.

The final group of reports to be discussed is useful to *advertising management*.

1. The Daily Flash Report (Exhibit 9). This report identifies the daily status of each promotion. The daily mail count is recorded by a bar chart. A trend line on an overlay records the total inquiries for the campaign. As time progresses the bar chart forms a bell-shaped curve which can be used to identify the halfway

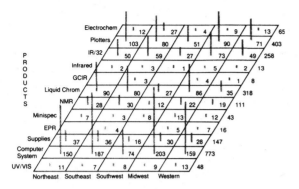

EXHIBIT 7. Product Inquiry Report

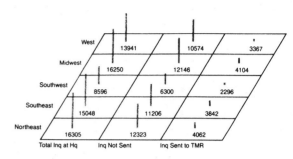

EXHIBIT 8. Regional Inquiry Report

point of the inquiry returns. Identifying this point is useful in projecting the life of the promotion.

2. The Publication Effectiveness Report (not shown). This report lists the various publications used and identifies the total exposure of a promotion. This is done by multiplying the circulation of a publication by the number of insertions. The report determines the comparative pulling power of each, while at the same time it compares the cost effectiveness of all.

3. The Cost to Potential Revenue Report (not shown). This report identifies the cost per thousand to reach the market with a promotion, the cost per inquiry, the percent of qualified inquiries, the cost per qualified inquiry, the sales potential resulting from the inquiries, and the forecast revenue-to-advertising cost ratio.

Reporting with Graphic Charts Has Many Advantages

Charts add a dimension to the meaning of a report. Executives who need to know the progress of inquiry promotion programs, as well as those involved in support of the inquiry system, generally have limited time to review results. It is a mistake to give them hard copy

reports loaded with columns of figures. Most managers manage by comparison. Graphic charts present easy-to-see relationships and encourage deeper involvement in the reports. It is easier to compare present position against past position and the intended objective with a chart than with a printout of hundreds of numbers.

Summary

The efficient handling and managing of inquiries in business-to-business marketing is a major problem for many companies. An inquiry management system can be a solution and also become a valuable company asset.

Such a system helps advertising to become more accountable for its expenditures and integrates the advertising and selling functions into a unified whole.

The system can increase sales productivity by the elimination of unproductive follow-up calls. It is also a positive aid in finding prospects ready to buy.

The application of an inquiry system to the advertising and marketing functions can become a valuable management tool for assessment of progress toward objectives.

In summation, an inquiry management system works because it measures results—the

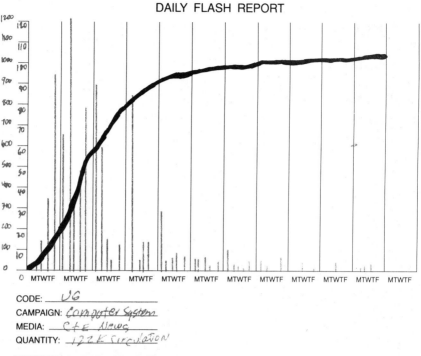

EXHIBIT 9. Daily Flash Report

ingredient most wanted in advertising and marketing today.

References

1. Center for Marketing Communications (1976), "Inquiry Cards' Sales Potential and How to Exploit It." Unpublished research study.

2. Hutchings, Robert H. (1981-83). The author's observations of inquiry qualifications from 287 responses to advertising programs.

3. Lavidge, Robert J. and Gary A. Steiner (1961), "A Model for Predictive Measurement of Advertising Effectiveness," *Journal of Marketing*, 24 (October), 59-62.

4. McGraw-Hill Research, Laboratory of Advertising Performance (1985), "Cost of Industrial Sales Calls," 8013.8.

Robert H. Hutchings, "The Application of an Effective Inquiry Handling System for Business-to-Business Marketing," *Journal of Direct Marketing*, Vol. 1, No. 2, Spring 1987.

Bingo Card Junkies Why They Could Be Your Best Prospects

ROGER W. BRUCKER

Contrary to common perception, people who circle a large number of bingo card numbers are very important prospects. Heavy bingo card circling reflects the inquirer's greater management responsibility and his/her anticipation of the need for problem-solving information. This anticipation of problems, rather than waiting for the problem to become "current," seems to explain why such circlers have no difficulty with the long processing times associated with bingo card inquiries. Heavy circling also causes some marketers to think that the literature they supply is money thrown away, but not responding to such inquiries leaves vendors "unqualified" from the buyer's perspective when the buyer's problem does get hot. They're not on the buyer's list because they took the inquiry too lightly. Sometime a multiple circler is a "squirrel"—a person who is known to have files when the need for information arises, and is looked to to provide problem-solving information. It is important that the person's files contain the seller's material when such requests come.

"PEOPLE WHO CIRCLE A LOT OF NUMBERS ON bingo cards are literature collectors and not worth my time or expense."

If you've ever said that, you're half right. "Bingo card junkies" *are* literature collectors. But you're probably wrong if you conclude that they are not worth your time or expense.

A recent survey by Odiorne Industrial Advertising, with the help of *Modern Machine Shop* magazine, finds that heavy users of reader service cards are involved in 35% more projects than average users. And heavy users plan to spend 40% more than average users.

Because they have strong purchase involvement, heavy users of reader service cards amass information on products they believe they will need because they want to build a comprehensive file. And because some advertisers process batches of reader service requests relatively slowly, compared to letterhead requests, those important buying influences know it may be some time before the information they requested arrives (from two weeks for a telephone request to more than a month for a bingo card inquiry). They also know that reader service inquiries generally spare them a salesman's visit.

A Frequent Question

We were curious about reader service card user behavior because our clients have often raised questions about it. Magazine space salesmen are also asked about heavy users and their value to an advertiser.

Our survey achieved a 37% response without an incentive (see accompanying table). We defined heavy reader service card users as those who circled 10 or more *Modern Machine Shop* reader service numbers in two of the previous 12 months' issues. We compared them to the average reader service card users who circles 3.6 numbers per card.

The survey's 56 heavy user respondents said they planned to spend about $19 million. The 72 average user respondents were going to spend approximately $14 million. That averages to nearly $340,000 per heavy user versus about $196,000 per average user.

The greater responsibility carried by important buying influences (more projects, more dollars) is sufficient explanation for their heavier bingo card usage. Faced with a greater number of projects and the accompanying purchase requirements, heavy users gather product information well in advance of their anticipated need because they want to make an informed decision.

Behavior in Perspective

Such anticipatory file-building results in two things:

1. It puts the problem of long reader service card processing times into perspective. The user expects that the advertiser will respond eventually, which is acceptable to the file-builder.

2. Yet it makes advertisers think that the literature they furnish vanishes into oblivion when they respond to heavy reader service card users.

Let's discuss the first effect. Smith at Acme Manufacturing has a thousand things to do. One emerging problem is finding a grinding machine to manufacture his product. He may not have to make a recommendation for eight months, but he doesn't want to be unprepared. In his experience, deadlines sneak up.

He gathers the needed information by using reader service cards. Doing so avoids having salesmen call before he's ready to see them, yet he'll get the information he needs prior to the problem becoming hot.

Then he moves quickly to the next problem: finding carbide tools for processing new product parts in time for a market introduction next year. He circles the numbers of some tooling ads along with the grinding machine numbers.

He circles 10 numbers in all. He knows he won't hear from the unreliable vendors. He'll build his files with the vendors who make his evaluation job easier by providing him with the information he needs to make good decisions.

Now let's take a look at the second effect: The ad manager of Ajax Grinding Machine Company has just received Smith's inquiry. He notices from the publication inquiry report that Smith circled 10 items. He thinks that if he sends out some literature to a heavy circler like Smith, nothing much will happen. If he tries to visit or call, Smith may not even remember that he circled that particular number.

What should Ajax do? It should get its literature out to Smith promptly. The lead time to the sale is probably going to be quite lengthy, but by responding, Ajax will at least be in the running for a sale at some point in the future. However, Ajax will probably respond to other inquiries first. And unless there's a policy against responding to heavy circlers, Smith's literature will go out, but it will go out last.

Qualifying Advertisers

At first glance, Ajax' action may seem logical because of the long lead time for selling to heavy circlers. However, considering that heavy circlers represent more dollars and more projects, it becomes essential to adequately inform those buying influences. They are attempting to compile as much literature as they can prior to seeing salesmen and asking for quotations. A manufacturer not in their files, may not be in on their deals. By not responding, or responding late, the advertiser has eliminated himself from consideration in many cases.

In much the same way that salesmen qualify prospects prior to calling, the heavy reader service card user qualifies vendors for his future purchases. He may not have the time or desire to chase down the vendors who didn't respond to his inquiries. In his mind, they have already ruled themselves out of consideration for his purchase by failing to answer his inquiry.

There is some evidence that others in the heavy user's company are aware of his literature "squirreling" habits and refer to him when they encounter problems. "People are always wanting to see my files or ask my opinion on who to consider," said one tooling engineer.

In contrast, the more "selective" reader service card user is faced with fewer projects and fewer purchase decisions. He can afford to be less methodical in his search for problem solutions because he doesn't have as many buys to make. He can wait until the need for a decision is near before seeking solutions. This kind of problem solving is less efficient because the

Modern Machine Shop obtained the names of all individuals who had circled 10 or more reader service items in two or more issues over a 12 month period. These "heavy circlers" numbered 150. A survey mailing June 6, 1983, without incentive, produced 56 (37.3%) usable returns after a three week cutoff. A duplicate questionnaire was then sent to a random sample of readers who were "average" (3.6 circles/card) in their card usage over the same 12 month period. A survey mailed November 1, 1983, without incentive, produced 72 (48%) usable returns.

1. Why do you use Reader Service (bingo) Cards? (More than one may apply.)	*Heavy Circlers*	*Average Circlers*
I collect information (catalogs) for further use.	79.3%	63.5%
I want to learn more about a product or process.	87.9%	83.8%
I am working on a specific project and need information.	53.4%	45.9%
Things are slow right now and I had nothing better to do.	0%	0%
I am ready to buy a product and need competitive information.	39.7%	29.7%
Other	10.3%	6.8%
2. How many projects are you currently involved in that may necessitate the purchase of a product?		
None	5.2%	13.5%
1 or 2	24.1%	24.3%
3-5	43.1%	33.8%
6-10	12.1%	12.2%
10 or more	12.1%	13.5%

3. These projects will result in the purchase of approximately how much capital equipment?

Heavy circlers: $19,073,000 total
$340,000 average per respondent

Average circlers: $14,142,000 total
$196,000 average per respondent

user is likely to make expensive phone calls if it's too late to use bingo cards.

At times the purchase decision is made without sufficient competitive information. The average user may welcome sales calls, but he's no more qualified as a prospect than the heavy user who had made his inquiry months before. Both seek information to make a purchase decision, but in quite different time frames.

4. When you are involved in a project, what are the three most important sources of information?	Heavy Circlers	Average Circlers
Salesman	46.6%	40.5%
Trade Shows	32.8%	37.8%
Material (catalogs) collected at an earlier date	89.7%	64.9%
Reader Service (bingo) Cards	48.3%	52.7%
Editorial in trade magazines	25.9%	17.6%
Direct contact with manufacturers	56.9%	48.6%
Discussion with others in my company	20.7%	33.8%
Other	3.4%	4.1%
5. As part of your job, is it common for you to request large amounts of information?		
Yes	82.8%	55.4%
No	15.5%	40.5%
6. How long have you held your present position?		
Less than one year	3.4%	1.4%
1-3 years	31.0%	31.1%
4-8 years	32.8%	33.8%
9-20 years	13.8%	20.3%
21 or more years	19.0%	12.2%

Dismissing heavy reader service card users as worthless "bingo card junkies" is a mistake. Heavy users are serious buying influences who represent more projects and more dollars than conventional reader service card users. By failing to adequately respond to heavy users an advertiser is snubbing an important part of his prospect market and failing to convert valuable leads into sales.

Of course there will be aberrations—the high school student who circles 25 numbers because he desires a full mailbox when he comes home from school, for example. But remember those are the exception, not the rule. The "bingo card junkie," representing $340,000 in purchases, isn't fooling around.

Roger W. Brucker, "Bingo Card Junkies: Why They Could Be Your Best Prospects," *Business Marketing*, February 1985. Reprinted by permission of *Business Marketing*. Copyright Crain Communications, Inc.

Research and Testing

Don't Change Your Offer without Testing

John Klingel

Changing a major and extremely sensitive element of a direct mail package, the order card, without testing is a cardinal sin. A small change, or at least what common sense dictates is a small change, can dramatically alter response. For example, changing "Send my free _____ and start my subscription" to "Enter my subscription. We'll send your free _____ when we receive payment" can result in substantial differences. Such changes should be tested before being rolled out.

Every now and then a campaign falls substantially below our expectations. At first we tend not to believe the results; we check to see if the fulfillment company entered all the orders, that the lettershop dropped all our mail, that the merge-purge operation put Zip Codes on all the labels, and so on. Then in desperation we blame the post office or assume that there's "a boxcar in Buffalo."

The "boxcar in Buffalo" reflects our wishful thinking that a large volume of our mail is in a boxcar that was accidentally put off on a siding in Buffalo—and that as soon as the railroad discovers their error, the mail will be delivered. Well, I've been through a few disasters in my direct mail career, and as many times as I've waited for them to find the boxcar, they never have.

Testing and Back Testing

The truth is that no matter how well we plan and how well we execute, occasionally the

129

results are simply horrible. And obviously when the results are poor, we want to know why. Because we are testing and trying to improve results, the poor results may be on a new package, offer or price. So one of the first things we suspect is that the lower response resulted from some change in the package.

The cardinal rule of direct mail is not to change any major element of the package without testing. But testing is never perfect, and there's always the chance that we used faulty test data and the new control caused the drop in response. So one of the oldest tricks in the book is to back test the old control by including the old control as one of the test panels. The back test allows us to confirm our previous tests and gives us a benchmark to see if the drop in response occurred because of a package change or other factors.

Changing Order-Card Copy

Recently I've run into a couple of situations that seem to indicate that there are a fairly large number of people who don't understand the risks involved in changing order-card copy. In one case, a magazine asked me to review a campaign that was 75 percent to 80 percent under budget. In the second case, I was called and asked if January was a bad season. When I asked why the question was asked, I was informed that their campaign was 50 percent under budget.

I've had campaigns fall 10 percent to 30 percent short due to economic conditions, but when a campaign misses by 40 percent or more, as both these did, I assume there's something besides a poor season. The first magazine dropped their campaign over a month late (early February) when it should have mailed just before Christmas. The second magazine dropped two weeks late but also dropped a tra-

ditional spring campaign on time. The spring drop was under budget to the same extent as the January campaign.

But there was more involved than timing. It turned out that both these magazines had committed the cardinal sin of direct response: They changed a major and extremely sensitive element of the package—the order card—without testing. The other elements of their packages were relatively the same, except for some changes in colors and relatively minor changes in descriptions and editorial content.

Furthermore, they did not include a test of the old package in the mailing. The basic problem in these situations is that we can't tell what caused the response to drop. We can only speculate and guess. Mailing counts have been verified, the merge-purge output checked, and there doesn't seem to be any problem with order entry at the fulfillment company. Both magazines have to plan future campaigns—and they don't have the reliable results on which to base their forecasts.

Many people in the publishing industry don't seem to know that the wording of order-card copy is extremely sensitive. As a result, they often change the wording of the order card from campaign to campaign. Sometimes the changes don't hurt, and sometimes they result in extremely poor response. Little changes, or at least what common sense may dictate as insignificant changes, can dramatically alter response.

In neither of the cases can I tell for certain what caused the drop in response. It was probably a combination of factors—maybe a poor season, plus a reduced response from mailing late and changes to the order card. But personally, I suspect that the order-card changes played a major role.

In the first case, the lateness of the mailing probably caused a significant drop in response. (I've seen as much as a 50 percent decline in response from early January to March, so I don't want to downplay the seriousness of mailing late.) But let's consider the order card.

When I first looked at the order-card copy for the magazine (whose response dropped 75 percent to 80 percent) my eye didn't pick up the problem. However, when I looked at the fulfillment reports, the percent of cash with order was 40 percent. When I asked if that was normal, the circulation manager said no, they usually got very little cash with order. So I asked to see the old order card. Then some of the changes became very noticeable.

As I've mentioned many times, a high percentage of cash with order usually means that the profitability of promotion can be increased. Pushing credit usually raises response more than enough to offset the higher billing costs and bad debt costs. As a result, when I see a high percentage of cash with order I suspect a problem. When this magazine rewrote the order card, they left off the words "and we'll bill you later." There was no indication on the order card that the magazine would accept credit. The magazine uses a premium offer and the wording was changed from "Send my free (blank) and start my subscription" to "Enter my subscription. We'll send your free (blank) when we receive payment." These two approaches are very different and may have resulted in a substantial difference in response.

The second magazine uses a choice-of-two-terms offer: one and two years. In 1983, the order card showed the first-year price first and the two-year price second. In 1984, the package that pulled 50 percent fewer orders had an order card with the two-year rate first and the one-year rate second. The wording of the offer is very complex because there are different premiums offered for each term.

In the letter that accompanied the two packages (the current package and the old package), the circulation manager commented that they got a lot more two-year subs this year.

My analysis is pure speculation, as the only

way to measure the impact of these elements of the order card would be to test them against one another. But neither publication should have changed their order-card copy without pre-testing to see if the changes hurt response. Or if their bosses forced them to change, they should have back tested by mailing a small quantity (*i.e.*, 10,000) of the old package. That way, when response dropped below expectations there would be something that could be used to measure the impact of the copy changes.

My advice to both these magazines was to go back to the old package on the next mailing and mail the most recent package to a test panel. (Just as an aside, neither of these publications are clients, and I didn't charge them for taking a quick look at their campaign to see if I could spot the problem. I'd love to show you the actual order cards, but I'm afraid that it would embarrass the magazines and the personnel involved.)

The circulation personnel who were involved are very bright. The problem is that their circulation experience is largely self taught. Neither they nor the people they work for have been trained in direct response marketing. As a result, they rely on common sense—and common sense is a poor guide in determining how to be effective in direct response marketing.

Unfortunately, very few people are lucky enough to be trained in direct response marketing. There are simply very few job situations where people with a good direct response background can pass on their knowledge and experience to others.

The most pathetic thing is that one of these magazines uses a so-called direct response agency. They should know better than to change an offer without testing. But it's obvious from the wording of the offers and the lack of testing that this direct response agency *doesn't* know—or at least doesn't practice the basics. But when magazine management doesn't know anything about direct response they can't judge the quality of advice they receive.

If you want to avoid the type of disaster that the two publications discussed above experienced, you have to respect direct response.

John Klingel, "Don't Change Your Offer without Testing," *Folio: The Magazine for Magazine Management,* October 1984. Reprinted by permission of John Klingel and *Folio.*

Research Methods

Joseph Castelli

Research should not replace direct response testing, but used in tandem with testing to produce more effective direct response campaigns. Research can contribute to the successful direct response campaigns in four main areas: (1) identifying the target market, (2) determining what to say in advertising, (3) determining corporate image, and (4) developing new products.

Research versus Testing

Most people in direct marketing are familiar with the concept of testing. Direct marketers test several mailing packages before deciding which one to use. We test a variety of mailing lists to see how well each list does before we rent entire lists. We test different offers and premiums to determine which ones generate the greatest response.

Research involves surveys that are conducted among consumers. Much of this research is conducted before the testing phase that often occurs in direct marketing. The question you may ask is, "Why do we need research when we can test in the mail?" The answer would be that research can help answer some critical marketing and advertising questions that cannot be answered as easily, if at all, by testing.

However, research should not replace testing. Instead, research and testing should be used in tandem to produce more effective direct-response campaigns.

Research Applications

There are four main areas in which research can contribute to the success of a direct-response program:

- Identifying the target market
- Determining what to say in the advertising
- Determining the corporate image
- Developing new products

Identifying the Target Market

You are more likely to reach your marketing goals if you determine which consumers represent your best opportunity. Therefore, one of the most important things research can do is provide a clear picture of the target market.

One way to identify the target market is by examining your current customers. For example, you can determine their demographic characteristics. It might be helpful to know whether your current customers are primarily:

- Men or women
- Young adults or older people
- College-educated or not
- Professionals or blue-collar workers
- Single or married
- City folk or rural dwellers

Beyond this, you also should learn something about their behavior and attitudes. For example, you should try to determine:

- What products they currently buy
- How often they buy the products
- How frequently they use the products
- On what occasions they use them
- What they like about the products
- What they dislike about them
- What needs, if any, are not being satisfied by the products currently on the market

You should learn about their lifestyles. For example, it might be helpful to know whether your customers are more likely to:

- Spend money or save money
- Go to parties or stay home
- Prefer gourmet cooking or meat and potatoes
- Have a broad or a limited range of interests
- Attend rock concerts or PTA meetings

Once you determine who your target is, selecting the right mailing lists and print media becomes much easier. You also will be more certain that the tone of your advertising is correct.

Here are some suggestions for conducting such a study.

- Ideally, the study should be conducted by telephone rather than by mail.
- The sample should be drawn from a list of current customers. You should interview at least 300 respondents. However, you may wish to segment the sample. For example, you may wish to see how the heavy buyers differ from the light buyers. In this case, each of these groups should be represented by at least 150 respondents.
- To avoid any bias in response, respondents should not be told for whom the study is being conducted.

- The questionnaire should consist primarily of structured questions.

Determining What to Say in the Advertising

Once you know your target market, the next thing to determine is what to say in the advertising. For this, we recommend a two-phase research program.

The first phase consists of qualitative research. In most cases, this would consist of a series of group sessions. Group sessions can be helpful in several ways.

- As was mentioned earlier, they can help one develop an understanding of consumer language. Therefore, they can help ensure that one knows how to talk to the consumer.
- They can help one identify the reasons why people buy a given product.

On the basis of these group sessions and creative judgment, a series of copy promises or product benefit statements are developed. We are now ready for the quantitative phase of the research program, in which the relative importance of each of these product benefits is determined. This is done with a technique called the copy promise test.

We begin by developing a series of copy promises or product benefit statements. These statements should be in the form of single sentences. Here are some examples of copy promises that might be tested for a new series of books on photography to be offered on a continuity basis.

This series of books:

- Is a handsome collection of volumes on your favorite subject
- Can help you become a better photographer
- Contains the latest information on photography

- Can show you how to improve your photographic skills

- Allows you to learn photography at your own pace at home

- Helps you develop a personal photographic style

- Is a comprehensive course in creative photography

While this list includes only seven promises, a copy promise test could evaluate as many as twenty-five promises at one time.

After the promises are developed, each is typed on a 3 by 5 card. The cards then are incorporated into a deck.

The copy promise test then can be conducted either on an intercept basis in shopping malls or by telephone. The decision about which method to use should take into account the difficulty one would encounter in locating members of the target market in a shopping mall. For example, if your target market consists of women 18 to 35 years of age, it may be relatively easy to locate a sufficient number of them in shopping malls. On the other hand, it would be very difficult to find a sufficient number of antique dealers this way. Given the fact that many direct-response campaigns are directed at fairly narrow target markets, you probably will find that a telephone survey is the most practical way of conducting a copy promise test.

A typical copy promise test is conducted among 150 respondents. Whether the survey is done in person or by telephone, respondents first are screened to ensure that they are in the target market. For example, if one conducted a study for a new series of books on photography, respondents might be screened to ensure that they own a camera, use at least six rolls of film per year, and regularly read at least one of the major photography magazines.

Before the promises are presented or read to these respondents, there is a brief introduc-tion. For example, in the case of the photography series, respondents would be told that a leading publisher is planning to introduce a new series of books on photography and that this series may offer its readers a variety of benefits. They then would be told that we would like to read some of the benefits that such a series might offer photographers and ask them to tell us how important each benefit is to them. They would be asked to use a 10-point scale. Therefore, if they perceived the benefit to be very important, they would give it a rating of 10. If they perceived it to be not at all important, they would give it a rating of 1. They would be told that they could give each benefit any rating from 1 to 10 depending on how important they perceived the benefit to be.

When all the promises have been rated, the respondents are asked to rate each promise in terms of its perceived uniqueness. That is, they are asked to indicate whether they believe that each benefit is available in all, most, some, few, or none of the photography books currently available on the market.

Ideally, a few promises are regarded to be both important and unique. We would consider these to be the most effective promises.

At this point, it should be mentioned that you should not accept the results of a copy promise test with blind faith. You should verify the results with an in-mail test. Select the three or four winning promises and test them in the mail. In one such test, the winning promise won by a significant degree in the mail. The response rate was 25 percent higher than that of the next best test mailing.

Here are some things to keep in mind in regard to promise testing.

1. The key to the success of promise testing is to start with a good set of promises. This means that the top creative people on the account should be involved in the development of the copy promises.

2. Each promise should be in the form of a simple sentence.

3. Each promise should contain only one benefit. Otherwise, it will be difficult to interpret the results.

4. Be sure that the promises to be tested can in fact be used in advertising. The promises should be discussed with your legal department before the promise test is conducted.

Determining the Corporate Image

It is important for a firm to know what image it has in the minds of the target market. Obviously, if your company is not well known or is perceived to be selling inferior merchandise or to be slow in fulfilling orders, your business will be affected adversely. Therefore, it is important to know how your firm is viewed by the prospective customers. To determine this, a corporate image study can be conducted among the members of the target market.

Corporate image studies can be conducted through personal interviews; a telephone survey, or a mail survey. For the reasons stated earlier, a telephone survey is often the preferred method.

The sample should consist of members of the target market. However, you should also include in the study a sample of current customers.

The study should be designed to obtain the following information:

• Top-of-mind awareness of companies in your industry. For example, you might ask, "When I mention sporting goods manufacturers, what companies come to mind?"

• Awareness of these companies on an aided basis. For example, you might say, "I'm going to read to you the names of some companies that manufacture sporting goods. As I read each name to you, please tell me whether you have heard of that company." Of the two measures of awareness, more confidence should be placed in top-of-mind awareness. However, if consumers do not recognize the name of your firm even on an aided basis, this would suggest that some effort should be made to increase their awareness of your firm.

• Perception of your firm and its competitors on a series of key attributes. You can begin by asking respondents to rate a series of attributes in terms of how important they are in the selection of a firm from which to buy sporting goods. The list of attributes might include:

1. Is a leader in the industry

2. Offers quality merchandise

3. Offers a wide selection of merchandise

4. Provides speedy delivery

5. Guarantees the products it sells

Once they have rated these attributes in terms of importance, you should ask them to rate your firm and its competitors on the basis of these same attributes. You then will know which attributes are the most critical and how well your firm stacks up against the competition in terms of these critical attributes. This information can be used to help identify potential problem areas or provide assurance that no outstanding problems exist in the awareness or perception of your firm.

Developing New Products

Another key area in which research can be helpful is new product development. A new product development program generally involves two stages of research.

The first stage is the idea generation stage. One way to develop new product ideas is through the use of qualitative research. For example, several group sessions or a series of in-depth interviews can be conducted with consumers. However, these should not be regarded as brainstorming sessions. That is, these consumers are not asked to provide ideas for new products. Instead, they are asked to discuss a range of topics such as:

- The products they use
- How often they purchase them
- How frequently they use them
- In what ways they use them
- What they like about them
- What they dislike about them
- What needs are not being satisfied by these products

On the basis of this qualitative research, a series of new product concepts are developed. These concepts may be ideas for entirely new products or ideas for improving existing products. After these concepts are developed, they should be discussed with the product development staff to be sure that the new products actually can be made. If any cannot be made, the concepts should be revised or dropped from the next stage of research.

We are now ready for the concept testing stage. The objective of this stage of research is to determine the relative interest in each new product idea on the basis of the concept alone.

This research generally is conducted among a sample of 150 members of the target market. While the ideal way to conduct such a study is through personal interviews, the cost of doing the study by telephone is considerably lower. The interview is similar to the one used in the copy promise test that was discussed earlier. After respondents are screened to make sure they are members of the target market, they are told that a leading company is planning to introduce a series of new products on the market and that we would like their reaction to these new products.

Respondents then are exposed to one concept at a time. After each concept is read, the respondents are asked to indicate their interest in buying the product. A scale is used to measure buying interest. For example, this scale might consist of the following five points:

- Definitely will buy

- Probably will buy
- May or may not buy
- Probably will not buy
- Definitely will not buy

In addition, reasons for interest or lack of interest usually are obtained. Respondents then may be asked to rate the product according to a series of product attributes. For example, if you were testing concepts for new office equipment, you might ask respondents to indicate how they perceive the product in terms of the following attributes:

- Easy to use
- Saves time
- Saves work
- Good value for the money
- Attractive appearance
- Reduces error
- Fewer repair bills

After the respondents evaluate the first concept, the next concept is presented, and the same procedure is followed. To avoid any bias arising from the order in which the concepts are presented, the order should be rotated. In other words, the first respondent would see concept A, then concept B, and finally concept C. The second respondent would begin with concept B, then evaluate concept C, and finally rate concept A.

In evaluating the results, one should keep in mind that this type of research, like much of the research we have discussed, is designed to provide a relative rather than an absolute measure. That is, the test will measure interest relative to the other concepts being tested. Therefore, it may be safe to assume that respondents prefer concept A to either concept B or concept C if that is what the results show. However, it would not be safe to assume that you could project the buying interest levels to the marketplace. For example, if 20 percent of those interviewed say they definitely will buy the product, that does not mean that 20 percent of the target market actually will do so. For many reasons, the level of interest you obtain in the research is likely to be higher than the one you will achieve in the marketplace.

Obviously, we have oversimplified the procedure. Beyond the research already discussed, there may be a need for product testing to determine whether the product lives up to consumer expectations. There also may be a need for name testing and research to determine product positioning.

Quantitative Direct Response Market Segmentation

Richard A. Hamilton

Geodemographic information, computers, rising marketing costs, multivariate analysis techniques, and other factors have combined to push geodemographic market segmentation into the forefront. The objective of such segmentation is to make already profitable lists more profitable, and marginally profitable lists profitable. Honing current lists loses customers but increases purchase probability. The primary technique used to analyze geodemographically coded "area records" is cluster analysis. The most prolific source of geodemographic market segmentation information is the *United States Census of Population and Households.*

COMPANIES HAVE LONG SOUGHT AN ACCURATE method of evaluating where potential customers in new markets could be reached. Marketers and direct marketers have begun to embrace *quantitative geodemographic market segmentation* as their method of evaluating current customers and applying the information to reach into new markets. The concept has been manifest for decades, as can be seen in the marketing strategy of the late Tom Crawford. He was the owner of two Kansas City-based maternity clothing outlets, one retail (The Blessed Event) and one mail order (Tom Crawford's Maternity Wear). During the 1940s and 1950s, Tom tracked severe winter storms geographically as indicators of where to send targeted mailings to expectant mothers three months later. Firms that provide this type of information based on scientific techniques today have grown to the point that their combined current annual revenues are estimated to exceed $200 million.[1,2]

Beginning in the 1950s, the power and speed of the computer enabled many institutions to analyze vast quantities of information in a timely fashion. These computerized systems also accommodated the utilization of high-powered multivariate quantitative techniques. At the same time, increasing costs and competition were requiring the sellers of goods and services to better understand their customers so that the most effective marketing plans could be developed. The emergence of many special interest media literally forced companies to more finely tune positioning and target market strategies. Additionally, the United States Postal Service (USPS) began requiring all users of second and third class mail to use the zip code on all items mailed starting in 1967.[3]

This new policy virtually assured that zip codes would gain legitimacy from their use by businesses nationwide. These factors, especially the arrival of the zip code, led to the foundations upon which geodemographic models have been built.

This article will focus on the general philosophy of geodemographic market segmentation systems, their objectives, the primary quantitative techniques used, and the types of data available for use in such systems.

Geodemographic Segmentation Systems: An Overview

The general philosophy advocated by users of geodemographic systems is that of matching those factors that make up the profile of a desired group with the same factors in other groups in an effort to find similar profiles. Those groups whose lifestyle profiles are similar to the profiles of the firm's current customers should have a high probability of having similar needs. Firms able to meet these needs can expect these prospects to become customers in the future. But these classifying factors, generalized across markets or individuals, may not have value when operationalizing marketing objectives and tactics. Because of this limitation, the objective of these systems for mail-order firms involves the honing of mailing lists in order to make marginally profitable lists profitable, and to make already profitable lists more profitable.

For example, assume that a company is contemplating a mailing of 195,000 to a list from which it received a 2.5 percent response previously when promoting a complementary item. If a 2.3 percent response were required to meet all marketing costs directly associated with this particular marketing effort, and a 2.5 percent response rate were expected, the company would not use the list if that 0.2 response differential did not meet the company's contri-bution margin and customer acquisition cost goals.

However, if the company used the data from the previous years' mailing of 200,000 using geodemographic market segmentation techniques, they could separate the most profitable portions of the list and mail only to them. If Table 1 were the results of such an analysis, by mailing only to segments 1, 2, and 3, this marginal list would be turned into a profitable list with a response rate of 3.17 percent.

TABLE 1. Sample Geodemographic Market Analysis

Cluster/ Segment	Mail Count	Cluster Percentage of Response	Cumulative Percentage of Response
1	46,073	3.71	3.71
2	32,838	3.09	3.45
3	29,115	2.41	3.17
4	63,214	1.88	2.69
5	28,760	1.34	2.50
Total	200,000		

It must be understood that honing currently used lists loses customers. In the previously mentioned example, removing individuals from the rented list this year would exclude the possibility of acquiring new customers from Segments 4 and 5. Therefore, the objective of geodemographic market segmentation systems for mail-order sellers is not to reduce the number of catalogs or letters mailed. The objective is to reallocate mailings from the unprofitable portions of current lists to the profitable portions of new lists, or to mail to profitable segments more frequently.

By targeting a larger proportion of mailings to more highly qualified prospects, the company can increase the average probability of purchase. From a marketing operation point of view, what good is it to know that one out of every three households in a metropolitan statistical area (MSA) is a customer without knowing in which one of the three households the customer resides? From a distribution and promotional targeting point of view, in particular, that knowledge would serve essentially no purpose.

The methodology is also used to make compiled lists and mail-responsive lists productive. In addition, a firm's best customers (in terms of the recency of their purchases, the frequency of separate purchases, or the total dollars spent) can be targeted more often for specialized promotions. These models have been used to target different advertising campaigns and messages to market segments that differ demographically, psychographically, and/or by lifestyle. Furthermore, the methodology is currently being used by many cablevision companies to tailor station offerings to different franchise territories based on geodemographic differences. Lastly, it has been used for product development strategies and retail store location selections.

The Statistical Geodemographic Segmentation Methods

The primary quantitative technique used to analyze geodemographically coded "area records" is *cluster analysis*. Cluster analysis may be one of two types:

1. The breakdown or tree-analysis method assumes that the entire market is completely homogeneous until portions of that market can be found to be statistically significantly different from the remaining market, based on some variable. Using a statistical technique such as Automatic Interaction Detection (AID), the total market, or one of its already divided submarkets, is divided at each successive level by splitting off the segment that will cause the greatest reduction in total least squared error. The process is continued until a prespecified stopping point has been reached.[4] Table 2 depicts the results of such an analysis.

2. The buildup, or Q-type factor analysis assumes that all submarkets (zip codes, for example) are different in terms of demographics until similar ones, as defined by a large number of variables, are found. Most cluster analysis methods operate on some variation of Euclidean distance measure. The median, centroid, or minimum-squared-error methods combines the two zip codes or clusters with the smallest summed squared, paired differences between descriptive variables, continuing the process until a prespecified stopping point has been reached.[5] Table 3 depicts one iteration of such a process.

The Sources of Geodemographic Information

The most prolific source of data currently available for use as the basis of a geodemographic market segmentation system is the *United States Census of Population and Households*. Virtually all statistics summarizing the nation in aggregate are a matter of public record. Because the Constitution assures the citizenry that the Census Bureau's pledge of individual and household confidentiality will be maintained, data begin to be suppressed at some point as the statistics summarize smaller and smaller geographical areas.

This suppression of data is the underlying reason for the development of geodemographics. It is essentially a coding system (called geocoding) which matches censuslike demographic and lifestyle characteristics of neighborhoods back to specific individuals and their households based solely upon where they reside. Codes are needed to match individuals and residences (defined by name; street name; and number, city, state, and zip code) with areas (defined by nonsequential government identifying numbers, such as census tract numbers).

Consumer behavior theory, in particular, reference group theory, holds that individuals

TABLE 2. The Tree-Analysis Method

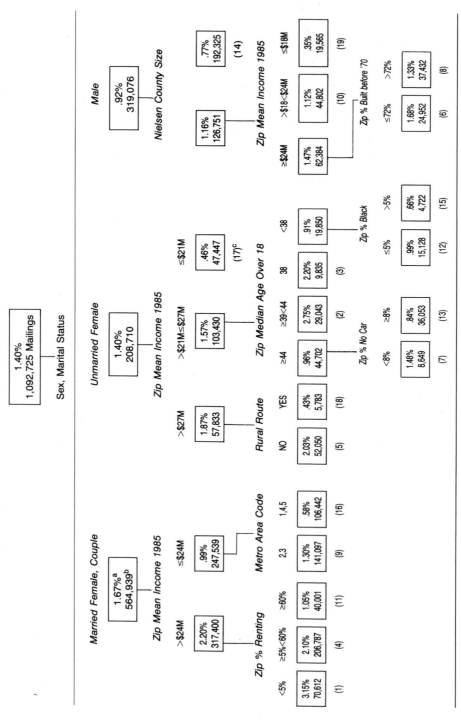

aPercentage figure (%) in cells indicates percentage response.

bNonpercentage figures in cells are mailing counts.

cFigures in parentheses below final cells indicate each cell's percentage response ranking.

TABLE 3. Q-Type Factor Analysis

Zip Code/ Cluster No.	Variable 1 — Median Family Income (000)	Variable 2 — Median Hours Household Worked/Week	Variable (N-1) — Percent Nonwhite	Variable N — Median Housing Occupancy Tenure (Yrs.)	
			Raw Data		
53192	10.0	29.7	17.6	5.3	
Clust. 847	16.7	34.9	22.8	7.7	
Clust. 216	26.4	36.1	7.0	3.2	
64110	21.9	38.7	7.9	4.0	
Paired Zip Code/ Cluster No.			*Differences*		*Square root of summed squared differences*
53192 & Clust. 847	6.7	5.2	5.2	2.4	10.2
53192 & Clust. 216	16.4	6.4	10.6	2.1	20.6
53192 & 64110	11.9	11.0	7.7	1.3	18.0
Clust. 847 & Clust. 216	9.7	1.2	15.8	4.5	19.1
Clust. 847 & 64110	5.2	3.8	12.9	3.7	14.9
Clust. 216 & 64110	4.5	2.6	2.9	0.8	6.0[a]

[a]Because 6.0 is the smallest distance between any two zip codes/clusters, zip code 64110 now becomes part of cluster 216 and the next iteration begins. The final output of such a system would be similar to Table 1.

live in or aspire to live in neighborhoods made up of persons they are like or whom they aspire to be like. Geodemographers assume that households within close proximity of each other share the same attitudes, interests, and opinions, and therefore must share similar wants, needs, and desires. Therefore, they reason that inputing the demographic and lifestyle attributes of homogeneous clusters of people or households back to their individual residences is theoretically and conceptually sound.

The data available as input to such systems

TABLE 4. 1980 Census of Population and Housing[6]

100 Percent Items

Population

Household relationship (T)
Sex (T)
Race (M)
Age (M)
Marital Status (T)
Spanish/Hispanic origin or descent (A)

Housing

Number of units at address (M)
Access to unit (T)
Complete plumbing facilities (P)
Number of rooms (P)
Tenure (whether unit is owned or rented) (A)
Condominium identification (T)
Value of home (owner occupied units and condominiums) (P)
Contract rent (renters—occupied units) (A)
Vacant for rent, for sale, etc.: and duration of vacancy (T)

Sample Items*

Population

School enrollment (T)
Educational attainment (T)
State or foreign country of birth (T)
Citizenship and year of immigration (T)
Current language and English proficiency (T)
Ancestry (M)
Place of residence five years ago (T)
Veteran status and period of service (T)
Presence of disability or handicap (T)
Children ever born (T)
Marital history (T)

Employment status last week (T)
Hours worked last week (T)
Place of work (T)
Travel of transportation to work (T)
Number of persons in carpool (T)
Year last worked (T)
Industry (T)
Occupation (T)
Type of employment (T)
Number of weeks worked in 1979 (T)
Usual hours worked per week in 1979 (T)
Number of weeks looking for work in 1979 (T)
Amount of income in 1979 by source (T)

Housing

Type of unit and units in structure (M)
Stories in building and presence of elevator (T)
Year built (T)
Year moved into this house (T)
Acreage and crop sales (T)
Source of water (T)
Sewage disposal (T)
Heating equipment (T)
Fuels used for house heating, water heating, and cooking (T)
Costs of utilities and fuels (T)
Complete kitchen facilities (T)
Number of bedrooms (M)
Number of bathrooms (M)
Telephone (T)
Air conditioning (T)
Number of automobiles (T)
Number of light trucks and vans (T)
Homeowner shelter costs for mortgage, real estate taxes, and hazard insurance (T)

*For most areas of the country in the 1980s, one out of every six housing units or households received the sample form. Areas estimated to contain 2,500 or fewer persons in 1980 had a three out of every six sampling rate, which is required in order to obtain reliable statistics needed for participation in certain federal programs.
(A) = reported at all levels; (P) = partially suppressed at the city block/enumeration district (CB/ED) levels; (M) = most suppressed at CB/ED levels; (T) = totally suppressed at CB/ED levels.

must start with the Census. Demographic subject items included in unsuppressed summary levels are shown in Table 4.

Table 5 shows that as the geographical subdivisions being summarized become smaller, the amount of data divulged for public consumption diminishes. The marketer using geodemographics must concentrate on analyzing geographic areas that are small enough that persons residing in the area are demographically homogeneous among themselves, yet heterogeneous relative to persons residing in other areas. Thus, at this

TABLE 5. Geographic Subdivisions—Below the State Level[7,8,9]

Geographic Areas/Sub-divisions	Definition Origin	Approximate Number of Geographic Units	Approximate Number of Demographic Subject Items	Average Population Size
Metropolitan Statistical Area (MSA)	Census Bureau	275	1,000,000+	50,000+
County/City Town/Place	Census Bureau/ Political	3,000	30,000+	varies
Sectional Center	Postal Service	800	1,000	varies
Zip code	Postal	35,000	1,000	varies
Census Tract	Census Bureau	45,000	13,000	4,000
Carrier Route	Postal	165,000	N/A	500–2,200
Block Group/ Enumeration District	Census Bureau	250,000	1,000	800
City Block	Census Bureau	2,500,000	30	90
Zip + 4	Postal	22,000,000	N/A	12

time, inherent in geodemography is a trade-off between the degree of homogeneity of the subdivision population and the amount of data about that population available to adequately describe it.

Most social scientists would agree that census tracts are small enough geographical subdivisions to have meaningful homogeneity for use in surveys and research. The other two smaller and therefore more homogeneous Census Bureau subdivisons are the block group/enumeration district (BG/ED), and the city block. BG/ED level subdivisions are the smallest Census Bureau subdivision for which most demographic data are available. City block data divulges only very basic housing statistics.[10]

Geographic subdivisions defined by the Postal Service have meaningful homogeneity at the zip code level. This was first argued by Martin Baier, and the zip code was used successfully and essentially exclusively as *the* geocode

from 1967 through the early 1980s.[11] This move was hastened by the 1967 postal regulation that required all second and third class mail be zip coded. At that time, no demographic data were available by zip code until Yuan Liang created ZIP-O-DATA, an annual estimate of demographic and lifestyle information for all zip codes.

Because zip codes were a creation of the USPS to expedite the delivery of mail, zip code boundaries were not designed to fit into the additive build-up system of the Census. Therefore, the data summarizing individual zip codes was originally (1967–1969) extrapolated from census data by ZIP-O-DATA.

In 1970 the Census data were made available for the first time from the Census Bureau on a zip code basis. However, it was only available for five zip codes within MSAs. Thus, early demographers during the 1970s were forced to use the extrapolated data of services such as ZIP-O-DATA or to use other relatively nonhomogeneous sectional center data to segment nonmetropolitan areas. The 1980 census data was sorted and divulged for all five-digit zip codes nationwide for the first time.

For the smaller and thus more homogeneous USPS carrier route and ZIP + 4 subdivisions, one major problem currently exists: All demographic data ascribed to carrier routes or ZIP + 4s are statistical extrapolations of census data.

One final but very important point about BG/ED or city block data versus carrier route or ZIP + 4: Even though USPS subdivisions smaller than the zip code suffer from the need for 100 percent statistical extrapolations, they benefit from the USPS subsidy for geocoding through postal discounts. In essence, the USPS subsidizes companies' geocoding efforts through postal rate discounts offered to mailers of carrier route and ZIP + 4 mail. Most companies would agree that the smaller geographical areas (carrier routes or ZIP + 4) must be more homogeneous than the larger zip code. That theory, plus the postal rate discounts, are swinging more and more geodemographers to the use of carrier routes and ZIP + 4. But studies of the extent to which the increased accuracy from more area homogeneity has offset extrapolation estimates used to describe their residents report mixed results.[12]

For example, a study reported in February (1987) *American Demographics* had six geodemographic data vendors (CACI, Claritas, Donnelly Marketing Information Services, National Decision Systems, National Planning Data Corporation, and Urban Decision Systems) confidentially share their between-census estimates of certain variables for certain geographical units (the metropolitan area, the major county, a group of census tracts, and a zip code). The metropolitan areas chosen for the study were Baltimore, Detroit, and Phoenix. For each specified geographical area in each city, the vendors were to supply estimations of current population, number of households,

average household size, number and percent of households within broad income ranges, average household income, and five-year projections of population and number of households.

Less variance between vendor estimates/predictions were found when (1) the population base is more stable (e.g., Baltimore or Detroit versus Phoenix); (2) the estimate/prediction area is larger (e.g., county versus a group of census tracts); (3) the time horizon of the estimate/prediction is shorter (current versus 5 years); (4) the units of geography are standardized with field data and boundaries updated by the census (group of census tracts versus a zip code); (5) percentage income distributions by vendor are compared as opposed to the number of households within income ranges; (6) using population as opposed to number of households (because different assumptions made by the vendors about average household size compound estimate/prediction variances).[13]

Because many companies have not kept databases, or at least not ones sufficient enough to aid in making marketing decisions, a new segment of the geodemographic market segmentation industry has begun to flourish. These companies are called (customer) list enhancement companies. As long as a company knows who its customers are and can identify them geographically by name and address, enhancement companies can overlay other demographic and lifestyle data (which actually describe the demographics and lifestyles of those in the neighborhood in which they live) onto individual customer records.[14]

One such example is National Demographics and Lifestyles' (NDL) "Lifestyle Selector." NDL's database contains ten demographic and fifty lifestyle characteristics on over fifteen million recent purchasers of major consumer products (see Table 6). The database is retrieved through customer questionnaires packaged with the products purchased. Merge-purge matches between NDL and client lists have been averaging 12.2 percent, enabling its

TABLE 6. National Demographic and Lifestyles Selector[16]

Demographic Characteristics	Lifestyle Characteristics		
Sex	Art/antique collecting	Foreign travel	Racquetball
Age	Automotive work	Gardening	Real estate investments
Income	Bible/devotional reading	Golf	Rec. vehicle/ 4-wheel drive
Marital status	Bicycling	Gourmet foods/ cooking	
Home ownership	Boating/sailing	Health natural foods	Running/jogging
Occupation	Book reading		Science fiction
Ages of children	Bowling	Home furnishing/ decorating	Science/new technology
Credit cards used	Cable TV viewing	Home video games	Self- improvement programs
Geography	Camping/hiking	Home video recording	
Religion/ethnic background	CB radio	Home workshop	Sewing
	Collection	Household pets	Snow skiing
	Community/civic activities	Hunting/ shooting	Stamps/coin collecting
	Crafts	Motorcycling	Stereo, records, and tapes
	Cultural arts events	Needlework/ knitting	Stock and bond investments
	Electronics	Our nation's heritage	Sweepstakes
	Fashion clothing	Personal/home computers	Tennis
	Fishing	Photography	Watching sports on TV
		Physical fitness/ exercise	Wildlife/ environmental issues
			Wines

users to make more precise discriminations between market segments.[15]

The information shown in Table 7 is available from CACI's Acorn market segmentation systems, which matches client lists with a large number of survey and panel data sources and with the constantly updated name and address files of over 74 million maintained by Metromail/R. L. Polk. Also linked to the Acorn system are data sources of catalog purchasers and their profiles, the products purchased, mail-responsive purchasers, media audience data, teenage purchasers, Gallup's convenience store and eating out database, and in-depth financial services usage, including the types of accounts held and the balances of individuals.

Conclusion

Geodemographcis has had a relatively short history of activity that has been growing exponentially, particularly in this decade. Although the sophistication of the computer, mathematical models, and the data itself have lead to the explosive growth of geodemographic market segmentation systems and their usage, two very important points must be stressed:

1. The primary growth in usage has come from corporations which already have valuable customer databases. These firms are primarily

TABLE 7.   CACI Source (Available by Zip Code or Census Tract)[17]

Annual Census Updated Items

Population*
Households*
Median household income*
Age distribution (10 groups)
Median age
Income distribution (7 groups)
Average household size

Annual Noncensus Updated Items

Purchasing potential indices
Investments
Savings
Loans
Apparel
Footwear
Sporting goods
Groceries
Drugs
Dining out
Department stores
Home improvement
Auto after-market
Furniture

*Item estimated for current year and for five years hence.

direct marketers, whose database knowledge about current customers is enhanced by using such systems to efficiently acquire new customers.

2. Companies with only sparse or no customer databases could greatly profit by building fairly nonsophisticated customer database, using such concepts as the Recency/Frequency/ Monetary formula and the 80/20 principle, or by collecting product category purchase or cross-selling information. These basic elements are more essential for unsophisticated firms, and would be more helpful than an immediate engagement with a geodemographer. Current

customers have far and away the highest potential for future sales.

Endnotes

1. "The ACORN Market Segmentation System," CACI, INC.—Federal, Washington, D.C. (an advertising circular).

2. Kimbrough, Ann Wead, "How Where You Live Tells Why You Buy," *The Atlanta Constitution*, October 24, 1985, pp. 1-B, 8-B.

3. Baier, Martin, "Zipcode . . . New Tool for Marketers," *Harvard Business Review*, January–February 1967, pp. 133–140.

4. Jackson, Barbara Bund, *Multivariate Data Analysis* (Homewood, Ill.: Richard D. Irwin, Inc., 1983), pp. 23–45.

5. Ibid, pp. 131–190.

6. *1980 Census of Population and Housing*, U.S. Department of Commerce, Census Bureau.

7. Weissmann, Joseph, "Geo-Select Confusion: Which G-Factor Is Best?" *Direct Marketing*, June 1985 (reprint).

8. Weissmann, Joseph, "Consumer Graphics of Census Data Aid Market Researchers," *Marketing News*, March 6, 1981, p. 1.

9. "Geographic Segmentation," *Summary of Computer Services* (part of a sales information packet from Direct Marketing Technologies, Inc., Rolling Meadows, Ill.).

10. Weissmann, Joseph, "Geo-Select Confusion: Which G-Factor Is Best?" *Direct Marketing*, June 1985 (reprint).

11. Baier, Martin, *Elements of Direct Marketing* (New York: McGraw-Hill, Inc., 1983), pp. 164–165.

12. Weissmann, Joseph, "Geo-Select Confusion: Which G-Factor Is Best?" *Direct Marketing*, June 1985 (reprint).

13. Chapman, John, "Casting a Critical Eye," *American Demographics*, February 1987, pp. 31–33.

14. "Geo-Coding and Census Data Implant Systems," *List Enhancement Systems* (part of a promotional package of Creative Automation Company, Hillside, Ill.).

15. "Customer List Segment Analysis," *The Lifestyle Selector* (part of a 1984 sales information packet from National Demographics and Lifestyles).

16. Ibid.

17. "How To Turn Your PC into a Market Analysis Tool for Only $395 . . . ," CACI, INC., (first quarter 1986 direct mail advertisement).

Richard A. Hamilton, "Quantitative Direct Response Market Segmentation," revised from "Geodemographic Market Segmentation," in *Marketing Issues and Trends* (vol. 3, R. Coulter and S. Greene, eds.), Atlantic Marketing Association, 1987. Reprinted by permission of author.

Production

Production
The Last Strategic Frontier

Mark Gruen

Graphic arts production (excluding overhead costs) commands an estimated 90 percent of a direct mail marketing program's budget. Production results are the last word on the manner in which image is communicated on paper to the market. In spite of the importance of this function, production people are normally underpaid and of low status, and production itself is too often treated as an afterthought. Production people should be brought into the process while strategy is being considered, and while their suggestions can still make a significant contribution to the bottom line. Production strategy can be the difference between success and failure. The state of mind that ignored the importance of production in the past is perpetuated today. To overcome the problem, basic courses, workshops, and seminars should include the topic, and caution against creativity without forethought to production. The emerging direct marketing curricula in universities should include production. And, the production job itself should be restructured with regard to career advancement opportunities and with respect to the status of the job.

IN A RECENT RESEARCH STUDY PUBLISHED BY THE Direct Marketing Association, catalog print buyers were surveyed regarding the most important factors involved in choosing a printer.

149

Responses were: 84 percent "dependability," 79 percent "production quality," 77 percent "competitive costs," and only 53 percent "technical capabilities."

With issues of quality, cost and capabilities down the list from dependability, it can be said that these statistics translate as follows: "We choose the printer who can save our necks when we're late with the material."

Agency or in-house production buyers of direct mail packages and collateral materials, as well as catalogs, probably would respond in the same manner. The fact is that, traditionally, production buyers are submitted to unnecessary pressures from marketing, account, media and creative colleagues and pass these pressures along to suppliers. New production technology hasn't changed the basic relationships of production buyers: They have little or no clout on their home ground and rely on printers and other production suppliers to meet unrealistic deadlines. They are underpaid, overworked and undervalued.

Even the authoritative article on printing and production in the recent 9th Edition of the *DMA Fact Book* describes production techniques and working with suppliers, without a reference to production as a key component within the overall management process.

Omitting one-half of the contribution and responsibilities of production doesn't acknowledge the reality of its importance in the direct marketing mix, quantitatively and qualitatively.

Whether talking about the direct marketing services industry as a whole, or a single package or catalog, an estimated 90 percent of direct marketing budgets (excluding postage and overhead costs such as rent and personnel) falls in graphic arts. How that money is managed directly effects cost per response.

Not only are production results critical to the bottom line, they are the last word on the manner in which image is communicated on paper to the marketplace.

It is, therefore, important for direct marketing services industry to position properly the role of production and the status of production professionals. Production management is not merely sending out specifications for price quotes. Like all effective management, it is the harnessing of available resources to get the job done right.

Production Strategy

By now, the practice of developing marketing, creative and media strategies is so common that prospective clients ask about them in initial agency interviews. Presenting a "road map," or action plan for total direct marketing communication is part and parcel of what agencies deliver, and, frequently, strategic thinking differentiates one agency from another, and wins, keeps and contributes to an account.

Virtually no agencies showcase, and few clients ask about, production strategy and capabilities. But production activities help answer the strategically significant questions good marketers, writers and designers ask, including:

- How will we properly position this situation?
- How will we project the image?
- How will we credibly approach the market?
- How will we achieve a reasonable cost per response?
- How will we meet the schedule?

A responsible agency should muster all its strengths, especially at the question asking and information gathering phases of a proposal to a prospective client, or a new campaign for an existing client. Why not make the most of production resources? It makes sense for experienced production professionals, at the management level, to become new members of strategic teams, to be there at the beginning, to be accountable throughout for developing, implementing and evaluating production strategy.

Making a Difference

In most outside and in-house agencies, creative creates and says to production, "Produce it!" Typically, time is running out, the design is tricky and either the budget runs high, or shortcuts are taken to meet the budget.

The production function is mismanaged when it is thus reduced to a buying function, positioned as an afterthought. To attract bright, productive managers who are strategic thinkers, the function should be on a par with account and creative personnel.

What would happen, for instance, if the situation turned around and production was called upon to set some parameters for creative? What if production said to creative, "Here are some alternatives that will help get the job done!"?

It seems that results based on sound production values would include lower costs and more appropriate images. And "overtime" would no longer be such an important word in the printers' lexicon.

• As a direct marketing agency for example, Gruen + Sells has examined magazine inserts, particularly for one of our financial services clients. The question was posed, "Just how important is the quality of the paper stock for the application? Yes, the image of the card is, and has to remain, high, but how high is high enough? Is it necessary to use the whitest white and the heaviest possible stock the designer has spec'd?"

Obviously, it was concluded that the answer is, "no." Production recommendations to the client, Sears Credit, resulted in recent application inserts printed on a less expensive grade and finish of paper. The costs were reduced by one-third. The final tally on response is not in yet, but at last count, they were up, attributed to the creative strengths of the ad itself.

• Lack of knowledge of special production effects can result in a prosaic approach where there could be an exciting image projected, at comparable or reduced costs.

Sears Telemarketing Services, as an example, needed a brochure stitched within a folder containing a back pocket to hold customized letters, quotations, schedules and other inserts. A typical solution would have involved costly hand-gluing. Instead, with production functioning at the conceptual stage, a format with an extended die-cut cover, folding to form not only the back pocket, but stitched to form a surface for a dramatic illustration opposite the inside front cover, was developed. In this case, compared with a traditional format, the image was enhanced at a lower cost.

• In some cases, special production effects might cost somewhat more, but their impact in terms of response is significant. A simple three panel premium brochure for the Parker Pen Company was given the feel of a point-of-purchase display when the third panel was die-cut to add dimension—and "sell"—to the product. The result was increased orders, particularly on the featured pens.

• It is often believed that low cost, superior quality and fast service are mutually exclusive, a myth perpetuated in the *DMA Fact Book* article on printing and production.

Recently, the media strategy for a client suggested that remnant space available in a major consumer magazine be taken advantage of. In a test of creative strategies, two headlines in a split run were tested. The color separations were sent out for bid and two quotes were received, one five times higher than the other. The lower bid supplier produced excellent separations in plenty of time.

High production estimates can be standard operating procedures when suppliers know production buyers are in a hurry. This may be compensation for the times production buyers cry "wolf." The first rule is: Don't be in such a hurry. However, if you have to be rushed, let a precedent of realistic deadlines establish standards for price, quality and service.

Solving the "Production Problem"

A so-called production problem frequently is the result of management problems all the way down the line, from a client who has inadequately formulated a marketing plan, to an account manager who has not called upon available agency resources at the right time, to a designer who has incorrectly specified ink, paper or format.

The state of mind that ignores the importance of production has existed for years and is perpetuated today. Only recently, a group polled prospective workshop attendees on interest in hearing a session on "Production for Non-Production Types." Because of low interest, the topic was dropped from the proposed list.

Such groups should take a leadership role by including production in basic courses, workshops and seminars. If planners of conferences do not recognize the importance of production, neither will the general membership.

Designers and writers, in school and on the job, should be cautioned against creativity without forethought to production. While new ideas are the lifeblood of our direct marketing services industry, and the mindsets of production managers, buyers and suppliers ought to be stretched, the constraints of the process ought to be acknowledged. Working relationships should be based on mutual understanding and respect.

Production Curricula

The emerging and growing university direct marketing curricula should make more than passing reference to production. Graduates entering the field should be conversant with the technology, terminology, procedures and requirements of production, since production effectiveness will influence success far more than creative or media.

By the same token, production curricula should cover management and the creative process, as well as the technical side of the graphic arts, preparing students to fill a broader role in the work environment.

Because potential production and allied professional personnel, so key to meeting industry needs, are learning their crafts in trade schools and art schools, groups that sponsor scholarships and other student benefits should include these students in their programs.

Once in a job, production personnel should be involved at the conceptual stages of direct response advertising programs. Participating in the development of total communication ideas can save time and money, and avoid mistakes.

Production managers should have the opportunity to reach the level of senior management, rather than getting stuck on a dead-end vertical track. It is no secret that many production jobs carry relatively low status and low salaries. Therefore, they will continue to attract people with relatively low talent and motivation, unless status and compensation are based on the comparable worth of production experts who are responsible for some 90 percent of the budget. While the reputation for free lunches and kickbacks might be exaggerated, users and agencies should never put production professionals in a situation in which they think they have to rely on such "favors."

Production managers are really agency managers, or company managers. They should be recognized as first-class citizens within a team environment geared to reaching goals by getting a quality job done on time, for the best price.

How to Avoid Production Problems

Here are some steps to a strategic approach to the production of direct marketing programs:

- Include production in the early stages of correspondence and meetings.
- Be sure the entire management team understands the goals of the program.
- Put production on the agenda of the conceptual discussion.
- Determine what *level* of quality best accomplishes your image or sales goals. Remember, quality is a strategic or tactical device.
- Have production evaluate thumbnails and sketches, rather than final boards, from the production point of view.
- Choose and evaluate suppliers on the basis, first, of capabilities and quality.
- Avoid last-minute changes from the approved strategy.
- Recruit, nurture and evaluate production managers with the same management criteria applied to account, creative and media staff.

Mark Gruen, "Production: The Last Strategic Frontier," *Direct Marketing,* January 1987. Reprinted by permission of *Direct Marketing* magazine.

Mail-Order Financial Analysis

The Dollars and Sense of Direct Mail

Practical Concepts of Math and Finance

Pierre A. Passavant

Every direct mail campaign should be preceded by a pro forma profit and loss (P&L) analysis to see if it makes sense, and to see in advance if there is a reasonable chance of success. Understanding how the numbers in the P & L link together, and are irrevocably tied to promotional expenses, is critical. Every expense that is added must "work," that is, it must get more business at the same profit level. One shot (go for the order) promotions are the easiest to analyze. Two-step (inquiry, conversion) promotions must be examined at two stages: (1) cost per inquiry and (2) conversion rate. The key distinction in the financial analysis of "club" promotions (any situation where there is an ongoing relationship with the customer) is the expression of all sales and expense statistics in terms of the average person (who, obviously, doesn't exist as a single, identifiable individual). Averages also come into play in planning and analyzing catalog promotions. In all cases, calculating a "contribution" allows you to determine what response you need, depending on what your profit goals are. Lifetime value of a customer, rather than profit from a single sale, is an integral part of financial analysis. This requires assumptions about additional offers that can be made to first-time buyers, percent response to those offers, and the dollar value of such offers. The most important of all financial relationships is the relationship between cost of promotion and response rate.

Introduction

PERHAPS YOU HAVE NOTICED THAT AN EXPErienced direct mail manager often sounds like a cross between a merchant and an accountant. A merchant who knows how to pick the right item and promote it effectively. An accountant who has a detailed knowledge of response rates and expenses.

Direct Mail marketers are, in fact, very number oriented. And there's a very simple reason for it. Most of the time, a direct mailer can *track* the results of individual modules of promotion. A typical example would be a mailer who gets 250 order cards back from a promotion sent to 10,000 names on the XYZ list. The order cards were "keyed" or coded so that the mailer would know that a specific mailing to a certain list pulled exactly a 2.5% response.

Knowing the response to individual promotions is very valuable information. It allows you, the mailer, to calculate profit and investment results for each effort you make. That allows you to repeat or expand on what has worked and to modify or avoid what has not. Building a file of historical results allows you to forecast the likely outcome of new promotions to different mailing lists—your own or others you might rent. Having the results of previous mailings also allows you to try to "fine-tune" subsequent promotions—in order to increase response and profits.

This booklet will give you a basic understanding of the key numerical elements that enter into every direct mail promotion. The booklet won't make you an accountant or full-fledged financial analyst, but it will give you a clear explanation of how to use "the numbers" to plan successful direct mail promotions, and how to analyze your results when they come in.

Developing a Campaign Profit and Loss Worksheet

Every direct mail campaign should be preceded by a pro-forma Profit and Loss (P & L) analysis—to see if it makes sense economically. On a new offer, the pro-forma P & L will be based on estimates because no actual experience has yet been recorded. After the campaign is over, a final P & L should be drawn up using actual results. This then becomes the basic financial input to future promotions that might be planned.

One-Shot Promotions

The simplest kind of direct mail promotion is a one-shot—where the seller makes an offer of a single item. If the prospect orders, the item is shipped and the entire transaction is complete. (This obviously differs from club or subscription or continuity or catalog marketing—where predictable additional shipments or renewals occur.)

Let's start with a P & L worksheet for a one-shot promotion that assumes the mailer is sending out a test of 50,000 direct mail packages offering a large, colorful book called *Great Vacation Places of the World*. The price of the book is $39.95 plus $1.95 postage and handling. If the test is successful, large mailings are planned and the cost of a mailing will then be $300 per thousand packages ($300/M) complete in the mails (that's 30 cents each—postage and amortized creative costs included). Let's further assume that the response to the mailing will be 2.5% or 25 orders per thousand packages mailed.

P & L Worksheet for One-Shot Promotion
(50,000 mailing with 2.5% response)

Income		Total Dollars	Per Net Sale	Notes
1,250 orders	@ $39.95	$49,938		
+postage & handling	@ 1.95	2,438		
Total value of orders	@ 41.90	52,376		
Minus 100 returns (8%)	41.90	4,190		
=1,150 net sales	41.90	48,186	$41.90	
Expenses				
1,150 books (delv'd cost)	@ 10.00	11,500	10.00	1.
Fulfillment— 1,250 orders	@ 4.10	5,125	4.46	2.
Promotion— per order	@ 12.00	15,000	13.04	3.
Bad debt— 2% of sales	@ 41.90	964	.84	
Overhead— 15% of sales	@ 41.90	7,228	6.29	4.
Total		39,817	34.62	
Profit Before Taxes		8,369	7.28	
% to Net Sales		17.4%	17.4%	

1. Assumes projected product cost with successful promotion and large press run. Damaged returns and lost shipments would increase product cost *per net sale.*

2. Includes reply postage, order processing, bank credit fee, shipping (at 4th class book rate) and handling, customer service, handling returns, and collection effort.

3. Estimated cost of direct mail package in large runs is $300/M. Response assumed to be 2.5%. This equals $12 per order for promotion.

4. All other expenses (management, building, utilities, non-sell departments, etc.).

While the numbers and relationships above might be typical for some large, successful book promotions—don't assume they would hold for all promotions. Here are just a few examples of possible large differences:

- Returned goods would be higher than 8% for fashion items. In some cases, as much as 30%-35% returns are "normal" in the fashion field.

- Cost of product would be more than 24% of selling price for a high ticket item (over $100). With higher price offers, cost of goods often approaches 50% (but there are offsetting decreases in fulfillment and promotion).

- Bad debt could be much more than 2%—depending on the type of offer, the quality of the list audience, etc.

The important thing for you to understand is that the numbers must fit together like the stones in an archway. For example, it would be all right, in the above P & L Worksheet, to enrich the product so that projected cost of goods became $11 (instead of $10) *provided that* the enrichment, when described in the mailing piece, increased the response enough so that promotion cost per sale became $12.04 (instead of $13.04). That would happen if the response rose to just 2.77% from 2.5%—an increase of 11%. But note that, if the product enhancement did not affect response at all, then the $1 incease in product cost would simply reduce profit by $1—lowering the percent profit to 15% (instead of 17.4%).

Understanding how the numbers in a P & L link together—and are irrevocably tied to promotion response—is so vital it is worth taking a minute to review another example . . .

Suppose the seller decided to add a premium (free gift) to the offer for people who actually pay for the book. Let's say it's an imitation leather passport jacket with built-in currency converter which costs $1.60 wholesale.

How can you tell, numerically, whether that promotion idea has a reasonable chance of working? And, in this case, let's define "working" as getting *more* business at the same profit of 17.4%.

The calculation is really quite easy . . .

- If the seller is going to spend $1.60 *more* per sale in order to give a premium—then the amount spent on direct mail promotion costs per sale must go *down* by $1.60. Note that the same $15,000 is being spent on media promotion in both cases, *but the promotion dollars spent per sale vary with response.*

- Without the premium, promotion
  cost is: $13.04
  The premium will cost (per sale):   1.60
  Therefore promotion cost must
   drop to: 11.44
  (for total expenses and profit
  to remain the same)

- Promotion cost per sale of $11.44 is achieved
  with a response of 2.85%. That's a 14% increase over the 2.5% response without a premium. Since a good premium offer can usually be counted on to increase response 15%
  or more, this looks like a good way of improving the offer—at least on paper.

Now, of course, we have to test to see
whether the enhanced offer, including premium, will really pull as many additional orders as
we hope. But at least we know in advance that
there is a reasonable chance of success.

If you are beginning to get a feeling for
how the different elements and lines in the P & L
fit together, it's time to move on and consider a
few important variations. (If you're not comfortable with what's already been covered, go
back and review it again right now. It's important that you grasp the foundation blocks before going further.)

Two-Step Promotions

Two-step promotions are those where the
seller first gets an inquiry and then tries to convert that inquiry to a sale. The essential difference between a one-step and a two-step P & L
analysis is simply that the promotion expenditure is divided into two parts: (1) inquiry solicitation and (2) conversion effort. And the efficiency
of the promotion effort can be examined in two
stages: (1) cost per inquiry and (2) conversion
rate.

Once again, let's take a simple example
and work through it. Suppose we are trying to
sell a home correspondence course (two-step

marketing is typically used for relatively complex and high-ticket products or services). The
course sells for $500 and we feel we can afford
to spend 14% or $70 of that on media promo-
tion. That promotion figure, by the way, is
often referred to as the allowable promotion
expenditure—and it can be expressed per order or per sale.

We might solicit inquiries through an expensive mailer sent to selected audiences at a
cost of $225/M. If the response to that Step 1
mailing were, say, 3% then each inquiry received would cost us $7.50. In addition, it will
cost at least 25 cents to capture and store each
inquiry. We will spend another 70 cents average
on each of 5 follow-up mailings (a total of $3.50
per inquiry). Follow-ups can be made by mail,
by phone or in person—but let's assume we'll
only use mail. Total promotion costs, then, are

Inquiry solicitation	$7.50
Capture name	.25
Follow-up promotions	3.50
Total	$11.25-per inquiry

That cost of $11.25 represents *total promo-
tion expenditures*—so we can figure the cost per
order by estimating how many inquiries will be
converted to orders. Here are the costs per order associated with several different conversion
pecentages (you simply divide the inquiry cost
by the conversion percent).

Conversion%	Promotion Costs per Order with $11.25 Cost per Inquiry
10%	$112.50
14%	80.35
16%	70.31
20%	56.25

Now we know that, if inquiries and follow-
ups cost $11.25 each, we must convert 16% of
them (within 5 efforts) to achieve the allowable
cost per order of $70. The process of direct

mail testing would allow us to tinker with the inquiry solicitation offer to see what happens if we get more or fewer inquiries per thousand in response to our first mailing.

You should already know that, if you get more inquiries per thousand, the cost per inquiry will decrease below $7.50—perhaps to $6.00 or less. If that happened, then total inquiry plus follow-up cost would be only $9.75 (instead of $11.25).

That *sounds* good ... because you only have to convert 14% of $9.75 inquiries to achieve a $70 cost (rather than the previous 16%). But it is often the case that less expensive (and, therefore, perhaps promotionally induced) inquiries do not convert nearly as well as those generated by less aggressive offers. So you have to test different promotional ways of getting inquiries and see how well each converts. And, again, examine the numbers at the end in the framework of a complete P & L analysis that takes all costs into account.

Shipment	No. of Starters Shipped	No. of Returns	No. of Bad Debt
1	1000	100	50
2	950	140	50
3	800	40	16
4	750	35	15
5	700	25	10
6	650	20	10
7	600	18	6
8	550	15	5
9	500	12	5
10	500	10	2
11	500	10	2
12	500	10	2
	8000	435	173
	Avg. 8 shipments per starter	5.4%	2.2% of shipments

If each plate in the series sells for $14.95, then the average starter spends 8 × $14.95 or $119.60—against which there will be returns of 5.4% and bad debt of 2.2% as indicated above. The amount of promotion dollars that can be spent to acquire a starter will depend on how much you can afford out of the average $119.60 order.

"Club" Promotions

Loosely speaking, "club" promotions can include any program where there is an on-going relationship with a group of "starters." Those "starters" may be book club members, insurance policyholders, telephone service subscribers, plate collectors, etc.

The key *distinction* that affects the P & L analysis in this case is the concept of the *average customer*. All your sales and expense statistics will be expressed in terms of that average person (who, obviously, does not exist as a single, identifiable human being).

Again, let's use a simplified example. Suppose we have a set of 12 plates to be shipped to customers one per month for as long as they choose to remain in the program. The pattern of customer retention might look like this:

Catalog Promotions

Averages again come into play in planning and analyzing catalog promotions. Plus much more. The world of catalogs is too varied and complex to give you more than a feeling for the subject in these brief pages.

Among the key averages that are developed and examined by catalog marketers are

• Average order size (this number times the number of orders received gives you the first line of the P & L table) and average expenses for filling orders.

• Average number of items per order (this directly impacts average order size and is an indicator of how good your impulse merchandising was).

• Average number of orders per buyer in a catalog season. This also directly impacts catalog productivity and is an indicator of customer satisfaction with shipments received as well as the effectiveness of the catalog itself, plus follow-up promotions, bouncebacks, enclosures, etc.

In addition to these averages, catalog marketers give a lot of attention to individual sections, pages and items. It is a common practice, for example, to develop a mini-P & L for each major department within a catalog—especially where there are significant differences in Gross Margin % (that's what is left over when you subtract Cost of Goods from Net Sales) or in average selling price from one department to another. In addition, the catalog marketer will determine the promotion cost for individual items and pages within a catalog.

For example, suppose a cataloger sends out 50,000 48-page catalogs at a cost of $650 per thousand—for a total of $32,500. That means each selling page (let's assume that 44 of the 48 are selling pages) costs $739 in the mails. The catalog marketer can relate that cost to the sales generated on each page, or portion of a page.

• If the desired P & L promotion expense for a department were, say, 14%—and some items had only 9% promotion expense (that is, promotion dollars divided by net sales) then customers are telling us they really like those items and they should have above average profitability.

Conversely, items (or pages) with an 18% promotion expense are not as appealing to customers—and not as profitable to the seller.

The preceding paragraphs give you the foundation for "numbers" thinking in direct mail promotions. As you get involved in intricate product and promotion plans, the quantity of numbers can get very large. And the financial tables and forecasts can seem jungle thick and bewildering. Remember, though, that at the base of any of those tables and calculations there rest some fairly simple concepts that interrelate revenues, expenses and response rates. Look for those basic elements and you will eventually master the "numbers game."

Let's move on and give you another important concept that will help you in planning campaigns.

Contribution to Promotion and Profit

The P & L Worksheet illustrated earlier showed how the Financial or Accounting Department would lay out revenues and expenses—admittedly in a somewhat simplified format. Now we are going to take those basic P & L components and slightly rearrange them so that you can calculate the "Contribution"—a key concept in determining how much response *you need to have* to achieve your campaign objectives.

To start, let's rearrange the P & L you saw on a previous page . . .

Calculation of Contribution to Promotion & Profit
(Refer back to P & L Worksheet)

		Total Dollars	Per Net Sale
Net Income			
1,150 net sales	@$41.90	$48,186	$41.90
Expenses			
1,150 books			
(delv'd cost)	@ 10.00	11,500	10.00
Fulfillment—			
1250 orders	@ 4.10	5,125	4.46
Bad debt—			
2% of sales	@ 41.90	964	.84
Overhead—			
15% of sales	@ 41.90	7,228	6.29
Total		24,817	21.59
Contribution to Promotion and Profit		23,369	20.31
—Per Order (+ 1,250)			18.69

The original P & L Worksheet we reviewed earlier assumed a specific rate of response (2.5%) and showed what the profit would be in that defined situation.

The "Contribution" calculation allows you to determine what response you need depending on what your profit goals are: 15%, 10%, break-even, or even a loss. (It's not unusual for direct marketers to be willing to accept a loss in a promotion designed to acquire new customers. The assumption is that customers will generate more than enough profit later to offset the initial loss and also contribute a handsome profit.)

In the above example, each sale of $41.90 generates "direct" or "volume" expenses of $21.59—which cover cost of goods, fulfillment, bad debt reserve and overhead. That leaves $20.31 as the "contribution" available for (1) promotion and (2) profit.

If all the contribution of $20.31 is spent on promotion, then you have neither lost nor made money. All income taken in has been spent . . . $21.59 on direct expenses . . . $20.31 on promotion. You have acquired a sale, paid something towards your overhead, and maybe you have a new customer. But up to this point you have not made any *profit*.

To make a profit, you will first have to subtract some amount from the total contribution and reserve it for profit. For example, out of a contribution of $20.31 you might reserve:

Reserve for Profit	Profit as % of Net Sales	Which Leaves for Promotion (out of $20.31)	
		Per Sale	Per Order (8% returns)
$2.10	5%	$18.21	$16.75
$4.19	10%	16.12	14.83
$6.29	15%	14.02	12.90

Once you know how much is available for promotion (given "x" direct expenses and "y" reserve for profit), it is easy to determine the response you need.

For example:

Profit Objective	Available Promotion per Order	Cost per Thousand of Mailing	Response Needed Orders per M	% Response
Break-even	$20.31	$300/M	14.77	1.48
5%	16.75	300/M	17.91	1.79
10%	14.83	300/M	20.23	2.02
15%	12.90	300/M	23.26	2.33

In the above table, we have determined that, with a net sale of $41.90 and direct expenses per sale of $21.59:

● The break-even response rate is 1.48%
● The 5% profit response is 1.79%
● The 10% profit response rate is 2.02%
● The 15% profit response rate is 2.33%

Knowing these numbers does not guarantee that any of the given response rates can actually be achieved. Experience and judgment must be applied to evaluate whether such results are probable. And even with experience and historical information available, there is no such thing as a "sure bet." However, at least if inside and outside wisdom tell you that no one has ever secured a response as high as the table says you need, you may avoid getting involved in a disaster. Or proceed in your testing with great caution.

The contribution and response-needed table also illustrates another important direct marketing concept. Namely that it takes very small increases in response to generate large increases in profit. After all, going from 2.02% to 2.33%—a 15% increase in response—increased profits from 10% to 15%, a hefty 50% jump!

It is for this reason that direct marketers test different offers, experiment with different segmentations of mailing lists, define new zip selections, and try new promotion formats and approaches. All in the hope of slightly increasing response and dramatically improving profits.

By this time, you're almost an expert. But it would be a good idea to put down in writing a few formula-relationships you have probably figured out for yourself from all the preceding material.

A Few Basic Formulas

The major numerical promotional elements that a direct marketer is concerned with are

1. The cost of reaching a given audience
   –total dollars
   –cost per thousand
2. The response generated from that audience
   –total number of responses
   –% response (to number mailed)
   –responses per thousand mailed
   OPM: orders per thousand
   SPM: sales per thousand
   IPM: inquiries per thousand
3. The relationship between the promotion cost and the response—which is the promotion cost per response
   CPO: Cost per order
   CPS: Cost per sale
   CPI: Cost per inquiry

These three basic factors can be manipulated to give you promotion productivity requirements—as was already demonstrated in some of the examples in the previous pages. The underlying formulas are these:

1. $\dfrac{\text{Promotional Cost}}{\text{Allowable Cost per Response}} = \text{Response needed}$

   $\dfrac{\text{CPM}}{\text{CPO}} = \text{OPM}$

2. $\dfrac{\text{Promotion Cost}}{\text{Response Estimate}} = \text{Cost per response}$

   $\dfrac{\text{CPM}}{\text{OPM}} = \text{CPO}$

One of the the things you should note from the above two formulas is that CPM—or cost of promotion—is a very important element. It directly affects both response needed and cost per response. That's why you'll find direct mailers trying to decrease costs (in addition to increasing response rates as we mentioned in the previous section). A decrease in promotion cost, with no change in response rate (that *is* possible!), leads to more profit. That's why, too, the large mailer who prints in large quantities has a decided advantage over the small mailer who must pay a much higher CPM for his direct mail packages.

Now that you have some appreciation for the numbers involved in individual campaigns, let's expand that information to one more key direct marketing concept.

The Life Value of a Customer

Any time a marketer talks (as we did earlier) about "break-even or "losing money" on promotions designed to bring in new customers, the question must arise: "when *do* I make a profit and how much?" The corollary is: "how can I determine whether customers acquired at break-even or less are worth acquiring at all?"

These may not be easy questions to answer. The further that profit is removed from the present, the more information you need to build up to the life value of a customer and the less certain you can be that the results will actually be achieved.

Essentially, building up the life value of a customer involves making assumptions about

● What additional offers can be made to the customers after acquisiton (You *do* have additional offers ready, don't you?)

● What percentage response you will get to those offers

● What the dollar value of the orders will be

With the above information, you can calculate sales and profits for a year, two years, five years, ten years, or more. Here's a very simplified example—which looks at just the first half-year or so for a group of new customers:

"Life" Value of a Customer Group

Offer	# Orders	$ Sales	% Profit	$ Profit
1,000 customers acquired at break-even				-0-
Bounceback	4	100	20%	20
Enclosure	5	150	20%	30
List rental		50	50%	25
Solo offer	50	2000	25%	500
Bounceback	4	100	20%	20
Enclosure	5	150	20%	30
List rental		50	50%	25
Solo offer	60	2400	30%	720
Bounceback	4	120	20%	24
Enclosure	5	170	20%	34
List rental		50	50%	25
		5340		1453
				(27% to sales)

The above activity could be accomplished by an aggressive direct marketer in six months . . . so it would not be unrealistic to multiply the final profit column by a factor of 5 or 10 or more to "guesstimate" the projected profit value of the original group of 1000 customers. Some companies actually use computer models to carry out detailed promotion assumptions for years into the future. In those more precise methodologies, assumptions are also made regarding the attrition of the original group of customers—since it obviously woud not be realistic to assume that you would continue to promote to an unchanging number of customers forever.

In the limited examples outlined above, the direct marketer would have to take the x "life value" forecast and blend it with the sales and costs of the initial acquisition promotion. If the over-all results are satisfactory (say, 15%-

20% profit in the long run) then the acquisition of customers at break-even would be justified.

Some of the profit percentages shown in the preceding table may seem a bit high to some of you (20%-25%-30%) but you should know enough about direct mail "numbers" at this point to realize that low CPM's or high response rates can give you very high profit results.

And that's exactly what you get when you re-promote your own customers—low cost opportunities like bouncebacks and enclosures and higher than average response rates. This is because you are going back to your own customers who (we hope!) were satisfied with their last experience with you.

A Closing Word—About Response Rates

In several of the examples used in this booklet we used what is often regarded as a "typical" or "average" response rate. Namely, something around 2%.

Don't let yourself be misled by that number. It may, in fact, be typical for some subscription mailings, book offers and catalog mailings— to outside lists. But response rates vary widely depending on

- The medium (direct mail or space)
- The product (insurance vs. recipe cards)
- The offer (inquiry vs. free trial vs. cash-with-order)
- The price ($195 vs. $39.95)
- The list (customer vs. prospects)

There are other factors too—but these are the main ones. Suffice it to say that normal response can easily vary from .1% (that's 1/10 of 1%—not unusual in insurance or offers in print media) to 50% or more (that's fifty percent, yes—which happens when good catalogs are mailed to long established customers).

The important thing for you to remember is that the really key element in the P & L is the promotion cost per response and what it represents out of the contribution available. CPM is important, yes. Response rate is important, too. But the most important number is the relationship between the two—cost per response and how it fits into your P & L worksheet.

Pierre A. Passavant, "The Dollars & Sense of Direct Mail: Practical Concepts of Math & Finance," Dependable Lists, Inc., New York, 1981. Reprinted by permission of Dependable Lists, Incorporated.

Telemarketing

When to Use Telemarketing . . . And When Not To!

Richard L. Bencin

Knowing how to "mix" telemarketing with the other direct marketing disciplines and marketing channels is often more important than asking whether or not it works. It does work if it's used properly. Even if you're caught in a marketing "deadend," it could be used to investigate, open, and sell new products in brand new markets. Telemarketing methods are categorized as inbound and outbound. The right one for your company depends on your products and services, markets, and special situations. Some caveats: provide complete management commitment to telemarketing; don't mix inbound and outbound; use part-time reps for outbound due to "burnout"; monitor every calling station; provide full-time supervision; develop a professional staff, not just a "boiler room" operation; use professionally prepared scripts.

Telemarketing Generally Works

GENERALLY, TELEMARKETING CAN WORK FOR most companies —almost always. The trick is to know when and how to use it.

Because there have been so many successes and failures with telemarketing (there has been a great deal of empirical experience) knowledgeable marketers should now be able to direct their telephone efforts to the most profitable use.

Assuming the proper application is selected, only the test cell enhancements need to be tested and honed. Examples would be:

- Is Script A better than Script B?
- Which list provides the greatest response?
- Does a prior mailer improve the success of the telephone call, and is it cost justified?
- Which SIC (type business) and size provides the best qualification rate, sale rate and size of order?

When Won't It Work?

Telemarketing should be part of an overall marketing strategy. Sometimes supportive of direct mail, catalog, print/broadcast response and field selling and sometimes used as a replacement for direct sales rep channels, i.e., handling marginal accounts.

Therefore, knowing how to "mix" telemarketing with the other direct marketing disciplines and alternate marketing channels is often more important than asking whether or not it works. However, there are certain types of situations that appear to be less telemarketing prone than others.

Let me try to provide a matrix for low-impact telemarketing application. Consider very technical, highly engineered products; long production development cycle (on part of the customers); very few prospects/customers; history of very close engineering contact/assistance for prospects and customers or very large accounts.

However, any business caught in this "marketing dead-end," should be opening up new product lines for much wider market segments. Having all of your eggs in one basket is certainly not a good, long-term marketing strategy.

Telemarketing, along with other direct marketing techniques, could help to investigate, open and sell new products in brand new markets, which is just the thing for a company with a too narrow client base and esoteric products/services.

Incredible Examples

Business jet companies have utilized telemarketing to sell multimillion dollar business aircraft. One such company uses retired Air Force officers to call Chief Executive Officers (CEOs) to determine their business jet requirements.

Of course, the telephone call merely *qualifies* the CEO for a potential aircraft test ride, but look at the power and potential profit of developing a premier prospect list. A call by an Air Force colonel certainly helps to break the ice and set the stage!

As long as we are on the subject of jet aircraft, how about selling military aircraft via telemarketing?

If you find it ludicrous to think that telemarketing and cable TV could help to sell military aircraft, think again. McDonnell Douglas ran a campaign to sell aircraft on TV with telephone response by running an ad during an Army/Navy football game.

The ad offered a booklet and received 50 replies. However, according to Buck Buchanan of J. Walter Thompson, *all* of the responses were serious requests from people who would influence purchasing!

Another good example of telemarketing expertise was recently evidenced by none other than Chrysler executive Lee Iacocca. Not only is Iacocca an outstanding example of a marketing strategist, but he is also a great spokesman for telemarketing.

While he was still at Ford, he told a reporter that he could pick up the White Pages, pick out any 10 names, call and get at least one demo ride as a prospect. He said this before telephone marketing was telemarketing.

Iacocca Sells Chrysler

But Iacocca doesn't only *talk* telemarketing. Recently, company presidents in the Chicago area were surprised by Iacocca, himself, selling Chryslers. He told them that one of his new Chryslers, with the works, was just rolling off his assembly line, and he offered to inscribe the CEO's name on a gold plate over the dash. The program apparently worked.

Of course, he couldn't make all of the calls himself—it's likely that Iacocca was simply experimenting personally with a telemarketing program—but the potential was clear. A recording of his voice could be used, for example, perhaps introduced live by hundreds of local telephone callers.

In an unrelated fleet sales program, Chrysler in 1982/1983 used qualification telephone calls to corporate owners of 10-plus car fleets to determine their near-term fleet purchases. Local dealers were then provided with hot leads so that their management could call the local executive to sell or lease Chrysler fleets.

The result? A 32 percent sales increase in fleet sales in 1982!

DEC has carried full-page ads in MIS Week with headlines asking: "When was the last time you saved $25,000 on a phone call?" The ads sold $86,000 computers at the 30 percent discount by utilizing an 800 telephone response number.

So, whether you are selling jets, car fleets or expensive computers, telemarketing can help you sell direct. And, I guess if "big ticket" items can be sold in the medium, I'm sure that more conventional industrial products could be sold in the same manner.

Telemarketing Methods

There are many ways to categorize business-to-business telemarketing, but one of the easiest ways is the following:

Outbound
- Handling marginal accounts.
- New account development.
- Market research.
- Lead generation and qualification.
- Collecting overdue accounts.

Inbound
- Direct response. (direct mail, catalog, print/broadcast).
- Customer service.
- Sales order desk.

Which one is right for your company? Of course it really depends upon your product/ services, markets and special situations. But oftentimes a mix of all can be undertaken.

Some caveats:
- Provide complete management commitment to telemarketing, and give it a chance to work.
- Don't mix inbound and outbound telemarketing.
- Consider part-time telephone sales reps for the outbound portion because of "burn-out."
- Make sure you've got complete data processing analysis, tracking and control.
- Provide station monitoring and quality control.
- Insure dedicated telemarketing supervision (not "part-time").
- Integrate telemarketing with other disciplines of direct marketing.
- Create a professional telemarketing staff, not just a "boiler room" operation.
- Utilize creative incentive programs for your telemarketers.
- Make sure you've got professionally prepared scripts (or prompts) and have anticipated questions with appropriate replies.

• Get professional assistance to help set up or enhance your telemarketing operation.

Summary

Yes, telemarketing will generally work if you utilize the proper applications for your individual business. The failures are often misapplied programs or one without proper planning, controls and execution.

My personal experience reflects that most companies are taking a too conservative approach to telemarketing. An example is using lead qualification for field sales when the products could be sold directly over the phone.

With field selling costs going through the roof, more direct marketing, with telemarketing as its centerpiece, should be implemented. However, do get all of the available expertise to help insure the proper positioning of your strategic telemarketing.

Testing telemarketing to see if it works is over—it does! Now is the time to implement telemarketing properly within your own operations. Care, patience and commitment will go a long way to insuring its success.

Richard L. Bencin, "When to Use Telemarketing . . . And When Not To!" *TeleProfessional,* Winter 1986. Reprinted by permission of *TeleProfessional* magazine.

How to Get More Direct Orders

Bob Stone

Telemarketing can be, but seldom is, a stand-alone medium. When complemented by direct mail, the telephone has produced phenomenal results. Of all the applications of the 800 number, none have proved more successful than the toll-free order privileges of catalog buyers. The average order is about 20 percent greater by phone than by mail, due largely to the ability of the order taker to upgrade the sale. Television and telemarketing have been married for some time. Success stories abound, ranging from the famous White Castle Hamburger story to Home Shopping Network, which currently reaches more than 17 million homes. Print advertising combines with telemarketing in ways that range from order taking to dealer location programs. There is no telemarketing application more important than getting qualified leads for salespeople. More so than any other medium, telemarketing has the ability to filter out suspects from prospects. In sum, telemarketing is the catalyst for making any medium work better.

THERE IS A PREVALENT MIND SET THAT TELE-marketing is a stand-alone medium. It can be, but evidence is strong that when telemarketing is integral to an advertising mix, two plus two equals five. The synergism is the source of the bonus.

Telemarketing and Direct Mail

Telemarketers learned early on that if you give direct mail recipients the choice of making a toll-free call or returning a reply card *total response* from the mailing is usually increased by 10 to 20 percent.

The increase in total response is exciting. But the real bonus comes from those who respond by phone in contrast to those who respond by mail. When AT&T keyed mail respondents and phone respondents separately they learned to their delight that sales resulting from phone inquiries were double those from mail inquiries. The bottom line is that phone respondents are better prospects.

The power of the phone, integrated with direct mail, goes beyond commercial endeavors. Philanthropic organizations, for example, have experienced the power of the mail/phone combination.

One of the most prestigious philanthropic organizations in the world is the Memorial Sloan-Kettering Cancer Center in New York City. Their annual operating budget is about $250 million. Their net operating loss is about $14 million. This deficit must be made up by contributions and income from investments.

To test the power of phone integration the center developed a promotion strategy involving three elements:

● A one-page, pre-approach letter to previous donors thanking them for their most recent gift and alerting them to a forthcoming important letter.

● A second letter one week after the first. This three-page letter is signed by Paul A. Marks, M.D., president of Memorial Sloan-Kettering Cancer Center. This letter alerted the prospect to the phone call they would be receiving in a few days and asked that the donor consider a specific amount based upon the donor's giving history.

● Ten days to two weeks later the donor was contacted by telephone and asked for a pledge commitment.

Results were outstanding. Of those reached by phone, 28 percent made a pledge: the average pledge was $277. The actual cost per dollar raised came to only 25 cents. Direct mail warmed the prospects up, telemarketing brought the dollars back.

Telemarketing and Catalogs

Of all the applications of the 800 number none have proved more successful than toll-free phone order privileges for catalog buyers. Amazingly, many catalog marketers are presently getting 50 percent and more of all their orders by phone. But the most dramatic figure is that the average phone order is around 20 percent greater than the average mail order. Thus, if a catalog firm gets an average order of $70 by mail, they can expect an average phone order of $84.

The reason for the larger order is easy to explain. A woman ordering a dress by phone, for example, places the telephone communicator into a natural consultative selling situation. Consider this dialogue:

> Fine, Mrs. Smith. You want size 18 in the royal blue. Have you considered the scarf on page 32, item 1628? This would really look beautiful with royal blue,—Good. I'll include it with your order. Thank you.

There is another unique way to increase the average phone order. Jack Schmid, a catalog consultant in Kansas City, Missouri, came up with this idea when he was catalog manager of Halls, a division of Hallmark.

Schmid printed the following legend in his catalog—"When you place your order by phone, ask our telephone communicator for the special of the week." Dialogue between the customer and the telephone communicator went along these lines.

CUSTOMER: I'd also like to order items 1202 and 1842. Also, I'd like to know what the special of the week is.

COMMUNICATOR: Our special is the set of six tumblers on page 21. You will note the catalog price is $24. Our special this week is $18.

CUSTOMER: OK. Add the tumblers to my order.

This program was a great success. Depending upon the special of the week, up to 29 percent of those who placed phone orders added the special of the week to their orders.

Telemarketing and TV Advertising

Telemarketing and direct response TV have been married for some time. The advent of the 800 toll free number has extended the honeymoon for many.

Success stories abound. But one of the most unusual success stories came from White Castle hamburgers. A Midwestern chain with a loyal following dating back to pre-World War II, White Castle found that thousands of Americans who had been raised on their hamburgers migrated outside of their trading area.

In a brilliant strategic move, Gail Turley, advertising and public relations manager, mounted a direct response TV campaign to the White Castle cult. The theme of the campaign was: "White Castle has the taste some people won't live without." Viewers were urged to phone 1-800 W CASTLE to learn how they could have frozen hamburgers delivered to their homes. They learned that the minimum order was 50 hamburgers for $57. Seventeen percent of the inquiries were converted to orders!

The hottest trend in direct response TV today is, without doubt, shopping at home via cable TV. Home Shopping Network (HSN), based in Clearwater, Florida is the leader. HSN produces two 24-hour programs. The first sells "down-and-dirty," liquidated or overstocked merchandise at huge discounts. The second program sells high-tech merchandise at a discount. HSN will soon be reaching more than 17 million homes.

Programming is reminiscent of the curious barker: there's all the excitement of the most popular game show. It takes 600 toll-free lines to handle the orders—estimated at $63.9 million for 1986. TV and telemarketing, what a combo!

Telemarketing and Print Advertising

The next time you are on a flight, just for the fun of it, pick up a seat pocket copy of an inflight magazine. Then count the ads that contain a toll-free number to get more information or to order.

I'll wager that you will find that somewhere between 70 and 80 percent of all the ads feature toll-free numbers. The practice is standard operating procedure for airlines, car rentals, hotels and credit card firms. Now the practice is becoming common among major banks, finance companies, brokerage houses and insurance companies. Even Ford, Chrysler and General Motors are beginning to see the wisdom of this marketing combination. Making it easy to get more information and making it easy to order is what it's all about.

Dealer locator ads have proved a Godsend for national advertisers. Before the advent of the toll-free number the only way a national advertiser could effectively tell the locations of local dealers was to run regional ads with dealer listings. This was costly and ate up valuable selling space. The toll-free number changed all that. Now one line in a national ad—"Call 1-800 ___ ____ for the name and address of your local dealer" has changed all that.

And national advertisers now carry the dealer locator application to Yellow Pages advertising routinely. Hilton Hotels, using the theme "Now you can make a reservation at any Hilton in the world, using this toll-free number" was among the first to see the value of an 800 number in the Yellow Pages. The dealer locator service soon followed.

Sometimes, of course, there are several dealers within a trading area. So the question arises, how does each dealer in each area get a "fair shake"? The computer has figured this out. Through simple programming, the computer selects dealers sequentially in each area so no one dealer is ever favored over another. Even more sophisticated is a computer program that can select the closest dealer by simply punching in the zip code and census tract of the prospect.

Telemarketing and the Salesforce

Direct mail, catalogs, broadcast, print advertising. All media can and do make telemarketing more cost efficient, more profitable. But regardless of which media or combination of media services is the original source, there is no telemarketing application more important than getting qualified leads for salespeople.

Our constitution states that "All people are created equal." It does not state that all prospects or customers are created equal. They're not!

As a matter of fact, it's a truism that, give or take a few percentage points, 80 percent of all sales come from a 20 percent customer base. And likewise, 80 percent of all new customers come from 20 percent of all inquiries. Telemarketing, more efficiently than any other medium, has the innate ability to filter out *suspects* from *prospects*.

Considering the fact that McGraw-Hill estimates the average industrial sales call today costs in excess of $200, the importance of the sales force devoting its time to qualified leads becomes critical. The advantages are self-evident: the more qualified the leads, the higher the percentage of conversions to sales. The higher the percentage of conversions to sales, the higher the income of each salesperson; and the higher the income of each salesperson, the

higher the caliber of sales person management can attract. It's a compounding advantage.

At AT&T National Sales Center there is continuous testing of the lead qualification process. They have found sketching prospect profiles to be the most effective process. They ask such questions as:

- How many locations does the caller's company have?
- What is the company's annual sales volume; its cumulative growth record?
- Does the company have any expansion plans?
- How much does the company spend annually on long-distance telephone service?

The answers to questions such as these give a clear profile of the prospect. And matching the prospect profile against the *ideal* customer profile tells the telephone communicator exactly how to rate the lead potential as well as what action to take. Any marketer, through experimentation, can construct four or five qualifying questions that will lead to accurate grading of lead potential.

The most efficient way to sort leads is by degree of potential. Here is how one very successful marketer grades leads by potential. And the disposition taken for each grade.

Code	Grading	Disposition
A	High Potential	Refer to sales force
B	Medium Potential	Sell by telephone
C	Low Potential	Resurface at later date
D	No Potential	Acknowledge by mail

Telemarketing is the catalyst with the power to make media work better!

Bob Stone, "How to Get More Direct Orders," *TeleProfessional*, Winter 1986. Reprinted by permission of *TeleProfessional* magazine.

The Mathematics of Telemarketing

BOB STONE
AND JOHN WYMAN

Cost and effectiveness norms can be established for both inbound and outbound telemarketing activities. The range of costs depends on the application and the complexity of the operation. The key norms to establish are cost per phone hour, cost per call, and cost per order (or response in the case of literature requests, product information, etc.). Telemarketing reps can make approximately five times as many decision-maker contacts as a field salesperson, with each call (when fully loaded) costing approximately 15 percent of the field sales call cost. Assuming a marketing task of acquiring 1,000 new customers and a $180.00 sales call cost, it can be shown that these results might possibly be realized through telemarketing for approximately $1.4 million less. Telemarketing should be measured in quantitative and qualitative factors. Qualitative factors such as providing product information, solving customer, wholesaler, and dealer problems, and fulfilling literature requests can often be better done with telemarketing.

THE MEASUREMENT OF SUCCESS IS THE NUMbers. In exploring telemarketing opportunities, it is best to work within a structure that will result in quantitative and qualitative data for the applications to be pursued.

The first step in this process, when exploring a new business opportunity, is to look for numbers that might be used as *norms*. To get these norms, we went to Rudy Oetting, president of R. H. Oetting & Associates, Inc., a leading telemarketing agency in New York City.

Inbound/Outbound Costs

There are two sets of numbers that are key to estimating telemarketing costs: (1) cost per call for handling *inbound* calls from business firms and consumers, and (2) cost per call per decision-maker contact in making *outbound* calls to business firms and consumers. Oetting provided the following range of costs for each.

Approximate Inbound Cost per Call

Category	Range of Cost
Business	$2.50 to $5.00
Consumer	$1.50 to $3.00

Approximate Outbound Costs per Decision-Maker Contact

Category	Range of Cost
Business	$6.00 to $10.00
Consumer	$2.50 to $4.00

The difference in cost range between inbound and outbound calls should be explained. In the case of inbound calls, the initiator is always a prospect or customer: The caller phones at a convenient time with a view to getting further information or negotiating an order. In the case of outbound calls, the initiator is always the marketer: The call may be made at an inconvenient time for the prospect, and the caller may have to generate awareness about a new product or service. Consequently, outbound calls are usually of longer duration and often require more experienced, higher-paid personnel.

The range of costs, whether for inbound or outbound, depends a great deal upon the telemarketing application and the complexity involved for each application. The following table indicates where ranges of costs are most likely to fall, on average, by application.

Application	Low Range	High Range
Order processing	X	
Customer service	X	
Sales support		X
Account management		X
Sales promotion	X	

Developing Worksheets

Knowing the average range of costs for inbound and outbound calls is key, but it is just the start. The operation of an in-house telemarketing center requires a full range of personnel, and is subject to taxes, fringe benefit costs, incentive costs, equipment costs and collateral material costs as well. To get a true picture of all monthly costs, worksheets are advised.

Rudy Oetting has provided us with two representative worksheets: one for inbound (Exhibit 1) and one for outbound (Exhibit 2).

It is easy to see how worksheets lead to capturing all the numbers. The key numbers to explore are (1) cost per phone hour, (2) cost per call, and (3) cost per order (or response). A review of the computations for *Exhibit 1* (inbound) shows a significant difference in cost, for example, when phone representatives are able to handle 15 incoming calls per hour as contrasted to 12 calls per phone hour. And the cost per order drops dramatically if the representative is able to close six orders per phone hour, for example, as contrasted to one per phone hour.

Likewise for *Exhibit 2* (outbound), significant differences are to be noted in costs at differing levels relating to total dialings per phone hour, total decision-maker contacts per phone hour and total orders per phone hour. Such computations provide a realistic approach to determining break-even point.

While these two worksheets relate to the sales of products or services, the same type of arithmetic can be structured to determine likely costs for literature requests, product information, customer service calls, sales support, full account management or sales promotion. The calls handled or made per hour might vary by application, but the principles are the same.

Call Ratios Favor Telemarketing

When comparing outbound sales calls to field sales calls, the pure ratios favor telemarketing. On the average, a field salesperson can make five to six calls a day—25 to 30 a week. On the average, a telemarketing salesperson can make 25 to 30 decision-maker contacts a day (DMCs)—125 to 150 per week.

Put another way, to achieve the same contact level, an average of five field salespeople would have to be added for every telemarketing salesperson.

Sales Cost Comparisons

Using the sales call ratio advantage of telemarketing as a base, sales cost comparisons can be made, using a hypothetical case to illustrate the point.

The Case

A very successful industrial chemical company has built a multimillion-dollar business through the employment of a professional field sales staff. They have identified several SIC categories with prospects too numerous to cultivate. They wish to explore the potential of establishing an in-house telemarketing sales staff whose charge will be to open new accounts in selected SIC categories.

The Starting Point

Knowing that management regards the present cost of acquiring new customers through a field sales force acceptable, the starting point is determining the present cost of acquiring new customers. And then following

EXHIBIT 1. Inbound 9:00 a.m. to 5:00 p.m. Monthly Expense Statement

Representative Phone Hours (1235) Direct Expenses	Cost	Cost/Phone Hour
A. Labor		
Manager (⅓ time)	$ 1,000	$ .81
Supervisor (full time)	2,500	2.02
Representatives (10 full time)	14,300	11.58
Admin. (2 full time)	1,906	1.54
Tax and fringe (⅓ of wages)	7,062	5.72
Incentive	1,500	1.21
Subtotal	$28,268	$22.88
B. Phone		
Equipment and service	500	.40
Lines		
• WATS	15,947	12.92
• MTS (Message Toll Service)	—	—
Subtotal	$16,447	$13.32
C. Other		
Lists	—	—
Mail/Catalogs	2,470	1.00
Postage	1,235	.50
Miscellaneous	1,000	.81
Subtotal	$ 4,705	$ 2.31
Total Direct	49,420	38.51
G&A (15%)	7,413	5.78
Totals	$56,833	$44.29

Basis for Expense Statement: Exhibit 1

Labor

Manager:	Annual = $36,000 × ⅓ allocation = $1,000/month
Supervisor:	Annual = $30,000 at full allocation = $2,500/month
Representatives:	$8.25/hour × 40 hours/week × 52 weeks full allocation = $1,430/month 6.5 phone hours/day × 19 days/month = 123.5 phone hours/ month
Administrative:	$5.50/hour × 40 hours/week × 52 weeks full allocation = $953/month
Tax and fringe:	33.3% of wages (including contest incentives)
Incentives:	Reps Only—$1,500/month

Phone *Step Rate 18 plus Band 5
WATS (800) = 42 minutes (70%) per labor hour
WATS Connect Time: 1,235 hours × 0.70% = 865 billable
WATS hours plus 10 lines @ $36.80/line access

Note: The average number of calls handled per rep phone hour is 12 @ 2.3 minutes each. As high as 15 per phone hour during peaks.

Computations:
1. 12 calls /hour = $3.69/call
2. 15 calls/hour = $2.95/call
3. @ 1 Order/rep; phone hour = $44.29 per order
4. @ 6 Order/rep phone call = $7.38 per order

EXHIBIT 2.   Outbound 9:00 a.m. to 5:00 p.m. Monthly Expense Statement

Representative Phone Hours (1,235) Direct Expenses	Cost	Cost/Phone Hour
A. Labor		
Manager (⅓ time)	$ 1,000	$ .81
Supervisor (full time)	2,599	2.02
Representatives (10 full time)	13,000	10.53
Admin. (2 full time)	1,906	1.54
Tax and fringe (⅓ of wages)	9,015	7.30
Incentive	8,667	7.01
Subtotal	$36,088	$29.21
B. Phone		
Equipment and service	350	.28
Lines:		
● WATS	12,729	10.31
● MTS (Message Toll Service)	3,075	2.50
Subtotal	$16,154	$13.09
C. Other		
Lists	3,088	2.50
Mail/Catalogs	617	.50
Postage	309	.25
Miscellaneous	1,235	1.00
Subtotal	$ 5,249	$ 4.25
Total Direct	$57,491	$46.55
G&A (15%)	8,624	6.98
Totals	$66,115	$53.53

Basis for Expense Statement: Exhibit 2

Labor

Manager:	Annual = $36,000 × ⅓ allocation = $1,000/month
Supervisor:	Annual = $30,000 at full allocation = $2,500/month
Representatives:	$7.50/hour × 40 hours/week × 52 weeks full allocation = $1,300/month
	6.5 phone hours/day × 19 days/month = 123.5 phone hours/month
Administrative:	$5.50/hour × 40 hours/week × 52 weeks full allocation = $953/month
Tax and fringe:	33.3% of wages (including contest incentives)
Incentive:	Reps Only—40% of Total Renumeration

Phone *Step Rate 18 plus Band 5

WATS =	35 minutes (50%) per labor hour WATS connect time: 1,235 hours × 0.50% = 617 billable WATS hours plus 10 lines @ $31.65/line access

MTS

(Message Toll Services) =	5 minutes per labor hour connect time: 1,235 × 8.3% = 102.5 Message Toll @ 0.50 Min. = $3,075

Computatations:
1. @ 12 TDs (total dialings) per rep phone hour cost per dial = $4.46
2. @ 15 TDs (total dialings) per rep phone hour cost per dial = $3.57
3. @ 5 DMCs (decision-maker contacts) per phone hour cost per DMC = $10.71
4. @ 6 DMCs (decision-maker contacts) per phoen hour cost per DMC = $8.92
5. @ 1 Order per rep phone hour cost per order = $55.53
6. @ 3 Orders per rep phone hour cost per order = $17.84

through to determine at what point the company recoups its original investment and reaches the break-even point.

The Assumptions

For this hypothetical industrial chemical company, we will punch in the following assumptions:

1. The cost per field sales call has been computed at $180 each.

2. On the average, five field sales calls to bona fide prospects are necessary to acquire one new customer.

3. A total of three sales calls are made on each customer over a 12-month period.

4. The average order written by the field sales force comes to $1,000.

5. The gross profit per order comes to $500.

6. For each 1,000 new customers acquired, 50 percent will order three times the first year; the other 50 percent will not repeat.

7. Of the 50 percent who become active customers the first year, 70 percent of those will remain active customers the second year, each reordering three times.

First-Year Results

Using the set of assumptions, let's now compute the investment on behalf of the field sales force in acquiring 1,000 new customers (see Chart A).

Very simply, the company has an original investment of $400,000 for each 1,000 new customers acquired by the field sales force, or an investment of $400 for each new customer.

But the 12-month cycle has just begun. According to the assumptions, two more calls will be made on each new customer before the first year of activity is completed. Chart B shows where the company stands at the end of the first year.

There's improvement. The investment for each 1,000 new customers is down to $260,000, or $260 per customer. But we haven't broken even. So we go into year two. Now the attrition rate drops off, and 70 percent of remaining customers repeat three times during the second year (see Chart C).

Obviously, two years is the magic period. For all practical purposes, the break-even point comes early in the third year. And with a hard core of regular customers having been "paid for," substantial black ink can be expected by the end of the third year.

Having computed these figures, the next logical step would be to use the norm of setting a goal for an in-house telemarketing sales operation.

The Differences

In computing figures for an in-house telemarketing sales operation, the major difference in cost involves the difference in number of calls per day by a field staff compared to an in-house telemarketing staff. So, if averages prevail, each member of the field staff would make five calls per day at a cost of $180 each. We'll assume each member of the telemarketing staff will make 30 decision-maker contacts per day at a cost of $10.71 each. (See "Computations" for Basis for Expense Statement: Exhibit 2.)

Obviously, results by phone need not be anywhere near as productive because of the differences in selling costs. The difference is shown in Chart D.

Time Compression Potential

Building on our hypothetical case, let us now explore the time compression potential as it relates to acquiring 1,000 new customers. Our assumptions are as follows.

1. Our objective is to acquire 1,000 new customers.

2. On the average, five field sales calls are necessary to acquire one new customer.

A. Cost and Revenue Involving Acquisition of 1,000 New Customers

	Cost		*Revenue*
5,000 field calls @ $180 each	$900,000	1,000 orders @$1,000	$1,000,000
		Less Cost of Goods	500,000
		Gross Profit	$ 500,000
		Less Sales Cost	900.000
		Investment Total	(400,000)
		Investment per New Customer	$ 400

B. Cost and Revenue from Making Two Additional Follow-up Calls

	Cost		*Revenue*
2,000 field calls @ $180 each	$360,000	Two additional orders @ $1,000 each from 500 customers	$1,000,000
		Less Cost of Goods	500,000
		Gross Profit	$ 500,000
		Less Sales Cost	360,000
		Profit on Repeat Business	$ 140,000
		Less Investment in New Accounts	400,000
		Investment First Year	($ 260,000)

C. Year Two for Original Group of 1,000 Customers

	Cost		*Revenue*
1,500 field calls @ $180 each	$270,000	Three additional orders @ $1,000 each from 350 customers	$1,050,000
		Less Cost of Goods	525,000
		Gross Profit	$ 525,000
		Less Sales Cost	270,000
		Profit on Repeat Bus.	$ 255,000
		Less First Year Investment	260,000
		End of Second Year	($ 5,000)

D. Difference In Cost

	Telemarketing	*Field Force*
Prospecting	5,000 DMC calls @ $10.71 ea.	5,000 calls @ $180
Repeat Business	3,500 calls @ $10.71 ea.	3,500 calls @ $180
Costs		
Field Force	8,500 calls @ $180 =	$1,530,000
Telemarketing	8,500 DMC calls @ $10.71 =	$ 91,035
	Cost Difference	$1,438,965

3. Field sales personnel will make five calls a day.

4. Telemarketing sales personnel will make 30 decision-maker contacts a day.

5. Both the field sales representatives and the telemarketing staff have a work year of 250 days (50 weeks × 5 days per week).

6. It is assumed that the field sales staff and the telemarketing staff will be equally sales-efficient.

Field Sales Situation. Some 1,000 man-days are needed to make 5,000 calls and thereby yield 1,000 new customers. If each representative makes five calls a day, it will take four field salespeople one year to complete the task.

Telemarketing Situation. Using four sales specialists in a telemarketing center—sales efficiency being equal—making 30 decision-maker contacts a day, the same objective of 1,000 new customers will be reached in two months instead of 12 months. (And, of course, repeat business will materialize faster.)

The Question of Sales Efficiency

Our hypothetical case raises many questions:

1. Will the closure ratio of the telephone staff be the same as the field staff: one new customer, on average, for each five calls?

2. Will the first order come to $1,000 from phone solicitation?

3. Will 50 percent of telephone-acquired customers buy twice more the first year?

4. Will 70 percent of the repeat customers from the first year repeat three times the second year at an average purchase of $1,000?

Only testing and time will provide the answers to these critical questions. But the favor-

able cost ratios of telemarketing say clearly that the sales efficiency need not be anywhere near that of a field staff to result in a more favorable bottom line.

Attacking the Marginal Account Problem

In the real sales world, it is rarely a case of considering field sales *or* telemarketing: More often than not, it is a case of considering field sales *and* telemarketing. Most of all sales organizations find that their customers break into three categories:

1. High-profit customers
2. Average-profit customers
3. Marginal-profit customers

It is in the marginal-profit customer category that the opportunity exists to change the numbers favorably for the entire sales organization. To explore this potential, let us structure another hypothetical case.

The Case

The ABC Company has a current list of 3,000 customers. One-third of their accounts are judged to be marginally profitable (i.e., this category does not result in the company's targeted profit of 15 percent). At present, sales calls made by the field force are scheduled as follows:

High-Profit Customers—twice a month
Average-Profit Customers—once a month
Marginal-Profit Customers—once every other month

Sales calls are estimated to cost $130 per call, well below the national figure of $205.40 per call.

Annual cost of sales calls—marginal accounts

1,000 customers × 6 calls per year = 6,000 calls @ $780,000 total cost

If Telemarketing Is Used

Assume these marginal accounts are turned over to a telemarketing center. And assume further that instead of a cost of $10.71 per decision-maker contact, used in the previous hypothetical case, a fully loaded cost of $20 per contact will be applied. The numbers look like this:

1,000 customers × 6 calls per year
= 6,000 calls @ $20 = $120,000 total cost
Profit improvement—$660,000

Chances for Success

Since our telemarketing contact costs are only 15.4 percent of those of the field force, chances for success are exceptional. And unlike our previous case, that called for the telemarketing center to open new accounts without previous field force contact, here the center would be servicing existing customers established by the field force. So the task of maintaining sales by phone would be simplified. Assuming equal productivity, this category of accounts would change from *marginal* to *high profit,* far exceeding the 15 percent profit goal.

But the advantages wouldn't end there, because the telemarketing center would have freed the field force from 6,000 sales calls. This would open the door for more calls throughout the year to high-profit and average-profit customers, thus resulting in more sales and profits.

Developing a Measurement System

Telemarketing should be measured on both a quantitative and qualitative basis. Quantifying sales is a simple matter. But qualifying factors should not be overlooked, such as more time available to call upon better customers.

Qualitative factors become major considerations when measuring the value of telemarketing applications such as providing product information, solving customer, wholesaler and dealer problems, fulfilling literature requests, making telemarketing a part of the sales promotion process and gathering market research data as part of the telemarketing process.

The GE Answer Center—a free telephone service provided by General Electric that allows consumers to call with their questions or comments about products before or after they buy them—shows the way to measure qualitative factors. When Powell Taylor, manager of the center, was asked, "How do you know that the millions of dollars spent in building and maintaining the Center have been worth it?" he cited these measurement factors: "Surveys have shown that 95 percent of the callers to the center express satisfaction with the service."

Speaking of the impact of the program on dealers, Taylor cited surveys that showed that "more than 99 percent of surveyed dealers regard The GE Answer Center to be a 'super idea'." These qualitative factors have convinced GE's top management that the program represents a competitive advantage for them.

An often-asked question is, "Is the cost of providing literature by phone request rather than by mail request justified?" How does one measure this? Surveys can give qualitative and quantitative answers: "Did you get the literature promptly? Did you get our literature quicker than other literature you might have requested by mail? Did our response prompt you to go to a dealer? Did you buy?" Answers to such questions will provide qualitative and quantitative measurement, but with no basis of comparison.

To get comparative answers, controlled tests are indicated. To construct controlled tests, parallel markets should be selected. Market A advertising, for example, would offer literature by mail request only. Market B advertising would offer literature by either toll free phone request or mail request.

Research would ask the same questions and make the same analysis for both markets. Such research would provide a measurement of: 1) total literature requests from Market A versus Market B, 2) total cost per request from Market A versus Market B, and 3) total sales from Market A versus Market B. Most marketers who have tested phone requests against mail requests have found that phone requests come from more qualified prospects, resulting in more sales at the dealer level.

Success is measured by numbers. Telemarketing is measurable, quantifiable, and qualifiable. The numbers count.

Bob Stone and John Wyman, "The Mathematics of Telemarketing," *Direct Marketing* magazine, December 1986. Excerpted with permission from *Successful Telemarketing*, by Bob Stone and John Wyman (NTC Business Books, Lincolnwood, Illinois, 1986).

Telemarketing SOS
Rudy Oetting
and Brad Turley

Telemarketing has gained a high profile as an effective marketing medium. However, there are some disturbing patterns and trends we should be concerned about. Too often, marketing and sales development practitioners take the flawed view that the telephone is a means of reducing cost of whatever activity is involved. Furthermore, they do not understand that telephone sales are different than field sales and therefore organize themselves ineffectively. The cost reduction view, as opposed to the traditional sales and revenue-enhancing roles, is a reason that the field has low attraction for "fast track" executives, and, worse still, leads to the conclusion that cost reduction means "low cost," virtually guaranteeing minimum results and low quality. When telemarketing is viewed only as a cost

reducer the major telemarketing investment is channeled into automation. The human relationship is placed second to technological support. Finally, the impact of illegal "scams" far exceeds their numbers, generating a flurry of legislation. Telemarketers can't control the scams, but they can control their own quality and ethics. The collective voice of telephone marketers must be heard if an antitelemarketing legislative trend is to be reversed.

WHILE THE USE OF THE TELEPHONE IN MARKETing and sales is not new, the economic, social, and technological developments of the past 15 years have caused the telephone to gain a high profile as a potentially effective marketing medium or sales channel. In addition, organizations such as the Telephone Marketing Council of the Direct Marketing Association (1973), the American Telemarketing Association (1984), as well as Bell and AT&T ad campaigns, numerous seminars, trade shows, and local groups are helping to shape what could become a major industry.

But there are some disturbing patterns and trends that we should be concerned about if the tremendous potential of this industry is to be fully developed. Interestingly these trends are all linked:

1. There continues to be severe constraints on quality telephone marketing and sales development by those corporate practitioners who:

● choose to view the telephone strictly as a means of reducing the cost of sales and leads, or as a unit cost of doing business (order handling and customer service);

● do not understand that telephone sales are *different* from field sales and therefore organize themselves ineffectively.

2. Legislation is gaining momentum, and

other than the yeoman lobby efforts of the DMA, there has been little other meaningful activity to-date.

The result of these roadblocks and the link of commonality is *limited investment in human resources* at all levels from management and supervision, to telephone representatives and support personnel. Since the power of the telephone medium or channel is one human being in a transactional relationship with another, that lack of human investment will provide minimum quality performance which in turn will heighten consumer irritation and increase the legislative momentum.

Cost Reduction

Viewed strictly as a means of cost reduction, as opposed to the traditional marketing and sales role of increasing revenue, a telephone marketing or sales unit will not attract the "fast track" executives who are essential to the long-term success of almost any corporate venture. Worse, such cost reduction will often be misinterpreted to mean "low cost." And thus the operation will be organized, staffed, built, and run on a low-cost basis, almost guaranteeing minimum results and poor quality.

Telephone marketing will also be positioned as a second-class citizen particularly with regard to field sales. The result will be that everyone in the operation aspires to be "promoted out of" telephone marketing, a situation which will continually drain the small resources available—again, a self-fulfilling prophecy.

Unit Costs

On the incoming call side, most telephone marketing units (including customer service) still report to the operations and administration functions, and not the marketing function. As such, they continue to be looked upon as unit costs of doing business: low cost personnel, high supervisor to rep ratios, little training and fast phone calls.

Rather, these units should be viewed as short and long-term revenue opportunities. In the short term, a trained, qualified, and effectively supervised rep can increase the average revenue per order and convert inquiries to orders; in the long term, customers can be maintained through a proactive, market-driven approach to service handled by those same highly-qualified and supervised reps—a positively fulfilled prophecy.

When an organization views its telemarketing efforts only in a cost-focused manner, the major investments, if any, are channeled into automation. The thrusts are usually several: reduced labor requirements, increased dials or calls per hour, controls and measurements, and verbatim scripts. Certainly there are benefits to this approach. But too often the means become the end.

The human relationship is placed second to the technological support. The computer takes the place of supervision. The reps have no sense of value, particularly when more attention is paid to the system than to them. The customers feel they are talking to a computer.

Telephone versus Field Sales

Often companies do invest solidly in the start-up of their telephone marketing and sales operations. Unfortunately these operations are organized, staffed, and run almost identically as a field sales force, a force which can be their undoing or which, at the very least, can be a critical limitation. The two channels are very different in presentation techniques, territory management, supervision, support requirements, productivity, and measurements.

Service Bureau versus Agency

Typical examples of what we have come to know as service bureaus are really computer data processing firms and medical labs. In these industries, these bureaus provide the service of processing data or materials and returning them to the customer in a specified format. These firms provide no interpretation or recommendations about the data. Most importantly, none of the employees in these companies are involved in conducting high volume, customized human transactions with their clients' customers.

Therefore, the fact that the nearly 400 third-party telephone operations do label themselves as service bureaus is costing them and the whole industry dearly. In 1970, the average cost per outbound rep hour was $25 to $30 for an average volume program in the business sector. Factoring for a 2.5 inflation, the current rate would provide a current billing range of $71 to $86 per hour. Right now, however, services are being sold for 35 percent of what they were in 1970.

The ramifications of this situation are several: the client doesn't get the best job possible and is therefore not educated to the true power of the medium. These service bureaus can't and don't invest in their single most important long term asset—people, because the profits are limited.

Finally, the perception of the service bureau deteriorates to "boiler room" status, which leads to legislative problems (below).

For example, a full-service telephone marketing agency develops, tests and implements complete telephone marketing programs for their clients directly or through their advertising agencies. In addition, these firms provide consulting services to do the same development work on the client's own in-house operation.

The practice of using outside suppliers is becoming more prevalent in all lines of business. Therefore, we expect that many client firms will start to develop and maintain a staff that coordinates, directs, and manages telephone agencies. These relationships will be similar to the relationships they have with their advertising agencies. The change from an internal to an external agency or the use of an external agency as a supplement will provide them with a more variable expense item, less

labor and benefit problems, and improve overall results.

Legislation

There is no question that the impact of illegal scams far outweighs their numbers. But even the efforts of legitimate telemarketing practitioners can't control these scams. What we can control is quality and ethics. Because of our volume, we should be able to prevent most legislation, which would adversely affect legitimate telemarketers. But, the current legislation problems facing telemarketing are broad. Laws are being passed at the state and local level, and they cover a wide variety of concerns. These laws range from taxing telephone marketers' usage in Illinois, registrating reps in California, to requiring call introduction in Utah.

The efforts of the DMA will continue to address these legislative issues in a positive way. The association's ability to identify potential legal conflicts significantly contributes to the industry's ability to deal with problems prior to legal action. In addition to the DMA's lobbying efforts, the Telephone Marketing Council continues to educate the industry.

The recent formation and acceptance of the American Telemarketing Association demonstrates that telephone marketers are interested in working together to solve their problems. We expect this organization to become an effective forum in the next several years.

We also expect that the collective voice of the telephone marketers will start to reverse the recent flurry of legislation. The concern demonstrated by these associations, an internal industry commitment to eliminate unethical practices, and an improved perception and acceptance of the telephone marketing industry by the public will reduce future legislative action.

Rudy Oetting and Brad Turley, "Telemarketing SOS," *ZIP Target Marketing*, March 1986. Reprinted by permission of *Target Marketing* magazine, published by North American Publishing Company.

Case
Analysis and
Presentation

Introduction to Case Analysis and Presentation

THIS SECTION OFFERS SOME SUGGESTIONS THAT ARE DESIGNED TO assist you in your case analysis and presentation efforts. Case analysis guidelines are presented first, followed by an interesting and useful article by Ron Hoff on how to make an interesting, and good, presentation.

Guidelines for Case Analysis

Although they may vary in length, scope, and degree of difficulty, different cases have many things in common and can be approached using the same general analytical framework.

There are five main stages in a well-developed case analysis.

1. Identification and specification of the problem or objective
2. Appraisal of the facts and opinions expressed in the case
3. Development of alternative approaches to the case problem
4. Selection and justification of best approach
5. Discussion of implementation schedule and organizational responsibilities

A brief discussion of the contents of each stage of the analysis follows:

Stage 1—*Identification and Specification of Problem or Objectives.* Defining the problem at hand and the objectives that are being sought for in a program are perhaps the most important aspects of case preparation. Usually, if these are ill-defined, the entire study can be considered useless.

Defining the problem is not quite as simple as one might expect because of the number of similarities between the underlying problems and their symptoms. Care must be taken to accurately distinguish between the two. Treating the problem should lead to a cure, but treating the symptoms will, at best, lead only to a temporary remission. A precise, tightly written statement of the case problem should be presented for each case.

Care must also be taken to distinguish between objectives for each of the components of the marketing effort, and between overall objectives and subobjectives. Product and pricing and list objectives are not the same as positioning objectives, for example, and each objective is reached within a specific component of the program, not the overall program. Together these combine to achieve program goals.

Stage 2—*Appraisal of Facts and Opinions.* Well-developed cases are built on a careful appraisal of the relevant facts and upon a cautious and selective interpretation of the opinions and organizational interrelationships uncovered in this stage. Information provided to you in the text should not be treated as "gospel." Never forget that human beings, with all of their biases, prejudices, and perceptual hang-ups are involved. A business is not a machine.

Stage 3—*Development of Alternative Approaches.* Although plans of action include a wide range of specific recommendations, all can be placed under the general headings of organizational structure and marketing actions. Organizational structure changes include, for example, a change in the personnel staffing of a particular function, such as list selection. Marketing mix changes involve alterations in the structure of the offer, list or data-base segment to be targeted, creative approach, package format, and the like. Numerous combinations of these types of changes may be potential solutions, or selections for solving the problem at hand. Each of these alternatives merit your comment on the "how" and "why" aspects of the choice.

Stage 4—*Selection and Justification of the Most Promising Alternative.* After you have examined in some depth the various alternatives at hand, the time has come for the selection and justification of the one you believe to be the most promising. Your decision must be substantiated by a logical, data-based set of suggestions and recommendations.

Your selection of the best alternative may be rather difficult for a variety of reasons. Information may be incomplete and time pressures great. Such is life in the direct marketing business world. These problems are recognized by the instructor, but they are unacceptable as excuses for not completing a case assignment. The student is expected to cope with the situation, to make and state the necessary assumptions, and to complete the case as if he or she were on the job.

Stage 5—*Implementation of Strategy.* Once the case analyst has chosen the best alternative solution, his or her attention must be turned to the implementation of the strategy required. Such elements as timing, organizational reaction, competitive reaction, resource requirements and availability, performance standards, methods of measuring and tracking performance, and the like, must be considered. Each of these elements, and any others that are pertinent to a particular case, must be analyzed in depth, and explicit recommendations for completion of each must be included in the case presentation.

Case Presentation

Cases may be presented in both written and verbal forms and may be prepared by individuals and by groups of peers. The prime criteria for evaluation of case presentations, in whichever mode, are the quality of the analysis *and* the communicative power of the presenter.

Written Cases

Written presentations may be written out in full or in outline form. A good topical outline for written or oral case analysis contains consideration of the five stages of case analysis previously presented. The case write-up should be concise and well organized. The following is a general format for written case development.

    I. Objectives
   II. Problems
 III. Changes to be made in the marketing program, or areas where actions must be planned and taken
    A. Product and Premium
    B. Price
    C. Media
    D. Lists
    E. Offer
    F. Package Format
    G. Testing
    H. Analysis
    I. Performance Standards

IV. Additional Research Needed

V. Conclusions

Evaluation of the presentation will consider the following dimensions:

1. Appearance, grammar, organization, and form. Such items as clarity of expression, sentence and paragraph structure, and readability will be judged.

2. Problem definition, objective setting, and fact identification. Such items as ability to distinguish between problems and symptoms, between subarea and program objectives, and between fact and opinion will be assessed.

3. Alternative selection and evaluation. Such elements as completeness, substantiation, and creativity of alternative identification selection will be reviewed. The skill used in critiquing each alternative will be judged.

4. Selection and implementation. Such items as the precision of strategy statement and the completeness of implementation considerations will be made. Weakness in this area is as harmful as weakness in the problem/objective definition areas.

Oral Presentations

Oral presentations, often difficult for students, are an important aspect of the learning process. Portraying ideas *persuasively* but *tactfully* is a delicate process the mastery of which can only be obtained through practice.

The oral presentations required will generally be in conjunction with written casework. Evaluation of oral presentations will be based on the following criteria:

1. Organization of presentation

2. Content (quality and thoroughness)

3. Quality of visual aids (visual aids are strongly recommended)

4. Speaking voice (delivery)

5. Courtesy to audience

6. Ability to answer questions

7. Posture, poise

8. Ability to defend position

9. Persuasive impact

10. Mannerisms

11. Practicality of recommendations

THE PRAY-ER
Folds hands in front of body; looks as though he's praying to just make it through.

THE KEY EXECUTIVE
Fiddles with keys, coins and other wonderful things found in pockets.

THE JEWELER
Plays with ring, watch, etc.

THE STERN PARENT
Stands with arms crossed over chest.

THE FIG LEAF
Stands with hands folded in front much as Adam must have looked in his first outfit.

THE SOLDIER AT PARADE REST
Holds hands behind back.

DISHPAN HANDS
Conceals hands in pocket so no one can see them.

THE ATHLETIC TYPE
Demonstrates athletic prowess with a running series of jabs, punches, upper cuts, karate chops, etc.

EXHIBIT 1. Mannerisms to *watch* and *watch out for*
Source: Adapted from *Personal Selling Power,* July/August 1984, pp. 8–9. Reprinted by permission of Bryan Flanagan of the Zig Ziglar Corporation and author of the "Effective Business Presentation" seminar.

Group Presentations   Group work is a vital part of a management preparatory course. We are all well acquainted with the problems and frustrations associated with group work. These problems, however, are not exclusive to students. They extend far into the "real" business world where one must contend with them on a daily basis. Therefore, students will be placed into working groups for completion of the assigned group cases. Individual roles, leadership functions, and the division of labor will be left up to the individual groups. Each student is, however, expected to make a visible contribution to each group project.

Other Suggestions for Doing Cases

You should approach cases as an analytical, decision-oriented, managerially/operationally relevant experience.

Doing a case is *analytical* in that you take a situation apart, study its components, draw individual conclusions, and put them together in an overall solution. Beware of brilliant flashes of intuitive genius. Intuition can lead you to creative paths of analysis or novel conclusions and/or solutions. However, intuitive flashes can blind you to errors in logic. Whenever you take an intuitive step, look back to see if there is any logical support for your step in terms of combinations of several bits of data from the case, a single bit of case data, combinations of suggestions from the case, a single suggestion from the case, your own carefully considered experience, or a combination of these considerations. In other words, look for evidence to bolster your argument. If you can find none, you can still include the idea. Be sure to state that it is intuitive. Don't be surprised if someone asks, "Says who?"

A *decision orientation* means that in each case you have to come to a decision. Your analysis should provide the basis for determining what decisions have to be made (i.e., the best alternative). No one course of actions will be all good or all bad. Consequently you should note the strengths and weaknesses of each. You must choose a course, explain why you chose it, and why you rejected alternative courses. Your reasoning should be supported by case data, not simply intuition. The data that support your decision should be part of your presentation. You may want to hedge your bet by presenting a contingency plan, if you are very uncertain about your choice. Or you may want to admit that your choice was based on what you consider to be inadequate data. (You can make assumptions to supplement case data, but be sure they are reasonable and that in your presentation you identify them as assumptions.) In the end, however, you must choose and recommend a specific course of action, regardless of how difficult the choice may be. Remember taking no action is a choice.

Your case analysis should be *managerially/operationally relevant.* Although your analysis and thought process may have been very sophisticated and abstract, your conclusion must be a concrete guide to management action. Your choice of a course of action should go beyond platitudes like, "Research should be done to measure consumer reactions," "Share of market should be increased," or "The advertising department should be upgraded." The manager wants to know your recommendations regarding "how." In other words, your recommendations or chosen course of action should tell him what to do Monday morning, next week, next year, and so on.

To evaluate your own efforts, pretend your analysis and recommendations have just been presented to you by one of your subordinates. Ask yourself, "Does this action plan help me know what to do to solve my problems, and is it presented and supported in such a way that I am confident it is a well-reasoned (rather than simple intuitive) approach?"

Attacking a Case

A case analysis requires a bare minimum of two readings and two thought periods. The following are suggestions regarding what to do during each period.

Reading 1: This is the time to get familiar with the company, its products, its industry, company people and their perception of the problem. Look particularly for things like unusual elements in the industry or its products which would affect company operations. Identify the company's objectives, goals, size, position in the industry, and competitive strengths and weaknesses. Also become aware of company personnel's strengths and weaknesses. At all times watch for signals of potential problem areas. Remember, management may not see the central problem.

Thought 1: Identify from your list of potential problems (or combinations of the first problems) the central problem(s). This is the problem that must be solved first. One way to identify it is to ask of each potential problem you have uncovered, "What causes this problem?" You will find that many problems are caused by a few elements (which are not caused by other elements). This is the central problem. Other problems are symptoms of it.

Of course, you need evidence to support your opinion. Therefore, at this point think of the questions which have to be answered if you are to (a) support your ideas of what the central and peripheral problems are, and (b) develop and support a course of action. Then determine the information you would need to answer the questions. Now you have a guide for the next meeting.

Reading 2: Search for the data you need to answer your questions. Remember that you may have to assemble information on several elements in the case, and do some calculations to develop a bit of the data you need. So don't give up if the information you need is not readily available. Also remember that you may want to change your identification of the central problem on the second reading.

Thought 2: This is the point where you put your conclusions together.

Writing a Case Analysis There are many ways to put together the case write-up. The order in the format below is only a suggestion. In one order or another, however, you should cover all the elements listed.

1. The problem—a brief statement of how you view central problems, peripheral problems, and why you view them as you do
2. Recommendation—your chosen course of action
3. Alternative—the course you did not choose (Elements 2 and 3 probably will be brief summaries to be expanded in 4 and 5.)
4. Why this choice—the chosen course's strengths and weaknesses in terms of the company's objectives and capabilities
5. Why not the alternatives—the alternative course's strengths and weaknesses in terms of the company's objectives and capabilities

Remember the two cardinal rules:

1. *Always* (if humanly possible) support your argument with relevant data from the case.
2. *Never* rehash the case.

It is also useful to use a check sheet to insure that you have touched all the bases. (See Strategic Planning Process Outline following.)

Strategic Planning Process

   I. Gather all potential sources of information
  II. Write general situation statement
     A. Comprehensive, but not deep
     B. Subjects in order of background index
     C. Written by plan manager
     D. Free flowing, after scanning all readily available background data
  III. Write a product definition
     A. What is it and what it does only
     B. Lean and skeletal
     C. "Product" used generally

IV. Marketing margins determined—preplanning mathematics
- A. Compute contribution to promotion and profit, and then breakeven response rate
- B. Develop pro forma P&L
- C. Ferret out industry response rates for "most similar" products with same price points
- D. Factor future customer value into analysis

V. Perform needs analysis
- A. Write "top-of-the-mind statement" about potential customer need
- B. Use list of basic customer needs to generate additional ideas
- C. Describe needs ideas more specifically
- D. Rank needs
- E. Rewrite top-of-mind statement of needs again

VI. Perform competitive analysis
- A. Identify direct and indirect competitors
- B. Develop summary competitors chart listing competitors in order by sales volume of specifically competitive products
- C. Create a comprehensive written précis for each competitor
  - 1. Media used
  - 2. Control offer and theme, others
  - 3. Marketing methodology
  - 4. Marketing budget and expenditures
- D. Distribute précis, summary, and samples to core-group members prior to assessment meeting

VII. Establish level of need perception
- A. Core-group members individually write perception of need evaluation
- B. Core group does adversary rap and ranks perception of need
- C. Rewrite perception of need
- D. Determine confidence level of perception of need
- E. If confidence level not extraordinarily high, indicate types of research needed, and list information objectives very specifically

VIII. Identify customer profiles
- A. Determine if any linear or cluster characteristics have impact on response levels

       1. Regression analysis
       2. Zip analysis
       3. Census tract analysis
       4. Other computer generated analysis
  B. Core group members individually study and review all profile related data vacuum cleaned to date
  C. Identify any key areas not yet searched and/or analyzed for assignment to core group member for vacuum cleaning
  D. Individuals jot down top-of-mind characteristics and conditions that relate to response for product from the five benchmark categories
       1. Response graphics
       2. Demographics
       3. Geographics
       4. Psychographics
       5. Special graphics
  E. Core group reviews each benchmark category for possible omissions
  F. Individuals combine characteristics and conditions into brief written thumbnail statements of discreet profiles of individuals or households
  G. Core group lists all profiles, then grid evaluates them, discusses and prioritizes profiles
  H. Specify profile research if confidence level not sufficiently high after previous phase
  I. Test standard approaches or existing control against combined profile
  J. Perform computerized multivariate analysis in parallel whenever possible

IX. Build customer profiles into market segments
  A. List profiles in order of ranking
  B. Define market geographically on basis of existing distribution reach (not media reach) for each profile
  C. Segment that geographic whole by any relevant special conditions (special graphics) other than standard demographics, psychographics, or response data for each profile
  D. Apply master demographic overlay to each segment when profile includes household demographics, and identify density of profile per SMSA (Standard Metro-

politan Statistical Area) and/or ADI (Area of Dominant Influence) within geographic segment

E. Categorize, search out, and evaluate all responder, psychographic, and occupation lists and other media

F. Prioritize lists and media

G. Core group explores all list grafting potentials

H. Core group evaluates media reach, efficiency, and effectiveness for each profile/segment

I. Quantify each market segment by reachable populations within each profile

X. Diagram the buying process for each profile/segment

A. Identify each person who could conceivably be an influence during the buying process for each profile/segment

B. Identify the exact function each influential person would perform during the process. Will person influence, recognize need, evaluate product, recommend product, select brand, approve purchase, or influence in another way?

C. Prioritize the buying influences

XI. Focusing benefits

A. Core group rap and free associate benefits and write down as they occur

B. Prioritize the benefits and isolate prime benefit

C. Determine if prime benefit is a unique selling proposition

D. Apply prime benefit to each profile/segment and each buying influence in that profile's/segment's buying process

E. Apply each succeeding benefit to each profile and each buying influence

F. Write a summary of each "benefits–profile-buying influences" tree

XII. Evaluate marketing database and back-end resources needed

A. Format (content and sequence) the most important marketing reports needed

B. Indicate all back-end capabilities needed, current state of applicability, and specify any resources needed

XIII. Write background summary

A. Written précis of all information acquired and assessed

prior to commencing strategy development
  B. Address all subjects from background index in sequence
  C. Should contain no detail whatsoever—brief
XIV. Develop the objectives
  A. Determine what phase we are in—related to product or service
      1. Entry level
      2. Rollout and second-stage testing
      3. Maturing market
      4. Saturation
  B. Determine what we know, don't know, and our confidence level on
      1. Customer profiles/segments
      2. Product leverage
      3. Repeat sales potential
      4. Media performance
      5. Competition
      6. Creative approaches
  C. Rank these in terms of excellent, good, poor
  D. Determine conditions of our market
      1. New
      2. New for direct response
      3. Immature
      4. Mature
  E. Review availability of resources
      1. Financial
      2. People skills
      3. Time
  F. Core group brainstorms and lists possible objectives; discuss and refine
  G. Individuals in core group rank objectives, discuss with group and group performs grid evaluation to determine ranking of objectives
XV. Develop obstacles
  A. Identify all obstacles core group can think of and discuss for refinement
  B. Relate each agreed upon obstacle to each specific objective it blocks
  C. Prioritize obstacles two ways: impact on response potential and difficulty to overcome
  D. Do any obstacles now become objectives?

    E. Identify all advantages core group can think of and discuss for refinement

    F. Relate each agreed upon advantage to objective it helps

    G. Prioritize each advantage on the basis of amount of leverage each advantage brings to each objective

XVI. Develop strategy

    A. Strategy may be marketing, creative, media, production, fulfillment, financial, or other

    B. Major tools for creating strategy

      1. Rubbing—adversary analysis and debate

      2. SCAMPER—substitute, combine, adapt, maximize/minimize, eliminate, reverse/rearrange

      3. Brainstorming

      4. Core group stressing—individual rank, group discussion, grid evaluate, group consensus

    C. List objectives in priority order then related obstacles and advantages

    D. Develop strategy for each

XVII. Develop tactics

    A. Develop the tactics for each strategy

    B. Tactics involve written specifications for

      1. Schedules for implementation

      2. Basic appeals

      3. Formats

      4. Copy approach

      5. Pieces in package

      6. Timing

      7. Estimates cost summaries

      8. Charge breakdown by segment

      9. Nonrecurring and recurring expenditure summaries

      10. Estimated charges per program/package segment

      11. Media to be used

      12. Offers

      13. Prices

      14. May develop storyboards, rough copy, and so forth

XVIII. Freezing the design

    A. Proof all selections, specifications, costs and schedules—two people should proof—identify sign-offs required

    B. Give plan P&L stress

      1. Parameter costing vs. response ranges throughout

  2. Formal costing vs. specifications after completion of tactics
  3. Predictive yield analysis
     a. breakeven: acquisition and life cycle
     b. profit or loss as minimum and maximum industry or corporate response level
     c. bottom-line impact for each one percent penetration of market
     d. core group should review in-depth and make judgment on risk/gain
C. Entire plan is then written in final form and reviewed by each core group
D. Present plan to management for approval and funding
  1. Distribute plan prior to meeting
  2. Approvers study and critique
  3. Core group creates summary in presentation format
     a. put the bottom line at the top
     b. present objectives, obstacles, advantages, strategy and tactics summary in that order
     c. answer questions using background and entire plan
  4. Plan manager presents plan: discuss and decide
E. Changes to the plan after freezing can be effected only by V.P. approval
  1. Core group recommendation
  2. Marketing manager and director recommendation
XIX. Implement the plan
A. Copy of plan should be sent and discussed with all corporate functions involved
B. Lower-level marketing personnel who carry out plan must understand they do not have authority to change it

What's Your Presentation Quotient?

Ron Hoff

YOU'D THINK ADVERTISING PEOPLE WOULD BE BETTER PRESENTERS than they are. They're bright, personable, usually articulate. But most of them are duds when it comes to making presentations.

This isn't just my opinion. As background for a presentation course I've put together over the past ten years, I interviewed some of the top people in the agency business and a fair number of important clients. The opinion, strongly held by most of these executives, is that we just don't present our work very well.

Creative people are overly sensitive to criticism when they're presenting—particularly when it's their own work. Account people are stiff and mechanical. Research people are dull. Media people are obsessed by numbers. And so on.

This is a weakness in our business that seems to be fairly universal. I've had over 500 requests from agencies, large and small, for the script of the presentation course I mentioned. I send it out free, figuring if it can help our business with a problem we all have—it's the least I can do.

Advertising Age has also been well aware of the problem and taken steps to draw attention to it and do something about it.

Advertising Age Workshops have devoted many hours to the subject. I and a Foote, Cone colleague—Paul Repetto—have occupied a few of those hours, talking about presentation techniques and trying to help individual agencies set up their own presentation courses.

Other people in the business have done the same—at various forums and industry gatherings. The interest is genuine and widespread.

Yet the problem persists. We just don't present very well. The following checklist isn't going to change that basic situation, but maybe it will prompt a bit more interest in presentation techniques and styles.

Give it a try. See how you do. It's really pretty elementary, and it won't take much time. But it might get you going on something that could be extremely useful to you and your agency.

1. Be honest now. Is there a bit of "ham" in you?

Call presentation "performing" or "selling" or what you will, those who do it best get a thrill out of doing it. If truth be told, they even like to rehearse (though they'd never admit it).

Most of the great presenters have a sense of theater. They move easily on a stage or platform. They enjoy the spotlight. It's a trip. It exhilarates them. Look into their histories and you'll probably find some summer stock experience, or a trophy for debating, or a try at broadcasting. Let's face it. There's a bit of ham in them.

2. Is there a bit of Clarence Darrow in you?

Presentation isn't just showing the work. Presentation is the gentle art of guiding minds to your point of view. This means you've got to get your audience nodding with you every step of the way—from the first simple statement of "why we're all here" to the last piece of work in your bag.

Don't leave gaps in your thinking. Don't expect your audience to make jumps over ground you haven't prepared for them. Don't expect your audience to give you the benefit of the doubt. Once your audience stumbles over your logic, you've probably lost them forever.

A side note: Ever notice how some presentations just sort of "get under way" without the slightest proclamation of purpose? It's like dropping into the middle of the ocean and hoping you'll find land.

3. Are you a good editor of your own material?

Most presentations are too damn long. In my presentation course, the students must limit their presentations to four minutes. This requires a lot of boiling down, a lot of tight organizing.

The majority of presenters would profit from having to fit their words into a set time frame.

David Ofner, general manager of the Foote, Cone office in Chicago, has my favorite quote on this subject: "Why is it so many presenters go on talking *after* they've won? More often than not, they snatch defeat from the jaws of victory."

4. Do you get nervous?

You should. A little nervousness gets the adrenaline going, gives your presentation a vitality it wouldn't have otherwise.

One small tip: Never start a presentation by telling your audience how nervous you are. You may get their sympathy vote, but they'll be more interested in your condition than the context of your presentation.

5. Do you have a system for "psyching yourself up" before you present?

Sounds silly, but it works. Pro football players do it. They'll prepare for a big game by talking to themselves, "I'm going out there and mangle that guy. I'm going to make Mean Joe Greene look like a buttercup. I'm going to be invincible. I'm going to have the best game of my life."

Same thing works for presenters. "I know more about this subject than anybody else in this room. I've got it down cold. I'm going to dazzle them out of their boots. I'm going to have the best presentation of my life."

There's only one little "must" in this technique. You *must* have your presentation so well prepared that you really won't have any doubts about it.

6. Do you rehearse your presentation at least 10 times before you give it?

David Ogilvy has some pungent peeves about presenters. He says most of them simply "don't take pains with their presentations." He's right, of course. A sloppy presentation is an insult to the audiences that must endure it. A bumbling presentation says that the presenter didn't think enough of his or her audience to spend much time in preparation.

Rehearsal is the key. If you haven't rehearsed your part at least *10* times, it probably isn't set in your mind. Invariably, rehearsal brings improvement. You'll discover little things that will make your presentation clearer, sharper, more colorful. Rough edges will get polished off. And you'll be more comfortable with the material.

All too often, presenters pooh-pooh the need for rehearsal, saying, "Don't worry. I'll get it right when it's the real thing." Sometimes they do. *Sometimes.*

7. Do you keep your cool under fire?

Very few presenters can lose their tempers and come away with anything except frayed nerves. The most effective presenters present with good-natured confidence.

There's good reason. Audiences usually reflect the attitude and manner of the speaker. If the presenter is nervous, the audience will be uncomfortable. If the presenter is arrogant, the audience will probably challenge him. If the speaker is at ease, the audience will relax and be receptive.

I've seen a few presenters win by getting angry. But there must be a very special relationship between presenter and audience. The speaker must be recognized as an absolute wizard in his or her field, and the audience must regard that person as vital to their future. Suffice to say, it's rare. *Very* rare.

8. Do you know what you really sound like—and look like—when you're making a presentation?

Most presenters have never seen themselves as others see them. When they do, on videotape or film, it usually comes as a rude shock. They decide to do a lot of things differently. And they become better presenters.

When your agency has a major presentation coming up, rent a videotape camera for a day and put the whole rehearsal on tape. Then play it back and have the presenters criticize each other. It's the single most useful thing you can do to improve the major presentations your agency will make.

Another tip: Get yourself a cassette player and record your voice as you present. Then play it back. Do this five or six times and you'll not only discover your delivery improves, you'll have your material set in your mind. Reason: We tend to remember our own voices.

9. Do you have dramatic substitutes for the storyboard?

Conventional storyboards are probably the worst things in the world to present to an audience of more than two people. They look complicated. They don't focus attention. They read up and down instead of across. The words are too small.

Fortunately, there are alternatives. Exceptional presenters will memorize the board and act out the story. Others will put individual frames on slides and memorize the audio so that they can flick through the slides quickly without fiddling with a script.

Some imaginative presenters like David Scott of Ogilvy & Mather have designed their own dramatic storyboards with synopsis sheets, enlarged key frames, horizontal action progression and acetate coverings which can be marked (with a grease pencil) as the presentation develops. A little imagination can improve the tired old storyboard a hundredfold.

10. Are you a student of body language?

Your body may be communicating signals that are contrary to what you're saying.

Presenters who hunch over lecterns, gripping each side like it was the *Titanic,* are telling the audience they are very unsure about the whole thing.

Presenters who cover two-thirds of their bodies with podiums and rivet their eyes on a script are saying, "I feel safer back here. I really don't want to get involved with you."

Next time you're rehearsing your part of a presentation, ask a couple of your colleagues to "tune out" your words and read your body language. It's something most presenters never even think about. But the good ones *do.*

11. Do you know when to use slides and when to use cards?

Slides discourage participation by your audience. This can be good or bad depending on the kind of meeting you're planning. There are some definite cautions to keep in mind about slides. Any kind of audio-visual aid that puts the lights out can also put your audience to sleep. Darkness induces dozing. A slide presentation after a heavy lunch is *not* a good idea.

Also, slides can give you some unsettling surprises. Unless you operate the slide changer yourself, you can discover your words are way out of sync with what's on the screen.

But slides have one big advantage. If you've got an audience of 12 or more, slides will be seen by everyone in the room (that is, if the slides are designed like billboards and not like long-copy ads).

Jumbo-size cards or charts are more informal than slides, more likely to generate discussion. They're also flexible. You can make marks on cards to stress your points. You can shift them around like a deck of cards. And you can leave them on display after you've presented them. But cards aren't good for a large audience. And they can break your back if you're going a distance.

12. Do you know where your hands are?

Hands have a way of getting in the way. Most of the time, the presenter isn't even aware of what the hands are doing.

There are the coin jinglers. Most of them aren't even conscious of what they're doing. But their audiences are.

There are also the gesticulators. They make the same little gestures over and over again. They don't know they're doing it. Put them on videotape and they'll say, "Was I really doing that?"

Restless hands are a subconscious response to nervousness. I've got a few suggestions for you:

1. Take everything out of your pockets before you begin. *Everything.*

2. If you're using a table or lectern, don't leave needless things around that will attract restless hands. Like pencils. Or paper clips. Or rubber bands.

3. If you're going to put a hand in your pocket, okay—but *both* hands in pockets make you look like Peck's Bad Boy.

4. Rehearse in front of a mirror and see what your hands are doing. They may have been doing things for years without your knowing about it.

13. Do you know how to keep your audience from leaping ahead of you?

They'll do it every time if you give them half a chance. If you have a number of itemized points on a slide or card, your audience won't stay with you while you stand there and talk about the first point. While you're talking, that audience of yours is going to be reading the second point and the third and right straight through the entire list.

To cope with the basic human instinct to "read ahead" no matter what you're saying, you can do two things:

1. Don't put more than one idea on a slide or board. That way, you can control things—and move to the next point when you're good and ready.

2. Read through *all* the items on your slide or card, word-for-word. Then, go back and elaborate on each point as you please. Your audience will have no reason to leap ahead. You've already done it for them.

14. Do you have a system for anticipating questions?

Let me recommend the system that seems to work for Presidents of the United States. Well, sometimes.

The day before the presentation, gather everybody on the team and spend at least one hour anticipating the questions you may get. Write them down. Make sure you've got strong, factual answers—not flabby generalities. If you really think about the personalities of the people who will be at your meeting, you'll probably guess at least 75% of the questions they'll ask.

This can be the crucial part of the meeting, particularly at new business sessions, but it's surprising how few agencies take the time to rehearse the question/answer part of the meeting.

Note: You should also decide *before the meeting* who's going to answer which questions. When everybody from the agency jumps in to answer a question, things can get a little messy—especially when the creative spokesman has just given a particularly lucid answer and the account man says from the other side of the table, "What I think Jim was trying to say . . ." Happens all the time.

15. Do you know how to say "don't know" without sounding like a dummy?

I've found that most presenters would rather impale themselves on a pointer stick than admit they don't know. This leads to wild guesses. Which usually lead to disaster. If you don't know, say it's a good question and you'll have the answer within 24 hours.

One of the best presenters I've ever known took out a pad and wrote the question down when he didn't know the answer. And he made sure that everybody saw him do it. A little thing, but it *proved* that he thought the question was important.

16. Do you always know what the other presenters in your meeting are going to say and show?

If you're the presenter of the creative work, do you know what the media presenter is going to say?

Do you know what the account executive who is "just going to say a few words at the start" is *actually* going to say?

More often than not, everybody "sort of knows" what everybody else is going to say—but they don't know precisely.

That's why you'll often see the creative person showing four-color spreads and the media director presenting a beautiful schedule of one-pagers.

That's why you'll hear a lot of overlapping in presentations, "The few words at the start" by the account executive often turn out to be just what the creative guru was going to use to introduce his material.

The only way to avoid croppers like these is to have at least one full-dress rehearsal where everybody on the team attends, and everybody says *exactly* what he or she is really going to say.

17. Do you always have a dossier on the key people in your audience?

Know your audience. Know who makes the decisions. Know who's likely to cast the dissenting vote(s). Know why. Know the personalities of the people who'll attend. Know what their titles are. What their job histories have been. Know what their hang-ups are. Know where they went to school. What their special interests may be.

This sounds like a big deal. Needn't be. Just assign a junior account man to talk to the old-timers on the account and make up a sheet with a capsule on each person who'll attend. Make sure everybody on the presentation team has a copy at least two days before the meeting will be held.

18. Do you know what to do when the audio-visual equipment breaks down?

And it's going to break down. You know it. I know it. What do you do when it happens?

Here are a couple of things *not* to do:

1. Don't get mad.

2. Don't just stand there like the great stone sphinx.

3. Don't start rattling off jokes that have nothing to do with the situation.

Here are a couple of things you *can* do:

1. Declare a five-minute break and see how long it will take to get things going again.

2. Go on to something else that doesn't require the incapacitated equipment and hope that repairs can be made in the meantime.

3. Open the meeting up for questions or discussion on the material covered up to that point. A trifle risky, but probably okay if the vibes have been good. If they haven't, maybe you can clear the air.

4. Tell a brief story that relates to the situation. Example: Tell them you're starting a presentation course back at the agency and this experience will be the first case study.

Above all, keep cool. Fate has not singled you out for disaster. It's happened to every presenter who ever said, "Lights, please."

19. Do you know how to avoid the "caught-in-a-coffin" look?

Most podiums, particularly hotel podiums, look like cheap wooden boxes—or, to be more precise, like coffins. Then, these wooden boxes have little blue-white lights in them that cast an eerie, upward glow on the speaker's face.

The result usually looks like Dracula rising from the dead for one of his nightly frolics. All of which may be fine for horror movies, but it doesn't do much for speakers who are trying to register as nice people.

Get out of "the box" if you possibly can. Move out from behind it—stand beside it—*anything* is better than looking like you're ready for Freddie the friendly undertaker. Additional lighting will help. Ask a technician to put some overhead spots on you to remove some of the ghastly shadows.

How you *look* is important in presentations. Don't let a boxy lectern with ghoulish lighting ruin an otherwise first-class presentation.

20. Do you make an effort to learn from actors, ministers, moderators, commentators, newscasters—even politicians?

Watch how actors use their hands. Notice how tv moderators control the flow of a discussion. Listen to how radio newscasters use their voices to sustain interest. Take a lesson from politicians in voice projection. Notice how ministers, the good ones anyway, speak to their congregations—person to person.

Presenters can learn to be better presenters from professionals in many fields. They're all around us—on tv, in films and plays, in churches and town halls. Say to yourself, "I'll learn at least one thing from this person—one thing that will improve my presentation technique."

Make a conscious effort to learn this fascinating craft from the people who are really good at it. You could turn out to be even better than they are.

Ron Hoff, "What's Your Presentation Quotient?" *Advertising Age*, Vol. 49, No. 3, January 16, 1978. Reprinted by permission of Crain News Service.

Direct Response "Rules" Test

OF COURSE WE'D ALL LIKE TO TEST EVERY VARIABLE IN EVERY DIRECT response program. But this is impossible. Sometimes the size of our mailing universe is too small to support much testing. Sometimes we have to meet mailing schedules that won't allow us the time to test. And sometimes—many times—the budget just can't afford it.

When you can't test you can rely on what usually works best in direct response. If your mailing package or ad or TV commercial incorporates the "tried and true" elements, your chances for success are increased.

How well do you know these "rules of thumb"? Answer the following statements true or false.*

True   False

Mailing Format

1. The most effective mailing package consists of an outside envelope, letter, circular, response form, and business reply envelope (or card).   ____ ____

---

*Author's note: We have been unable to locate the original source of this material. If any reader can provide us with this information, we shall be delighted to acknowledge our indebtedness.

True False

2. The circular or brochure ranks first in importance.   ____ ____

Letters

3. Form letters using indented paragraphs usually outpull those in which indented paragraphs are not used.   ____ ____

4. Underlining pertinent phrases and sentences usually increases results slightly.   ____ ____

5. A combined letter and circular will generally do better than a separate letter and separate circular in the same package.   ____ ____

6. It is best to disclose the price and payment terms early in a sales letter.   ____ ____

7. A form letter with a display headline will ordinarily do better than a filled-in, personalized letter.   ____ ____

8. Authentic testimonials in a sales letter ordinarily increase the pull.   ____ ____

9. A one-page letter ordinarily outpulls a two-page letter.   ____ ____

10. Computer letters always outpull printed letters.   ____ ____

Brochures

11. A brochure that deals specifically with the proposition presented in the letter will be more effective than a brochure of an institutional nature.   ____ ____

12. Employing all art or all photography in a circular will usually result in a better brochure than one employing a combination of art and photography.   ____ ____

13. Deluxe, large-size, color brochures most always prove cost efficient in the sale of big ticket products.   ____ ____

Outside Envelopes

14. Illustrated envelopes always detract from a mailing's effectiveness.   ____ ____

15. In a series of mailings, it is important to standardize the type and size of the outside envelope.   ____ ____

True   False

Order Forms

16. Reply cards with receipt stubs will usually increase response over cards with no stubs.   ____ ____

17. Adding a toll-free "800" response telephone number to the order form will increase response.   ____ ____

Reply Cards or Envelopes

18. Postage-free business reply cards or envelopes will generally bring in no more responses than those to which the respondent must affix postage.   ____ ____

19. An airmail reply envelope usually increases responses to impulse offers.   ____ ____

Color

20. One-color letters usually pull as well or better than two-color letters.   ____ ____

21. A two-color brochure generally proves more effective than a one-color brochure.   ____ ____

22. Full color brochures are most always cost effective, regardless of offer.   ____ ____

Postage

23. Third-class mail ordinarily pulls as well as first-class mail.   ____ ____

24. In business-to-business mailing, bulk postage stamps usually pull better than metered postage.   ____ ____

General Information

25. Nothing is more important to the success of a mailing than good, sound creative.   ____ ____

26. In a two-step lead generation offer, it's important to involve the sales force to assure maximum success.   ____ ____

27. In most cases for most products, mailing in July and August is just as good as mailing in January or September.   ____ ____

True   False

The Offer

28. Before a catalog is started, the theme is the most important element.   ____ ____

29. You should look at a direct-response television ad more like an audio and visual direct-response mailing package than as a normal consumer TV commercial with a phone number at the end.   ____ ____

30. The most effective direct-response TV spots are usually 60 seconds or less.   ____ ____

31. The telephone can serve as a supplement or alternative to other direct response media.   ____ ____

32. Anyone can make an unscripted telephone solicitation call.   ____ ____

33. Next to direct mail, newspapers are more widely used by direct marketers than any other medium.   ____ ____

34. Bind-in magazine insert cards usually are cost efficient.   ____ ____

35. Direct response newspaper ads tend to produce orders nearly as quickly as with television advertising.   ____ ____

36. Co-op mailings, card decks, and package inserts are relatively expensive direct response media.   ____ ____

Warm-Up Exercises

I. Take the "frequent flyer program" developed by the airlines, define it very carefully, describe what it is that the concept is designed to overcome, and show how it could be used (develop an example of how it could be applied) in each of the following contexts:

A. Consumer Durable Product

B. Consumer Perishable Product

C. Nonprofit Organization

D. Service Organization

E. Business-to-Business Organization

II. Find at least five direct response newspaper or magazine ads and critique them, proving that each either is or is not consistent with direct-response advertising "rules."

III. Go to a local retail store, such as an automobile aftermarket store of some sort, and select a product from items you see on the shelf that you feel could be sold successfully with a classic, solo mailing package. Defend your belief that the product is amenable to the method, and outline your essential strategy for selling it.

IV. Research the literature on "what's new" until you find a cutting edge new product or process, such as a new form of plastic which will dissolve when soaked in water containing a certain chemical agent, or something such as electronic mail, and "blue sky" about how this product could be used in the direct marketing field as a selling or product enhancement tool.

V. Research the literature on social/economic trends. Then pick out one trend, such as the increasing percentage of children living with only one parent, or the increasing number of single person households, and "blue sky" the effects of this trend on the direct marketing processes involved on a selected product. Be specific.

VI. Locate a classic direct response package of any type, then analyze and critique each of its direct marketing components, making a case for each component's probable effectiveness, or, perhaps, why it is likely to fail.

VII. Locate a self-mailer of any type, then analyze and critique each component of the package, making a case for each component's likelihood of being effective or ineffectual.

VIII. Assume that you have been asked to write an ad to sell cakes as gifts. Your client can make and package delicious cakes that will be moist and firm upon arrival. He/she can even personalize your cake with a message of your choice. Choose an audience and a medium and write a short magazine ad designed to one-step the sale of these cakes as gifts to others from the buyer.

IX. Select at least five direct mail catalogs, two or more of which are business-to-business catalogs, and write an analysis of the apparent strengths and weaknesses of their covers as direct-response tools.

X. Evaluate the direct marketing potential of each of the following new product and service concepts:

● *Vitamin Dispenser.* Activities that must be repeated daily frequently have no natural "trigger" or cue to remind people to do them. A habit must be formed and reinforced if such activity is to be done faithfully. One such activity is the taking of vitamins. For example, persons suffering from what dentists describe as bone loss should take magnesium/potassium vitamins daily. However, because the problem is painless, most people forget as often as they remember to take their vitamins. A solution to this problem (for vitamin takers) could well be commercially lucrative. A device is needed that reminds the taker to take his/her vitamins, or both dispenses vitamins and cues the taker to take them. The device could be either mechanical or electronic. It is visualized as being used in a conspicuous place (bathroom, etc.) where it would automatically remind the vitamin taker and be his or her "silent friend."

● *Automatic Do List.* People appear to have a need for an automatic task reminder service. A solution to this could be a programmable electronic or mechanical device. The device would serve as its user's automatic do list. Lists would be programmed into it. A signal would be emitted at the appropriate time (or the device could simply come on) indicating that a planned task has not as yet been done, or that it is time to do it.

● *Imported Stemless (Cordial) Cognac/Brandy Glasses.* People are always looking for a gift idea that is unique and different. Stemless cognac or brandy glasses are difficult to find. Sometimes even exclusive gift shops don't sell them. But they do sell at retail, at prices that range from $40 to $75 for a set of four. These items are readily available from wholesale suppliers in New York. Your cost would be approximately $25 for a set of four. Packing (for shipment) costs would be about $2 per set.

● *Financial Planning By Mail.* Financial-planning-by-mail computer programs that can take personal investor investment objectives and investment data and churn out model strategies in a few seconds are now available. The cost of data entry (from mailed in data), computer analysis, and a modicum of human interpretation should run from $10 to $15 per plan.

● *Gutter Nails.* Driving through any neighborhood, one can normally see the long nails used to affix gutters to the edge of roofs "backing out." This is a problem that home owners have learned to live with. But there is a solution: injection molded plastic screws. These screws, like the nails they replace, are about eight inches long, but unlike the nails, they aren't driven in so that they can "backout." They are screwed into the wood. These screws will break but only if severely torqued. They won't rust, however. These can be manufactured in quantity and packaged for shipment for $5 per hundred nails.

XI. Assume that you are preparing to write some lead-generating ads for a rental furniture company. The company rents to both businesses and to individuals. Identify at least *five different positioning themes* that might be effectively developed in an advertisement designed to get leads. Do this for both the business and consumer markets.

XII. You own a store which specializes in "designer chocolates." You can design chocolate favors, and about anything else that chocolate can do for a large party. Your chocolate processing expertise is tops and you have excellent creative skills. You are Jewish and your clientele is comprised largely of Jewish people with upscale incomes. You operate out of a downtown Chicago store. Currently your business is good but not outstanding. You're thinking of turning to direct marketing. But before you do, you'd like to determine if this product/service is amenable to the direct response method? Is it?

XIII. You sell industrial product liability insurance. Your business is highly dependent on referrals from people you value as customers who are happy with your products and services. You sense that you need to be more organized in your approach to obtaining referrals and begin to think about developing an "offer" to your customers that would be designed to melt away their resistance to giving you the leads you need. What would this "offer" look like? Assume that you are making it over the phone.

XIV. You are a major seller of cookware. Your basic marketing program involves a sales representative/dealer structure that recruits hostesses to hold parties at which your cookware is sold. Currently, your dealers are generating their own leads. You decide to launch a national TV ad campaign to generate leads for your dealers. This campaign generates leads far in excess of your expectations. These leads are then fed to your dealers. Almost instantly, sales begin to decline. Define the cause of this, and recommend something that might be done to alleviate it while retaining the TV-generated leads program.

XV. You have just bought a feed store which sells livestock feed to farmers. It also sells water softener salt to smaller retailers. The business has been in the same family for over 65 years and has never really been promoted. (Last year's total promotional budget was $2300.) Over the last fifteen years the business has gradually fallen off. At this point, it is right at breakeven. What are some of the ways that direct marketing might be effectively used to promote this store?

XVI. Tinnitus is an "ear buzz" problem that is said to afflict 36 million Americans. The problem, which includes ringing and whistling in the ears, is totally invisible to all but the sufferer. The "buzzes, whistles and rings" vary from person to person, and normally, are not debilitating. However, they are a constant source of irritation. No one really knows a cure for tinnitus, but treatments include surgery (rarely), listening to a radio set to approximately the same frequency as the buzz, and doing nothing, depending on which professional the sufferer happens to see. The professionals apparently don't talk to each other about their treatments, so it's difficult for the sufferer to get a total analysis of the solutions that exist relative to the particular problem. Suppose you put together a booklet that surveys all the efforts being made in the United States to deal with the tinnitus problem. How would you go about offering this booklet to the market?

XVII. Assume you are charged with marketing a new dog control product. The product is an electronic device involving two basic ingredients: one is a wire buried in the ground surrounding the area where the dog is allowed to run. The other is a collar worn by the dog. When the dog approaches the buried wire, an electronic signal is triggered and the dog is warned to go no farther in that direction. There is some dog training involved, of course, but the device is simple to install and works very well. Assuming that the product can be manufactured for $40.20, including allocated costs, how would you proceed to price and market the product? Can it be sold by direct-response methods? How?

XIX. Every year a "Country Concert in the Hills" is held near your home town. Such names as George Jones, Loretta Lynn, and John Schneider are typically on the bill. You happen to know the individual charged with promoting advance ticket sales, most of which are sent out by mail. In all cases, tickets go out in an envelope. In conversations with the ticket sales director, you learn that she's thinking of ways to get more sales by using the contacts she already has with current ticket purchasers, who, because they have bought tickets, are known to have an interest in country music, and probably have friends who are also interested. She is wondering if there is an offer of some sort that could be inserted in the envelope with the tickets—whether the tickets are handed over at a counter or sent to the purchaser in the mail. Think about this for her, and suggest some profit-increasing offers that the ticket sales director might make.

XX. You determine that it may be possible to save real estate professionals some time and money if you do a regular weekly telephone survey of all financial service organizations in your market area. You would then offer the results of this survey in newsletter form to all financial service competitors in your market area. Competitors would know at a glance the loan rates of their competitors on loans ranging from one-year adjustables to second mortgages. Assess the potential of this service and whether or not it could be sold by direct response methods. Suggest a specific direct response strategy that might be used to market the service.

Direct Marketing Cases

Case 1   Bull Markets

AL BINKLEY THOUGHT HE HAD A GREAT IDEA. IT INVOLVED DIRECT response marketing of vitamins—more specifically, a vitamin designed especially for the financial community. The product was a multivitamin similar in content to such well-known brands as "One-A-Day," "StressTabs," and the like. He called his brand "Bull Markets." The product's label described it as "a high-potency, multimineral formula containing twenty-five essential daily vitamins and minerals—with no preservatives, starch or sugar added."

Introducing... **Bull Markets**

30 Day Trial Offer

...an important **new** addition to your success.

Most executives and successful businessmen function at greater extremes than average people. The result is fatigue, your body weakening, etc...

Bull Markets is a powertul multivitamin/multimineral formula created to strengthen you, keep you ahead where you belong.

FDA aproved, the result of 30 years of vitamin experience, a combination of 25 essential vitamins and minerals with extra vitamins B¹, B², E, C, B₆, B₁₂, and iron, it's everything you need.

We'd like you to try a 30 day supply of Bull Markets. The cost is $5.00 plus $1.00 for shipping and, of course, a money back guarantee. A small price for your health

If you don't think you need Bull Markets to protect your health, to strengthen you, and to help you think clearer on long days... think again, and buy it before your competition does.

Call Now! Order Toll Free, Operator Standing By.   1-800-426-4010

MasterCard or Visa accepted. Please give your number to operator when calling.

or send coupon

One bottle at $5.00, plus $1.00 handing. Enclose check, money order, or MC No.
Two bottles (one for a friend) save $1.00. Total for two is $11 00

Name _____   MasterCard or Visa No _____

Address _____   Zip Code _____

Send To: **Kinser Pharmaceutical Inc.**
P.O. Box 211, National Rd.
Englewood, Ohio 45325

•Limited while trial samples last.

EXHIBIT 1. *Columbus Dispatch* Newspaper Advertisement

Each bottle contained thirty tablets. Al purchased his vitamin supply with his "Bull Markets" label on the bottle from a repackager.

Al planned to sell the product for a $5 per bottle list price. He estimated his in-the-mail fulfillment costs to be $2 per bottle, so he had a $3 per bottle contribution to pay for his promotion costs. Thus, his first effort at selling the product, which cost him $800 to design and place in the paper, had a 267-bottle breakeven requirement. This effort was an ad in the financial section of a Sunday edition of the *Columbus* (Ohio) *Dispatch*. (See Exhibit 1.)

Al fully expected his ad to work, but it didn't. Al was the "operator standing by" mentioned in the ad. Thus, when he had received no calls at all by 4 P.M. on the day the ad was placed, he was sure his 800 phone number wasn't working. So, just to make sure, he had friends call him on it to test it. Unfortunately, it turned out that the number was working but the ad wasn't. In fact, the ultimate number of orders received was zero! Al is now trying to figure out what happened and what, if anything, he should do next in his effort to sell vitamins by mail.

Analyze the ad shown in Exhibit 1 and the media in which it appeared for their consistency with good direct mail and direct marketing principles. Then come up with a total direct-response strategy for selling vitamins that you think will work!

Materials in this case reprinted with permission of Kinser Pharmaceutical, Inc.

Case 2   Sealant Marketing

SEALANT SPECIALTIES CORPORATION DEVELOPED A WINDOW CRACK (joint) filler that was easy to use, long lasting, and attractive in appearance. They successfully marketed this product in bulk to manufacturers of windows—all of whom produced windows by the thousands and all of whom already owned the proper product application equipment.

The product manager for the product thought there must be a profitable market for the product among small storm door and storm window fabricators and applicators—firms who sold a few hundred windows a year perhaps, but normally no more than enough to equip one or two houses at any one time. Because of their size, he was sure that this market would buy only if a self-contained application gun were supplied as part of the product, and this feature was added.

The problem, it seemed, was how to test the market, how to reach and sell relatively small home improvement contractors economically, and how to keep the start-up investment low. The number of such applicators in the three state area surrounding the firm's main location was estimated to be a few hundred at best. The manager also determined that there were 120 prospects within sixty miles of the main plant.

The product manager first tried selling the product by making cold personal sales calls on prospects, but results were poor. Too often, the buyer was "out on a job," "already using a satisfactory sealant," or not interested "at this time of the year." In view of this, it was decided to try a direct mail campaign.

The mailing went out in two stages. The first consisted of an inexpensive white folder, sealed with a Band-Aid. The message said the offer would be in the next mailing. The second mailing consisted of an inexpensive blue folder, also sealed with a Band-Aid. The recipient was invited to use an 800 number to take advantage of a demonstration and to receive a free first-aid kit.

Success was to be measured by the number of sales appointments made. It was hoped that prospects would see the first aid kit as a valuable incentive, for which they would be readily willing to trade a few minutes of time listening to a salesperson.

Evaluate the probable effectiveness of this program. What other strategies and offers might have been considered?

This case prepared by Roger W. Brucker, president, Odiorne Industrial Advertising.

Case 3 Dudes

EARNEST AND JULIE CRANDALL MADE A MID-CAREER MOVE FROM Houston, Texas to the highlands of Colorado in 1968, where, together, they have operated a dude ranch—now known as Tomeche Hot Springs Ranch—for nearly fifteen years.

It had taken all their savings to buy what at the time was a run-down cattle ranch in the Colorado highlands, but it was everything they had ever hoped for. The ranch sat at the bottom of Tomeche Dome, an inactive volcano whose geothermal action fed a variety of ground springs with a year-around, unlimited supply of 105-degree water. One of these springs was less than a hundred yards from the ranch house. The ranch was near the Continental Divide, forty-five minutes by van from scenic grandeur that rivaled that available anywhere on the North American continent. It was also located close to abandoned gold mines and historic, but no longer used, railway tunnels through the Rocky Mountains. Furthermore, the ranch was near the "backside" of the "Vail" slope which offered, according to skiing aficionados, the best snow skiing in Colorado.

Earnest and Julie had not set out to become dude ranchers, but became involved in the business as a way to make ends meet early on in their adventure. The geographic setting of the ranch and the need for extra money combined to encourage Earnest and Julie to try the business in summer of 1973. They immediately liked it and found it relatively easy to manage. Earnest handled the outdoor operations and Julie handled the hotel and food service, and marketing, aspects of the operation. Over the years, they prospered and built the business into one that produced a very good living for themselves and their three sons—ages 2, 3, and 5, when they came to the mountains, but all now young adults.

All three—Rob, Les, and Ron—were bright, outgoing young men; all had gone off to college, but having grown up on the ranch and in the mountains—loving it all the while—they wanted to make it their lives' work. Rob, the oldest, and Les, the second son, were already married; Ron and his fiancée were very involved in planning their wedding. The wives were all very supportive of their husbands' staying on the ranch; they felt that they, too, could combine marriage with careers by participating in the dude ranching business with their husbands. The only question was whether dude ranching could support them all.

The ranch set-up could now accommodate forty families of up to six people at a time—$350 per person was the average weekly rate. An average of twenty-five families visited the ranch each week during the summer season. The horseback riding aspect of their operation was very seasonal, limited largely to the summer months of June, July, and August. Hunting and skiing activities offered by the ranch were, for the most part, fall and winter activities.

Over the years repeat business, and business generated from

the recommendations of satisfied customers, were the primary bases of the ranch's growth. Essentially Julie's marketing efforts consisted of sending a very personal, homey letter and brochure to former visitors telling them of happenings on the ranch, and inviting them back for another visit. She was also supplied with leads by the Colorado department of tourism which received general inquiries about vacationing opportunities in Colorado. Those who made such inquiries were mailed a brochure—the same one that went to former customers—and a price list. The "doings" Julie talked about in her letters were largely personal items about family members; or if not that, about developments at the ranch, such as the completion of a new stable, or the addition of a new attraction for their guests.

Every ranch visitor was made very welcome by the entire family. Guests noted that all of the ranch employees, including nonfamily members, acted less like employees of the ranch than like friends and informal group leaders. In fact, the entire operation was conducted in a manner that left virtually all visitors with the feeling of having had a very entertaining, carefree visit with the Crandall family, rather than merely having spent an entertaining time at a facility in the mountains.

The entire week—a week being the length of the typical stay—was conducted as if it were one big family get-together—having a good time on mountaintop horseback rides; on van trips to mountain passes and abandoned gold mines; on chuckwagon breakfasts; riding the rapids on the Gunnison River on rafts; camping out overnight in mountain canyons; taking fishing trips to nearby trout streams; or lounging around the ranch's geothermally heated, constant 105-degree pool, waiting for the next all-you-can-eat meal cooked under the supervision of a lady who had earned her reputation cooking for various gangs of hardy Colorado goldminers.

But now things were "a-changin'." More people were getting into the dude ranch business—and doing a better job at it. Furthermore, if all of the Crandall sons and their families were to earn their livings on the ranch, business would have to be sought after much more vigorously.

Develop a direct response strategy for the Crandall family that will increase the operation's business—first to present capacity, then to whatever expanded capacity you feel is merited in this particular situation.

Case 4   Reliable Bearings
Sales Support Telemarketing

RELIABLE BEARINGS CORPORATION MANUFACTURES TAPERED roller bearings for many kinds of machines, such as off-road machinery, construction equipment, and chemical process equipment. The sales manager, Jim Race, grew increasingly apprehensive about the increase in usage of foreign bearings. He decided to put together a combination sales and technical presentation, a "road show" that could be staged for larger customers and prospects in their plants. The seminar presentation would highlight new developments in Reliable's product line, their investment in a new steel mill, the findings of a technical study of bearing life improvement, tips on how to apply different kinds of bearings in various designs, and finally a practical analysis of defects found in some of the foreign bearings.

The problem was how to get invitations to put on the seminar. Race asked a key salesperson if he would spread the word about the availability of the seminar to his customers and prospects as he called on them. "I know my customers," said Sam Smooth, salesperson for the Michigan territory. "If they hear I want to bring something like that in, they'll claim it's just a sales pitch for Reliable Bearings. I'm not going to destroy my credibility with them that way."

"Direct mail might work," said the advertising manager. "If we have an attractive brochure describing the seminar and enclose a return postcard for the names of those who want to attend, we should get an audience."

"Why not try telemarketing?" said the marketing manager. "You get some silver-tongued persuader on the phone, and I'll bet you can talk lots of prospects into attending the seminar."

Race considered the three alternatives: he could force the sales force to issue invitations, but at what cost? He might prepare a direct mailing, but would it work? Could you really explain enough on the telephone to get anyone to accept a seminar invitation?

While he was considering these alternatives the advertising manager stopped by to say he had purchased a Dun and Bradstreet mailing list of companies with 100 or more employees, within the top ten SIC groups that use roller bearings in their products. "It's a good list. It has the name and telephone number of the chief engineer, exact title, company, address, city, state, and zip code," said the advertising manager. "I figure that whether you use direct mail or telemarketing that list will be useful to you."

What should Jim Race do next? What steps might reduce the risk and increase the reward to Reliable Bearings in its effort to hold seminars in customer and prospect plants? Can you prepare some materials that would be useful in getting the program rolling?

This case prepared by Roger W. Brucker, president, Odiorne Industrial Advertising.

Case 5   Direct Woodworking

A DIRECT MARKETING COMPANY, DIRECT WOODWORKING, IS currently selling the nation's leading multipurpose woodworking tool. Direct Woodworking's model is top quality and carries a $1,000 price tag. There is very strong consumer loyalty to Direct's brand and to the company, and Direct is perceived as the unchallenged quality leader.

Research reveals that there is market interest in a new model of Direct's product that carries a lower price tag. New product engineering comes up with a new product model which can be made and sold profitably for approximately $700. It does almost exactly the same things as the current model. The only major difference is in the new model's lessened overall convenience of operation.

Sixty-five hundred people who were on Direct's prospect list (people who had inquired about Direct's current product after reading magazine ads, seeing a product demonstration, and the like) were interviewed and asked to state the likelihood that they would buy the new product. (At this point, the prospects were unaware of the possible availability of the new product.) They were then presented with a description of the new product and asked to state their purchase probability for it.

The following results (the number of people who responded, and their responses) were obtained:

832 definitely will buy the old product
1,868 probably will buy the old product
1,800 might or might not buy the old product
1,000 probably will not buy the old product
1,000 definitely will not buy the old product

290 definitely will buy the new product
1,500 probably will buy the new product
2,220 might or might not buy the new product
1,510 probably will not buy the new product
1,000 definitely will not buy the new product

65 say definitely will buy to both old and new
300 say probably will buy to both old and new
400 say might or might not buy either product
300 say probably will not buy to both products
250 say definitely will not buy to both products

Direct doesn't want to invest in a product unless it will give them substantial additional market penetration, meet the needs of a new market, or protect them against a competitive threat.

Based on the above data, do you feel that the new product should be introduced? What additional information do you think is needed most in order to adequately reduce the risk of being wrong?

Case 6   The Skirting Man Cometh

KEN BLANCHARD'S COMPANY NAME, "THE SKIRTING MAN," suggests a flamboyant marketing style, and indeed that is true. Ken had been a promoter of sorts ever since his first paper route, and nonstop promotion of his company suited his style perfectly. His efforts were designed to create himself as the company personified. And, he succeeded.

Ken created a high personal profile for himself, and therefore for his company, at every opportunity, especially at trade shows where mobile home dealers congregated. A kilt and the rest of the uniform of the men of the Scottish Highlands became his trademark. He used this costume and his unique personality very effectively to establish a mental association between himself and his product among dealers, and to build a distinct market identity for his company.

His company sold mobile home "skirts" to mobile home dealers who in turn sold them to individual mobile home owners. Skirts are interlocking vinyl sheets which attach to mobile homes like a skirt to prevent either elements or animals from going beneath the home, thus the skirting man and the kilt associations.

The skirt business is very competitive, with a variety of dealers offering vinyl skirting products that are very similar in function and in price (see Exhibit 1). Market awareness and image are key factors in the business. Because Ken was good at developing this, his company did very well, especially at trade shows, which produced the bulk of his early success. But as time passed, he turned more and more to print advertising and direct mail orders.

"Mix or Match Systems to Receive Unit Discount."
- DEALER'S PRICE LIST OF COMPONENTS & SYSTEMS -
PRE-PAID FREIGHT OFFER GOOD ON ORDERS OF 6 HOMES OR MORE
PRICES BELOW BASED ON 162 LINEAL FEET* (14x70 HOME)

ECONOMICAL GRECIAN OVERLAP SYSTEM	1-6 Units	Special 10 Unit
WHITE-BEIGE	Prepaid	Discounted Price
28" Job	209.80	189.80 Prepaid
35" Job	234.96	212.72 Freight
One piece-rail Kit (TBRA) 11'8" (162 Lineal ft.)	96.58	86.66
Grecian Overlap Panels - 11'8" 18/Carton (18GR12)	113.22	103.14
Single 11'8" Panel	6.29	5.73

ALCOA® Harbourtown System		
WHITE-BEIGE	Prepaid	
28" Job 24 panels	229.95	209.95 Prepaid
35" Job 31 panels	266.21	243.13 Freight
Rail Kit (ALRK) 162 Lineal ft.	105.63	96.19
Carton of 12 Panels (ALPP)	62.16	56.88
Single 11'8" Panel	5.18	4.74

QUALITY VINYLOK SYSTEM		
WHITE-BEIGE V-LOK	Prepaid	
28" Job	245.99	225.99 Prepaid
35" Job	274.15	251.91 Freight
Rail Kit (TTBRA) 162 Lineal ft.	119.27	109.35
Carton of 18 Panels (18VK12)	126.72	116.64
Single 11'8" Panel	7.04	6.48
BROWN V-LOK	Prepaid	
28" Job	285.25	265.25 Prepaid
35" Job	317.69	297.69 Freight
Rail Kit (TTBRA) 162 Lineal ft.	139.27	128.09
Carton of 18 Panels (18VK12)	145.98	137.16
Single 11'8" Panel	8.11	7.62

EXHIBIT 1. Dealer's Price List

Using direct mail, he could multiply his reach over the number of dealers who attended any single trade show, and he could reach them throughout the year. Ken thought, however, that he could do even better. In view of this, he has turned to you to assist him in deciding what his offer and creative strategy should be, and to create a complete direct mail package designed to implement the strategy. The package should include inbound telephone scripts and any other marketing materials that are deemed necessary.

Material in this case reprinted by permission of Kenneth Blanchard, the "Skirting Man," Minerva, Ohio.

Case 7   Keowee Grinding

KEOWEE GRINDING MACHINE COMPANY IS A MANUFACTURER OF MA-chines designed to grind cylinders—any kind of cylinder including step, thread, and tapered cylinders. Customers bought Keowee's machines to grind pump shafts, compressor shafts, hydraulic valve spools, engine crank shafts, and the like. These machines ranged in price from $150 to $300 thousand.

In early 1987 Keowee began to experience a difficult and expensive marketing problem. Though Keowee's machines were standardized to a degree, no two customers had exactly the same application, resulting in significant customization in virtually every case. Still, the company had to offer price information up front. This wasn't as simple a problem as it seemed to be.

Early on in the informing stage of marketing, prospects usually asked for an approximate price, which presented no major problem. But very frequently, prospects would ask for a "quotation." A quotation is a formalized step in the negotiation process, usually undertaken after the prospect has become informed about the product's features, advantages, and benefits (usually from a sales rep or from mailing pieces, etc.). It was the preparation of these formal quotations that was turning into a major marketing cost problem.

According to President Jeff Ridge, "When prospects ask us for a quotation on the price of a grinding machine we build, that's a two-day ordeal, requiring careful analysis of the job, proper technical recommendation, and selection of the proper accessories. And, if we leave anything out, it could cost us thousands of dollars." On the other hand, Ridge could not recall any customer *ever* buying exactly what was specified in their original, full-blown, and costly quotation. "As we get into the application we find that an accessory here and an option there will do a better job. The customer, when convinced, goes along. Oftentimes, too, items have to be cut out to save money, or added to meet a specific performance requirement."

According to Ridge, "Our problem is how can we shortcut our time and money investment in making formal quotations that are never an accurate description of the final order?" To solve this problem, it was decided that a survey that probed how customers and prospects made use of quotations in their buying process should be taken. This revealed some useful information. For instance:

● A few prospects recognized that if they asked for a quotation the salesman would go away for a while. Their request was a brush-off.

● Most customers and prospects recognized that quotation preparation would be a substantial undertaking. They needed the quotation figures primarily for internal planning, budgeting, and justification, not for making the ultimate buy decision. They fully expected to be involved in an ongoing negotiation of details, and to pay either more or less than the quoted figure.

● A few customers had already received a quotation from one or more competitors. For them, the quotation was a key element in the justification process for a decision that had already been made, to buy the competitor's product.

Knowing these facts, marketing management decided to qualify prospects with a telemarketing program. This required a script designed to learn what the prospect had in mind when asking for a quotation. Was the request a brush-off? Was only ballpark information needed? Was this request part of a head-to-head competitive, decision-making situation where only a detailed quotation would serve?

Management also reviewed the company's fifty most recent orders. They then divided the final price on these orders by the machine shipping weight. This data, when plotted, revealed that very light and very heavy machines were very expensive per pound, while the per-pound price of intermediate weight machines was typically much lower.

The information from the price-per-pound analysis was then used as the basis for a script strategy designed to separate legitimate grinding machine prospects from tire kickers. The script language included: "Can we discuss price for a minute? We made a study of our last fifty machines shipped. Our machines tend to be 30 percent to 40 percent heavier than competitive machines, which is one secret of our rigidity and accuracy. These machines price out at $12.50 per pound on the average. In your case, we guess your machine will weigh about 8,000 pounds. If that's true, we'd be looking at a price around $100,000. Is that reasonable for doing a good job in your application?"

The company also created a boiler-plate "letterhead" or short-form quotation for use with prospects identified by telemarketing as being more than merely tire kickers. But expensive, detailed, formal quotations were reserved for those situations identified through telemarketing as requiring them.

Evaluate the Keowee program. Will it work? Why or why not? How can the program be improved?

This case prepared by Roger Brucker, president, Odiorne Industrial Advertising.

Case 8   Major Computer

MAJOR COMPUTER IS A COMPANY THAT SELLS A LINE OF PERSONAL computers in competition with IBM. It got into the business late with a good, but not spectacular, product line, and established a national network of dealers to sell it. As was true for most of the early PC dealers, when this company's dealers first got into the business, they knew a lot more about computers than they did retailing. Thus when the "bloom fell off the PC rose," many dealers went by the wayside. But many did survive—though most now tended to carry other brands in addition to that of Major Computer.

Some of these dealers sell aggressively, but most do not. Those that do often don't give Major Computer's product line as much attention as it needs. Major Computer has not been overly concerned about this situation because it has a new line of PCs which it plans to unveil in about four months, and it wants all the corporate effort focused on this line, the future of the PC division of the company. The new line of products is capable of matching, even beating, IBM's product line capability in a variety of ways significant to the typical PC buyer, both business and consumer. In sum, when this line is out, the dealers will truly have something to sell.

A national mass media campaign is being planned to announce the new line and direct likely prospects to Major Computer dealers. But unless the dealers themselves make a concerted effort, results are not expected to be spectacular, or even good. Thus the company is planning a program designed to help the dealers "attack their base," that is, their database of past and prospective customers' names which they have accumulated over the years. Not all of these buyers are the same, however. In fact, the market (the names in a typical dealer's database) appeared to be readily segmentable into the subgroups that are shown below:

● *Home Computer Owners/Users.* Machine was purchased for games, entertainment, and personal financial management. (If these requirements have not changed, there is no need for trading up.) Memory limitations and being tied to a particular hardware vendor are problems for this segment.

● *Home/Office Computer Owners/Users.* Machine of some sort was purchased to meet home and office needs. Entry price was lower than office but higher than home. IBM PC Jr. and Apple IIc owners typify this segment. This segment faces both limited software availability and significant incompatibility with office software. These owners have outstanding game machines which suffer when used as office machines.

● *CPM-based Machines.* Machines were purchased by early PC adopters at a time when the CPM was considered the standard. Machine examples include: Intertec, Zenith 289 and 290, Televideo, Kaypros II, 4, and 10, Osborn, and North Star. Owners of these machines face memory limitations, limited availability of peripherals, no future software development, and slow service on parts. Such owners can benefit through an upgrade to the Major Computer product line by obtaining the ability to utilize the largest available software base, the ability to take advantage of more peripheral options, and by having a dealer network with the ability to provide support and service with a "de facto" standard product.

● *MS-DOS-based Machine Owners/Users.* Machines were purchased before the acceptance of PC-DOS as the de facto standard. Machine examples include: HP-150, Vector 4, DEC Rainbow, 100+, TI Professional, Zenith Z-100, and Major Computer's DATAMATE-5. Users face problems of being committed to the hardware vendor for new products, future enhancements and updates, plus lack of "freedom of choice" in choosing software. Dealers will have to special order low volume parts plus face a lack of purchasing choices because additional products are usually supplied by hardware vendors. The principal reason the segment has for upgrading to the Major Computer line is to get "freedom of choice" in hardware purchases.

● *IBM or IBM (operationally) Compatible Owners/Users.* Machines were purchased to be compatible with the de facto standard in the industry. Such owners want enhancements without sacrificing compatibility and a large software base. They buy on value after operational compatibility requirements are met. They're concerned about future changes in the de facto standard. They have a wide variety of buying options. Their dealers also have a wide variety of options. Their supply of product exceeds demand, so dealers are under a margin squeeze. Reasons for upgrading to the Major Computer line vis-à-vis IBM include better price/value relationship, and Major Computer's product enhancements such as: On-Line Help and Autotutor. Reasons for upgrading to the Major Computer product line vis-à-vis an IBM compatible include better price/value relationship, nationwide support and service, Major Computer's commitment to the industry, its financial resources, and its responsiveness to potential changes to a new "de facto" standard.

Major Computer has an excellent new product entry for each of the segments described earlier. While plans are being made for a national media blitz to inform the public of the new products, the company decides also to develop a program to energize, and help, its dealers support the new line. It decides that it will recommend intense dealer use of the phone and hires you to develop a phone strategy to show them how. Your strategy is to include an overall approach and also a script, or scripts, should more than one be needed, which can be given to dealers to help them address each of these apparent market segments.

Case 9   Letters

WITH ONE EXCEPTION, THE LETTERS DISPLAYED IN EXHIBITS 1–4 don't take a direct marketing posture as they deliver their message. Rewrite each of those that don't reflect direct marketing principles, putting as much direct response technology into them as you feel is appropriate. Evaluate the probable effectiveness of the letter with the greatest direct marketing flavor.

```
TO:  MERCHANTS                              Re:  Outerbelt Center
                                                 Downgrading

     Time and time again I have written the merchants about downgrading the
shopping center, criticizing the landlord, and in other ways undercutting
your own livelihood here.

     Every time a prospective tenant walks around the Mall and talks to the
merchants, all he ever gets is criticism.   Don't you realize the criticism
is hurting you?  I realize that there are many of your who are not doing
well and who would rather blame me for your own inadequacies than your own
inability to operate a business properly.  If you want to do that, there is
nothing that says you can't write me about it or even tell me about it
personally.  But why you would run down even your own place of business.  In
an obvious effort to get at me, only results in your cutting off you nose to
spite your face.

     Prospective tenants come and tell me they have talked to the merchants
and from what they hear from the merchants, they do not feel they want to
come into the shopping center.  If that is what you want, I can assure you
that it will happen.  They will not come into the shopping center, stores
will be vacant, and I will not get any additional rent, but remember, you
will lose sales because vacancies are not a compliment to a shopping center.

     And another thing.  I do not ever want to hear any merchant tell me,
"Why don't you rent vacant stores?"  You know why, so do not ask me.  I do
not want to hear about it.

                         Yours very truly,



                         Sidney J. Bromley


SJB:mv
CC: Main office
```

EXHIBIT 1. Outerbelt Center Letter

NEW PRODUCTS INCORPORATED
Box 256
Iowa City, Indiana 54680

Dear President:

The Tat'l Tail safety flag which is described on the attached brochure is an
excellent premium item. Many Savings & Loans are using it to promote
bicycle safety and at the same time promote thrift among your people. They
work with local police departments and fraternal organizations to provide
public safety campaigns. Many times these are done through the school
system, and the group will present a safety program and follow it up with an
offer allowing each of the students to come into their Savings & Loan and
pick up a Tat'l Tail safety flag as either a gift or a premium for saving.

We've designed the Tat'l Tail to be high quality item. The pennant (sample
enclose) is made of vinyl impregnated nylon, resistant to weathering,
tattering, tearing, fading and stretching, and is permanently attached to
the fiberglass whiprod. A unique attachment holds the rod securely to
prevent theft and can be attached to almost any vehicle such as bicycles,
snowmobiles, motorcycles, agricultural equipment and other vehicles. If you
compare the Tat'l Tail with other similar products, you will find it to be
the best.

Our normal terms of sale call for full payment within 30 days of shipping.
We will ship by the most convenient method and will add freight to the
purchase price or bill it collect. To place you order, just fill out the
attached order blank and send it to the address listed below. We will be
looking forward to your order, and we wish you the best with the Tat'l Tail
safety flag.

                              NEW PRODUCTS INCORPORATED
                              Box 256
                              Iowa City, Indiana 54680

EXHIBIT 2. New Products Incorporated Letter

HAIRCOR HEATING CO.
1251 Weton Center
Palantine, Nebraska

Gentlemen:

Enclosed is our latest illustrated and descriptive catalog sheet of items we
manufacture.

Haircor products have been successfully manufactured and installed for over
25 years.

The Haircor Silencers are manufactured in various sizes. They eliminate the
problem of hammering in water lines.

In keeping with the present fuel oil shortages, it is to the advantage of
the consumer to have installed Haircor motorized zone-controlled gate
valves, which help keep fuel consumption down. Specific zoning sections in
residential or commercial buildings can be heated when necessary. This too
is a savings in fuel costs.

The Haircor fuel oil tank gauge will show at a glance the amount of fuel oil
in the tank regardless of its location. This gauge should be installed at
the same time of the tank installation.

For satisfaction and excellence in performance, specify HAIRCOR PRODUCTS.

Kindly contact your wholesale distributor for further information.

Sincerely yours,

                                    HAIRCOR HEATING CO.
                                    1251 Weton Center
                                    Palantine, Nebraska

EXHIBIT 3. Heating and Air Conditioning, Inc.

800 South Wacker, Apt. 710
Chicago, Illinois 60607

Are you looking for a
Senior Direct Marketing
Manager? Like one that
took a start-up situation
to $60 million in sales in
nine years!

...If you are, I think you'll want to use the enclosed postage-paid reply
card to learn more about a seasoned pro who could be <u>very valuable</u> to your
company.

This person developed and implemented direct marketing programs for a
manufacturer of big-ticket consumer power tools when distribution through a
dealer network became unprofitable.   The results... <u>sales grew from $3
million dollars to $60 million in 9 years</u>. He managed a sales and marketing
staff that went from 3 to 285. He's a hands-on manager that's experienced
with lists, space, creative, direct mail, telemarketing, television,
catalogs. He's even developed and integrated a retail network into the
direct marketing sales channels.

> In short, this guy <u>knows direct marketing from A to Zip</u>! As you
> may have guessed, the person I'm describing is myself. If you are
> looking for a talented senior direct marketing manager, I feel I
> have a lot to offer. What's more, I'm prepared to prove it with a
> <u>SPECIAL FREE OFFER</u>.

I don't expect you to thoroughly evaluate my talents by the few paragraphs
above, but I'll be happy to send you an <u>interesting, detailed resume</u>. Look
it over and see if there isn't a place for my talents in your company ... or
with someone you know.

To get the resume, just complete and return the postage-paid reply card
enclosed. Or for even faster action, you can phone me at 312-431-3384.

Sincerely yours,

Frank Helbig

P.S.   Since I'm presently employed I've used a pseudonym for
         confidentiality.

EXHIBIT 4. Frank Helbig's Job Hunt

Case 10   Total Fitness Machine

REGGIE WILLIAMS IS VICE PRESIDENT OF MARKETING WITH CONSUMER Products, Inc. CPI is an established, successful manufacturer of outdoor gas grills and related consumer products. Much of CPI's product assortment is sold through mass merchandisers, such as K-mart, plus a variety of smaller but operationally similar retailers. CPI enjoys a strong positive reputation in the retail trade.

After an intense period of research and study, CPI management concluded that the most promising consumer goods growth areas of the 1980s was the physical fitness products and services category. The in-home exercise apparatus facet of this market appeared to present CPI with a particularly promising growth opportunity as well as a synergistic fit with its manufacturing competencies. In view of this, a venture team was set up to develop and introduce a new CPI physical fitness product line.

The team's mandate was to develop a very versatile fitness apparatus which (a) delivered the exercise options and benefits sought by the ultimate consumer/buyer, (b) could be sold in the $99 to $299 price range, and (c) could be sold through CPI's current channels, or perhaps through mass-market-oriented sporting goods stores.

After eighteen months of consumer research and engineering work, a very promising physical fitness product was ready for market introduction. The product was based on an inclined rails, rolling platform, cable and pulley design concept (see Exhibit 1) which permitted the user to tone, stretch, and flex every part of the body. Furthermore, with the addition of four accessory items, exercise alternatives on the equipment were virtually unlimited. But even without these, the basic product provided a large exercise variety.

Four different models of the product were developed.

- The CPI 1350 was the line's lowest priced and most Spartan item. This product incorporated the cable and pulley, inclined rails, and rolling platform concept but was restricted to three incline positions. However, it offered buyers a highly versatile, effective exercise apparatus.

- The CPI 1450 was a nearly complete expression of CPI's engineering design concept. (See Exhibit 1.) It was designed to hold manufacturing costs to the lowest possible level consistent with good quality. This model offered nine inclined plane positions, and also folded away for storage. "Folding away" on this model meant that the rails and rolling platform could be stood upright and locked in place when not in use. The 1450 was to be CPI's "sell model"—the model they had designed to be, and expected and wanted to be, their volume seller.

• The CPI 1550 was also a complete expression of CPI's engineering design concept. Materials of different types differentiated this model from the 1450. Rails, for example, were $1'' \times 2''$, and chrome plated, in contrast with the 1450's $1'' \times 1''$, regular run steel, painted rails. It also had the advantage of folding rails. Rails were hinged at about the midpoint of their length which permitted the whole unit to fold away much more compactly and inconspicuously than the 1450. This product was slightly larger than the 1450. It offered twelve inclined plane positions.

• The CPI 2000 was the 1550 with a superelegant look. Rails, for example, were black anodized; the rolling platform cover was made to look more expensive; and so forth. This product was to be directed toward the direct marketing distribution channel. The CPI 2000's perceived market was the direct response responsive, affluent, managerial/executive type.

Four major accessories were available for all models. These were a leg pulley, a bench press, a curl bench, and a squat stand. The bench press and curl bench were necessary to give a product a complete "body building" capability.

CPI's planned retail list prices, probable retailer promotional prices, and dealer costs for its basic machine and major accessories are shown here:

Model	Retail List	Retail Promo	Dealer Cost	CPI Cost (Full)	CPI Cost Direct Variable
1350	$149	$119	$ 80	$ 45	$ 40
1450	$199	$169	$100	$ 50	$ 45
1550	$269	$249	$170	$110	$100
Leg Pulley	$ 30	$ 20	$ 12	$ 8	$ 7
Bench Press	$ 40	$ 30	$ 16	$ 11	$ 10
Curl Bench	$ 50	$ 40	$ 20	$ 13	$ 12
Squat Stand	$ 50	$ 40	$ 20	$ 13	$ 12

The planned retail prices did not include the Model 2000. This model was turned over to a separate direct marketing organization which purchased units from CPI for resale under it's own name, Kenne Enterprises, with CPI's brand name, *Home Spa,* on the product. This organization agreed to set its price so as to minimize potential conflict between CPI and CPI's traditional retailers; or, in other words, to set a price which complemented CPI's retail channel pricing program to the maximum possible degree consistent with profitable direct marketing of the 2000 model.

Competitive information available to the venture team indicated that their *nearest* direct marketing competitor was listing its product for $695, and selling it for $495 during promotions. The *strongest* direct response competitor was very successfully selling a "body building machine" for $495, including freight which ranged from $30 to $50 per order. CPI's engineers believed this product cost less to make than the CPI 2000 *Home Spa.*

Assume that you have been hired to develop a test direct marketing program for the CPI 2000 *Home Spa.* Make your first order of business the discovery of alternative positioning concepts, and develop a test to determine which of the several concepts that you come up with is the best. Following that, decide what pricing and direct marketing strategies you think are needed for the Model 2000. As you consider the problem, assume that CPI is also open to suggestions about its retail price plan. In addition, while examining the problem, make the further assumption that CPI has no objections to supplying you with a more "gussied up" product, providing you're willing to pay for it.

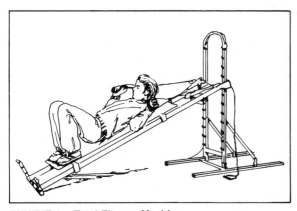 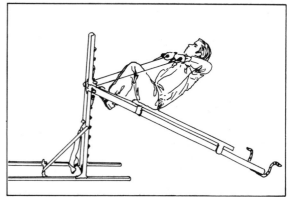

EXHIBIT 1. Total Fitness Machine

Case 11   Magna Deca

THE HOME FITNESS EQUIPMENT MARKET CONTINUES TO GROW, AND the success, in particular, of direct marketers in the field attracted the attention of Jim Sherwood, the marketing manager of Magna Deca, a large consumer goods company. Jim's company marketed largely through traditional channels, but wanted to get into direct response, and felt it had found an appropriate product.

The product was an at-home physical fitness product selling for less than $500. Magna Deca had acquired the product and was prepared to give it the necessary marketing push if the market appeared to be there, but only if it were "there" in the direct response channel. To find out, Jim Sherwood commissioned a local direct response advertising firm to come up with a test direct marketing plan. The plan they suggested involved simultaneous testing of four positioning concepts and five books from five different media groupings—all at the same time. The names of twenty-thousand subscribers of five different magazines were to be rented and one-quarter of each of these twenty-thousand subscriber sets were to be exposed to one of four positioning concepts. (See Table 1 following.)

TABLE 1.   Test Marketing Plan

Publication Category	Test Book	Positioning Concepts			
		Body Building	Health Improvement	Alternative to Jogging	Family Gym
Bus and Travel	*Business Week*	5000	5000	5000	5000
Men's Pubs	*Playboy*	5000	5000	5000	5000
Sports Pubs	*Sports Illustrated*	5000	5000	5000	5000
Science and Elect	*Mechanics Illustrated*	5000	5000	5000	5000
News Weeklies	*Time*	5000	5000	5000	5000

It was decided that five thousand subscribers from each test book would be mailed a lead-generating piece built around each of four positioning themes. In this way it was felt that both the media and the message could be tested at once. The test program was to be run under the name "Personal Fitness Systems" (PFS), rather than the Magna Deca name.

Criticize this testing approach, and suggest other test approaches that might be more appropriate and/or more effective.

Materials in this case used by permission of SEI.

Case 12   The Royer Corporation

THE ROYER CORPORATION MAKES AND SELLS SWIZZLE STICKS, HORS d'oeuvre pics, steakmarkers, and waitstaff personnel badges for night clubs and food service establishments all over the world. Its clients include major casinos in Las Vegas, and other instantly recognizable watering holes of the rich and the famous. All of the firm's business is done using a combination of direct mail and telephone.

The corporation is located in Madison, Indiana, a picturesque town overlooking a scenic bend in the Ohio river on Indiana's southern border. Royer's president and co-owner, Guy Kitchens, along with Frank Geist, vice president, and also a co-owner, took over the company nine years ago, at a time when it was about to fold. Kitchens' first basic decision was to stop using reps and dealers and go direct—a decision that worked and has brought the firm to its current $1 million annual, and growing, sales level.

Kitchens, who was only 25 years of age when he took over the operation, had always operated the firm on the basis of common sense rather than a business school philosophy he never developed. (He was a philosophy major in college, but hadn't ventured near the business school.) His total marketing staff consisted of two people—a sales director and a marketing assistant, neither of whom had had any formal marketing or direct marketing training. Both of these people spent the majority of their time on the phone, with little time left for thinking about marketing. Given his, and their, lack of marketing training, or time to think about it, Kitchens was always—in spite of his success—a little insecure about how he was handling the firm's direct marketing.

It looked like a promising idea, then, to call in Professor Alfred Soloman from a nearby university, and have him take a look. Soloman had a variety of experience in the direct marketing field, and Kitchens had heard enough good things about his direct marketing acumen to believe that an evaluation of the firm's marketing by Soloman might be useful. So he called the professor in for a two-day visit.

Soloman and Kitchens, and his staff, spent the two days talking over every aspect of the operation, and even did some on-the-spot "noodling" on some ways to improve some of the specifics of the Royer operation, especially its telephone procedures. When Soloman left, he left, as Kitchens put it, a full plate of things to work on. But nothing had been formally written down, so Soloman was asked to provide a written report outlining his sense of where the company was in its quest for direct marketing excellence. He agreed to do this. Some of the observations he made in his report are highlighted below.

Basic Attitudes

The consultant's observation is that Royer Corporation possesses the basic, critical attitudes that underpin successful direct marketing practice. Attitudinal and operational signals that customer satisfaction is the pathway to growth and profits were constantly in evidence. In fact, better than virtually any firm the consultant has observed, the corporation's leadership seemed to understand that the three most critical success factors in direct marketing are

1. Taking care of your customer,
2. Taking care of your customer, and,
3. Taking care of your customer.

Personnel

Many direct marketing firms get staff-heavy very quickly. This certainly didn't appear to be the case at Royer. Furthermore, the lean marketing staff of the company all appeared to be relaxed and enjoying their work. None appeared to be uptight and anxious—as is often the case—and all appeared enthusiastic and willing to work hard. Minds all seemed to be open to new possibilities. No one seemed to be threatened by change or by the prospect of being measured—a critical success factor for people who tend to succeed in direct marketing.

Decision Making

It was the consultant's observation that all persons involved in marketing program implementation at Royer are given ample opportunity to influence the direction and content of the program.

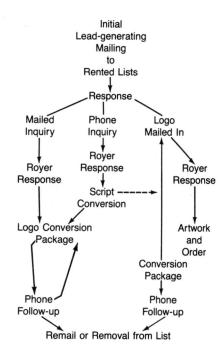

Initial
Lead-generating
Mailing
to
Rented Lists

Response

Mailed Inquiry — Phone Inquiry — Logo Mailed In

Royer Response

Royer Response

Script - - - - - ▶ Conversion

Royer Response

Logo Conversion Package

Artwork and Order

Conversion Package

Phone Follow-up

Phone Follow-up

Remail or Removal from List

EXHIBIT 1.   Royer's Direct Marketing Program Structure

This is a very positive situation in a direct marketing operation, as it provides opportunities for everyone to make a creative contribution, or at least to act as a stimulus to others' creativity. It also gives employees professional growth opportunities, lets them gain confidence, and readies them for greater freedom of action, and management responsibility in the future.

Overall Program Match with Direct Marketing "Rules"

Though it needs to be shored up a little, there appears to be nothing inherently flawed in Royer's current multistage direct marketing approach (mail-generated leads, mail offer of free art work with telephone follow-up to nonrespondents, and mail/phone conversion of free artwork recipients). (See Exhibit 1.)*

---

*Casewriter's note: The package that Royer used to generate leads included the cover letter shown in Exhibit 2, plus price lists, and eight four-color sheets illustrating each of Royer's eight series of food and beverage accessories. This material was all packaged together in a folder. (There were flaps on the bottom of the folder which folded up to create a pocket.) The folder's cover was designed to communicate elegance, which it did, but there was no "sell" on it, nor was there any sell on the back side of the folder.

Thus, from an overall perspective, it is the consultant's opinion that only a modest amount of direct marketing sharpening is needed to bring the Royer program into conformance with the experience-based rules of effective direct marketing. Furthermore, most of what needs to be done can be done without a large increase in mailing/phoning costs.

List, Offer, and Positioning

Royer's offer and positioning strategies are somewhat fuzzy and not clearly related to specific program objectives. Royer's initial, lead-generating mailing to prospects should be built around a specific, attractive offer of a clearly defined "something," even if that something is nothing more than very useful information to exchange for the prospect's making him- or herself known to Royer Corporation as a prospect.

It is also the consultant's opinion that the principle benefit the prospect will obtain, or the principle problem or irritation Royer's product will relieve, does not stand out in the present materials. This forces prospects to figure out for themselves what "itch" Royer is offering to scratch. And when this happens, too often, no doubt, their figuring leads them to conclusions other than those Royer wants them to reach. This leads to fewer responses. The rule in direct marketing is to pick out one major story about your product and build your package around it. This is the essence of what is called "positioning."

Lists/List Segmentation

Royer management has a good, solid, "gut grasp" understanding of lists, and this has served them well to this point. But the company needs considerable work here. The list is the "market" of the direct marketing firm. In direct marketing, to understand a targeted market is to understand a targeted list. This means careful attention to measurement and quantification of market characteristics, that is, more attention to market/list segmentation.

In Royer's case, list segmentation would involve much more careful delineation of the characteristics of the Royer Corporation's

---

When the recipient opened the folder, he or she found the product information shown in Exhibit 3. The inside back of the folder contained the general information shown in Exhibit 4.

Inquiries generated with this mailing came in either by phone or mail. An attempt was made to convert phone inquiries as they came in. Conversion meant agreement to send in a corporate logo. Mail inquiries were followed up by telephone. (Again a corporate logo was requested.) When a logo came in, Royer prepared artwork showing how the prospect's swizzle stick or badge design would look, and mailed it back to the prospect—along with a request to order. Nonresponding recipients of logo artwork were followed-up by phone.

Approximately 10 percent of all mail and telephone respondents to the initial mailing were interested enough to send in their logo and get the free artwork. Approximately half of these converted to buyers after seeing their free artwork.

typical "good" prospect, firms with which Royer has had the most success. This will permit the firm to concentrate on finding more of them. This means wasting fewer resources, buying fewer lists, and so forth, populated with prospects whose affinity for the Royer program is mild to nonexistent. It will also permit Royer to write copy, use telephone scripts, ad headlines, and the like which address the issues that really concern their "best" customers. The direct marketing aphorism is "If you can't sell your best customers, you can't sell anybody."

A Caveat

Considering the above criticism, Royer should reflect on direct marketing's 40–40–20 rule. This rule states that 40 percent of a direct marketer's success is because of the list, 40 percent is due to the offer, and 20 percent is explained by everything else that the direct marketer does.

Assuming that the 40–40–20 rule is valid, it is quite clear that Royer *is* currently making *good offers* to pretty *sound lists,* otherwise it wouldn't be having the success that it is. The consultant believes, however, that there is room for improvement in both areas. Furthermore, because they each constitute such a large chunk of the success basis of an operation, significant improvements in either offers or lists will increase sales dramatically.

Computer Support

At this time, Royer appears to be totally manual in its marketing information management. This is a situation most direct marketers find intolerable when entering a rapid growth phase—which is where the Royer Corporation appears to be poised at this time. Thus, investigation of electronic data processing support seems to be a matter that should not be delayed for more than a few more months, if that long.

Database Marketing

Automation also makes it possible to become a true database marketer. Getting new customers is a major part of direct marketing. Database marketing is often an even larger part.

Database marketing involves thinking about old customers as a special market, or as a set of special markets, and it involves special approaches to marketing to old customers. This usually takes the form of doing something special for old customers, a la the butcher who offers special cuts to his best customers.

Database marketing is part of the process of creating a customer *after making a sale.* It's part of relationship building. This issue was not explored deeply by the consultant, but it appeared that, at Royer, getting new customers may be emphasized relatively more than marketing to old ones. This might be better stated that, at the Royer Corporation, marketing to old customers *may not be emphasized enough.*

Testing

More automation would also make *testing* of program changes more easily undertaken. At present, Royer appears not to be using the testing concept as a routine part of its programming. Normally, as much as 10 percent of the marketing budget is allocated to the search for breakthrough ideas for getting business. It is strongly recommended that the testing concept become part of Royer's thinking. This means that testing of new lists, new headlines, cover letters, and the like, should become a constant process.

Comparison of Program against Some Established Criteria

One of the ways to evaluate a direct marketing effort is to compare it against a set of established criteria that have proven effective for direct marketing firms. These criteria are expressed in the following questions and comments as they relate to the overall program and marketing materials used by Royer.

1. Does the program/package communicate *perceived value,* that is, is the copy saturated with, and focused on, benefits—rather than on features? This approach begins with the development of a company image of customer/prospects as being *value* buyers rather than as *price* buyers.

2. Does the program/package handle the *perceived authority* problem—does it answer the question, "What gives Royer the right to make its product/service claims?" Testimonials are *one* way to deal with this.

3. Does the program/package handle the *perceived satisfaction* problem—that is, prove to the prospect that they will not be dissatisfied with the action they take? This might include proof that, indeed, no commitment is being made when the customer/prospect sends in a logo.

4. Does the program/package handle the *perceived limited availability* question? Does it create the strong impression that you can't get the value package that Royer offers from anyone else. Ways should be found to show just how unique the Royer offer is.

5. Does the program/package "merchandise" Royer's guarantee of satisfaction/no obligation, thereby reducing *perceived risk*? Official looking "guarantee seals" which talk about customers being satisfied or "else" represent a typical tool used for this purpose.

6. Does the program/package come across as a one-on-one piece, that is, as having been written by one person,. say Royer's president, to one person—the prospect/suspect.

7. Does the program/package come across as having been written by someone who understands the world (pressures, stresses, strains, and problems) of the prospect.

8. Does the program/package contain a reason for *taking action now,* to overcome the death knell of direct marketers, procrastination—the natural tendency of even good prospects to put off taking

action until "later"—at which time it frequently does not happen.

Careful study of the materials and approaches Royer is now using reveals that significant potential for improvement exists in *all of the areas outlined above.* Exactly how, and where, is a part of a creative process, and thus, cannot be totally specified here.

Examine the overall thrust of Royer's program, Soloman's comments, and the content of Exhibits 2, 3, and 4, then decide what specifically needs to be done to truly invigorate its direct marketing. Is the brochure/folder content consistent with good direct marketing principles? What do you think the objective of Royer's initial lead generation mailing should be? How about going for the order vis-à-vis lead generation? How hard should a lead be? What might Royer use as a premium and how should a premium be used. What should the envelope teaser, if any, say? Does the cover letter say what a good direct response letter should say? What should the cover letter say? What about scripts for the telephone follow-up of the initial inquiry? If needed, what should it contain?

```
                          ROYER CORPORATION
                         122 West Fifth Street
                         Madison, Indiana 47250
                      (812) 265-3133·Cable:ROYER
         January 28, 1986

         Mr. Paul Paveroti
         Vice President of Purchasing
         FSO International, Inc.
         480 Southwest 2nd Street
         Seattle, Washington 97201

         Dear Mr. Paveroti:

         We are a leading manufacturer of custom design cocktail stirs, hors d'oeuvre
         pics·and personnel name badges. By way of introducing you to our company we
         have enclosed a copy of our latest catalog and representative samples of our
         products.

         For more than ten years the Royer Corporation has specialized in the design
         and manufacture of custom designed cocktail stirs, hors d'oeuvre pics, and
         name badges. Information regarding design, pricing and terms is contained in
         the catalog. However, there are several points which deserve special
         emphasis:

             We have complete design facilities and our artists are at your
             disposal. We will quote on your design or submit a design for your
             consideration at no cost or obligation.

             There are no mold charges on stirs, pics or badges designed with the
             specifications of our Sovereign, Sculpture, Script or Medallion
             Series style categories.

             We do all design, mold construction and manufacturing ourselves
             under one roof and sell directly to you. This gives you the highest
             quality at the lowest possible prices.

             Royer Corporation is committed to excellence in product and service.
             Your satisfaction is guaranteed.

         If you would like to discuss our products further, give me a call at our
         toll free number: 1 800 457-7997. Let us show you how easy it is to design
         your own custom stir, pic or name badge.

         Sincerely,


         Carl C. Sutton
         Director of Sales
```

EXHIBIT 2. Package Cover Letter

ROYER CORPORATION

THE ROYER COLLECTION OF FOOD AND BEVERAGE ACCESSORIES

The beauty and personality of custom designed cocktail stirs, hors d'oeuvre pics, steakmarkers, and name badges uniquely enhance your food and beverage service. Functional as well as decorative, these individualized items are a graceful reminder to guests of your attention to detail and concern for their dining experience.

Royer custom food and beverage accessories are available in low minimum quantities and, in most cases, without initial mold or design charges. This portfolio illustrates the various style categories available, and our custom design skill provides virtually unlimited choice with each category.

The Sovereign Series. Your emblem and name carefully crafted in raised line and lettering and tipped in contrasting foil color. These are our finest cocktail stirs and pics. A distinctive touch for the most distinguished establishment.

The Sculpture Series. Custom designed to capture your unique image, each Sculpture series Stir or Pic is a faithful reproduction of your logo or theme in three dimensional art and raised lettering.

The Script Series. Cocktail stirs that put your signature on every drink with raised lettering to match any style script or type at an unusually affordable price. Plain or color tipped.

The Impression Series. Cocktail stirs and name badges imprinted with your name and logo at attractively low prices. Available in low minimum quantities for smaller establishments.

The Engraving Series. Name badges of two-ply engraving stock with your name and logo imprinted. Suitable for engraving with individual names for a most professional appearance.

The Medallion Series. Badges with your name and logo raised and color tipped to convey dramatically the warmth and personality of your service.

The Emblem Series. An original series of badges styled with your emblem and name embossed in molded polystyrene with channel for name tape. A quietly effective statement that will show absolutely no wear during extended use.

The Standard Series. Stir Rods and Steakmarkers that add color and excitement at convenient prices.

At Royer we have been committed to the highest standards of excellence in the design and manufacture of personalized accessories for the hotel and restaurant industry for more than ten years. A specialized staff and complete studio are available for consultation and preliminary artwork. Each step in the manufacturing process, from construction of individually engraved dies through molding and decorating, is performed in our plant to insure the integrity of product and service at reasonable prices.

If you would like to receive a full scale color sketch of your design for evaluation, simply send us material bearing your logo (matchbook, letterhead, napkin, etc.). Please specify the series and color of your choice. Of course, there is no cost or obligation.

You are invited to call our sales representative. Enquiries are welcome, and our staff is always happy to advise on your selection and design. Please call toll free 1-800-457-7997.

EXHIBIT 3. Text—Inside Front Cover of Folder

GENERAL INFORMATION

Reference Key

Custom Series:	Sovereign, Sculpture, Script, and Emblem series items
Imprinted Series:	Engraving and Impression Series Items
Standard Series:	Standard Stir Rods, Steakmarkers, and Name Tags
Colors:	Additional standard colors or special color matches are at extra costs
Quantity Discounts:	Stock items may be combined for quantity discounts. For example, 10 cases of Standard Stir Rods and 10 cases of Standard Steakmarkers on the same order will earn the 20-case price for both items. No combination discounts are allowed on Custom or Imprinted Series items.
Annual Contract Option:	Sovereign, Sculpture, and Script series items are available on Annual Contract in quantities of 100M or more. Under the terms of this option, the customer receives the quantity discount for the total amount ordered but receives the merchandise in equal installments on a split ship/split bill basis. For example:

Annual Contract Quantity	*Quarterly Shipment*
100M	25M
300M	75M
500M	125M

Over-/Underruns:	All Custom and Imprinted Series are manufactured to order. Allow 10 percent over-/underrun.
Pricing:	All prices are FOB factory. Prices on Annual Contract. List prices are subject to changes without notice.
Shipping:	Merchandise is shipped prepaid and added to open accounts unless otherwise specified. Allow the following shipping time:

New Custom Series items	8 Weeks
Custom Series reorders	4 Weeks
New Imprinted Series items	6 Weeks
Imprinted Series reorders	4 Weeks
Standard items	7 Days

Shipping Weight:	Custom items vary in size and weight depending upon the design. Shipping weights shown are approximate and actual weight may vary considerably.
Routing:	Routing will be determined by the shipper unless otherwise specified.
Special Orders:	Special sizes, shapes, shanks, and two-sided moldings are available at additional cost which may involve mold charges. Our sales representative will be happy to assist you.

EXHIBIT 4.   Text—Inside the Back of Folder

Now look at Exhibits 5 through 7. These materials were subsequently developed for generating leads, which were then followed up with a mailing and a telephone call. In your opinion are these

---

Royer Corporation

OUR STUDIO WILL DESIGN A

CUSTOM COCKTAIL STIR FOR YOU

ABSOLUTELY FREE AND WITH

NO OBLIGATION TO PURCHASE.

Dear Executive:

Royer custom cocktail stirs can increase your alcoholic beverage sales for just pennies a glass. And you can evaluate your design free of charge and without any obligation to purchase.

Sales of alcoholic beverages average 40% to 50% higher profits than food sales. As the manager of an establishment serving liquor, you are doubtless well aware of this fact.

As the individual responsible for purchasing bar supplies and amenities for your organization you also know that proper packaging and merchandising of cocktails and specialty drinks increases your liquor sales dramatically.

Royer custom cocktail stirs are an important part of effective merchandising. They garnish, add color, excitement and increase the customers perception of value received. At a cost that leaves the profits for you.

Royer custom cocktail stirs build repeat business by providing a graceful reminder to your guests of their experience. They put your signature on every drink in a personal and distinctive manner.

As an effective manager you don't buy a pig in a poke. You want personalized amenities, but you are not going to purchase something you haven't seen. Nor do you want to spend a small fortune for a professional designer to create an item you may decide against.

Royer will design your stir or pic free of charge, without obligation. Working with your logo, our staff will prepare a full scale color layout of your custom cocktail stir or pic at no cost. And, there is absolutely no obligation on your part to purchase.

Royer won't waste your valuable time. We'll do it through the mail and over the phone. It's simple and it's painless.

I invite you to take the first step to increasing the most profitable segment of your business.

122 West Fifth Street, Madison, Indiana 47250

EXHIBIT 5. New Package Cover Letter—Page 1

materials appropriate for the task? Where are they strong? Where are they weak? Does Mr. Kitchens need to go back to the drawing board?

Return the enclosed card today or call us toll free at 1 800 457-8997. We will send you a complete catalogue, samples, price list, and Design Request Form. The literature explains the three easy steps necessary to have us design a custom cocktail stir or pic for you. Included also are many examples of unique beverage stirs we have created for our customers across the country.

Thank you for your time. We look forward to working for you.

Very truly yours,

Guy M. Kitchens
President

GMK/bh

P.S. I URGE YOU TO HAVE YOUR CUSTOM COCKTAIL STIR DESIGNED TODAY. IT'S SIMPLE. IT'S FREE. AND, THERE IS ABSOLUTELY NO OBLIGATION. TAKE THE FIRST STEP AND SEND FOR OUR FREE CATALOGUE.

EXHIBIT 5 (cont.).   New Package Cover Letter

BUSINESS REPLY MAIL

FIRST CLASS   PERMIT NO. 232   MADISON, IN

POSTAGE WILL BE PAID BY ADDRESSEE

Royer Corporation
122 West Fifth Street
Madison, IN 47250

NO POSTAGE
NECESSARY
IF MAILED
IN THE
UNITED STATES

Detach and mail portion above

ROYER™

Personalized Beverage Stirs and Pics

Please accept my personal invitation to explore Royer's creative design services at no cost or obligation. Return the attached card and we will send you our color catalogue, price schedule and detailed information on how to take advantage of our free offer.

Sincerely,

Guy M. Kitchens
President

Detach and mail portion at right in envelope provided.

Postage will be paid by Royer Corporation

Literature
Request

☐ Please send me a copy of your catalogue and information explaining how I can have a personalized cocktail stir or pic designed without charge. Upon receipt of your literature I am under no obligation to use your design services. Should I decide to have a cocktail stir or pic designed I am under no obligation to purchase the product.

_____
Your name if different from label below

_____
Telephone Number

GUARANTEE: Royer Corporation will provide upon request a full scale color layout of your custom cocktail stir or pic free of charge and without any obligation to purchase.

Royer Corporation 122 West Fifth Street, Madison, Indiana 47250

EXHIBIT 6. Response Card—Front and Back

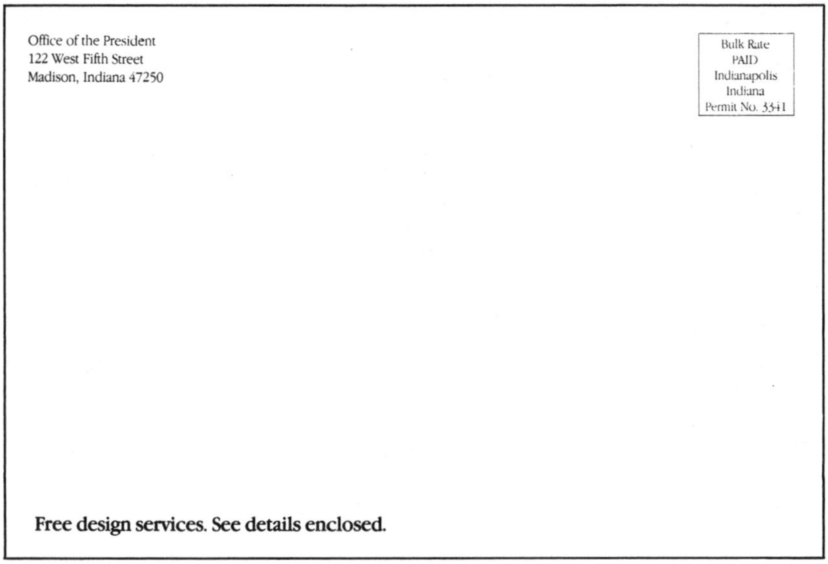

Office of the President
122 West Fifth Street
Madison, Indiana 47250

Bulk Rate
PAID
Indianapolis
Indiana
Permit No. 3541

Free design services. See details enclosed.

EXHIBIT 7. Mailing Envelope

Materials in this case used with permission of the Royer Corporation.

Case 13   WENCO, INC.

NELSON WENRICK HAD WORKED IN THE CONSTRUCTION INDUSTRY for virtually all of his life. After working with his father and brother in a family-owned firm for over thirty-five years, he elected to go into business for himself under the name of WENCO, INC. Nelson had previously earned a bachelor's degree in civil engineering, an uncommon accomplishment among building contractors, most of whom learn their craft on the job. Nelson was thus able to offer his customers the combined benefits of his degree and his many years of valuable experience.

In establishing his own firm, Nelson decided to specialize in the erection of prefabricated metal buildings supplied by a nationally known manufacturer. He also chose to focus primarily on the commercial/industrial market. Much of WENCO's business is referred to as design/build, for it involves significant analysis of a client's needs coupled with architectural work to ensure that the function of the proposed structure will be served by the design a customer desires.

From the company's inception Nelson assembled a talented staff to handle finances, estimating, job supervision, and the like. He demonstrated considerable foresight by investing a large share of the company's early profits in computerized accounting and estimating systems, modern construction machinery and equipment, and an attractive, professional-looking office building. Nelson quickly developed a reputation for knowing what he was doing and for giving his customers what they wanted in a building. There were many previous customers who were willing to provide testimonials to the fine job that WENCO had done for them.

WENCO's annual sales volume reached nearly $2.5 million by the end of the company's third year of operation. The summer of the following year proved to be an interesting and pivotal one for both Nelson and the company. For reasons which were not immediately clear, the company's level of business activity showed no apparent increase over that of the previous year. After carefully examining the situation, Nelson realized that WENCO had spent a relatively small amount in marketing. Much of what was done in this area was what "just came natural." A significant percentage of the firm's work was obtained by competitively bidding on projects against several other area contractors. Nelson had also hired one salesman who followed up on inquiries and made cold calls to prospective clients.

Nelson, however, wanted to see his company grow by seizing a bigger share of the existing market. He felt that he could easily double the size of his business with very little additional investment in personnel and equipment. It became apparent that a more aggressive marketing program could provide the solution he was seeking. Nelson thus contacted a marketing consultant who met with the WENCO staff on two separate occasions. The consultant offered both general and specific direction but left the actual creation and execution of the program up to Nelson and his employees. Nelson soon discovered that the implementation of an aggressive marketing program can be an expensive proposition. He therefore set a limit on the percentage of total sales which he could afford to earmark for marketing expenses.

A lead generation package was soon assembled. A folded brochure in the form of an architectural rendering (blueprint) was

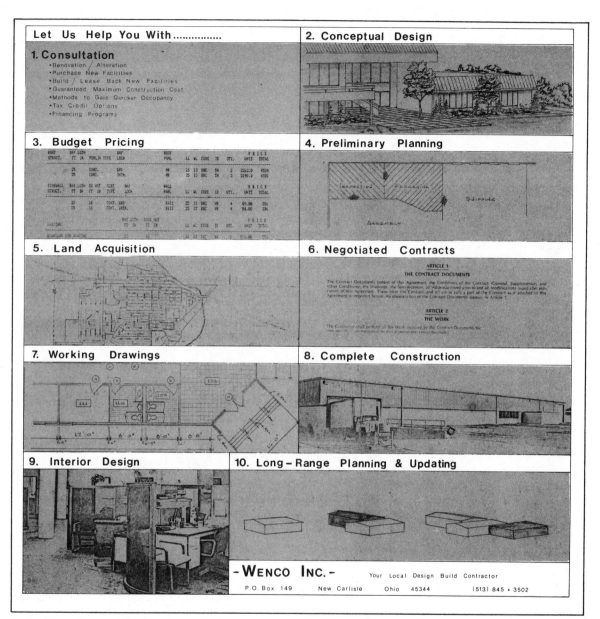

EXHIBIT 1. Unfolded Brochure (detail)

designed by one of the company's draftsmen. Unfolded, the rendering measured 18″ × 24″ and carried the potential customer through every step of the design/build process, listing the various services which WENCO offers its clients. (See Exhibit 1 for detail

W E N C O ,   I N C .

Post Office Box 149, 9791 Sigler Road, New Carlisle, Ohio 45344
(513) 845-3502

Dear

WENCO, INC. is a design/build general contractor representing over 150 years
of combined construction experience in the Miami Valley.

As president of WENCO, I am extremely proud of the reputation our company
has earned among its peers. Our people are hard-working, highly skilled and
genuinely committed to customer service. Our buildings are attractively
designed, competitively priced and carefully tailored to meet the owner's
needs.

WENCO does not use fancy buzz words, flashy advertisements or fast-talking
salesmen. Our solid record of performance speaks for itself. Last year,
repeat business from satisfied clients accounted for nearly 50% of WENCO's
total sales.

After reviewing the enclosed brochure, I invite you to examine WENCO more
closely. Come to our office and exchange ideas over a cup of coffee. Visit
a WENCO job site. Tour a completed project and speak frankly with the
building's owners.

For more information, please return the enclosed postcard or call our office
at (513) 845-3502. I am confident that you, too, will find WENCO's simple,
direct approach a refreshing way to do business.

Cordially,

Nelson D. Wenrick
President
WENCO, INC.

EXHIBIT 2.   Cover Letter

from this brochure.) WENCO originally intended to send this
rendering out with a memo of transmittal attached to it. Both of
these items were things that design/builders and architects understood well. It soon became obvious, however, that WENCO was
not marketing to other design/builders and that the average manager of an industrial facility might not be familiar with such specialized documents as a memo of transmittal. Thus, the memo of
transmittal was scrapped in favor of a carefully composed cover
letter which stressed WENCO's many years of experience and the

Envelope

I would like more information.

☐ Please call me to discuss my building needs.

☐ Please send me a free copy of Building Profit magazine.

NAME   TITLE

COMPANY   BUSINESS PHONE

ADDRESS   CITY   STATE   ZIP CODE

WENCO, INC.   (513) 845-3502

Response Card

Brochure Front Fold

Brochure Back Fold

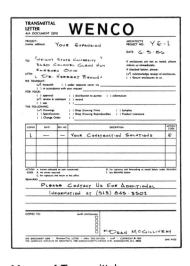

Memo of Transmittal

EXHIBIT 3.   Envelope and Contents

company's reputation for quality craftsmanship and customer service throughout the area (Exhibit 2).

Potential customers were encouraged to respond either by mail or by telephone. A stamped, self-addressed postcard was thus enclosed, enabling the individual to request more information on WENCO or a free subscription to a building trades magazine (bottom of Exhibit 3). The principal aim was to elicit a response from as many prospective clients as possible and qualify them at a later date. The package was mailed in a hand-addressed, 6″ × 9″ manila envelope with the WENCO logo on a silver return address label (top of Exhibit 3).

Evaluate the proposed program and enclosed materials. What else do you think should be done to generate and qualify leads? To convert leads to sales?

Materials in this case used with permission of WENCO, INC.

Case 14   Allwood Chef, Inc.

IN 1980 ED PHILLIPS, WHO RAN A SMALL WELDING SHOP OPERATION in southern Illinois, was stricken with a rare disease. It took several years, and all of Ed's savings, before doctors diagnosed his problem. The illness, it turned out, was potentially curable, though it left Ed in a weakened condition.

No longer able to do heavy work, Ed, a proud man, began doing any kind of light work he could find to earn a living and pay for his continuing medical treatments. While working in a pizza parlor in 1972, Ed suddenly hit on the idea of catering company picnics and other social events where large numbers of people were gathered for meals cooked on site. Ed's idea quickly turned into a reality and after six months, "Ed's Catering Service" became a thriving business. As it grew, Ed toyed with several different cooking methods and cooker concepts; his goal was to find a way to cook enough meat to serve up to 600 people at one time, and still get a distinctive, flavorful result.

One day while discussing a catering job for a company that produced household fuel oil tanks, an idea occurred to Ed. Fuel oil tanks just might be configured in some way to produce the result he wanted. After considerable thought, Ed decided that he must separate the fire from the food in such a way that the grease would not drop onto the fire. Thus, Ed designed a "separator" (technically a "baffle") which he placed one-third of the way down in the fuel tank. The baffle permitted the fire to burn in the upper one-third of the fuel tank, but allowed the heat and smoke to circulate down to the lower two-thirds of the tank where the meat was cooked. The smoke would escape through an exhaust at the bottom end of the tank.

After experimenting with various ways of dampering the contraption and lowering and raising the height of the baffle, trying several exhaust locations, and developing various sizes and types of access doors, Ed developed a primitive version of the cooker. Ed placed the cooker on wheels to facilitate its movement.

Because one of his cookers could serve up to 100 people, Ed decided to construct six of them so that he would be able to serve up to 600 people at one time. Not satisfied with this arrangement, Ed decided to combine the six cookers into one giant cooker that could be towed to a site and used to cook for any size group. He proceeded to string three of the tanks end to end, and then place the two strings side by side on a specially built trailer. By adapting the proportions of his "one fuel tank cooker" to suit an end-wise combination of three fuel tanks, he was able to get the same taste and flavor as before. Ed immediately dubbed the new cooker the "Gourmet Cooker."

Ed thought he might have something that was patentable, and it was. He then obtained one.

Ed attempted to sell a license on his patented process to others; however, there were no takers. He learned later that several restaurants were using his cooker idea in some of their units. After several caustic confrontations with the owners/managers of these restaurants, Ed sued one of them for infringing on his patent and won! Unfortunately for Ed, although the restaurants stopped using Ed's idea (presumably because of his suit), they did not show much interest in making a deal with Ed for rights to use his "new" gourmet cooking concept.

Ed's patent was somewhat strange in that it patented a *result* (the double-spiral, heated gas flow), not the *cooker*. Thus, the patent precluded any charcoal burner maker from producing a cooker that used his heat movement process unless they paid Ed a royalty. None of them wanted the process, however, until reports began to circulate that a chemical produced when grease dropped from cooking meat onto hot charcoal was potentially carcinogenic. This report made Ed feel he really did have a good idea; his cooker placed the fire *above* the meat where grease could not drop on the fire. Further, his cooker could be fired with wood as well as with charcoal. With these considerations in mind, Ed Phillips proceeded to design a backyard-size "Gourmet Cooker."

The model he constructed was 36″ long, 14″ wide, and 20″ deep. Because he couldn't buy ready-made fuel tanks for a cooker this size, he proceeded to develop primitive presses and molds to make his model in quantity. Ed's cooker, which was made of steel and weighed over 100 pounds, cost over $75 to build—assuming a production rate of about twenty cookers per day. Because Ed believed he would have no trouble selling a product such as his cooker with so many positive features, he proceeded to produce over 200 units. At a price of $120, Ed succeeded in selling a few units; however, the going was rough. In fact, two years passed before he was able to sell his total inventory of 200 backyard units, most of which he sold at his catering jobs where people saw how they worked. Obviously frustrated, Ed could not understand why his cookers were not selling.

Everyone who owned a Gourmet Cooker raved about it! But orders were not coming in. His dealers, about twenty small retailers in southern Indiana and Illinois, were very enthusiastic about his cookers; however, they weren't moving them. The reason, presumably, was the price. During this period, several charcoal cooker makers approached Ed with offers to buy his operation. However, the money they offered was minimal. None was willing to give Ed a reasonable per-unit royalty or minimum annual guarantee. Ed strongly suspected that all they wanted to do was "cubbyhole" his idea until his patent expired in 1990.

It was not until 1978, five years after getting his patent, that Ed saw any real hope of making money on his idea. Alfred Wisdom, a marketing professor at a nearby university, happened to notice with particular interest a backyard cooker which a friend he was visiting had purchased from Phillips. Noticing the strange cooker, Wisdom asked his friend how the cooker functioned, and what led him to purchase it. Although Professor Wisdom found his friend's story about the cooker interesting, he thought little more about it until about a month later. While having lunch with Larry Savage, an executive at Woodworks, Inc., a direct response firm for whom he was doing some consulting work, Wisdom mentioned the cooker as a possible novelty item which the firm might be interested in. His description of this unique cooker (see Exhibit 1) piqued Mr. Savage's interest. As a result, Professor Wisdom was invited to enter into exploratory discussions with the Woodworks president and production manager concerning the availability of adding such a product to the firm's line of woodworking equipment and supplies.

John Mercer, the company president, was moderately enthusiastic about the idea but felt that his company should explore the opportunity further. Mercer asked Wisdom to visit Ed Phillips and to enter negotiations with him about the possibility of Woodworks, Inc. buying a license to market Phillips' patented product. Wisdom telephoned Phillips and found that, indeed, he was looking for someone to market his cooker. However, Phillips was very evasive in answering most of Wisdom's other questions. To Wisdom it was apparent that Phillips feared Woodworks, Inc. was just another company that wanted to buy his patent for "pennies," only to market the cooker after the patent had expired.

After talking with several local people who either knew or had known Professor Wisdom, Phillips began to feel that Wisdom was a trustworthy person. After considerable thought, Phillips called Wisdom and agreed to bring his cooker to the company's headquarters to demonstrate how it worked. After explaining the merits of his unique cooking process, Phillips sat down with company management to discuss a possible licensing agreement.

Ed was quite explicit in stating that unless he could earn at least $100,000 per year, he would not be interested in selling his patent rights. (He intimated, however, that his figure was somewhat negotiable.) Ed also wanted Woodworks, Inc. to satisfy a $3,000 loan he had incurred to build his primitive producton equipment. Finally, Phillips wanted to continue to produce his cooker until his royalty payments exceeded what he was currently making on the units he was selling. Woodworks, Inc.'s executives believed Phillips's demands posed a set of serious problems for them. They also were unclear as to the ease with which another company might find a way around his patent and therefore imitate his cooker.

After considerable discussion of these and other issues with his chief executives, Mercer asked Professor Wisdom to outline in writing a tentative offer to Phillips. However, while Professor Wisdom was wording this important document in the most precise terms, Woodworks, Inc.'s executives were having second thoughts. They concluded that at the present time it was not wise to depart from their rapidly growing woodworking lines. Thus, no offer was made to Phillips.

Having learned of the Woodworks decision, Professor Wisdom began to entertain thoughts of marketing Phillips's cooker. The more he thought about taking the entrepreneurial leap, the more enthused he became. The potential for success of this innovation, he felt, was tremendous. However, Wisdom needed both financial and "nitty-gritty, know-how" help. Larry Savage had both, so he and Wisdom agreed to set up a firm for the express purpose of negotiating a deal with Ed Phillips to market the "Gourmet Cooker." Finding Phillips agreeable to their proposal, they immediately hired a patent lawyer to research the product and a corporation attorney to draw up a licensing agreement and to get them incorporated with an initial capitalization of $10,000. They traveled to southern Illinois to negotiate a deal between Phillips and their new corporation. Allwood Chef, Inc. was on its way.

In your discussion of the Allwood case, consider the following:

1. Identify every conceivable unique feature of the "new" product and translate these into consumer benefits.

2. Determine the market position toward which the new cooker should be directed.

3. Develop an alternative name for the new product.

4. Develop a two-step space ad, which asks consumers to clip and send for more information, for placement in a magazine.

5. Develop a brochure to send to people who clip coupons and send for more information.

6. Develop a sales letter to send with the brochure going to coupon clippers.

7. Assume you are going to market this product by direct mail—develop a break-even analysis based on various assumed costs of marketing and distributing such a product by mail.

EXHIBIT 1. Product Description and Comments

The Gourmet Cooker (GC) is a truly multipurpose food preparation product. Either charcoal or wood may be used in it to generate cooking heat. Food may be cooked directly over charcoal or cooked indirectly with either charcoal or wood. It can be used to cook or smoke food. It will cook and smoke food simultaneously. It will cook meat, poultry, fish, and vegetables. It can be used to dry fruit such as apples, apricots, and prunes. A variety of foods can be prepared on it at one time. Bread can be baked on it. Food can be smoked and preserved with it.

The GC's unique double spiral heat flow produces even heat throughout its cooking/smoking chamber. As a consequence, food does not have to be turned or "rotisseried" to get evenly cooked meat or other food. Also, because the GC's firebox is not under the food, flame-ups produced when grease hits charcoal are eliminated.

The GC gives the user flavor options equal to the variety of woods found in nature. Hickory wood imparts the delightful and traditional hickory flavor to whatever is being cooked. Sassafras and maple produce equally unique and delightful, flavorful taste treats.

Large hams, roasts, chickens, and the like can be cooked and/or smoked to perfection and then frozen until needed. At serving time, users need only microwave, oven heat, or pan heat the foods; some meats like ham and chicken are good served cold.

Unlike other cookers, particularly those that are gas fired, as well as charcoal burners, to some extent, the GC does not consume a nonrenewable natural resource. Woods are available virtually everywhere and are easily replenished. Also, it is not completely necessary to burn raw wood to get the wood-smoked flavors; these flavors can be obtained to some extent by sprinkling available sawdust from various tree varieties on charcoal.

The sight and aroma of burning wood and food in a natural state bring the GC user into much closer contact with nature. This product is not for those who take a rush-hour view of dining. It slows the user down, allows him to relax and do things the way our forefathers did them, and enjoy them the way they did.

The GC is for those who appreciate good food; who take some pride in preparing food to flavor perfection; and who find an escape from the hustle, rush, and bustle of modern life in their preparation of nutritious, natural, and naturally flavored foods.

Alfred Wisdom
Professor of Marketing

_____

Materials in this case used by permission of SEI.

Case 15   Workmate Pricing Problem

WORKMATE, INC. SELLS A MULTIPURPOSE WOODWORKING TOOL. INITIALLY, this product was sold in shopping malls using on-site demonstrations by factory sales personnel. This very successful strategy was then complemented with a direct mail program designed to sell people who expressed interest at the malls but did not buy, and to sell people who inquired as a result of magazine and other types of advertising. Still later a telephone marketing program was established. All of Workmate's marketing effort melded together quite well with the exception of its price quotation program.

Mall sales teams sold the product for $1,195 and induced buyers to "buy now" with a $100 discount if the buyer purchased during the demonstration period (teams usually spent one week in each mall, then moved on).

The direct mail group found the "$100 off for a limited time only" strategy effective and ran such programs periodically. The direct mail inquiree was sent a package of promotional materials among which was a $100 coupon good for sixty days.

Approximately fourteen days before the coupon discount period ended (coupons were stamped), the telemarketing group took over and attempted to sell the prospect on placing an order before the sixty days were up. This program was only marginally effective, so the telemarketing group was permitted to offer an additional $50 inducement to buy now. This worked well.

The problem was that inquirers frequently turned up at malls holding a $100 discount coupon and, also, frequently aware of an additional $50 discount if they ordered via the telephone, making it difficult for mall teams to make their $100 inducement "to buy now" effective.

This problem got a lot of study with one conclusion being that the mall teams must always have the lowest and best offer, that is, the lowest price of the three channels. The problem was how.

Diagnose this problem and suggest a solution to it.

Case 16   Shopsmith, Inc.
Direct Marketing Company Renewal

THE SHOPSMITH MARK V MULTIPURPOSE WOODWORKING TOOL DIED quietly in 1966. An ingenious, multipurpose power tool, it had been the rage of the home-woodworking set in the 1950s, but apparently, the novelty had worn off. So after nearly twenty years of production and three changes of ownership, the tool just wasn't selling.

Ironically, woodworking craftsmen and hobbyists who owned the Shopsmith Mark V woodworking tool were so enamored with it that a cult of sorts had grown up around it. The tool was unusual only in that five basic woodworking tools (lathe, disc sander, table saw, vertical drill press, and horizontal drill press—sometimes called a horizontal boring machine) were combined into one machine driven by a central power source. With just a little practice, the typical user could shift the tool's orientation from one operation to another in a matter of seconds, for example, from sawing to lathe work, and so forth. In addition, woodworking accuracy using Shopsmith was truly excellent. Furthermore, the tool was extremely durable, so durable in fact that by 1970, twenty-three years after the first Shopsmith was produced, not a single machine, so far as anyone could determine, had been retired.

People who owned Shopsmith Mark Vs bragged about them constantly, and just as constantly kept on the lookout for other owners. When owners did find each other, lasting friendships often were formed and, sometimes groups with memberships spread across a hundred miles or so were organized to socialize and discuss any and all aspects of Shopsmith—its uses, its strength, its weaknesses, its inventor, his success, his failure, and so forth.

John Folkerth, a young stockbroker in Dayton, Ohio, was one of those who had grown fond of the woodworking and of Mark V. Fortuitously, John needed a part for one of his woodworking tools at the very time that the Mark V was no longer being produced. His pursuit of the part led him to the discovery that the Shopsmith line had been discontinued and that it's tooling was available for purchase. Itching to strike out on his own, John moved quickly to acquire the rights to the product and the equipment to produce it. He accomplished this by the fall of 1971, made the decision to quit his stockbrokering job, and began planning his next moves.

In March 1972 Folkerth engaged the services of Jack Tritle to help set up a production operation. Tritle agreed to work for nothing while organizing the production process, with a promise of backpay when and if the operation earned a profit. Tritle and Folkerth got the production system set up and turned out their first unit on March 20, 1973. This was in a very old, and modest, Tipp City, Ohio building which Folkerth joked would have caved in "if the termites had quit holding hands."

While Tritle and Folkerth had been working to get production of the Mark V off the ground, Larry Blank, a Folkerth colleague at his stock brokerage firm, began to show some interest in the project. Starting with Saturday visits and some suggestions on marketing the product, Larry was hired as vice president of marketing and began work in that role on April 1, 1973.

During this start-up phase, sales had been made largely to individuals and to selected hardware and similar stores, here, there, or anywhere, just to get volume. These were expensive sales, for the most part, and with Shopsmith's marketing margin on retail selling price slightly less than 50 percent, profits were meager. Though enough orders were obtained to sustain the new company, at the end of over one full year of operation, it appeared that the company had merely been pipeline filling. Dealers who had bought and stocked the product simply weren't moving it out of their stores. As Blank put it, instead of LIFO (Last In-First Out) or FIFO (First In-First Out), FISH (First In-Still Here) had been the accounting approach during that first year. This, combined with a cost-accounting error, put the struggling company into a financial bind in the summer of 1974, and moved Folkerth to inform Tritle and Blank, "We're just about belly up."

But the young company hung on and in the early fall of 1974, Larry Blank tried a new marketing approach that changed the company's fortunes. He convinced the management of a local enclosed-mall shopping center to let Shopsmith, Inc. set up a demonstration area in a high traffic zone within their mall. He then worked up a combined sales and demonstration talk, and trained three sales demonstrators to make product demonstrations in the mall. The program was an instant success. Forty-three Shopsmith Mark Vs were sold in five days. This success led to other similar demonstrations with the overall results being excellent.

The mall program was soon the heart of Shopsmith's overall marketing strategy. Buoyed by the success of the program, Blank worked to refine it, eventually hitting on two devices to make it easier to "set up shop" in shopping centers. One of these was a trailer that could be opened on site to provide an instant stage, with curtains for background, and so on. The other was a portable storefront for use in shopping centers where an empty store provided an apparently excellent display location. These efforts, combined with major refinements in the "canned" sales/demonstration talk, were marked by continuing success.

By 1976 Blank's marketing staff had grown to include a sales manager and an advertising manager. He had also established a telemarketing group which was working effectively. Blank carefully monitored his new staff's efforts, but turned his attention more and more toward finding new ways for Shopsmith to grow.

In late 1976 a little over three years after its revival, the overall success of the company was truly astonishing. Sales were so good, in fact, that new, modern manufacturing facilities and offices were built to house an organization grown to well over 200 people. The organization was so successful that it was beginning to run into "problems of success." Specialization of, and growth in, functions such as purchasing, finance, labor negotiations, advertising, pricing, sales management, mall marketing, and the like were producing communications and other problems new to the management.

Problems in the marketing area began to crop up, too. Although Blank could define them, he neither had the skill nor the time to solve them. His mall marketing strategy, for example, was still working well, but he knew a lot of marketing money was being wasted there. Shopping malls welcomed and often recruited Shopsmith demonstrations. The problem, then, was not finding demonstration sites but selecting the best ones. This problem became obvious after one weekend in Tennessee. Demonstrations were simultaneously made in a Nashville regional mall and in a small and somewhat isolated Tennessee town over 100 miles away.

The Nashville program produced a total of eight unit sales, barely enough to meet expenses; the other produced thirty-seven units in sales. Many other similar experiences across the country proved conclusively that some malls were good ones, some were poor ones, and some were absolutely awful. But the question was, which ones and why? Blank's in-house discussion produced a variety of potential explanations. One, for example, was that the presence of a lot of men's shoe stores in a mall explained the problem. Another was that sales seemed to depend on whether the demonstration corresponded with crop harvests in the local area. Blank concluded from these discussions that no one really knew and decided to call in a consultant to diagnose the problem. The consultant never found a really convincing answer either.

The marketing organization's other major problem was interchannel conflict. Sales contractors were protesting that the mailorder program was taking business out from "under their noses." Shopping mall demonstrations in contractor territories were receiving criticism for the same reason. Contractor sale prices and demonstration sale prices differed; and any special deal offered by the company that took business away from these contractors was a source of potential conflict.

In addition, it was becoming increasingly evident to Larry Blank and his marketing group that a stronger "local presence" of some type, perhaps in the form of a large number of very small, permanent sales offices all across the country, or possibly, the placement of retail stores in strategic locations around the country, were going to be necessary to continue the growth of the company. It was also obvious to Blank that the telephone and other emergent direct marketing methods should be installed and integrated into Shopsmith's marketing program. If done, this would further disturb the current arrangements—already high in conflict and possessed with the potential for much more. As an example, contractors were already upset that the mall demonstrations were "stealing their business." If the firm sold the machine through mall demos, contractors, mail order, and retail, how could the firm keep all these channels, and perhaps more, functioning in a complementary, synergistic way?

In spite of these conflicts and other problems, by 1978 Shopsmith had managed to develop four vigorous and profitable channels: mail, telephone, direct mall sales, and retail stores. In 1980 800 demonstrations were held at shopping centers, motels, home shows, and other locations around the country, reaching an audience of approximately 750,000 people. These people saw how the Shopsmith Mark V, with a list price of $1145.00, could be easily converted to do the work of five tools, and how it could be expanded with add-on accessories such as a band saw, jigsaw, belt sander, and a jointer. From 1975 to 1981 sales had grown from only 1.6 million to 60 million, the company had gone public and everything looked rosy.

Shopsmith had a mailing list of approximately one-half million owners (see Table 1), containing both those it had generated on its own, and those generated by predecessor companies going back over twenty years. As shown in Table 2, Shopsmith Mark V owners were overwhelmingly male, married, homeowners, and slightly upscale in income, with substantial discretionary income. They are also described as being family/home oriented and stable, and plan well in advance for the future. They enjoy gardening and are upwardly mobile. (The company had an even larger list of nearly 2 million inquiries that were less than four years old. See Table 3.)

TABLE 1.   Owner Breakdown by Year of Purchase

25,000 Hotline Buyers
35,000 1986 Buyers
53,000 1985 Buyers
71,000 1984 Buyers
75,000 1983 Buyers
55,000 1982 Buyers
100,000 1978–1981 Buyers

TABLE 2. Owner/Buyer Profile	**TABLE 3. Inquirer Profile**
99% Males 94% Married 92% Homeowners Median Annual Income $25,000 + Average Age Range 36–42 Average Order $1600	94% Males 94% Married 90% Homeowners Median Annual Income $25,000 + Average Age Range 32–38

Periodicals such as *Fine Woodworking* and do-it-yourself maga-zines, had traditionally been about the only print media that proved useful in reaching Shopsmith's market. The company just recently commissioned a study on do-it-yourselfers (D-I-Yers) that indicated that the woodworking market could be divided into five different major woodworking segments (see Table 4), as follows:

1. *Rather Not D-I-Yers.* Would much rather hire even minor work done but can't afford it—are forced into it. Not sophisticated D-I-Yers, but surprisingly active.

2. *Conscientious D-I-Yers.* Sophisticated D-I-Yers. Know good values. D-I-Y is a focal point of their lives. Continuously involved in home repair and improvements. Want high quality for the best price in town. Value sensitive. Use consumer reports and D-I-Y magazines for product information.

3. *Moderate D-I-Yers.* Moderately active home maintainers. Mostly routine; not major. Sees D-I-Y as a leisure activity in the same class as tennis, sailing, and so forth (for him or her). Does D-I-Y because it's the "in" thing to do. Buys on impulse. Likes "new" items. Price a minor issue. Convenience is a big issue. Sales ads don't work with this group.

4. *Economic D-I-Yers.* Strong believers in D-I-Y home repair and improvement. Does D-I-Y for economic reasons but likes it. Usually young, in debt, and price sensitive., Frequent patron of the "Home Center." Responds to sales. Usually desire to learn and do more D-I-Y. TV ads a big information source.

5. *"Good-Ole-Boy" D-I-Yers.* The "Good Ole Boys" of D-I-Y. Has always done D-I-Y. Neither likes it or dislikes it. Just does it, whenever it needs to be done. Typically blue collar. D-I-Y technique/equipment knowledge high. Likes to buy from the "authorities"—companies perceived to be the authority in relevant product fields.

TABLE 4. Market Potential of the Segments

Segment	Size of Household*	Buying Power Market Potential*
Rather Not	35.9	23.9
Conscientious	21.3	26.8
Moderate	17.9	21.4
Economic	11.9	12.9
"Good Ole Boy"	13.0	15.0

*Expressed as a percentage.

In spite of its various problems, things sailed along quite nicely for the Shopsmith Company until late 1981 when interest rates reached historic levels which made credit sales much harder to accomplish. (Sales resistance led to a price decrease, followed, shortly thereafter, by decreased profitability.) Despite the lower price and other purchase incentives, sales of the company's "cash cow," the Shopsmith Mark V five-tools-in-one woodworking tool continued to slacken in all channels—mail, mall demos, the telephone, as well as its latest channel, woodworking stores. (By now the company had five stores in three states.)

In addition, the firm was selling a complete line of woodworking tools and accessories. In 1984, to combat increasing market resistance, the company introduced a new, replacement model of the Mark V which sold for approximately 20 percent more than the model it replaced. The new product had several new bells and whistles, but as far as raw woodworking capabilities were concerned, it was difficult to discern any major advantages of the new product over the old.

Despite efforts to stop the trend, sales continued to decline from close to $80 million annually in 1983 to approximately $40 million in 1986. During this period, most of the company's original cast of characters, including Larry Blank, left the company and a new president was named. Unfortunately, the new president was unsuccessful in arresting the decline and left the company in early 1987, after an apparently frustrating year on the job. John Folkerth reassumed the presidency in early 1987, and began to ponder his options for getting his company on track again.

1. Diagnose Shopsmith's current strategic directions and define improvements that appear merited.

2. Develop an offer strategy for Shopsmith, a positioning strategy for Shopsmith, and a list strategy for Shopsmith.

3. Pull together a sketch of a classic direct mail package, including a cover letter, brochure, order form, incentive/premium, and other envelope stuffers, outside envelope teaser concepts, and so forth.

4. Develop fully a direct response print ad to generate inquiries, a cover letter for a classic package, and a method for building perceived authority into the program.

5. Prepare a comprehensive test direct marketing plan for Mr. Folkerth. He's interested in seeing three different programs, small, medium, and large ($50,000, $150,000, and $300,000). Coordination and cooperation of all channels involved in the strategy is important.

Materials in this case used by permission of Shopsmith, Inc.

Case 17   Blue Chip Grinding

BLUE CHIP GRINDING MACHINE COMPANY COMPLAINED THAT PROSpect requests for machine demonstrations were becoming a serious problem. Ten demos were already backlogged. Each demo required careful planning, review of the prospect's part prints, development of fixturing, working out the grinding process, dressing the grinding wheel, and writing a CNC program. Only experts could do all this.

"This problem is acute because no prospect will buy our machine without witnessing a demo. They want to *know* if our machine will do their work," said George Moore, president of Blue Chip. He explained further that the best experts at staging demos were already working overtime on production. "We can't use just anybody, because if there's a hitch in the demo, the prospect may lose confidence and not buy." The problem was how to solve this demonstration problem without hiring some people.

Moore decided to bite the bullet and call in some consultants. The consultants came up with a report. Read the report, which follows, and determine whether or not it should be implemented, and why.

Consultant's Proposal for Getting on Top of the Demo Problem

Objectives

1. Reduce the costly aspects of demos—custom process development, custom tooling, special wheel, personnel time, entertaining, and so forth.

2. Use machine demonstration as a positive marketing tool to qualify prospects and shorten sales order lead time.

Present Situation

1. Machine demos with customer parts require lengthy analysis, preparation, setup, and run time.

2. Time spent on individual demos is time unavailable for other tasks.

3. Lengthy delays and backlog may raise questions about Blue Chip's capability—may alienate prospects.

4. Any hitch in the demo proceedings, such as bad programs or parts, can postpone or kill the sale.

5. If higher ranking buying influences do not attend the demo, they may offer additional questions and issues, further delaying the sale.

6. Consultants interviewed machine tool buyers and salespeople to learn *why* they want to see a demonstration (see Appendix). They want to be assured of *reliability* and *capability* to fully satisfy the *critical aspects* of their application.

7. Sales leads from old customers, advertising, publicity, and trade shows are being qualified quickly with a telemarketing script. Reps have sufficient information for on-target follow up. For qualified prospects they can supply data sheets to show how Blue Chip has solved similar problems. The stage is set for obtaining the prospect's part prints, presenting the demo part, and inviting demo visit.

Proposal

1. *Adopt a preemptive demonstration strategy.* Try to force the prospect to attend a demonstration *before* the quotation is prepared, or as early as possible in the sales negotiation. This is to qualify the prospect and get him involved in a substantial way *before* he can formulate his own demo (probably running his own parts).

2. *Use a telemarketing script to force the demonstration, to find the key elements of reliability, the critical aspects of the application, and the buying influence.* The script provided in Exhibit 1 can be used by sales reps or Blue Chip. The objective is to schedule a standard demonstration at the earli-

est possible time to head off the need for a special demonstration with customer parts.

3. *Organize a standard demonstration around two or three parts.* These should be selected to show machine capability in relation to prospect's needs. The prospect is *never* told these parts are standard. Rather, the prospect's part print is examined, then they're given a machine's part to touch, heft, and examine. We tell him: "We want to demonstrate the critical elements for you in person. You will see firsthand our ability to hold this kind of tolerance (concentricity, steps, etc.). The plant demo also includes presentation modules by Blue Chip engineers in response to specifically identified reliability concerns (rigidity, repeatability, hydraulics, etc.).

4. *Hand the prospect a video cassette of his demo for review back at the home plant.* Set up a video cart consisting of two VCRs, a camera, and a small color monitor. Tape the prospect's demo. The front end of the tape includes some standard boiler-plate on Blue Chip's capability. The prospect will show this tangible evidence of his demo to buyers at home that our salesmen may not be able to reach. Equipment cost is around $2000 total.

a. Qualifies prospects quickly. Willingness of a company to spend time and money to send its people is a good indicator of genuine intent to buy. Reps can call back to close on demo where need is farther down the road.

b. Simplifies the demo procedure by standardization.

c. Early demo permits faster demo, uncomplicated by having to work on nonstandard parts.

d. Provides hard evidence for the prospects back home.

e. Sets up the "actual parts" demo as something extraordinary. Policy is to charge for extraordinary demo with credit against machine purchase.

f. Places the competition at a disadvantage. (Can the competitor make Blue Chip's demo part?) Prospect places order with people they have met, confident of capability and reliability.

g. Can head off competition by quickly engaging prospects with our solution. Can help sell special modifications to further differentiate our machine.

h. Shortens order lead time. Shrinks informing and negotiating.

i. Should sell more machines, require less lengthy interruptions of key personnel at Blue Chip since responses are modular.

Recommended Action

Decide on standard demo parts.

Sales Process

Current Sequence	*Proposed Sequence*
Sales leads from old customers, advertising, publicity, shows	Sales leads from old customers, advertising, publicity, shows
Qualification (consultants phone script)	Qualification (consultants phone script)
Supply data sheets	Supply data sheets
Receive prospect's part print and RFQ	Requalify: close on standard demo, (phone or rep) and receive print
Evaluate application, propose solution, quote	Standard demo establishes capability and reliability; supply AV tape
Determine prospect's actual interest	Quote or no-quote
Custom part demo at Dayton	Negotiate order or no-order
Negotiate order or no order	

Appendix: Consultant Interviews

Interview with Gene Godfrey,
Cortland Corp.

(Roger Brucker is asking the questions; Gene Godfrey, answering.)

Q: *I'm trying to find out about how people like you use machine tool demonstrations when you are considering buying machine tools. Do you always ask for a demonstration?*

A: Most of our machines are special. You often can't get a demonstration of something special. Now, if it's a standard machine, I want to see it. I want to talk to the user.

Q: *What do you do with the results of the demonstration?*
A: What do you mean?

Q: *Do you make a formal written report, an oral report, or what?*
A: It's a brief report to management. Sometimes I give them my notes. They may have some questions, and I may have to get more information. They're no dummies. Generally it's not a formal report. If it were government, I suppose there would be a long written report.

Q: *If your report is favorable, they authorize the buy?*
A: No, all purchasing is from headquarters. They sometimes overstep our recommendation. More likely on standard machines than specials. They may have made a special buy or something we don't know about. Now, the hub of special machine builders is Detroit. Even so, we know that no special press is as good as a Minster. Minster supplies components to some of the special press people.

Q: *What if your reaction to a demonstration is negative. What happens then?*

A: Take Martin Machine down the street. We went over there to see a machine. The frame didn't seem heavy enough. It wasn't my project, so I don't know the whole story. But they went to Cincinnati for the grinder. I think it was a case of "too local," that is, you have to go out of town to get the good stuff.

Q: *Was there a written report on that conclusion?*

A: No, it was reported verbally to management.

Q: *How many layers of management do you report to on these demonstrations?*

A: We report to the plant manager, without too many layers between. I report to my supervisor, who is primarily in quality, so he doesn't have a lot to say. His supervisor is third in command of this plant. He's plenty smart, so I'm always reporting to him, and he reports to the plant manager. The top man [plant manager] may challenge something, or he may just sign off on the buy. Often he'll say, "OK, if that's what you want, but you guys have to make it work."

Q: *Why do production executives like you want a demonstration?*

A: We want to see if the machine is reliable. How well built is it? What components do they use, and are they good? Like cylinders, valves, controls and so on. If those are not what we have standardized around here, we'll specify to use Vickers valves. You see, we have to standardize because otherwise we'd have to stock everybody's controls. We use Allen-Bradley on most machines, so we can stock those. I also check to see how things fit, whether the ways are generous, and whether it looks like the machine would hold up. In specials, I realize I won't see the machine we are discussing, but I want to be sure they can do the main thing.

Q: *You mean the critical thing?*

A: Yes, the thing that makes it special. I suppose there are some guys who like to go to demos to get a steak dinner. That may be the real motive in some cases.

Q: *It's not your motivation?*

A: (Laughs) No, I don't much like going out of town. We did have a rebuild that was my project. The rebuilder farmed the job out to a sister division plant in Portland, Maine. I went up there and had a good time. They stood on the lake and pointed to the island where Vice President Bush had his home. If I had been there longer, I might have seen it.

Q: *Thank you, Gene, for your time. I appreciate it.*

A: No trouble at all, Roger. Goodbye.

Interview with Bill Cardigan,
Chief Manufacturing Engineer, Chemical Equipment, Inc.

(Bill Brown is asking the questions; Bill Cardigan, answering.)

Q: *Do you ever ask for a demonstration on a particular part when you are buying a machine tool?*

A: We have a design for a very simple part, a cylindrical piece with a couple of steps, that we ask them to set up for. We supply the tooling, and the process information, and the material to run twenty-five parts. We ask the vendor to program the machine that he proposes for this work, and to run twenty-five of them, in our presence, without interference from engineers. We number the parts as they come off, and time the cycle. We examine the parts for drifting from specification, and for finish. I realize this takes a lot of time and money on the vendor's part, but our experience has shown that this assures us the cycle time and quality we need.

Some machine buyers can be satisfied with a "standard" demonstration, where the machine tool builder shows special parts of his own choosing being made. These parts always show the machine off to its best advantage, and if the buyer is sharp, he can determine whether this machine is good at the part he wants to make on the machine in question. Chemical Products prefers the more elaborate and time consuming way. Chemical Products will ask three or four vendors to do this same demonstration.

Q: *What do you look for in a demonstration?*

A: Reliability, consistency, repeatability, and predictability. Reliability is the most important thing. We assume that all machines are rugged, that all control systems can do the same things, and that electrical and hydraulic systems are essentially the same among vendors. We generally buy turning centers, NC lathes and drills—all fairly standard machines available from a number of sources. There is never any question as to whether the machine can do the job. The questions are "How reliably?" and "How fast?"

Q: *After a demonstration, to whom do you report?*

A: I don't have to make a report internally. The vendor usually asks me to write up the results of the demonstration, which I do, and file a copy of this report in the folder on the purchase of this machine and give a copy to the vendor, not identifying his competition.

Q: *Is there anything else you'd like to tell me?*

A: A machine vendor should develop a standard demonstration and try to use it when it will satisfy the needs of the prospect. Many buyers can look at a part slightly different than their own and assure themselves that the machine will do what the quotation says it will do.

For a builder to offer to build the machine and guarantee that it will produce as promised is bad business for both builder and buyer. I always call other purchasers of this type machine and ask them what their experience has been.

Vendors always resist doing demonstrations, and sometimes ask to be reimbursed for the trouble. I usually tell them that the competitors have offered to do it free, and that solves the problem. I don't know what I'd do if they all wanted to charge.

Interview with Waldemar Gould,
former sales engineer and sales manager for New Age Machine Company (a Blue Chip competitor)

(Bill Brown is asking the questions; Waldemar Gould, answering.)

Q: *Did you do demonstrations for prospects?*

A: Yes. We generally had to use a machine which was being built for someone else, as we did not have a stock of "demonstrators" available. Sometimes we did not have the exact model he was going to buy, but he would accept a part being run on a different model. Sometimes we could run parts for which we were building the tooling, but sometimes we had to run his specific part. For the automotive industry we always had to run off seventy-five or more parts when the machine was finished, so the customer could verify the dimensional accuracy of the machine before it left our plant.

We sometimes charged for the presale demonstration and credited this against the cost of the machine if the prospect bought. Otherwise we billed him. The tooling could be pretty expensive and not usable for anything else.

Q: *What did prospects look for in a demonstration?*

A: They looked at the quality of the part.

Q: *To whom did the witnesses at the demonstration report?*

A: The witnesses were generally manufacturing engineers and they made a written report to the chief manufacturing engineer in large plants and the plant manager in smaller plants. The latter was the person who made the buying decision.

Q: *Is there anything else you'd like to tell me?*

A: Screw machines are different from crush grinders. Most people know the quality they'll get from a screw machine, but they aren't sure about a grinder. Consequently it may be more difficult for Blue Chip to sell without a demonstration on the actual part than for New Age. Another way to provide a demonstration is to take the prospect to a satisfied customer, and let him see the machine in action (on someone else's part). Sometimes this is hard to arrange.

EXHIBIT 1. Script to Schedule Demonstration

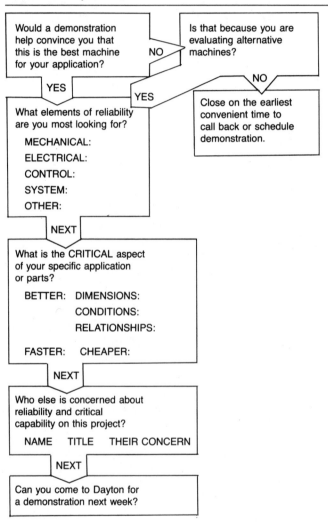

This case prepared by Roger Brucker, president, Odiorne Industrial Advertising.

Case 18   Kestnbaum & Company—
Children's Apparel by Mail

Background   KESTNBAUM & COMPANY* WAS GIVEN THREE WEEKS TO REVIEW AND comment on material outlining a new product concept, children's apparel by mail, prepared by the direct marketing group of a major brand name apparel manufacturer. Input was required in time for division management to meet a critical go/no-go deadline. The material presented here is extracted from that data.

Basic background on the parent corporation is as follows:

• A manufacturer and nationwide distributor of several major lines of men's and women's apparel. The company's brands are well known and highly respected.

• The firm has developed an extremely successful group of specialty mail-order businesses based on a handful of its own product lines augmented by some outside purchases.

• With only one exception, not substantially relevant to this case, the company did not manufacture children's apparel. All items considered for the catalog business would be purchased from outside vendors.

Consulting Objectives   The consulting objectives, based on available data, were as follows:

1. Determine the basic viability of the proposed business as a mail-order enterprise.

2. Evaluate the reasonableness of costs, rates, and factors assumed by the company.

3. Determine whether there are any serious omissions or inaccuracies in the assumptions.

4. Suggest alternative approaches and methods to building the proposed business. (Note: Alternatives *must* be limited to direct marketing channels.)

5. Recommend a go or no-go decision.

---

*Kestnbaum & Company is an international management consulting firm wholly specialized in direct marketing. The company concentrates on the introduction and upgrading of consumer and business-to-business direct marketing activities.

Extract from the Company-prepared Project Summary

- Objective
  - —Develop a proven children's apparel program using direct marketing methods that has the potential to achieve $40 million in sales within five years with an ROI of 20 percent or better after taxes.
- Strategies
  - —Position the children's apparel catalog to offer above average quality of basic children's apparel and related products at less than department store prices. The benefits will be the combination of selection, variety and value, convenience, improved fit charts, ease of return, and status. Final positioning and emphasis is to be determined by qualitative research.
  - —All catalogs will feature the company's leading popular brand name and all products will carry the brand's guarantee as an endorsement.
  - —Create a status image for the catalog and products by developing a separate brand name for products designed and made exclusively for the mail-order catalog.
  - —Purchase from outside suppliers a majority of all products, but, where feasible, develop special specifications (sizing, status symbol, etc.) and garment sizes so that sizing will be as consistent as possible throughout the catalog.
- Concept Strengths
  - —Focus groups have shown that women are favorably disposed to the idea of children's apparel carrying the company's brand. There are no known mail-order companies whose product lines are devoted *exclusively* to children's apparel. (Sears, Wards, and Penney's catalogs are not considered mail order.)
  - —There are fourteen million children in only those audiences identified as primary targets (e.g., high income, education). Hence long-term sales potential is great.
  - —The risk associated with rollout in direct marketing is less than in competing channels.
  - —Emerging capabilities in all phases of direct marketing (fulfillment, systems, marketing) minimize the risk of entering this channel of distribution.
  - —Incremental manpower resources required to test the program are relatively small until the program has proven itself.
  - —A mail-order catalog of children's apparel from a recognized brand name manufacturer offers a logical solution to women's problems associated with taking children shopping.
  - —The mail-order catalog will provide the consumer with a wider selection of merchandise than is available in most current retail outlets, especially in smaller cities.
  - —A problem exists in sizing information provided by various manufacturers, a problem that will be addressed in the proposed catalog.

—The size of the children's market is five times larger than the market for the company's primary branded products.

—Many companies have been successful in selling apparel through the mail.

—Parents of young children can be identified and reached via a wide variety of compiled, subscription and mail-order response mailing lists; via mass circulation publications; and, potentially, through such additional direct response media as coop mailings and package inserts.

—Research has indicated that a two-year wear guarantee (i.e., a no questions asked refund for any item which wears out before two years) generates high customer interest and offers a somewhat unique appeal. The percentage returned is estimated to be low.

● Potential weaknesses

—Strong retail and some catalog competition from Sears, Wards, and Penney's.

—Reluctance of many women to buy apparel for anyone in the family through the mail.

—Initial lack of many exclusive products.

—Estimated three years of losses prior to positive payback.

Basic Assumptions

Customers will be acquired through a two-step approach: inquirers via mail and space advertising programs, followed by conversions via catalogs.

Space Ad Inquiry Development

Plan: Place ads in publications with a total circulation of 100 million per year to generate 300M inquiries/year.

Response Rate after three years:

90% of target reached
80% of those reached note catalog offer
15% of those noting send for catalog
Target market estimate—8.8 million households

Cost: $7.50 per 1000 circulation.

Solo Mailing Inquiry Development

Plan: Mail 1 million prospect names, twice a year
Response Rate: 15 percent
Cost: $425 per thousand names

Conversion Mailings to Mail/Space Inquirers

Plan: Mail series of four regular catalogs
Response Rate: 33 percent conversion over four mailings with the following individual response rates: 13.3, 10, 6.7, 3
Cost: $400 per thousand catalogs sent
Average First Order: $30

Customer Mailing (i.e., mailings to those who buy)

Plan: Three regular catalogs in March, August, October; a sale catalog in late December

Response Rate: percent on regular catalog, 5 percent on sale catalog. These rates are assumed for the *entire* customer (buyer) file. A customer would be mailed at this level for five years after acquisition. If no additional order were received in five years, the name would be dropped.

Cost: $400 per thousand catalogs mailed

Average Order: $40

Single Order Cost Assumptions

Item	Plan	Explanation
Shipping & Handling Charge	$2	
Margin	45 percent	
Order Processing and Delivery	$2.17	
Order Card Postage	$ .25	Postpaid reply card assumed on all orders
Payment Terms	50 percent Cash 50 percent Bank Card at 2.75 percent discount	
Merchandise Returns	15 percent	Assumes 2 percent return for refund, 4 percent return for merchandise, 9 percent return spread over two years due to wearability guarantee
Return Handling and Refurbishing	$3.10	On *all* returns
Postage Refund on Returns	$1.70	Full postage costs refunded to *all* customers who return merchandise
Departmental Overhead	7.5 percent	On *net* sales
Corporate Overhead	0 percent; 4 percent	Company assumed to absorb corporate overhead during start-up period; 4 percent starting third year

Flash: Results of a dry catalog inquiry test mailing available just prior to the deadline showed that 19 percent of those receiving the piece requested a catalog.

EXHIBIT 1. Contribution Analysis

	New Customer Order	Old Customer Order
Average Order Size	30	40
Shipping & Handling	2	2
Cash Inflow	32	42
Cost of Goods Sold	16.5	22
Gross Margin	15.5	20
Processing & Delivery	2.17	2.17
Reply Card Postage	.25	.25
Charge Card Fees	.44	.5775
Return—First Year	.60	.80
Wear Return—First Year	1.35	1.80
Deferred Return (Prior Yr.)	1.35	1.80
Return Handling	.3255	.3255
Return Postage	.1785	.1785
Def. Return Handling	.1395	.1395
Def. Return Postage	.0765	.0765
Total Processing Charges on Average Order	6.88	8.1175
Average Contribution to Overhead—Second Year & On	8.62	11.8825
First Year	8.836	12.0985

To help evaluate this proposed business and to participate fully in examining the case in class discussion, come prepared to discuss:

1. Which concept strengths are
   (a) Strongest? (b) Most dubious?
2. Which potential weaknesses are
   (a) Most risky to the venture's success?
   (b) Least important to the go/no-go decision?
3. Did you spot any other potential strengths or weaknesses?
4. Which assumptions are:
   (a) Most solid/reliable? (b) Least solid/reliable?
5. What other information or assumptions would be helpful to the evaluation of this venture?
   Calculate
6. The expected cost for *each:*
   (a) Space ad inquirer? (b) Solo mail piece inquirer?
7. The total selling cost (i.e., catalog costs) per order for
   (a) An old customer? (b) A new customer?

8. Expected contribution per order to advertising cost and profit. Contribution subtracts from net sales *all* merchandise, operating and overhead costs, but not the cost of acquiring or promoting a customer. (See Exhibit 1.)

Calculate the

(a) Contribution for each
   1. $30 new customer order
   2. $40 old customer order

(b) Break-even response percentage and sales per thousand pieces mailed for 8a.

9. The approximate size of the customer file needed to meet the five-year objective?

Material in this case prepared by Robert Weinberg, Kestnbaum & Company. Copyright 1987 by Kestnbaum & Company. Reprinted by permission.

Case 19   Western Wear Inc.
Developing a Print Media Test Program

Assignment   DEVELOP A PRINT MEDIA TEST PROGRAM THAT WILL GENERATE REquests for Western Wear Inc. "family" catalog. For this assignment, women's publications will be the only publications considered. Women are the prime audience segment for this promotion. They are reputed to be the most active catalog responders and often make purchase decisions for other family members. (The media budget is $160,000, maximum.)

Individual publication data sheets, arranged alphabetically, are provided. They outline editorial profiles, selected demography, competitive information, mail-order activity, and advertising rates.

Select what you believe to be the appropriate publications, and give rationale for your plan.

Strategy   The proposed print media test strategy can be broken down into the following broadly defined stages:

Stage 1. determination of print program viability, identification of better performing publications, and demographic profiles.

Stage 2. format and creative tests in those publications that have performed in Stage 1, selective retests of marginal and poor-response publications, expansion of test publication universe.

Stage 3. rollout of best-performing format(s) and creative, continued publications testing.

Test Objectives

- To establish the viability of print promotion
- To develop a media plan that will lead to a continual and measurably cost-efficient flow of leads
- To establish best prospect demographic profile(s)

Selection Strategy

All of the publications recommended in this plan meet the criteria demanded of a successful direct marketing promotion. They are (a) mail-order responsive; (b) demographically targeted to the perceived Western Wear Inc. catalog customer (family-oriented, middle income, ages 25–44); and (c) they have the appropriate editorial environment.

It is our considered opinion that these magazines are most likely to produce profitable return. They also provide direction for expansion programs in the near future.

Creative Format

As noted throughout this test proposal, one-half page black-and-white ads are now planned as the basic space unit for Stage 1. This format offers the following advantages:

- It is large enough to accommodate catalog selling proposition. Catalog graphic and coupon (toll-free number for catalog requests is not recommended as a basic component because no monetary qualifier is now planned. No-cost phone ordering of catalogs will lower conversion rates).

- Its relatively low cost (vis-à-vis larger or four-color formats) allows testing of a wide range of publications.

- It has proven cost effective for a wide variety of lead generation programs.

The main disadvantage is that most of the publications recommended do not provide A/B splits on this size. Consequently, extensive copy/creative testing will not be possible in Stage 1. Therefore, versioning is now planned in a few selected publications.

Two test copy approaches have been developed emphasizing different positionings of the catalog:

● A history of quality—first quality goods now available by W.W. Inc. catalog

● Product breadth—a wide variety of Western Wear Inc. products dispelling the common belief that W.W. Inc. is a shirts-only manufacturer

Differentiation between these two approaches is handled primarily in the headlines because copy space is limited. Subtle changes within the body copy help support each position. However, the primary function of the body copy is to provide concise and complete information in order to elicit a consumer response. Graphics will be identical in both versions. Each will display the cover of the book to pique consumer interest.

Ideally, a test program would be structured in order that both versions could be tested on a one-to-one basis. However, as mentioned previously, most publications will not split test a one-half page size ad (Exhibit 1).

EXHIBIT 1.   Test Program

THIRTY-FIVE YEARS IN THE MAKING

At last.
The Western Wear Inc. Catalog. Ninety-six big pages filled with quality Western Wear Inc.'s shirts, jackets, sweaters, pants, and blue jeans—for everyone in your family. Send in the copy below for your *free* copy.

Please send me my *free* copy of the Western Wear Inc. Catalog.

Western Wear Inc., 1813 Hinman, Evanston, IL 60201

Name (please print)		
Address		
City	State	Zip

MORE THAN SHIRTS

At last.
The Western Wear Inc. Catalog. Ninety-six big pages filled with quality Western Wear Inc.'s shirts, jackets, sweaters, pants, and blue jeans—for everyone in your family. Send in the copy below for your *free* copy.

Please send me my *free* copy of the new Western Wear Inc. Catalog

Western Wear Inc., 1813 Hinman, Evanston, IL 60201

Name (please print)		
Address		
City	State	Zip

Appendix: Magazine Data Sheets

CATEGORY Women's

PUBLICATION Mademoiselle   CIRCULATION 1,100,000

EDITORIAL PROFILE

Mademoiselle is edited for the woman 18-34, and addresses the needs of this fat-growing consumer segment with coverage of career topics, fashion, beauty, health, hone decorating, travel, entertaining and the arts.

RATE:
1/2 page, B/W, 1x -- $13,520

PUBLISHED: Monthly

DEMOGRAPHICS

% M/F: 7/93
Median Age: 27.7
Median Income: 29,375
% of Children: 41.9
(under 18)

SELECTED COMPETITIVE ACTIVITY

Advertiser	# of Insertions	
	1984/Jan.-Dec	Jan.-May, 1985
Avon	8	3
Eddie Bauer	N/A	N/A
LL Bean	4	1
Lands End	N/A	N/A

MAIL ORDER ADVERTISING PAGES
1984: 58.18
Jan-May '85: 42.26

Sources: PIB Brand Detail, Mail-Order, 1984 and May, 1985
Demography: Simmons '85 and some independent publications surveys.

CATEGORY Women's

PUBLICATION Vogue   CIRCULATION 1,000,000

EDITORIAL PROFILE

Vogue is edited for the woman who considers fashion a way of life. The magazine's editorial pages cover fashion, beauty, health, fitness, travel, the arts, money, entertaining and food.

RATE:
1/2 page, B/W, 1x -- $13,700

PUBLISHED: Monthly

DEMOGRAPHICS

% M/F: 10/90
Median Age: 30.7
Median Income: 30,568
% of Children: 42.7
(under 18)

SELECTED COMPETITIVE ACTIVITY

Advertiser	# of Insertions	
	1984/Jan.-Dec	Jan.-May, 1985
Avon	N/A	N/A
Eddie Bauer	N/A	N/A
LL Bean	2.0	N/A
Lands End	6.0	2.0

MAIL ORDER ADVERTISING PAGES
1984: 62.37
Jan-May '85: 50.13

Sources: PIB Brand Detail, Mail-Order, 1984 and May, 1985
Demography: Simmons '85 and some independent publications surveys.

CATEGORY   Women's

PUBLICATION   Family Circle   CIRCULATION (Rate Base) 7,100,000

EDITORIAL PROFILE   Family Circle is a service magazine covering major areas of interest to women, such as food, home, decorating, good loods, health, child care, money management, family relationships, crafts, travel and careers.

RATE: 1/2 page, B/W, 1x -- $12,925	Fall Run
-- 4,020	Western Edition (Circulation -- 1,268,000)
-- 5,830	Eastern Edition (Circulation -- 2,402,000)
-- 6,190	Central Edition (Circulation -- 2,630,000)

PUBLISHED: 17 times a year

DEMOGRAPHICS

% M/F: 12/88
Median Age: 42.9
Median Income: 26,667
% of Children: 46.6
(under 18)

SELECTED COMPETITIVE ACTIVITY

Advertiser	# of Insertions	
	1984/Jan.-Dec.	Jan.-May, 1985
Avon	4	n/a
Eddie Bauer	n/a	n/a
LL Bean	1.0	n/a
Lands End	n/a	n/a

MAIL ORDER ADVERTISING PAGES
1984:   77.58
Jan-May '85:   87.67

Sources: PIB Brand Detail, Mail-order, 1984 and May, 1985
Demography: Simmons '85 and some independent publicaiton surveys.

CATEGORY   Women's

PUBLICATION   Good Housekeeping   CIRCULATION (Rate Base) 5,000,000

EDITORIAL PROFILE

Good Housekeeping is edited primarily for homemakers interests: food, fashion, beauty, decorating, diet, health, social problems, personalities, fiction, and current affairs. Repairs. Regular column subjects include psychological self-help, etiquette, medicine and consumer problems.

RATE:

1/2 page, B/W, 1x -- $13,160

PUBLISHED: Monthly

DEMOGRAPHICS

% M/F: 14/86
Median Age: 40.7
Median Income: 26,486
% of Children: 48.8
(under 18)

SELECTED COMPETITIVE ACTIVITY

Advertiser	# of Insertions	
	1984/Jan.-Dec.	Jan.-May, 1985
Avon	4	1
Eddie Bauer	n/a	n/a
LL Bean	2.0	n/a
Lands End	n/a	n/a

MAIL ORDER ADVERTISING PAGES
1984:   96.10
Jan-May '85:   76.67

Sources: PIB Brand Detail, Mail-Order, 1984 and May, 1985
Demography: Simmons '85 and some independent publication surveys.

CATEGORY   Women's

PUBLICATION   Ladies Home Journal   CIRCULATION (Rate Base) 5,000,000

EDITORIAL PROFILE

Ladies Home Journal is edited for today's women, addressing the challenges she actively faces in her multifaceted life. Each issue has a wide spectrum of service and feature material including food, decorating, health and diet, beauty & fashion and child care.

        RATE:
                1/2 page, B/W, 1x -- $19,670

PUBLISHED: Monthly

DEMOGRAPHICS

            % M/F: 10/90
            Median Age: 41.3
            Median Income: 26,307
            % of Children: 45.2
            (under 18)

SELECTED COMPETITIVE ACTIVITY

                                        # of Insertions

Advertiser	1984/Jan.-Dec.	Jan.-May, 1985
Avon	1	1
Eddie Bauer	n/a	n/a
LL Bean	2.0	n/a
Lands End	n/a	n/a

MAIL ORDER ADVERTISING PAGES

            1984:   44.79
Jan-May '85:   47.91

Sources: PIB Brand Detail, mail-Order, 1984 and May, 1985
Demography: Simmons '85 and some independent publication surveys.

CATEGORY   Women's

PUBLICAITON   Harper Bazaar   CIRCULATION (Rate Base) 700,000

EDITORIAL PROFILE

Harper's Bazaar is edited for the success-oriented woman. Editorial features emphasize fashion, beauty, health, diet, travel and entertaining.

        RATE:
                1/2 page, B/W, 1x -- $12,955

PUBLISHED: Monthly

DEMOGRAPHICS

            % M/F: 13/87
            Median Age: 31.4
            Median Income: 30,750
            % of children: 40.1
            (under 18)

SELECTED COMPETITIVE ACTIVITY

                                        # OF Insertions

Advertiser	1984/Jan.-Dec.	Jan.- May, 1985
Avon	n/a	n/a
Eddie Bauer	n/a	n/a
LL Bean	1.0	n/a
Lands End	n/a	n/a

MAIL ORDER ADVERTISING PAGES

            1984:   43.82
Jan-May '85:   31.18

Sources: PIB Brand Detail, Mail-Order, 1984 and May, 1985
Demography: Simmons '85 and some independent publication surveys.

CATEGORY Women's

PUBLICATION Redbook   CIRCULATION 3,800,000

EDITORIAL PROFILE

Redbook is edited for young women today, who are juggling the demands and rewards of husband, child and jobs. Articles are geared towards helping her make "first time" decisions in her complicated life ranging from personal relationships, home money mangement, beauty, fashion, fiction, food and nutrition.

        RATE:
                1/2 page, B/W, 1x -- $18,609

PUBLISHED: Monthly

DEMOGRAPHICS

            % M/F: 10/90
            Median Age: 36.9
            Median Income: 26,371
            % of Children: 49.7
            (under 18)

SELECTED COMPETITIVE ACTIVITY

                                    # of Insertions

Advertiser	1984/Jan.-Dec	Jan.-May, 1985
Avon	4	1
Eddie Bauer	N/A	N/A
LL Bean	N/A	N/A
Lands End	N/A	N/A

MAIL ORDER ADVERTISING PAGES
            1984: 56.11
Jan-May '85: 48.74

Sources: PIB Brand Detail, Mail-Order, 1984 and May, 1985
Demography: Simmons '85 and some independent publications surveys.

CATEGORY   Women's

PUBLICATION   McCall's   CIRCULAION (Rate Base) 6,200,000

EDITORIAL PROFILE

McCall's is edited for the contemporary woman. Each issue features food, beauty, fashion and home management service, fiction, book exerpts and in-depth profiles of personalities in the news.

        RATE:
                1/2 page, B/W, 1x -- $16,500

PUBLISHED: Monthly

DEMOGRAPHICS

                                        # of Insertions

Advertiser	1984/Jan.-Dec.	Jan.-May, 1985
Avon	n/a	n/a
Eddie Bauer	n/a	n/a
LL Bean	n/a	n/a
Lands End	n/a	n/a

MAIL ORDER ADVERTISING PAGES

            1984: 45.61
Jan-May '85: 48.29

Sources: PIB Brand Detail, Mail-Order, 1984 and May, 1985
Demography: Simmons '85 and some independent publication surveys.

CATEGORY Women's

PUBLICATION Soap Opera Digest   CIRCULATION 840,732

EDITORIAL PROFILE

Soap Opera Digest synopsizes the "soaps," and gives in depth behind the scenes reports on the daytime industry and its participants.

RATE:
1/2 page (digest), B/W, 1x -- $15,655

PUBLISHED: Every Second Week

DEMOGRAPHICS

% M/F: 13/87
Median Age: 29.4
Median Income: 20,217
% of Children: 55.5
(under 18)

SELECTED COMPETITIVE ACTIVITY

Advertiser	# of Insertions 1984/Jan.-Dec	Jan.-May, 1985
Avon	2.0	N/A
Eddie Bauer	N/A	N/A
LL Bean	N/A	N/A
Lands End	N/A	N/A

MAIL ORDER ADVERTISING PAGES
1984: 31.66
Jan-May '85: 12.60

Sources: PIB Brand Detail, Mail-Order, 1984 and May, 1985
Demography: Simmons '85 and some independent publications surveys.

CATEGORY Women's

PUBLICATION Seventeen   CIRCULATION 1,600,000

EDITORIAL PROFILE

Seventeen is a general service magazine edited to inform, enlighten and entertain America's young woman. Articles include tips on fashion, beauty, fabric/patterns, food and decorating.

RATE:
1/2 page, B/W, 1x -- $13,400

PUBLISHED: Monthly

DEMOGRAPHICS

% M/F: 10/90
Median Age: 24.6
Median Income: 26,875
% of Children: 60.5
(under 18)

SELECTED COMPETITIVE ACTIVITY

Advertiser	# of Insertions 1984/Jan.-Dec	Jan.-May, 1985
Avon	10	3
Eddie Bauer	N/A	N/A
LL Bean	3.0	1.0
Lands End	N/A	N/A

MAIL ORDER ADVERTISING PAGES
1984: 53.25
Jan-May '85: 50.90

Sources: PIB Brand Detail, Mail-Order, 1984 and May, 1985
Demography: Simmons '85 and some independent publications surveys.

CATEGORY Women's

PUBLICATION Weight Watchers   CIRCULATION 825,000

EDITORIAL PROFILE

Weight Watchers magazine is a food and contemporary lifestyle publication targeted to women who are concerned about their weight, what they eat, and how they look. Special emphasis is placed on nutrition and current fitness trends. It also contains articles on at-home entertaining, beauty and fashion, and tips for the working woman.

RATE:
1/2 page, B/W, 1x -- $13,035

PUBLISHED: Monthly

DEMOGRAPHICS

% M/F: 18/82
Median Age: 39.1
Median Income: 24,000
% of Children: 43.0
(under 18)

SELECTED COMPETITIVE ACTIVITY

Advertiser	# of Insertions 1984/Jan.-Dec	Jan.-May, 1985
Avon	3	N/A
Eddie Bauer	N/A	N/A
LL Bean	N/A	N/A
Lands End	N/A	N/A

MAIL ORDER ADVERTISING PAGES
1984: 47.02
Jan-May '85: 23.98

Sources: PIB Brand Detail, Mail-Order, 1984 and May, 1985
Demography: Simmons '85 and some independent publications surveys.

CATEGORY Women's

PUBLICATION Self   CIRCULATION 1,000,000

EDITORIAL PROFILE

Self is edited for the active woman of the 80's, and concentrates editorially on information designed to assist a busy woman living in two worlds: business and home: Editorial features self-improvement in the areas of health and beauty, diet and nutrition, money management and entertaining.

RATE:
1/2 page, B/W, 1x -- $13,140

PUBLISHED: Monthly

DEMOGRAPHICS

% M/F: 10/89
Median Age: 28.5
Median Income: 29,559
% of Children: 51.0
(under 18)

SELECTED COMPETITIVE ACTIVITY

Advertiser	# of Insertions 1984/Jan.-Dec	Jan.-May, 1985
Avon	4	3
Eddie Bauer	N/A	N/A
LL Bean	N/A	N/A
Lands End	N/A	N/A

MAIL ORDER ADVERTISING PAGES
1984: 23.22
Jan-May '85: 21.77

Sources: PIB Brand Detail, Mail-Order, 1984 and May, 1985
Demography: Simmons '85 and some independent publications surveys.

CATEGORY Women's

PUBLICATION Savvy   CIRCULATION 300,000

EDITORIAL PROFILE

Savvy is edited for executive women. Savvy features corporate management
strategies and tactics for the professional female decision-maker.

        RATE:
            1/2 page, B/W, 1x -- $11,830

PUBLISHED: Monthly

DEMOGRAPHICS

        % M/F: 3/99.7
        Median Age: 35.3
        Median Income: 39,700
        % of Children: 34.8
          (under 18)

SELECTED COMPETITIVE ACTIVITY

                                      # of Insertions
Advertiser   1984/Jan.-Dec.   Jan.-May, 1985

Avon   N/A   N/A
Eddie Bauer   N/A   N/A
LL Bean   N/A   N/A
Lands End   N/A   2

MAIL ORDER ADVERTISING PAGES
        1984: 33.13
    Jan-May '85: 26.20

Sources: PIB Brand Detail, Mail-Order, 1984 and May, 1985
Demography: Simmons '85 and some independent publications surveys.

CATEGORY   Womens

PUBLICATION   McCalls Needlework & Craft CIRCULATION (Rate Base)709,589

EDITORIAL PROFILE

McCalls Needlework & Craft is designed for the active woman who wants to
create beautiful things to wear and to decorate the mome. Each issue
emphasizes leisure time activities; fashions to knit and crochet, decorating
idas, bazaar items, and gift ideas.

        RATE:
            1/2 page, B/W, 1x -- $11,455

PUBLISHED: Bimonthly

DEMOGRAPHICS

        % M/F: 0/100
        Median Age: 42
        Median Income: 30,000
        % of Children: 51.70
          (under 18)

SELECTED COMPETITIVE ACTIVITY

                                      % of Intersections
Advertiser   1984/Jan.-Dec.   Jan.-May, 1985
Avon   N/A   N/A
Eddie Bauer   N/A   N/A
LL Bean   N/A   N/A
Lands End   N/A   N/A

MAIL ORDER ADVERTISING PAGES
        1984: 97.27
    Jan-May '85: 42.49

Sources: PIB Brand Detail, Mail-Order, 1984 and May, 1985
Demography: Simmons '85 and some independent publication surveys.

CATEGORY   Women's

PUBLICATION   Cosmopolitan   CIRCULATION (Rate Base) 2,500,000

EDITORIAL PROFILE

Cosmopolitan is edited for youg women, single or married, and concerns self-
improvement, careers, clothes, beauty, travel, entertainment an the arts.

        RATE:

            1/2 page, B/W, 1X -- $16,790

PUBLISHED: Monthly

DEMOGRAPHICS

        % M/F: 17/83
        Median Age: 28.7
        Median Income: 28,051
        % of Children: 51.4
          (under 18)

SELECTED COMPETITIVE ACTIVITY

                                      # of Insertions
Advertiser   1984/Jan.-Dec.   Jan.-May, 1985

Avon   8.0   3

Eddie Bauer   n/a   n/a

LL Bean   1   n/a

Lands End   n/a   n/a

MAIL ORDER ADVERTISING PAGES

        1984:   141.17
    Jan-May '85: 145.17

Sources: PIB Brand Detail, Mail-Order, 1984 and May, 1985
Demography: Simmons '85 and some independent publication surveys.

CATEGORY   Women's

PUBLICATION   Essence   CIRCULATION (Rate Base) 800,000

EDITORIAL PROFILE

Essence is the magazine for today's black woman. The editorial content
included career and educational opportunities, fashion & beauty, investing &
money management, health and fitness, parenting and travel.

        RATE:

            1/2 page, B/W, 1x -- $12,710

PUBLISHED: Monthly

DEMOGRAPHICS
        % M/F: 27/73
        Median Age: 30.8
        Median Income: 21,042
        % of Children: 57.6
          (under 18)

SELECTED COMPETITIVE ACTIVITY

                                      # of Insertions
Advertiser   1984/Jan.-Dec.   Jan.-May, 1985

Avon   2   n/a

Eddie Bauer   n/a   n/a

LL Bean   n/a   n/a

Lands End   n/a   n/a

MAIL ORDER ADVERTISING PAGES

        1984:   18.91
    Jan.-May '85: 15.21

Sources: PIB Brand Detail, Mail-Order, 1984 and May, 1985
Demography: Simmons '85 and some independent publication surveys.

CATEGORY Women's

PUBLICATION Working Mother   CIRCULATION 550,000

EDITORIAL PROFILE

Working Mother is edited specifically for today's women who work and have children under 18. Articles focus on careers, child rearing, family health care, beauty care, work and familty fashions, food preparation and home management.

    RATE:
        1/2 page, B/W, 1x -- $12,830

PUBLISHED: monthly

DEMOGRAPHICS

        % M/F: 13/87
        Median Age: 34.7
        Median Income: 29,444
        % of Children: 76.0
        (under 18)

SELECTED COMPETITIVE ACTIVITY

	# of Insertions	
Advertiser	1984/Jan.-Dec	Jan.-May, 1985
Avon	N/A	N/A
Eddie Bauer	N/A	N/A
LL Bean	N/A	N/A
Lands End	N/A	N/A

MAIL ORDER ADVERTISING PAGES
        1984: 20.07
    Jan-May '85: 14.66

Sources: PIB Brand Detail, Mail-Order, 1984 and May, 1985
Demography: Simmons '85 and some independent publications surveys.

CATEGORY Women's

PUBLICATION Parents   CIRCULATION 1,675,000

EDITORIAL PROFILE

Parents is edited for young women 18-34 with growing children. Editorial coverage emphasizes family information & growth, focusing on the day-to-day needs and concerns of today's woman and her family. Regular departments include: beauty, family finance, food, love and marriage and lifestyle.

    RATE:
        1/2 page, B/W, 1x -- $15,640

PUBLISHED: Monthly

DEMOGRAPHICS

        % M/F: 19/81
        Median Age: 30.1
        Median Income: 25,625
        % of Children: 84.7
        (under 18)

SELECTED COMPETITIVE ACTIVITY

	# of Insertions	
Advertiser	1984/Jan.-Dec	Jan.-May, 1985
Avon	N/A	N/A
Eddie Bauer	N/A	N/A
LL Bean	N/A	N/A
Lands End	N/A	N/A

MAIL ORDER ADVERTISING PAGES
        1984: 60.01
    Jan-May '85: 39.13

Sources: PIB Brand Detail, Mail-Order, 1984 and May, 1985
Demography: Simmons '85 and some independent publications surveys.

CATEGORY: Women's

PUBLICATION: Glamour   CIRCULATION (Rate Base) 2,000.000

EDITORIAL PROFILE

Glamour is edited for the personal interests of young women 18-35 with a "how-to" approach. Emphasis is placed on fashion, beauty, careers, travel, lifestyle, decorating, entertaining, sewing & crafts, and consumer information.

        RATE:
            1/2 page, B/W, 1x -- $13,930

PUBLISHED: Monthly

DEMOGRAPHICS

        % M/F: 7/93
        Median Age: 27.9
        Median Income: 29,716
        % of Children: 49.7
        (Under 18)

SELECTED COMPETITIVE ACTIVITY

	# of Insertions	
Advertiser	1984/Jan.-Dec.	Jan.-May, 1985
Avon	7	3
Eddie Bauer	n/a	n/a
LL Bean	5.0	2
Lands End	5.0	2

MAIL ORDER ADVERTISING PAGES

            1984:   78.40
    Jan.-May   '85:   56.34

Sources: PIB Brand Detail, Mail-Order, 1984 and May, 1985
Demography: Simmons '85 and some independent publication surveys.

CATEGORY Women's

PUBLICATION Woman's Day   CIRCULATION 6,900,000

EDITORIAL PROFILE

Woman's Day is written and edited for the contemprary woman. The magazine's editorial centers around the traditional values of home, family, children, food, health, and nutrition. How-to beauty, fashion and fitness features are also part of the basic service mix.

    RATE: 1/2 page, B/W, 1x -- $52,140   Full run

                    -- 21,745   Western edition
                                (Circulation - 1,228,000)

                    -- 23,725   Central Edition
                                (Circulation - 2,621,000)

                    -- 23,520   Eastern Edition
                                (Circulation - 2,476,000)

PUBLISHED: 17 times a year

DEMOGRAPHICS

        % M/F: 8/92
        Median Age: 41.4
        Median Income: 27,052
        % of Children: 48.6
        (under 18)

SELECTED COMPETITIVE ACTIVITY

	# of Insertions	
Advertiser	1984/Jan.-Dec	Jan.-May, 1985
Avon	2	2
Eddie Bauer	N/A	N/A
LL Bean	1.0	N/A
Lands End	N/A	N/A

MAIL ORDER ADVERTISING PAGES
        1984: 73.09
    Jan-May '85: 58.99

Sources: PIB Brand Detail, Mail-Order, 1984 and May, 1985
Demography: Simmons '85 and some independent publications surveys.

Case 20   PQ Systems

Managing, Compensating, and Providing Advertising Support for Telemarketing Representatives

PRODUCTIVITY QUALITY SYSTEMS (PQ SYSTEMS) IS A DAYTON, OHIO firm dedicated to improved quality management through the implementation of Statistical Process Control (SPC) methods. The company began in 1980 as Productivity Quality Associates. Its initial efforts were focused on instructional seminars that addressed the concept of Statistical Process Control and offered practical problem-solving techniques. It now offers a nearly complete line of Statistical Process Control "products."

Company Background

Everything PQ Systems does is based on the philosophy of Dr. W. Edward Deming, the leading quality control expert who is heralded as the "Father of SPC" and who is credited with introducing Japanese industry to Statistical Process Control in the 1950s. Dr. Deming's philosophy departs radically from the "inspection" approach to achieving quality, and instead focuses on prevention, combining statistics and participative management in a system that increases quality, lowers costs, and gives workers greater job satisfaction simultaneously.

One PQ Systems' press release describes the effect Dr. Deming's philosophy and Japanese industry has had on American industry this way:

> American industry is in the midst of a battle to retain its competitive position in World Markets. If its industrial base is to survive, efforts must be swiftly undertaken to achieve greater product quality, productivity and lower production costs. Statistical Process Control is the single most important tool with which to achieve these objectives. It is a mathematical process whose success has been borne out time and time again by one country in particular which has come full circle to surpass American industry in both productivity and quality. This country is Japan.

The release goes on to describe what Statistical Process Control is all about:

> Statistics is the science of making data or information more understandable and useful. It is a mathematical process that first describes

things as they are in their current state . . . and secondly, as they probably will be in their future states. Statistics provide the formulas, charts, and diagrams necessary to transform vast collections of data into useful information for problem-solving purposes.

SPC is the science of using statistical methods to monitor production processes in all types of manufacturing and service industry. SPC, more than any other process, provides the tools to achieve optimal quality, productivity, and profitability. In manufacturing, for example, SPC is used to monitor production processes to PREVENT defective parts from being produced. SPC methods help evaluate production equipment and products to detect variances in quality. When product quality begins to shift farther from the ideal and closer to the outer limits of acceptability, the responsible equipment or process can be adjusted and the process brought back under control before a single unacceptable product is produced.

Compare this with America's more common practice of DETECTION where products are inspected at the final stage of the production process. Under this system, equipment and processes may still be adjusted, but only after several pieces of unacceptable product have been produced. The lack of feedback during the actual production process means no corrective measures can be taken to avoid scrap until it's too late.

Flaws in this method become even more evident when defective parts are used in the assembly of large items. A detection system generates tremendous—and unnecessary—costs due to excessive scrap, rework, inspection, customer returns, warranty costs, and many intangible losses.

Studies provide a report card on just how expensive the outmoded process can be . . . 15–40% of all production costs under a "Detection System" are attributed to waste. It is this waste that can be avoided through enhanced quality control practices.

SPC, on the other hand, is the single most effective tool with which to achieve (1) greater product quality, (2) reduced production costs, (3) increased productivity, and (4) greater profitability.

Individual workers have been blamed unfairly and all too often for poor quality and low productivity. The Deming philosophy of SPC places the blame squarely on the shoulders of those with the power to correct the problem. Management, preaches Deming, is 85% to blame for the perpetuation of poor quality, poor productivity, runaway production costs and declining profits.

America has fallen behind. Statistical Process Control is not an entirely new concept. For nearly four decades SPC has enjoyed enthusiastic acceptance and widespread use in Japanese industry. SPC, coupled with the teachings of Dr. W. Edward Deming, proved to be the catalyst in Japan's transformation from a producer of poor quality products to one of unfaltering—and to date unmatched—product quality. To move from detection to prevention to the ultimate state in quality management, that of never-ending search for improvement, demands the mastery of new skills; knowledge of Statistics and Statistical Process Control methods top the list.

Building on Deming's philosophical foundation, today PQ Systems offers expertise, products, and services to assist American Industry in every step of its transformation process to more streamlined competitive operation. Its product line includes Statistical Process Control computer software, video tape training system and support manuals, and quality/productivity films. A brief description of individual products is given below.

I. Statistical Application Software

  a. SQCpack™: The SQCpack™ is a software package designed to utilize the speed, accuracy, and power of personal computers to perform complex statistical calculations fundamental to SPC. Introduction of the SQC pack in 1981 marked a substantial advancement in SPC, uniting for the first time the speed and reliability of computers with the power of statistical applications.

  b. SQC Report: The SQCpack™ Report is an optional software expansion for the standard SQCpack™. It consolidates extensive control chart information into simplified report form for greater ease in the use and analysis of the statistical data.

  c. GAGEpack: GAGEpack is the software system created to manage, evaluate and control the dependability of gaging equipment for more accurate product quality monitoring. GAGEpack enables businesses to build a complete database on their inspection equipment, generate equipment and management reports, and determine gage reliability/repeatability for greater process control.

II. Video Tape Training System and Support Manuals

  a. The TRANSFORMATION OF AMERICAN INDUSTRY™: The "transformation" training system offers a comprehensive training in statistical process control techniques based on the Deming philosophy. Classroom-setting instruction is captured on a series of twelve video tape modules and are supported throughout with paralleling workbooks and text. The system includes an Instructor's Guide and a one-week Train-the-Trainer Seminar.

III. Quality/Productivity Films

  a. *Right First Time*: Dramatization of a fictional company's struggle to implement statistical methods within its manufacturing facility. Offers a basic introduction to

Statistical Process Control methods and philosophy and demonstrates the significant impact that SPC can have on management style.

b. *People & Productivity*: Focuses on key ideas from Japanese business philosophy and examines how these attitudes help improve productivity and employee relations. The film highlights leaders in business, industry, unions, and education—both Japanese and American—as they express their views on this new, profitable approach to industrial productivity.

c. *Roadmap for Change*: This film uses a case study to examine how Dr. Deming's fourteen obligations of management are being implemented in one American corporation. It captures reaction of managers and employees at the Pontiac Motor Division of General Motors to the Deming approach adopted in their new Fiero plant.

d. *Management's Five Deadly Diseases*: A look at the common management practices in corporate America that prevent the attainment of greater product quality, productivity, and competitive position in the world market.

e. *Participative Management*: Nissan's $660 million manufacturing plant in Smyrna, Tennessee marked the largest Japanese industrial investment ever made outside of Japan. This film case-studies the implementation of Nissan's participative management system at its Smyrna plant, and is particularly informative for American corporations hoping to develop their own alternative management styles.

IV. Consulting

a. Consulting Services: PQ Systems consultants, operating individually or as a team, analyze in-house operations to provide professional guidance in the following areas: implementation of complete SPC programs; selection and assessment of applicable SPC computer systems; and personnel training in basic statistics, charting, advanced statistical analysis, and design of experiments.

V. Training Seminars

a. SPC Using the Microcomputer: A seminar offering training for those with little knowledge or experience in statistical applications. Participants are offered an introduction to quality control and various statistical charting techniques. Computers and SPC software are provided to all for the additional benefit of hands-on learning.

b. "Train the Trainer" Seminar: An instructional seminar designed to provide company representatives with the knowledge, materials and instruction necessary to fully implement an SPC program in their respective facilities. The seminar includes actual training experiences by all of the participants.

c. User Conferences: Conferences offer instructional training for users of PQ systems' various products and services. Objectives of the conference include user familiarity with the products' capabilities, special features, and real-life applications as well as the creation of an open forum in which the exchange of user ideas, questions, and developing needs may be shared.

VI. Computer Sales and Rental

a. Computers that run the PQ Systems' software are sold as needed, or rented to buyers who wish to use that option. Either purchase or rental is also available to anyone wishing to rent, whether they are customers for PQ Systems products or not—through a newly created, separate, computer rental/sales division.

Current Situation

Sales Volume   PQ Systems' current sales volume is approximately $2½ million per year.

Management   The president of PQ Systems is Dr. Michael Cleary, who is also a professor of Management Science at Wright State University in Dayton, Ohio. Dr. Cleary and Craig Tickel, a former Cleary student with extensive background in the automotive industry, founded the firm in 1980.

Dr. Cleary's background includes vast experience and research in quality control methods. He had in-depth involvement with the Ford Motor Company as it charged ahead of General Motors (due in major part to its successful attempt, using the Deming philosophy, to improve the quality of its products), and

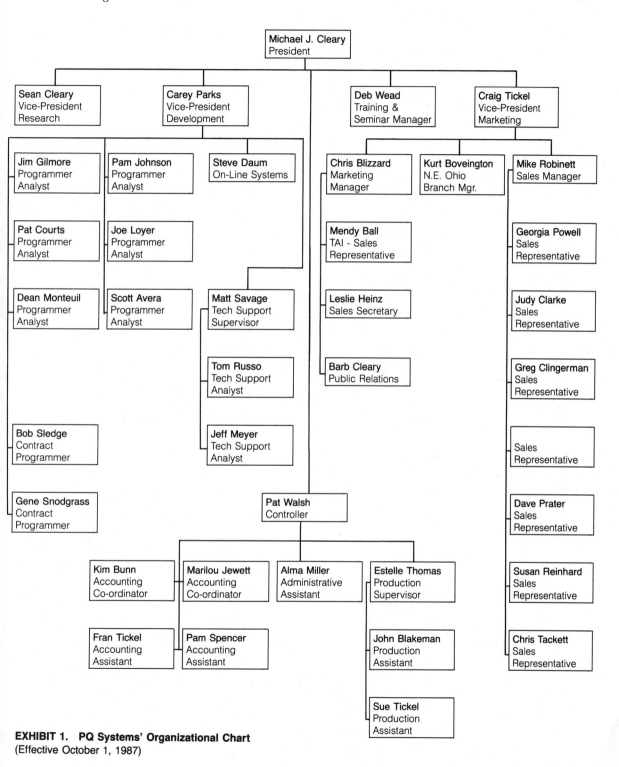

EXHIBIT 1. PQ Systems' Organizational Chart
(Effective October 1, 1987)

has served as consultant and trainer for numerous other major companies, such as Uniroyal, Eaton, and the like. He has an international reputation, having done in-house seminars and consulting for a variety of major companies in the U.S. and in such other countries including Great Britain, Australia, Japan, Korea, and several countries on the European continent.

Craig Tickel is vice president for operations and manages the day-to-day operations of the company. Other key players in the firm include Carey Parks, vice president and development manager; Chris Blizzard, marketing manager; Pat Walsh, controller; Debra Wead, seminars and training manager; Mike Robinett, sales manager and acting telemarketing manager; and ten young and enthusiastic telecommunicators who man the phones and on whom the day-to-day responsibility for making sales happen rests. (See Exhibit 1.)

The firm's management style is very participative. Participation is encouraged in a variety of ways, including a daily morning company meeting where problems and successes are shared with others. At the present time, these meetings include virtually everybody in the firm. The telemarketing group also holds frequent meetings to discuss company developments, selling techniques, and management concerns such as the sales compensation plan, and the like.

Leading Products

The firm's number one seller is the SQCpack™ computer program. This program was originally programmed by Dr. Cleary's son, Sean, a precocious computer enthusiast, while he was still in high school. It has undergone many revisions since then, and is today, many think, unarguably the best Statistical Process Control computer program available in the world. It sells for $695. All of the firm's product prices are listed in Table 1. The SQCpack™ and all the firm's other software products are constantly being updated by a team of professional programmers. Users who choose to do so can get these updates for fees ranging from $25 to $150, depending on their situation, and on which update they are seeking.

Some common prospect questions and answers about the SQCpack™

Q: *Why do I need the SQCpack™?*
A: Research has shown that 20 percent of all charts manually prepared contain one or more errors. SQCpack™ saves you time

TABLE 1. PQ Systems Pricing

SQC Pack $695
SQC Report . . . . $695   (used with SQCpack™—
                                                                        under development)
GAGEpack . . . . $695   (free standing)

Video Tapes
  TRANSFORMATION OF AMERICAN
  INDUSTRY tapes . . . . $5000*   (12 Module Set)

Films
  Right First Time $375
  People & Productivity $500
  Roadmap for Change:
    Part 1 . . . . $500
    Part 2 . . . . $500
  Management's Five Deadly Diseases $500
  Participative Management $500

Consulting Services (6–7 day in-house
  seminar) $1000/Day

Training Seminars
  SPC Using the Computer
    Regularly Scheduled (3-day seminar) . . $500/person
  SPC Using the Computer
    In-house (2–3 day) seminar $1000/Day
  Training the Trainer Seminars:
    Scheduled—4/Yr $750/Person**
    In-house—on demand $10,000

User Conferences . . . . FREE

Computer Rental/Sales . . . . Negotiated (separate company)

---

*Includes 5-day Train-the-Trainer Seminar.
**One enrollment free with purchase of TRANSFORMATION OF AMERICAN INDUS-
  TRY tapes.

and is more accurate than doing calculations by hand. We estimate
that SQCpack™ can cut your time per chart in half, even without
advanced data collection devices. It gives detailed professional outputs which allows you to spend more time doing analysis and
problem solving, not calculations. SQCpack™ gives you structured
uniformity for your quality control department.

Q: *How much computer knowledge is required to operate the
SQCpack™ effectively?*

A: When you receive the SQCpack™, simply place the systems disk in your computer and turn it on. The SQCpack™ is
menu driven and function key oriented; you can enter data and
obtain printouts the first time you sit at the keyboard. In order to
assist you in learning about our product, we have included a demonstration dataset that allows you to generate the screens dis-

played in the user's manual. Ease of use is a major reason cited by our customers in selecting our package. At the same time, the SQCpack™ has enough flexibility so that it can be changed to match your hardware configuration.

Q: *How good is the SQCpack™ documentation?*

A: The user's manual walks the user step by step through the package. Screens are displayed within the manual which match the demonstration datasets. All formulas used within the package are included in the documentation. In addition, a reference manual is included with the documentation. This manual published by Ford Motor Company is the most straightforward and useful reference available in the marketplace today.

Q: *Why do I need the SQCpack™ and computer hardware on the production floor?*

A: As products continue along a production line, variation in the process occurs. Early detection of this variance is the key to reducing scrap and salvaging materials before they become defective. This is the difference in the philosophy of prevention versus detection on the production floor. Using the SQCpack™ with the IBM 5531 will allow the operator to receive immediate feedback on his process and allow him to take necessary action. Properly applying statistical analysis is the only method to keep his process "in control." SQCpack™ gives him the proper tools necessary to do the job.

Q: *What statistical techniques will the SQCpack™ use?*

A: The SQCpack™ utilizes all of the standard statistical quality control techniques which include variables, attributes, and problem solving.

Q: *How much data can I input on the SQCpack™ program?*

A: SQCpack™ has been written so that there is no finite limit to the amount of data that can be placed in one file. The only limit is the amount of storage capacity available on your data diskette or hard disk.

Q: *Can I interface with other software packages?*

A: Yes. SQCpack™ includes utilities so that you can interface to data stored in ASCII format. Utilities are available to access data from such packages as Dbase II and Lotus 1-2-3.

Q: *Can I collect data with hand-held data collectors?*

A: Yes you can. By utilizing the RS 232 serial part of your IBM 5531 computer and a hand-held data collector, you can download a program to collect data using your data collector.

After collecting the data on the floor, it can be uploaded to your IBM 5531 computer and analyzed using the SQCpack™. The SQCpack™ performs the same as if you had entered the data via the keyboard.

Q: *Can I utilize both a parallel and a serial printer?*

A: The SQCpack™ software is configured to work with a parallel printer. A serial printer can be utilized by assigning the "LPT1:" device to the serial port prior to entering the SQCpack™.

Q: *Does the SQCpack™ support plotter outputs?*

A: The SQCpack™ supports Hewlett-Packard 7470A six pen and compatible plotters.

Q: *Can I make a backup copy of the software?*

A: The SQCpack™ is copy protected. The copy protection does allow for a backup copy to be made. The original diskette must be present to start the software package. Should the original diskette be inadvertently erased, the programs could be restored from the backup diskette to the original diskette.

Q: *What is the average payback period for the IBM 5531 PC used with the SQCpack™?*

A: Even if you only have one person who spends four hours per day doing charts manually, SQCpack™ can cut this time in half. This amounts to a savings of 510 hours/year or a savings of $10,200 per year. The payback of the IBM 5531 PC and the SQCpack™ is therefore less than one year.

But the real savings are in what statistical methods can do for your operation. Studies show that the cost of producing defective parts can be as much as 20 percent of sales. If a $10-million-dollar company can reduce its costs to 10 percent of sales using statistical methods, this would result in a savings of $1 million per year!

Realistically a reduction to well below the 10 percent level is achievable through continued process control and a commitment to "never ending improvement."

Q: *How do I obtain updates?*

A: Each SQCpack™ includes a registration card. When a new version of the software is released, each user will be contacted.

Q: *Can I put the SQCpack™ on a hard disk?*

A: Yes. Instructions are included in the user documentation to transfer the system to the hard disk. Like many copy protected systems, the original diskette must be present in order to start the system. Once the software is started the original diskette may be removed.

Q: *Is the SQCpack™ sufficiently supported with technical expertise?*

A: Yes. We believe this is one of the strongest points of our company. Whether your question is in the area of statistical application, use of computers, or the SQCpack™ software, we have the expertise to provide you solutions. You will find help and support from 7:30 A.M. until 6:30 P.M. EST, Monday through Friday (even sometimes on the weekends) at 1-800-547-1565. Our 800 number is only for SQCpack™; you'll receive help not an operator.

Q: *Why is PQ Systems better than the competition?*

A: PQ Systems is committed to "never ending improvement" in respect to our product. The SQCpack™ currently utilizes more graphics and color capability than the others. The SQCpack™ is constantly enhanced, so new capabilities are always being added. SQCpack™ is the easiest to use because it has been designed to be "user friendly." The package is backed by technically qualified professionals who will help you with the applications of the SQCpack™ as well as correctly and efficiently answering questions about SPC and hardware. PQ Systems corporate expertise is quality management and quality control software.

Q: *What are some future developments I can expect on the SQCpack™?*

A: Due to the increasing technological developments in computer hardware and software, our goal is to stay a cut above the competition. We will continue to do this by offering features our competitors lack. We want to offer a more sophisticated interface with hand-held data collectors including DataMyte, BetaMate, 0S4, and the GageTalker. Personal computers are moving toward real-time systems which will permit multiple users and larger amounts of data stored in an organized and easily accessible fashion. As these systems mature, so will our product. Technology is providing the path to real time manufacturing systems of the future. PQ Systems and the SQCpack™ is committed to be a part of that future.

Other Major Products   The TRANSFORMATION OF AMERICAN INDUSTRY™ tapes set, priced at $5,000, and the GAGEpack program, priced at $695, sell well too, but at this time, are only a fraction of the business. In sum, the SQCpack™ is the firm's "cash cow." All of the other products are thought to have excellent potential. Furthermore, virtually all of the firm's customers for one product are logical prospects for the rest of the product line. The firm wants to give all of its line more emphasis. Currently, however, there is no overall printed sales piece which bring them all together and merchandises them as a collectivity. A new video tape will do this to a certain degree, however.

Another particular product that definitely appears to offer much potential, if emphasized, is the *Right First Time* film. This is a black-and-white film dramatization of a fictional company that discovers that it has to improve its quality and how it goes about putting a system in place. This British-made film is about thirty years old, a fact that adds to its value. Being in black and white, the film delivers a subverbal message that "we could have been doing this all along," and firmly implants the notion that the time to get started is *now*. The British accents and setting of the film also add to the sense of drama and need to get moving. The film also suggests that U.S. quality may now also be behind that of Europe too, which puts U.S. firms in a quality cross fire between Japan and Europe, and possibly, even, some Third World countries.

New Products under Development

The SQCpack™ was designed to run primarily on the IBM^{AT} and IBM^{XT} and compatible machines. Current product development efforts are devoted to developing the software to run on larger on-line, multiuser systems. This program is written in a higher level language, making it faster and more efficient than the original SQCpack™. However, it will be a much more expensive product, probably being priced at $30,000 or more. It is felt that this product will sell to people who are truly sold on the Deming approach, and who for the most part will already be PQ Systems customers.

Growth Strategy

At this point in time the firm's growth strategy is largely one of penetrating its current markets with improved products and improved marketing effort. It appears also that the firm has unofficially decided to become a direct marketing company, using that channel almost exclusively. The use of dealers has been discussed, however.

The Market for PQ Systems Products

It is thought that virtually any operation from production plants to offices that engage in repetitive processes can be significantly affected by the introduction of the Deming Statistical Process Control method and philosophy. These include service companies/organizations (including the IRS), chemical/process industries, job shop companies, and manufacturing firms. Thus, the market for SPC products is a very large one, with manufacturing and process operations the most readily available.

Major and direct benefits users of all sorts can obtain are savings by reducing scrap, saving time, and the like. Other equally important, but indirect, benefits include reducing the invisible losses from lost customers and bad word-of-mouth which result from unnecessarily low quality.

Competition In total, there are approximately sixty competitors in the SPC computer package market. Of these, the most significant brand names are

Quality Alert

Zontec

MetriStat

Northwest Analytical

Spc PC

To date, only MetriStat and Zontec are known to be marketing both nationally and aggressively. All of these firms have SPC software, which competes against the SQCpack™. None, however, have an SPC product line that can compare with the depth of PQ Systems line which currently contains software, films, seminars, consulting and the like, and is expanding. The PQ Systems leading product, the SQCpack™, is objectively and substantially superior to most of its competitors, and head-to-head, is at least the equal of any competitive product. Furthermore, PQ Systems has the unofficial imprimatur of Dr. Edward Deming on its program. This connection comes through especially clear in the TRANSFORMATION OF AMERICA videos where Dr. Deming is prominently featured both as a speaker and in silent background pictures.

Marketing Program Although there is a variety of exceptions, such as orders taken at seminars and the like, virtually all of PQ Systems' sales are made via the telephone. (See Exhibit 2.) The vast majority of these are made (at list prices) to (a) inquiries generated by print advertising in *Quality Progress* magazine (see Exhibit 3), and (b) inquiries who have been referred to PQ Systems by satisfied users, or by someone who happens to know about the firm. Ads running in *Quality Progress* magazine are the only advertising being done, and this advertising is limited to the SQCpack™ and the TRANSFORMATION OF AMERICAN INDUSTRY tapes.

Marketing Materials. A brochure exists for

• The SQCpack™ software program (eight pages, front and back)

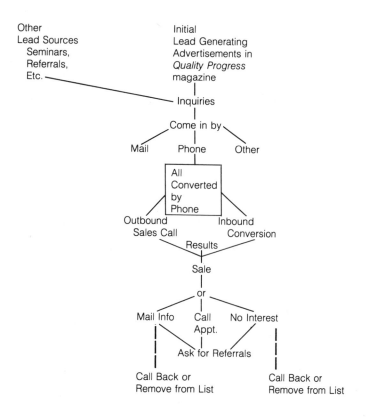

EXHIBIT 2. PQ Systems Marketing Program Structure

- The GAGEpack software program (four pages, front and back)
- The TRANSFORMATION OF AMERICAN INDUSTRY™ video tape program (four pages, front and back)
- The (scheduled) five-day TRANSFORMATION OF AMERICAN INDUSTRY™ Train-the-Trainer Seminars.
- Basic SPC using the SQCpack™ (scheduled three-day seminar)

Additional promotional tools include cover letters for the SQCpack™ and GAGEpack (see Exhibits 5 and 6); and Preview Video Tape—preview (thirty minutes) selling SPC, the PQ Systems' product line, and providing an overview of the TRANSFORMATION OF AMERICAN INDUSTRY tapes. (This tape is a very recent, professionally done and very convincing, sales tool.)

The cover letters, shown in Exhibits 4 and 5, are sent depending on the prospect's interest, along with the appropriate brochure or preview tape to unsold inquiries. (All mail inquiries are followed up by phone, and an attempt is made to sell them, before

EXHIBIT 3. TRANSFORMATION OF AMERICAN INDUSTRY Lead-Generating Ad
(*Quality Progress* magazine)

information is sent!) No product is sent without obtaining a purchase order number from the prospect—even for the thirty-day free trial.

The Prospect for the Firm's Products

The typical current prospect is a reader of *Quality Progress* Magazine, where most leads are generated. Most prospects can be assumed to be quite familiar with production processes. Thus, most should be fairly knowledgeable about the problems that PQ Systems products can solve. However, except for an occasional prospect, very few know exactly what a PQ Systems' product, particularly the SQCpack™, can do, or how it can benefit them.

Telecommunicators describe their current leads as being very diverse. Some leads come from purchasing agents who have been asked to get information for someone else. Others come from someone who only marginally understands what SPC is, and who are in firms which feel no real current need. Some come from people who have circled ten or fifteen numbers on a bingo card,

Dear Quality Professional:

Thank you for your interest in PQ Systems.

International Industry is presently facing a great challenge in the international marketplace both in the quality and price of their products. This challenge faces producers in virtually all sectors of manufacturing. The improvement in quality and the effectiveness of pricing by international competitors, is due in large measure to their application of statistics to solving problems.

PQ Systems is a quality management corporation dedicated to helping companies implement Statistical Process Control programs in their organizations. Through the use of our software, training systems, and seminars, PQ Systems has helped numerous companies improve quality and decrease costs. I have enclosed some brochures explaining our products and services in greater detail.

One of the enclosed brochures describes the latest release of the SQCpack^{tm}. The SQCpack^{tm} is statistical process control software designed to help you control your processes and reach these goals of improved quality and decreased costs.

To better evaluate our SQCpack^{tm} I suggest you take it in house. This will allow you to look at our package at your convenience, input your data, and work with your hardware set up.

To order the SQCpack^{tm} for a 30 day trial contact me at 1-800-547-1565. We require a purchase order or credit card number to reference shipment.

The TRANSFORMATION OF AMERICAN INDUSTRY^{tm} Training System brochure is also enclosed. For further review, we offer a preview tape accompanied with a set of student and instructors materials for a nominal fee. These materials are available for a 60 day evaluation.

If you have any further questions after reviewing these brochures please call me at your convenience. I look forward to having you join our list of industry-wide users. Thank You.

Sincerely,

Ken Reed
National Account Rep.

Productivity-Quality Systems, Inc.
470 Windsor Park Dr.; P.O. Box 633
Dayton, Ohio 45459
(513) 435-9717   1-800-547-1565
Telex 5101007458

Dear Quality Professional:

Thank you for your interest in PQ Systems.

American industry is presently facing a great challenge in the international marketplace both in the quality and price of their products. This challenge faces producers in virtually all sectors of manufacturing. The improvement in quality and the effectiveness of pricing by international competitors, is due in large measure to their application of statistics to solving problems.

PQ Systems is a quality management corporation dedicated to helping companies implement Statistical Process Control programs in their organizations. Through the use of our software, training systems, and seminars, PQ Systems has helped numerous companies improve quality and decrease costs.

An important step toward these goals involves the accurate gaging and inspection of your gaging equipment. Such a task is at times neglected due to the lengthy, manual effort involved.

The enclosed information describes the GAGEpack. This is a powerful, yet easy-to-use software package designed to help you manage, evaluate, and control your gaging equipment.

To order the GAGEpack, simply contact us directly at 1-800-547-1565 or in Ohio at 513-435-9717. All purchases are supported by a 30 day trial period. If you are not satisfied with the GAGEpack, sign the warrantee/return form and return it along with the complete program via insured, prepaid UPS within 30 days, and there will be no further obligation.

If you have any questions after receiving the enclosed information please feel free to give us a call. We look forward to helping you implement quality programs in your organization.

Sincerely,

Marketing Representative

Productivity-Quality Systems, Inc.
470 Windsor Park Dr.; P.O. Box 633
Dayton, Ohio 45459
(513) 435-9717   1-800-547-1565
Telex 5101007458

EXHIBIT 4.   PQ Systems Cover Letter/SQCpack™

EXHIBIT 5.   PQ Systems Cover Letter/GAGEpack

one being the PQ Systems ad. Some come from firms whose management has recognized a problem and are looking into SPC, but appear to be in no hurry. On the other end of the continuum are leads from firms under pressure from their customers to use SPC—a lead from an auto industry supplier, for example, is likely to be in this category. These are obviously the easiest to sell. Finally, some leads are from firms that are really not ready for the SQCpack™. What they really need is training.

In addition, many prospects, and the firms they represent, often have only a rudimentary knowledge of statistics. Many, in fact, also may even fear the word "statistics," and thus, may have some initial emotional reluctance or buying resistance that comes from fear of getting into something over their heads.

Frequently, too, it turns out that many prospects in large organizations are convinced of a product's value, and are ready to buy, when they are called on the phone, but don't have the authority to make a decision to buy, or so they say—and thus must get the approval of a superior.

What Do Prospects Have to Know before They Will Say Yes

Here are some typical *questions* telecommunicators say they face:

Are there quantity discounts?

Cost of the package? Discounts?

What is the cost of an SQCpack™?

What is the maintenance agreement for this package?

What's your policy on upgrades of the software?

Dealer program?

What are the hardware requirements?

How much memory is needed?

Can I install it on a hard drive?

Does SQCpack™ offer regression, correlation, and so forth?

Can I access info from a mainframe?

Will your pack network?

Does your pack work with data collectors?

What type of plotters are supported?

Does the SQCpack™ support plotters?

Do we have J-D graphics?

What type of printers does it support?

Is the SQCpack™ compatible with the Hercules Graphics Board?

Is SQCpack™ compatible with the laser printer?

Difference between TAI (community college) and PQ Systems five-day TTT?

How does your pack compare to the competition?

Is there a licensing agreement or is it copy protected?

Can you bring information in any other way besides the keyboard?

Do I have the ability to choose colors for charts?

How does the system test for normalcy?

Can I have subgroups?

Can I put my Spec lines on the charts?

Does the SQCpack™ do "trends testing" or out of control tests?

Can I choose my labeling for the charts?

Does the SQCpack™ do individual charts?

Here are some typical *objections* faced by telecommunicators:

Just gathering information—have no need.

Am already evaluating *X* number of packages.

I'm only evaluating literature right now.

Don't have enough time to evaluate.

I want to evaluate some more packages.

We are just evaluating what's out there.

"On the back burner"—not high priority right now.

We will be making our decision in a couple of months.

Can't get PO on trial—has to be purchased.

Can't get a P.O. number for thirty-day trial.

It's difficult to get approval.

Management has tightened the purse strings for the time being.

I want to know more about SQCpack™. Do you have any more information I could have?

I need what your pack provides, plus high statistics.

The package doesn't do regression.

Would like a demo disk instead of an entire package to evaluate.

I don't have management support of SPC.

The SQCpack™ doesn't work with my data collector . . . , Mettler balances . . . , QMS . . . , and so forth.

We need "real-time" SPC.

I only have an IBM PC with monochrome monitor and Hercules graphics board. Your pack won't work on that.

Package not tutorial enough.

Costs too much.

I can get better price through a dealer.

Don't have any PCs at this time.

Success of Current Methods

At the present time magazine ads and unsolicited referrals are generating more leads than the telemarketing department can cover. In fact, it appears that for the short term at least, the firm's current, most pressing marketing issue is fine-tuning the telemarketing effort to take advantage of existing potential. This means, in large measure, finding out how to convert a larger percentage of inquirers into buyers over the telephone.

Lead Assignments

Incoming leads for all products are distributed first come, first serve to each of the five reps, who call them as they see fit. One of the five reps is currently producing an average of sixteen SQCpack™ sales a week. This particular rep has an "assistant" who provides on-the-phone backup as well as clerical assistance. Two others are averaging eight SQCpack™ sales per week. One is selling about six each week. The remaining two are selling about four per week.

Lead "Tightness" or "Hardness"

Little is currently known about what type of lead is the hardest or best, except for one interesting pattern noted by the TSRs. This is that someone who calls them is much easier to sell to than is a mailed-in lead whom they call. This is true despite the apparent fact that phone inquirers know no more about the product than mail inquirers do before they talk with a PQ Systems' representative.

Marketing and Telemarketing Organization

The marketing manager and the telemarketing management roles are now both the overall responsibility of Operations Vice President Craig Tickel. Chris Blizzard currently performs the duties of the marketing manager role. Likewise Mike Robinett is currently performing in the role of telemarketing supervisor. Like Mr. Blizzard, he too, has not yet been given full authority or responsibility for the function. Mr. Robinett, who is the top phone rep, says he likes his telephone sales representative (TSR) job and does not want to be considered for permanent telemarketing management responsibilities.

The telemarketing representatives are each assigned to one of three regions comprised of several states. There is no particular pattern to these regions. Time zones and the like did not influence decisions concerning their size or locations much at all. Instead, these regions were put together so that the total apparent potential would be similar, that is, a similar number of big cities. Thus, it would not be at all unusual for a TSR to talk with a Texas prospect followed immediately by a call to a prospect in Oregon.

Physical Set-up for Telemarketing

The five telemarketing representatives now share a large $35' \times 70'$ room with other marketing and public relations personnel. Their five spacious $8' \times 8'$ cubicles (really small rooms) line one side of the room. Each room has ample desk, storage, and shelf space. One telecommunicator cannot see the other unless he or she physically exits their cubicle. A supervisor cannot see individual telecommunicators except through an open door on each of the cubicles. (The supervisor, who has other duties, is only occasionally present.) The communicators use standard hand-held telephones.

Telecommunicator Backgrounds and Training

To date, telecommunicator training has focused on product knowledge. All reps are schooled in the PQ Systems product line. All know how to use the SQCpack™, and in fact do use it, to monitor their calling activity. All of the current communicators have had some sales experience prior to joining the firm. No formal in-house sales training has been given to any of them. However, meetings, led by the top representative, are held once or twice a week to discuss how to best handle various kinds of prospects and calls. Craig Tickel feels that the reps do a very good job of talking about the products. Therefore, he feels that the training his reps need most is "How to close the sale" effectively. It has also been suggested that reps might not be strong enough on how PQ Systems' products benefit their users.

Scripts

No definite scripted approach to achieving sales has been put down on paper, though one rep seems to have found an approach that works when he uses it consistently. He has related his approach to his colleagues, and they have attempted to implement this approach as often as they can. However, at this time, no one gives the reps detailed help in working wrinkles out of their sales approaches. Management personnel have expressed an interest in scripting their TSRs and are looking into its feasibility and value for their products.

Telecommunicator Motivation

Sales are recorded as they are made on a chalk sales board located on the opposite wall in back of the telecommunicators. No bell-ringing or other motivation oriented special recognition is given as sales or other significant objectives or results are achieved.

Performance Standards

Neither calling activity nor standards of results are imposed on the telemarketing reps. This is an area that President Cleary is especially concerned about. There appears to be a need for standards such as minimum daily calls and minimum weekly results and the like. Cleary believes in the Deming philosophy of quality control, and he knows from experience that the Deming philosophy can work brilliantly when properly installed in a production setting and given time to develop. Why not in a telemarketing operation? His preference, therefore, is to not think in terms of more quota-type standards, but to think in terms of providing his telecommunicators with more and better "tools"—training, prepared answers to objections, and the like. In other words, Cleary does not want to focus on "inspection" but on "prevention" of poor quality calls. Prevention would involve using statistics and participative management in a system that increases call quality, lowers costs, and gives communicators greater job satisfaction.

Telecommunicator Compensation

Telemarketing compensation is an area of concern to the firm's management, and they are searching for a compensation strategy that is fair to the telecommunicators, makes the firm an attractive place for TSRs to work, and permits the firm to prosper when the sales people do.

Currently, the company telemarketing representatives receive a guarantee of $800 every two weeks, paid regardless of sales, or 9½ percent commission on total dollar volume, whichever is greater. This plan is generous enough that the top rep earned $36,000 in 1986. Frequently, however, the commissions of some reps don't reach the level of their salary. In other cases, individuals making sales involving multiple copies of SQCpack™ to the same large firm, say fifty at one time, go soaring over their guarantee for the two-week period during which such sales are made, that is, $50 \times 695 \times .095 = \$3301.25$.

Promotional Selling

To date there has been no apparent use of especially created (limited time only) offers designed to increase closing ratios. The basic offer on all products is a thirty-day free trial of the product of interest.

Currently, customers are required to give a PO number as a condition for receiving the SQCpack™ for a thirty-day free trial. What the prospect receives is not a sample. It is the real product, with one caveat. The firm does not permit the prospect to "install" the product on their computer unless they have decided to buy it. However, because the installation disk is sent with the package, the customer could violate this rule. But in so doing the customer would be breaking the law.

Public Relations Efforts

Newsletter. A short newsletter, called *Quality Line* is published quarterly. This features authority-building short articles on major

users of SQCpack™, and such things as having the TRANSFOR-
MATION OF AMERICAN INDUSTRY™ program translated
into Spanish. It also includes personal profiles of PQ Systems'
officers, news on upcoming seminars, and some subtle sell material on, for example, a comparison of steps involved in charting
manual versus computer techniques. Typically, also, articles discussing technical problems users often run into, such as insuffi-
cient computer memory, are included.

President's conference appearances. President Cleary
makes frequent appearances at national and international meetings and conferences, making speeches and presenting academic
papers. Other principles in the firm, especially those who teach
the Train-the-Trainer and SQCpack™ Seminars, continue to do
this as well.

User conferences. Free user conferences are held annually
in Dayton. These are used to share ideas and experiences of users,
and also as an opportunity to learn what the customers' needs are.

News releases. News releases are prepared and released as
the opportunities arise.

Materials in this case used by permission of PQ Systems, Inc.

Case 21   Wall Drug Store

THE WALL DRUG STORE IS A COMPLEX OF RETAIL SHOPS LOCATED
on the main street of Wall, South Dakota, population 770, owned
and managed by the Hustead family of Wall. It includes a drug
store; a soda fountain; two jewelry stores; two clothing stores; a
restaurant with four dining rooms; a western art gallery; a book-
store; and shops selling rocks and fossils, camping and backpack-
ing equipment, saddles and boots; and several souvenir shops. In
1983 a major expansion was undertaken which added five more
shops and a chapel.

**Wall Drug
History**

Ted Hustead graduated from the University of Nebraska with a
degree in pharmacy in 1929 at the age of 27. In December of 1931
Ted and his wife Dorothy bought the drug store in Wall, South

Dakota, for $2,500. Dorothy and Ted and their 4-year-old son Bill moved into living quarters in the back twenty feet of the store. Business was not good (the first months receipts were $350) and prospects in Wall did not seem bright. Wall, South Dakota, in 1931 is described in the following selection from a book about the Wall Drug Store.

> Wall, then: a huddle of poor wooden buildings, many unpainted, housing some 300 desperate souls; a 19th century depot and wooden water tank; dirt (or mud) streets; few trees; a stop on the railroad, it wasn't even that on the highway. U.S. 16 and 14 went right on by, as did the tourists speeding between the Badlands and the Black Hills. There was nothing in Wall to stop for.[1]

Neither the drugstore nor the town of Wall prospered until Dorothy Hustead conceived the idea of placing a sign promising free ice water to anyone who would stop at their store. The sign read "Get a soda/Get a beer/Turn next corner/Just as near/To Highway 16 and 14/Free ice water/Wall Drug." Ted put the sign up and cars were turning off the highway to go to the drugstore before he got back. This turning point in the history of Wall Drug took place on a blazing hot Sunday afternoon in the summer of 1936.

The value of the signs was apparent and Ted began putting them up all along the highways leading to Wall. One sign read "Slow down the old hack/Wall Drug Corner/Just across the railroad track." The attention-catching signs were a boom to the Wall Drug Store and the town of Wall prospered too. In an article in *Good Housekeeping* in 1951, the Hustead's signs were called "the most ingenious and irresistible system of signs ever derived."[2]

Just after World War II, a friend traveling across Europe for the Red Cross got the idea of putting up Wall Drug signs overseas. The idea caught on and soon South Dakota servicemen who were familiar with the signs back home began to carry small Wall Drug signs all over the world. Many wrote the store requesting signs. One sign appeared in Paris, proclaiming "Wall Drug Store 4,278 miles (6,951 kilometers)." Wall Drug signs have appeared in many places including the North and South Pole areas, the 38th parallel in Korea, and on Vietnam jungle trails. The Husteads sent more than 200 signs to servicemen requesting them from Vietnam.

---

[1]Jennings, Dana Close; *Free Ice Water: The Story of Wall Drug* (Aberdeen, South Dakota; North Plains Press, 1969) p. 26.
[2]Ibid., p. 42.

These signs led to news stories and publicity which further increased the reputation of the store.

By 1958 there were about 3,000 signs displayed along highways in all fifty states, and two men and a truck were permanently assigned to service signs. Volunteers continue to put up signs. The store gives away 14,000 6″ × 8″ signs and 3,000 8″ × 22″ signs a year to people who request them. On the walls of the dining rooms at Wall Drug are displayed pictures from people who have placed signs in unusual places and photographed them for the Husteads.

The signs attracted attention and shortly after World War II articles about Ted Hustead and Wall Drug began appearing in newspapers and magazines. In August, 1950 *Redbook Magazine* carried a story which was later condensed in October's *Readers Digest.* Since then, the number of newspapers and magazines carrying feature stories or referring to Wall Drug has increased greatly. In June of 1983 the Wall Drug Store files contained 543 clippings of stories about the store. The number per ten-year period was as follows[3]:

1941–1950	19 articles
1951–1960	41
1961–1970	137
1971–1980	260
1981 through April 1983	59

The store and its sales have grown steadily since 1936. From 1931 until 1942 the store was in a rented building on the west side of Wall's Main Street. In 1941 the Husteads bought an old lodge hall in Wasta, S.D. (fifteen miles west of Wall) and moved it to a lot on the east side of the street in Wall. The building which had been used as a gymnasium in Wasta became the core around which the current store is built.

Tourist travel greatly increased after World War II, and the signs brought so many people into Wall Drug that the Husteads claim they were embarrassed because the facilities were not large enough to service them. The store did not even have modern restrooms. Sales during this period grew to $200,000 annually.

In 1951 Bill Hustead, now a pharmacy graduate of South Dakota State University at Brookings joined his parents in the store.

---

[3]Twenty-seven clippings were undated.

In 1953 Wall Drug was expanded into a former storeroom to the south. This became the Western Clothing Room. In 1954 they built an outside store on the south of the Western Clothing Room. This was accompanied by a 30 percent increase in business. In 1956 a self-service cafe was added on the north side of the store. In the early 1950s sales were in the $300,000 per year range and by the 1960s had climbed to $500,000.

In the early 1960s, Ted and his son Bill began seriously thinking of moving Wall Drug to the highway. The original Highway 16 ran by the north side of Wall, about two blocks from the store. It was later moved to run by the south side of Wall, also about two blocks from the drugstore. In the late 1950s and early 1960s a new highway was built running by the south side of Wall paralleling the other highway. Ted and Bill Hustead were considering building an all-new Wall Drug along with a gasoline filling station alongside the new highway just where the interchange by Wall was located.

They decided to build the gasoline station first, and did so. It is called Wall Auto Livery. When the station was finished, they decided to hold up on the new store and then decided to continue expanding the old store in downtown Wall. This was a fortunate decision, because soon after that, a new interstate highway replaced the former highway and the interchange ran through the site of the proposed new Wall Drug.

In 1963 a new fireproof construction coffee shop was added. In 1964 a new kitchen, again of fireproof construction, was added just in back of the cafe and main store. In 1964 and 1965 offices and the new pharmacy were opened on the second floor over the kitchen. In 1968 the back dining room and backyard across the alley were added. This was followed in 1971 with the Art Gallery Dining Room.

By the late 1960s and early 1970s, annual sales volume went to $1 million. In 1971 the Husteads bought the theater that bordered their store on the south. They ran it as a theater through 1972. In early 1973 they began construction of a new addition in the old theater location. This is called the "Mall." By the summer of 1973 the north part of the Mall was open for business. The south side was not ready yet. That year the Wall Drug Store grossed $1,600,000 which was an increase of about 20 percent over 1972. Bill believes the increase was due to their new Mall addition.

The development of the Mall represents a distinct change in the development of Wall Drug. All previous development had been financed out of retained earnings or short-term loans. In effect, each addition was paid for as it was built or added.

The Mall The owners of Wall Drug broke with their previous method of expansion when they built the Mall by borrowing approximately $250,000 for ten years to finance the Mall and part of twenty large new signs which stand 660 feet from the interstate highway.

During the last half of the 1960s and early 1970s, Bill Hustead had thought about and planned the concept of the Mall. The Mall was designed as a town within a large room. The main strolling mall was designed as a main street with each store or shop designed as a two-story frontier western building. The Mall is thus like a recreated western town. Inside the stores various woods are used in building and paneling. Pine (from Custer, South Dakota), American black walnut, gumwood, hackberry, cedar, maple, and oak are among the various woods used. The storefronts are recreations of building fronts found in old photos of western towns in the 1880s. Many photos, paintings, and prints line the walls. These shops stock products that are more expensive than the souvenir merchandise found in most other parts of the store. The shops are more like western boutiques.

The northern part of the Mall was open for business shortly after July 10, 1973. In the fall of 1973 Bill was uncertain as to whether or not to open the south side. The Husteads perceived a threat to the tourist business in the 1974 season. They agonized over whether to finish the Mall and order the normal amount of inventory, or to hold up the mall and order conservatively. Among the conditions that seemed to threaten tourism were rising gasoline prices, periodic gasoline shortages in parts of the country, and trouble with the American Indian Movement (AIM) at Wounded Knee on the Pine Ridge Reservation. The more long-term threat to the businesses that depended on tourists, especially Wall Drug, was the highway beautification laws of the 1960s that threatened the removal of roadside advertising signs.

Bill finally decided in the winter of 1973 to prepare for a full tourist season, therefore had the Mall finished and ordered a full inventory for the 1974 season. The decisions the Husteads confronted in the fall and winter of 1973 marked the first time they had seriously considered any retrenchment in their twenty-seven years of growth.

In May and June, the opening of the 1974 tourist season, there were nine shops in the Mall. Bill estimated in the winter of

1974 that the year's sales would be a record breaker of $2 million. June, July, and August sales were up 15 to 20 percent. September business was up 20 to 30 percent, October was up 40 percent, and November was a record setter for that month.

Bill gave the following reasons for the 1974 season:

1. Many other businesses bought light, Wall Drug bought heavy. Therefore, while others ran short, Wall Drug had merchandise toward the end of the summer.

2. Expensive items sold well in spite of the recession scare of the late 1974 period. Bill indicated that articles in eastern merchandising journals indicated luxury items were doing well all over. Wall Drug had to reorder even into the fall on hot items, such as books, jewelry, and western clothes.

3. Wall Drug had more goods and space than it ever had before, and each person was buying more.

4. There were more hunters than ever before in the fall. Signs on the highway advertising free donuts and coffee for hunters brought many in and they bought heavily.

5. Although visitations to Mt. Rushmore were down in the summer of 1974, Wall Drug sales were up. Why? Bill speculates that more people from South Dakota and bordering states took shorter trips this year, and thus went to the Black Hills. These people had likely been in the Black Hills before and had seen Mt. Rushmore on their first trip. However, these people wanted to pay another visit to Wall Drug to eat, see what has been added, and shop.

In the fall of 1974 Wall Drug invested in more large signs to place 660 feet back from the interstate. By 1976 they had twenty-nine of these signs. These were the only legal signs that they could put up along the interstate, but by the spring of 1976, the language of the Highway Beautification Act was changed to put these signs outside the law also. Wall Drug signs (smaller ones) in neighboring states were removed.

In 1975 and 1976 expansion continued with the addition of the Emporium, more dining area, and more rest rooms at the north end of the store. (See Exhibit 1.) In 1978 the location of the Wall post office at the south end of the store beyond the Mall, which had been purchased previously, furnished expansion for the western clothing stores' boots and harness shop.

In 1983 there was further expansion under construction east of the Mall to the alley. The new area features a chapel modeled after a church built by Trappist monks in Dubuque, Iowa in 1850. Also featured are a replica of the original Wall Drug Store, which will be called Hustead's Apothecary and will serve as the Drug Store Museum. The store sells Caswell-Massey products from the store of that name in New York, which is the oldest drug store in the U.S. Other shops include a western art gallery, a poster shop and western gift shop, an iron and pottery shop, and Hustead's Family Picture Gallery. The shops will be modeled after famous old western establishments. There will also be a new set of rest rooms (see Exhibit 1). In effect, the new addition will be an extension of the Mall.

Mall Operation

Wall is a small town of 770 people (as of 1980). The economic base of the town is the Wall Drug Store and is dependent on tourist business.

Wall is situated right on the edge of the Badlands and fifty-two miles east of Rapid City. For miles in either direction, people in autos have been teased and tantalized by Wall Drug signs. Many have heard of the place through stories in the press, or have heard their parents or friends speak of the Wall Drug Store. In the summer of 1963, in a traffic count made on the highway going by Wall, 46 percent were eastbound and 54 percent were westbound. Of the eastbound traffic, 43 percent turned off at Wall. Of the westbound traffic, 44 percent turned off at Wall.

When people arrive at Wall (those westbound usually after driving forty miles or more through the Badlands), they are greeted by the large Wall Drug sign on the interchange and an eighty-foot-high, fifty-ton statue of a dinosaur. The business district of Wall is two blocks long and is three blocks to five blocks from the interchange. The town has eleven motels and a number of gasoline filling stations.

Cars from many states line the street in front of and several blocks on either side of the drugstore. Tabulation of state licenses from autos and campers parked in front of Wall Drug, June 1, 1983, at 12:00 noon are summarized as follows:

South Dakota (not local county)	20%
South Dakota, local county	22%
Balance of states and Canada	58%

Wall Drug is more than a store. It is a place of amusement, family entertainment, a gallery of the West, a gallery of South Dakota history, and a place that reflects the heritage of the West. Nostalgia addicts find Wall Drug particularly interesting. Children delight in the animated life-size singing cowboys; the tableau of an Indian camp; a stuffed bucking horse; a six-foot rabbit; a stuffed buffalo; old slot machines that pay out a souvenir coin for 25 cents; statues of cowboys, dancehall girls, and other characters of the old West; a coin-operated quick-draw game; and souvenirs by the roomful which make up part of the attractions.

The food is inexpensive and good, and, although as many as 10,000 people might stream through on a typical day, the place is air-conditioned and comfortable. The dining rooms are decorated with beautiful wood paneling, western art is displayed, and western music plays. One can dine on buffalo burgers, roast beef or steak, and five-cent coffee, or select wine and beer from the rustic, but beautiful, American walnut bar.

Food accounts for about one-fourth of the sales in Wall Drug, about another 5 to 10 percent for beverages and soda fountain treats. (This varies with the weather.) About 10 to 15 percent is jewelry, 15 percent clothing and hats, 35 to 40 percent for souvenirs, and 5 to 10 percent for drugs, drug sundries, and prescriptions.

The store is manned by a crew of 201 people, 76 of whom are college women and 25 are college men who work there in the summer. Student help is housed in homes that have been bought and made into dormitory apartments. There is a modern swimming pool for their use, also. The clerks are trained to be courteous, informed, and pleasant.

Ordering for the summer season begins in the preceding fall. Orders begin arriving in December, but most arrive in January, February, March, and April. Many large souvenir companies postdate their invoices until July and August. Each year brings new offerings from souvenir companies and other suppliers. Much of the purchasing is done by Bill, who admits he relies on their suppliers' trusted salespeople who advise him on purchasing. Many of these companies have supplied Wall Drug for thirty years or so. Wall Drug generally buys directly from the producers or importers, including photo supplies and clothing.

Years ago much of what Wall Drug bought and sold was imported or made in the eastern part of the country. In recent years, much of the merchandise sold is made regionally and locally. Indian reservations that now have small production firms, and individuals, produce much handicraft that is sold through Wall Drug. (Examples of such firms are Sioux Pottery, Badlands Pottery, Sioux Moccasin, and Milk Camp Industries.)

The Husteads rely heavily on the department managers for buying assistance. The manager of jewelry, for instance, will determine, on the basis of last year's orders and her experience with customer reaction and demand, how much to order for the next season. All ordering is done through Bill.

Mall Promotion

In 1965 Congress passed the Highway Beautification Act, which was designed to reduce the number of roadside signs. Anticipating the removal of the many Wall Drug advertising signs, Bill Hustead invested in new signs that were allowed under that legislation. These signs were to be placed no closer than 660 feet from the road. To be read, these signs had to be larger than the older signs, and cost close to $9,000 each. Now even these large signs are included for regulation or removal in beautification laws.

Many states, including South Dakota, have been slow to comply with this legislation because states in less populated areas have many tourist attractions, and find road signs the only practical way to advertise these attractions. Since Ronald Reagan has been in office, there has been little money available for federal enforcement of sign legislation. New legislation, proposed by the Federal Highway Administration of the Department of Transportation in 1983, could have an impact on Wall Drug and other tourist-dependent establishments.

Bill and Ted also decided that they must gain as much visibility and notoriety as possible, and to help achieve this, they began using advertising in unusual places. In the 1960s Wall Drug began taking small ads in unlikely media such as the *International Herald Tribune* and the *Village Voice*, in New York City's Greenwich Village (see Exhibit 2), advertising five-cent coffee and forty-nine-cent breakfasts as well as animal health remedies. These ads brought telephone calls and some letters of inquiry. They also brought an article in the *Voice* and probably attracted the attention of other media. On January 31, 1971 (Sunday), the *New York Times* carried an article about Wall Drug. This article may have led to Bill Hustead's appearance on Garry Moore's television program "To Tell the Truth." In 1979 there were seventy-five articles in newspapers and magazines about Wall Drug. In the August 31, 1981 edition of *Time,* a full-page article in the "American Scene" featured the store and the Husteads. Also, in 1981 Wall Drug was featured on NBC television's "Today Show" and Atlanta Cable "Winners."

For a while, the Wall Drug Store was advertised in the London city buses and subways, Paris Metro (subway) in the English language, and on the dock in Amsterdam where people board sightseeing boats.

Mall Personnel

Recruiting and training the seasonal work force is a major task at Wall Drug. College students are recruited through college placement services. Training is of short duration but quite intense. Summer employees are tested on their knowledge of store operations and their ability to give information about the area to tourists.

Bill Hustead commented:

> I really think that there isn't anything more difficult than running a business with twenty to thirty employees in the winter and then moving into a business with 180 to 200 employees, and you have to house a hundred of them and you have to supervise them, and train them. This lasts through June, July, and August, then the next year you start all over. It's kind of exciting and fun for the first twenty-five years but after thirty years you begin to think it's a tough racket.

The store had a permanent nucleus of twenty to thirty employees. Although the business could operate with fewer employees during the winter, the Husteads believed that they needed the experienced employees to give stability to the operations in the summer. Permanent employees with seniority could get as much as six weeks paid vacation. Commenting on this policy Bill said:

> We probably go through the winter with more employees than we really need, but we give them time off in the winter because a seasonal business is so demanding. When the Fourth of July comes, you're working, when Memorial Day comes, you're working; when all those summer fun times come, you're working six days a week and it's quite a sacrifice. So, we try to be very generous with our paid vacations.

Finances

Exhibits 3 and 4 present summary income statements and balance sheets from 1973 through 1982. The Wall Auto Livery was consolidated into Wall Drug Store, Inc. in May 1975. Had this transition occurred prior to 1973, sales for 1973, 1974, and 1975 would have been about $192,000, $248,000 and $52,000 larger, and net profit would have been about $19,000 larger in 1973, and $21,000 larger in 1974, with a negligible effect in 1975. The value of the acquired net assets was about $180,000.

The company's growth and expansion has been financed primarily by retained earnings, temporarily supplemented at times with short-term borrowing. A major exception was a $250,000, ten-year installment loan secured in 1973 to help finance the mall and some large highway signs. In 1975 this loan was prepaid through 1980. At the end of 1982 only $34,000 remained to be paid on this loan. Other long-term debt at the end of 1982 include installment contracts for the purchase of real estate and a stock redemption agreement (which occurred in 1979) for the purchase by the company of some Class B, nonvoting stock. As indicated on the December 31, 1982 balance sheet, current maturities of long-term debt were $43,436. Of this amount, $34,496 is the final payment on the 1973 loan due in 1983.

Both the growth and the volatility of the business should be apparent from the income statements presented in Exhibit 3. Exhibit 5 presents the income statements as a percentage of sales. Exhibit 6 is an analysis of the rate of return on equity broken into the component parts using the format:

$$\frac{sales}{assets} \times \frac{gross\ profit}{sales} \times \frac{operating\ income}{gross\ profit} \times \frac{net\ income}{operating\ income}$$

$$\times \frac{assets}{equity} = \frac{net\ income}{equity}$$

Between 1973 and 1982, prices, as measured by the Consumer Price Index, increased by about 115 percent. Percentage increases in some balance sheets and income accounts for Wall Drug over this period are

Sales	163
Total G. + A. expense	145
Net income	159
Total assets	115
Equity	169

These percentages are based on combining Wall Auto Livery with Wall Drug in 1973 as if the merger that occurred in 1975 had already taken place.

The following are changes in percentages in some of the general and administrative expenses from 1976 through 1982:

Total G. + A.	37
Utilities	137
Officers' salaries	2
Other salaries	42
Depreciation	5
Advertising	116
Profit sharing contribution	49

The items mentioned accounted for 77 percent of total general and administrative expenses in 1982 and 76 percent in 1976. These same items as percentages of sales were

	1982	1976
Utilities	1.7	1.0
Officers' salaries	2.9	3.8
Other salaries	18.5	17.7
Depreciation	2.3	2.9
Advertising	2.1	1.3
Profit sharing contributions	2.0	1.8

Depreciation methods on various assets vary from straight line to 200 percent declining balance and over lives of from fifteen to forty years for buildings and improvements to five to ten years for equipment, furniture and fixtures. Although not evaluated or recognized on the financial statements, it is likely that some assets, such as the western art and the silver dollar bar, have appreciated.

Current Situations

Dependence on seasonal tourists for the major portion of Wall Drug's business has inherent risks, and uncertainty over the future of the roadside signs, which have brought customers to the store for nearly fifty years, is a grave concern to the Husteads.

> We will try to have ideas to modify our outdoor advertising program to adapt to changes in the law which we are sure will be forthcoming. If they are drastic changes, they could put us out of business. If they nail down so there isn't a sign on the interstate, that will do the job.

Asked about diversification as a hedge against this risk, Bill replied,

> We will try to diversify within our own community. By that I mean probably on our highway location in and around our Auto Livery.

We have several hundred acres there (in sight of the interstate), and a motel and a modified drug store would be our last straw if we were wiped out in town.

The Husteads hoped to be able to create a fund to provide self-insurance for their dormitory houses. This fund would then also provide some measure of security from business risks as well.

Although over 80 years of age, Ted Hustead is still active in the management of the store, involved in everything from physical inspections of the premises to acting jointly with Bill in making policy decisions. Ted can frequently be seen on the grounds picking up litter. Dorothy, Ted's wife, comes to the store every day, summer and winter, helps with the banking and spends from two to six hours each day on various chores. Bill's son Rick, age 33, joined the store in 1980 and now shares in the management. Rick has a master's degree in guidance and counseling and spent four years as a guidance counselor and teacher in high school. Rick also spent two years in the real estate business and one year in the fast food business before returning to Wall. During his school years, Rick spent ten seasons working in Wall Drug. His wife, Kathy, is a pharmacist and also works in the store.

Bill Hustead expressed his continuous concern with the future of Wall Drug in light of future action concerning roadside sign advertising. Can the store expansion continue? Should diversification be attempted in the community? Should diversification unrelated to tourism be considered? Will Wall Drug be able to continue to gain publicity as it has in the past to keep people aware of its "attraction" characteristics? The costs of doing business, such as a sizable increase in utilities, are rising. How can they plan for a bad year or two given the increasing uncertainty in tourist industry?

With these thoughts in mind, Bill Hustead also wondered about numerous suggestions (usually from unpaid advisors wherever he spoke to groups) that the Wall Drug operation was an ideal candidate for the direct response marketing field.

Assume the role of professional advisor and develop an analysis of the direct marketing potential of the Wall Drug operation. Then, based on your conclusions, develop a test direct response plan for Wall Drug to use to determine whether or not direct marketing is something Wall Drug should be pursuing. Be sure to assess the potential of a catalog or catalogs, and come up with at least one good catalog concept.

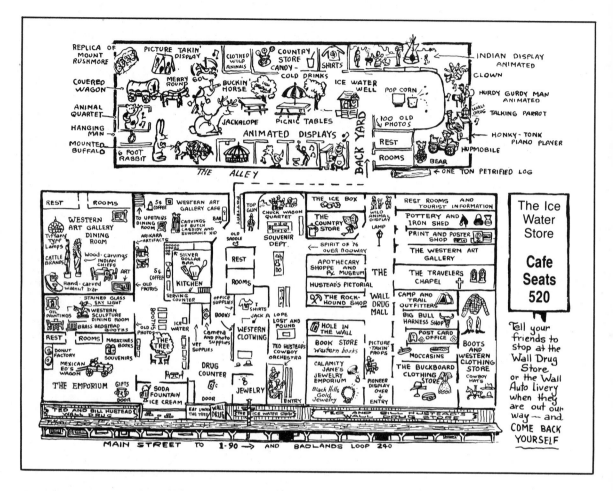

EXHIBIT 1. Wall Drug Store Map

EXHIBIT 2. Page One News (*Sioux Falls Argus Leader*, 7/8/81)

WALL DRUG ADS MYSTIFY NEW YORKERS
by Ruth Hamel

SoDak is a long way from SoHo, where west can mean New Jersey and Wall Drug could reasonably be thought to exist near Wall Street.

But, as usual, mere distance has not deterred Wall Drug owner Bill Hustead from advertising his business. Off and on for the past 20 years, Hustead has bought advertising space in the *Village Voice*, a New York City weekly based in Greenwich Village.

In every recent issue, a Wall Drug advertisement can be spotted between the columns devoted to Manhattan's vegetarian lunchspots and sushi bars. The small box may advertise petrified wood clocks one week, flying jackalopes on another and free ice water on another.

The tiny advertisements do not tell *Voice* readers where Wall Drug is, nor that it is more than a subway jaunt away for any New Yorker who might want to shop around for a petrified wood clock on a Saturday afternoon.

And the *Voice*'s accompanying Manhattan map that shows where various restaurants are located denotes Wall Drug with a small arrow that simply points west from New York's Hell's Kitchen.

All of which adds to the Wall Drug mystique.

"We do get inquiries from time to time," Katherine Rogers, *Village Voice* restaurant sales coordinator, said. "'What is that?' We give them the address."

Once told where Wall Drug is, people respond with the same question, she said: "'Why?'"

But the baffling ads work. Over the July 4th weekend, Wall Drug served five busloads of New York-area youth, some of whom knew of the drugstore from reading the *Village Voice,* Hustead said.

"One time, late at night, a guy from Massachusetts called" after spotting one of the *Voice* ads, Hustead said, "He wanted to know, 'What is a horse hitch?'"

New Yorkers passing through South Dakota will stop at Wall Drug to read the copies of the *Village Voice* Hustead receives every week and advertises on Interstate-90.

(Wall Drug signs, of course, are legendary. The small town drugstore with the multinational advertising campaign has placed signs in Amsterdam, London, and along the French Riviera, among other places.)

Hustead's account with the *Village Voice* began about 20 years ago.

Always a fan of New York City, the drugstore owner was sitting in a Greenwich Village coffeehouse reading the paper when "I thought it might be a good move to advertise in the *Voice*," he said. "I knew that a lot of writers take that paper."

So Hustead placed an ad that emphasized the reasonable price of Wall Drug food compared to New York food.

Eventually, the *Village Voice* ads led to a *Newsweek* article about Wall Drug.

Ms. Rogers said a recent ad for Wall Drug's rattlesnake bite kits prompted many calls to the *Village Voice* offices.

Another recent ad boasting of free ice water hit a chord when New York was in a drought and its restaurants would only give customers a glass of water if they asked for it, Ms. Rogers said.

Hustead is proud of the *Village Voice* ads but has reservations about the paper itself.

"I'm a little conservative," he said. "I feel it's not as wholesome a paper as it used to be. The language . . . it isn't something you want to lay around and let your 10-year-old girl read."

On a given week, Wall Drug may share *Voice* advertising space with naughty bakeries and naughtier film houses. And the newspaper that Hustead said used to resemble the paper in Wall now contains articles that might make some South Dakota jaws drop.

But the *Voice* association has allowed Hustead to meet interesting people between his forays to New York and New Yorkers' forays to Wall.

Wall Drug, Hustead says, "is a stop that those New Yorkers will make" as they pass through the state.

EXHIBIT 3. Income Statement (in thousands)

	1986	1985	1984	1983	1982	1981	1980	1975	1973
Sales	5611	5272	5055	4852	4733	4821	3970	2679	1607
Cost of Sales	2854	2793	2553	2587	2644	2676	2230	1484	806
Gross Profit	2757	2479	2502	2265	2089	2145	1740	1195	801
G&A Exp.	2459	2308	2150	1905	1802	1857	1473	1000	691
Income from Operation	298	171	352	360	287	288	267	195	110
Other Income Exp.	83	60	75	60	36	81	43	3	-10
Income before Tax	381	231	427	420	323	369	310	198	100
Tax	149	69	143	162	120	144	125	80	41
Net Income	232	162	284	258	203	224	185	118	59

EXHIBIT 4. Balance Sheet on December 31 (in thousands)

	1986	1985	1984	1983	1982	1981	1980	1975	1973
Cash & Short Term Inv.	815	618	501	647	240	282	449	93	74
Inventories	968	718	615	405	631	547	369	248	144
Other Current Assets	82	138	57	46	60	57	53	32	26
Total Current Assets	1865	1474	1173	1098	931	886	871	373	244
Property, Equipment	3773	3577	3467	3174	2907	2591	2380	1484	1130
Accumulated Dep.	-1870	-1732	-1609	-1475	-1355	-1254	-1147	-576	-428
Other Assets	19	20	21	23	24	25	27	31	34
Total Assets	3787	3339	3052	2820	2507	2248	2131	1312	980
Current Mat. of LTD	2	2	10	40	43	40	46	7	20
Note Payable	310	175	85	50	0	0	0	5	20
Accounts Payable	54	41	40	61	56	58	63	42	23
Accr. + Other Cur. Liabs.	304	261	251	262	252	244	310	193	110
Total Cur. Liab.	670	479	386	413	351	342	419	247	173
Long-Term Debt	171	173	173	182	191	149	179	136	244
Deferred Tax	56	27	6	10	7	1	-	-	-
Stockholder's Equity	2890	2660	2487	2215	1958	1756	1533	929	563
Total Liab. & Equity	3787	3339	3052	2820	2507	2248	2131	1312	980

EXHIBIT 5. Percent of Sales Statements

	1986	1985	1984	1983	1982	1981	1980	1975	1973
Sales	100.0	100.0	100.0	100.0	100.0	100.0	100.0	100.0	100.0
Cost of Sales	50.9	53.0	50.5	53.3	55.9	55.5	56.2	55.4	50.2
Gross Profit	49.1	47.0	49.5	46.7	44.1	44.5	43.8	44.6	49.8
G&A Exp.	43.8	43.8	42.5	39.3	38.1	38.5	37.1	37.3	43.0
Income From Oper.	5.3	3.2	7.0	7.4	6.0	6.0	6.7	7.3	6.8
Other Income Exp.	1.5	1.1	1.4	1.3	.8	1.7	1.1	.1	- .6
Income before Tax	6.8	4.3	8.4	8.7	6.8	7.7	7.8	7.4	6.2
Tax	2.7	1.3	2.8	3.4	2.5	3.0	3.1	3.0	2.5
Net Income	4.1	3.0	5.6	5.3	4.3	4.7	4.7	4.4	3.7

EXHIBIT 6. Components of Return on Equity

	1986	1985	1984	1983	1982	1981	1980	1975	1973
Gross Profit Sales	.491	.470	.495	.467	.441	.445	.438	.446	.498
Income from Oper. Gross Profit	.108	.069	.141	.159	.137	.134	.153	.163	.137
Sales Assets	1.48	1.58	1.66	1.72	1.89	2.14	1.86	2.04	1.64
Income from Oper. Assets	.079	.051	.115	.128	.114	.128	.125	.148	.112
Net Income Income from Oper.	.778	.947	.807	.717	.707	.778	.698	.605	.536
Assets Equity	1.31	1.26	1.23	1.27	1.28	1.28	1.39	1.41	1.74
Net Income Equity	.080	.061	.114	.116	.103	.128	.121	.126	.105

This case, originally prepared by James D. Taylor, Robert L. Johnson, and Philip C. Fisher of the University of South Dakota as a basis of class discussion, is used with their permission.

Case 22 Fairfax Cab Company

TOM HALLER PURCHASED THE FAIRFAX CAB COMPANY AT A TIME when widespread automobile ownership had generally reduced small town taxicab company profits to very modest levels. This was especially true for Fairfax Cab Company, located as it was in a sleepy middle-class suburb of a major Ohio city. Haller had driven cabs for years and thought he could make a go of it if given a chance. He got that chance when the owner decided to sell out and retire rather than be bothered by the personnel and other problems related to owning and managing the company. Buyers were hard to find; it finally came down to selling the company to Haller on a long-term contract, or selling the franchise and the company for a song to better-heeled investors. The owner chose Haller who was in business for himself.

As sole proprietor Haller succeeded in earning a living, but that was about all, for the next fifteen years or so. In fact, had it not been for the tax and other advantages that accrue to business owners, the company would have not been worth the effort. But somehow Haller succeeded in paying off his contract and was total owner of his company by 1984.

At that time, Haller approached the Fairfax city council for approval of a rate increase. (The Fairfax Cab Company's original owner had been granted an exclusive taxicab franchise in the city of Fairfax and this had been part of the purchase package and price. The council, the elected leaders of the city, then set the prices the franchise could charge for services.) The council questioned Haller, but did not delve very deeply into the business before perfunctorily granting him a cab fare increase.

But by 1987 Haller decided he needed another fare increase and once again approached the city council. Council membership, which had changed substantially, now included two very successful businessmen, two senior government employees, and a college professor of Business Administration, plus two others with modest business and marketing acumen.

Haller's approach to previous councils had been on the "I need the increase" and "I'm a good ole boy" basis, and the "good ole boys" had responded with approvals. But this council was different. They asked for definitive cost and revenue data, as well as information concerning operating style and philosophy, Haller had little of either down on paper, and had it not been for tax laws, probably wouldn't have had any.

The council asked City Manager Burnell Williams to investigate the situation and try to get a definition of Haller's operating condition and service strategies. Williams assigned this task to Assistant Finance Director Ham Michaels. Michaels struck out on service strategies, because Haller apparently had no plan, not even in his head, but did get some cost and revenue data. These were presented to the city council in the form of a memo. (See Exhibits 7–1 to 7–3.)

When he next appeared before the council, Haller felt his case was so strong that he thought it necessary only to refer to the memo and say it is obvious that "I can't make a living and must have the requested fare increase." He was dumbfounded when one of the council members suggested his rates were too high already and might even be reduced. Another chimed in that promotion of this service might be the answer to his problem. A third had sampled the cab company's service and remarked that the whole operation needed polishing up. The college professor noted that the whole effort of the company could be improved best by carefully identifying and promoting the cab company's wares to selected markets, perhaps, even coming up with "products" for different groups. Another council member said, "I think he needs a fare increase. He's a hardworking man. Let's give it to him."

The discussion, ranging from one aspect of the situation to another, lasted for over an hour. It was pointed out that a growing state university now existed in the community. It was observed that a major military installation which was located adjacent to Fairfax was also continuing to grow. The fact that the city's population had doubled (15,000–30,000) in ten years (1970–1980), and that a significant senior citizens' component had emerged in the population were also factors one or another member of the council felt should affect, in some way, the cab fare increase that faced them and the problems that faced Haller.

Study and analyze Exhibits 1 and 2 and the other relevant information and develop basic recommendations for what price structure the Fairfax City Council should permit Haller to use; and how Haller might proceed to promote his cab company effectively, with particular reference to how he might use direct response techniques as promotional tools. Then design a specific direct response promotional program that you feel Haller can afford and that will work.

EXHIBIT 1. Memo to City Manager

April 19, 1987

Memo to: Burnell Williams, City Manager
From: Ham Michaels, Assistant Finance Director
Subject: Proposed Taxicab Rate Increase

In reference to Mr. Thomas Haller's request to increase the rates of fares of taxicabs for the Fairfax Cab Company, I have examined the financial records of Mr. Haller for the past three years and report these findings as outlined [in Exhibit 2]. Mr. Haller, as a sole proprietor, reported net income of $9,954.12 in 1984, $6,923.51 in 1985, and $8,504.25 in 1986. From these net income amounts Mr. Haller had to pay federal, state and city income taxes.

In addition, I have contacted other cities for a comparison of taxicab fares and report those findings [in Exhibit 3].

For the Fairfax Cab Company the drop charge to start the meter would be increased from $1.20 to $1.50 for each fare or a 25% increase. The per mile charge would be increased from $1.00 to $1.20 or a 20% increase. Under the old rates, which became effective February 25, 1984, if a person were to travel three miles the fare would be $1.20 plus $2.00 for a total of $2.20. The same three miles under the proposed rates would cost $1.50 plus $1.20 for a total of $2.70 or an increase of approximately 23%.

EXHIBIT 2.   Fairfax Cab Company: Income Statement for the Year Ended December 31

	1984	1985	1986
Gross Receipts			
Fares Earned	$131,263.96	$111,410.55	$116,245.74
Sale of Asset		200.00	
Total Receipts	$131,263.96	$111,610.55	$116,245.74
Operating Expenses			
Depreciation	$ 4,489.75	$ 3,928.86	$ 3,240.00
Taxes	7,977.58	6,577.43	8,051.79
Repairs	8,800.16	5,248.62	5,089.98
Salaries	68,023.79	59,982.23	61,044.21
Insurance	7,126.00	6,414.00	6,390.00
Legal & Professional	260.00	210.00	90.00
Interest	702.25	159.55	646.50
Gas & Oil	16,890.18	15,988.37	16,396.12
Radio Expense	682.92	746.46	682.92
Cab Washes	370.20	279.85	272.35
Laundry	115.94	64.60	75.00
Advertising	640.38	311.92	455.52
Utilities	556.75	740.02	755.52
Telephone	1,204.09	1,282.05	1,429.19
Tires	1,206.56	824.85	940.62
Supplies		211.38	362.13
Miscellaneous	913.29	516.85	619.64
Total Expenses	$121,309.84	$104,687.04	$107,741.49
Net Income	$ 9,954.12	$ 6,923.51	$ 8,504.25

EXHIBIT 3.   Comparison of Area Taxicab Rates

Central City	For the first one-tenth mile	$1.50
	For each subsequent mile	1.00
or	For each subsequent one-tenth mile	.10
Vidalia	For the first one-sixth mile	$1.40
	For each subsequent mile	1.20
or	For each subsequent one-sixth mile	.20
Manor Hills	For the first one-fourth mile	$1.20
	For each subsequent mile	1.20
or	For each subsequent one-fourth mile	.30
Spring Valley	For the first one-fourth mile	$1.20
	For each subsequent mile	1.20
or	For each subsequent one-fourth mile	.30
Fairfax Cab Company (Per Ordinance No. 6-84)		
	For the first one-tenth mile	$1.20
	For each subesquent mile	1.00
or	For each subsequent one-tenth mile	.12
Fairfax Cab Company (Proposed)		
	For the first one-tenth mile	$1.50
	For each subsequent mile	1.20
or	For each subsequent one-tenth mile	.12

TITLES OF INTEREST IN MARKETING, DIRECT MARKETING, AND SALES PROMOTION

SUCCESSFUL DIRECT MARKETING METHODS, Fourth Edition, by Bob Stone

PROFITABLE DIRECT MARKETING, Second Edition, by Jim Kobs

CREATIVE STRATEGY IN DIRECT MARKETING, by Susan K. Jones

READINGS AND CASES IN DIRECT MARKETING, by Herb Brown and Bruce Buskirk

STRATEGIC DATABASE MARKETING, by Robert R. Jackson, and Paul Wang

SUCCESSFUL TELEMARKETING, by Bob Stone and John Wyman

MARKETING CORPORATE IMAGE: THE COMPANY AS YOUR NUMBER ONE PRODUCT, by James R. Gregory with Jack G. Wiechmann

HOW TO CREATE SUCCESSFUL CATALOGS, by Maxwell Sroge

PROMOTIONAL MARKETING: IDEAS AND TECHNIQUES FOR SUCCESS IN SALES PROMOTION, by William A. Robinson and Christine Hauri

BEST SALES PROMOTIONS, Sixth Edition, by William A. Robinson

INSIDE THE LEADING MAIL ORDER HOUSES, Third Edition, by Maxwell Sroge

NEW PRODUCT DEVELOPMENT, by George Gruenwald

NEW PRODUCT DEVELOPMENT CHECKLISTS, by George Gruenwald

THE COMPLETE TRAVEL MARKETING HANDBOOK, by Andrew Vladimir

HOW TO TURN CUSTOMER SERVICE INTO CUSTOMER SALES, by Bernard Katz

THE MARKETING PLAN, by Robert K. Skacel

ADVERTISING & MARKETING CHECKLISTS, by Ron Kaatz

SECRETS OF SUCCESSFUL DIRECT mail, by Richard V. Benson

U.S. DEPARTMENT OF COMMERCE GUIDE TO EXPORTING

HOW TO GET PEOPLE TO DO THINGS YOUR WAY, by J. Robert Parkinson

HOW TO WRITE A SUCCESSFUL MARKETING PLAN, by Roman G. Hiebing, Jr., and Scott W. Cooper

101 TIPS FOR MORE PROFITABLE CATALOGS, by Maxwell Sroge

HOW TO GET THE MOST OUT OF TRADE SHOWS, by Steve Miller

MARKETING TO CHINA, by Xu Bai Yi

STRATEGIC MARKET PLANNING, by Robert J. Hamper and L. Sue Baugh

COMMONSENSE DIRECT MARKETING, Second Edition, by Drayton Bird

NTC'S DICTIONARY OF DIRECT MAIL AND MAILING LIST TERMINOLOGY AND TECHNIQUES, by Nat G. Bodian

For further information or a current catalog, write:
NTC Business Books
a division of *NTC Publishing Group*
4255 West Touhy Avenue
Lincolnwood, Illinois 60646-1975 U.S.A.